THE
ESSENTIAL
THEATRE

THE ESSENTIAL THEATRE

SECOND EDITION

Oscar G. Brockett
University of Texas at Austin

Holt, Rinehart and Winston
New York Chicago San Francisco Atlanta Dallas
Montreal Toronto London Sydney

Editor: Roth Wilkofsky
Senior Project Editor: Marjorie Marks
Art Director: Lou Scardino
Production Manager: Nancy Myers
Picture Editor: June Lundborg
Text Design: Caliber
Cover Design: Albert D'Agostino

Library of Congress Cataloging in Publication Data

Brockett, Oscar Gross
    The essential theatre.

    Condensed version of the author's The Theatre.
    Bibliography.
    Includes index.
    1. Theater—History.   2. Drama—History and criti-
cism.   3. Theater—United States.   I. Brockett, Oscar
Gross   The theatre.   II. Title.
PN2101.B72   1980   792'.09   79-17766

ISBN 0-03-049371-4

In Memory of My Wife,
Lenyth Brockett

Preface

In *The Essential Theatre* I have sought to provide an introduction to the theatre and to arouse the wide range of interests—critical, historical, artistic, and practical—needed for a well-rounded view. It is a condensed version of *The Theatre: An Introduction,* which is now in its fourth edition. The brief edition was first published in 1976 at the suggestion of instructors who found *The Theatre* too extensive for the scope and length of their courses. This second edition has been prepared to bring the material more nearly up-to-date, to sharpen some discussions, and to provide new and more varied illustrations.

In making this version I have retained the main features of *The Theatre* while reducing its size considerably. Part 1 provides a rationale for theatre studies, outlines critical approaches, and discusses dramatic structure, form, and style. Thus, it serves as preparation for subsequent chapters. Part 2 surveys the development of theatre and drama from the beginnings to the present. It treats representative dramatists, forms, and styles, and gives an overview of theatrical practice through the ages. Part 3 describes how each of the theatre arts is practiced in America today. It emphasizes principles, goals, and working procedures. An Appendix summarizes opportunities open to those who wish to work in the theatre, and the Bibliography lists books that may be useful in further study or as sources of additional information.

Each chapter in Part 2 includes detailed discussions of one or more plays. Thirteen of these—*Oedipus the King, The Menaechmi, The Second Shepherds' Play,*

King Lear, Tartuffe, The School for Scandal, The Wild Duck, From Morn till Midnight, The Good Woman of Setzuan, Death of a Salesman, The New Tenant, Raisin in the Sun, and *Streamers*—are included in their entirety in an anthology, *Plays for the Theatre,* edited by Oscar G. and Lenyth Brockett and published by Holt, Rinehart and Winston in 1979.

It would be impossible to list all of those to whom I am indebted. The bibliography indicates some of the sources I have used, and the captions to the illustrations list others. A few persons deserve special mention: Roth Wilkofsky, Marjorie Marks, Lou Scardino, Nancy Myers, and June Lundborg of Holt, Rinehart and Winston, for assistance with illustrations, for editing the manuscript, and for other kinds of assistance.

I hope this new edition of *The Essential Theatre* will gain the approval accorded the first version.

Austin, Texas   Oscar G. Brockett
January 1980

Contents

CONTENTS

PART 3 THE THEATRE ARTS IN AMERICA TODAY

THE
ESSENTIAL
THEATRE

BASIC
CONCEPTS

PART **1**

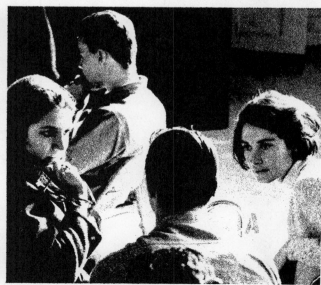

Theatre, Audience, and Critic

1

The theatre is so old that its origins are lost in prehistory; when human records began people were already performing rituals which involved most of the elements required for a fully developed theatre: a performance space, performers, action, masks or makeup, costumes, music, dance, and an audience. The function of these early rites was only partially dramatic, however, since they were usually addressed to those supernatural powers thought to control the return of spring, success in hunt and war, or the fertility of human beings and their environment. Only gradually did theatre pass out of this ritualistic phase and become an activity prized for itself. Nevertheless, it was probably in these rites that theatre had its beginnings, although it may also have stemmed in part from other impulses, such as the human love of storytelling and imitation.

Though its origins may be shadowy, the theatre has been with us in some form throughout human history. At times it has been highly devel-

3

oped and highly prized; at others it has been reduced to little more than a skeleton existing on the fringes of respectability. It has as often been denounced as praised, and its value — even its right to exist — has frequently been questioned.

During most of its existence the theatre has had to contend with contrasting responses: it has been consumed as an attractive delicacy even as it has been accused of being a distraction from more important activities. This ambivalence has been encouraged in part by theatrical terminology (such as *play, show,* and *acting*) which suggests that theatre is the product of grown-ups who have prolonged their childhood by dressing up and playing games to divert themselves and others. On the other hand, in most periods theatre has been considered by at least some segments of society to be one of the most effective tools available to human beings in their attempts to understand themselves and their world. In the twentieth century, it has been accepted as a legitimate field of study in university curricula alongside other more traditional subjects.

The theatre, then, has had both its detractors and its strong advocates. Nevertheless, those who value it often find themselves on the defensive with those who question whether it has any valid place in a college curriculum or whether a world dominated by film and television would miss it were it to disappear altogether.

THE BASIC ELEMENTS OF THEATRE

One reason for varying responses can be found in the theatre's complexity and diversity. These characteristics can be seen, first of all, in the three basic elements of theatre: what is performed (script, scenario, or plan); the performance (including all the processes involved in preparation and presentation); and the audience (the perceivers). Each affects conceptions of the whole — the theatre.

What is performed may be extremely varied, running a gamut from variety acts to Shakespearean tragedy. An entertainer may sing a song, play music on an instrument, dance, turn cartwheels, or juggle; or several performers may improvise a story or act out a complex script. Any or all of these things may occur in a place we call a theatre. Probably for this reason, we have great difficulty in defining precisely what is meant by theatre or in specifying where theatre ceases and some other type of activity begins.

Although variety entertainment is often labeled theatrical, most frequently theatre is thought to involve some degree of storytelling or impersonation. Most typically it utilizes a written text. Nevertheless, theatre does not necessarily require a script or dialogue. But, even if variety entertainment were ruled out and our conception of theatre restricted to material in some degree dramatic, we would still be faced

Marcel Marceau, who
performs pantomimes,
does not rely on dialogue
or a written script.

with great diversity, for dramatic entertainments may range through improvised scenes, pantomimes, vaudeville sketches, musical plays, and spoken dramas. Furthermore, they may be brief or lengthy; they may deal with the commonplace or the unusual, the comic or the serious. With so much diversity, it is not surprising that attitudes about the theatre vary markedly, or that some people conceive of theatre almost entirely as popular entertainment whereas others discount this aspect and find the essence of theatre in its capacity to offer penetrating insights into humanity and the world. In both instances, a part has been substituted for the whole.

The second ingredient, *the performance,* is equally complex and diverse. It gives concreteness to what is presented by translating the potential of a script, scenario, or plan into actuality. What the audience sees when it goes to the theatre is a meshing of script or plan with theatrical processes. A performance normally requires the cooperation and creative efforts of many persons: playwright, director, actors, designers, and technicians. The components involved in this process may be manipulated to create quite varied effects. All the components may be so skillfully integrated that the spectator is aware only of a single unified impression, or one or more of the components—such as acting or spectacle—may completely over-

The Schaubühne am Halleschen Ufer, a German theatre, performed Euripides' *Bacchae* as a dramatic conflict between the Apollonian and Dionysian lifestyles. (Courtesy German Information Center)

shadow the others. The components may be handled in a way easily understood by almost everyone, or in ways so strange that all but the most sophisticated are puzzled. A performance may therefore seem to one part of the audience clear and entertaining and to another overly obvious and entirely unoriginal; conversely, what to one group may seem strange and incomprehensible may by another be judged insightful and brilliant. Again, it is the diversity and complexity of the theatre that gives rise to such differing responses.

The third basic ingredient of the theatre is *the audience,* because until material is performed and seen by a public we usually do not call it theatre. For all the arts a public is imperative, but for most this public may be thought of as individuals—the reader of a novel or poem, the viewer of a painting or a piece of sculpture—each of whom may experience the work in isolation. But a theatre audience is assembled as a group at a given time and place to experience a performance.

The audience affects the theatre in many ways, but above all by giving or withholding support—both in the theatre and at the box office. Some audiences want merely to be entertained. They want to forget their personal cares and the problems of the world around them. They view the theatre as a form of recreation or escape. Other audiences wish the theatre to provide new insights and provocative perceptions about significant topics, to advocate action about political and social issues, or to increase awareness of and sensitivity to others and their surroundings.

6

Thus, they are apt to support a different kind of performance than those seeking escapist entertainment. Ultimately, audiences make their opinions known through their attendance or nonattendance. They support what appeals to them and fail to support what they do not understand or like. Thus, audience tastes significantly have influence on both what is performed and how it is performed.

Since there is such diversity in what is performed, in performances, and in audience tastes, we should acknowledge that not all theatre is likely to appeal to all segments of the public and that responses to it are almost inescapably varied.

POPULAR ENTERTAINMENT AND ART

Perhaps the reasons for this will become clearer if we divide theatre into two broad (though admittedly oversimplified) categories: *popular entertainment* and *theatre as an art form.* The two may and often do overlap, and to like one does not necessarily mean disliking the other, although audiences often seem to divide along these lines.

Actor-audience contact, illustrated here by an actress surrounded by the audience. (Courtesy French Cultural Services)

7

As the term implies, popular entertainment seeks primarily to provide diversion for a mass audience. It draws on (either consciously or unconsciously) the dominant attitudes, prejudices, and interests of the day; it usually employs easily recognizable (even stereotyped) characters, situations, and theatrical conventions, while manipulating them with sufficient novelty to be entertaining but usually without offering important new perceptions or raising any disturbing questions that challenge the audience's views. Because it intends primarily to provide diversion, it can easily be grouped with games, sports, and other recreational pastimes. This is not to imply that recreation for large numbers of people is an unimportant function, for to divert audiences from their cares and to offer release from the routine of existence is to provide an important service, both psychologically and sociologically. Nor is it meant to suggest that theatre need not be entertaining; if it cannot capture and hold attention it cannot command a following. Nevertheless, if theatre is merely recreational or entertaining and does not offer any additional appeals, it may be (and often is) dismissed as lacking in true significance.

A complete picture of the theatre's potential demands that it also be looked at as one of the arts. But what is art? Probably no term has been discussed so frequently or defined so ambiguously. Until the eighteenth century, *art* was used almost always to designate the systematic application of knowledge or skill to achieve some predetermined result. The word is still used in that sense when we speak of the art (or craft) of medicine, politics, or persuasion. During the eighteenth century it became customary to divide the arts into two groups, "useful" and "fine." Into the latter category were placed literature, painting, sculpture, architecture, music, and dance. At the same time the idea arose that while the useful arts may easily be taught and mastered, the fine arts, as products of genius, cannot be reduced to rules or principles that can be learned. As a result, since about 1800 art has often been depicted as too lofty to be fully understandable. Many critics also have implied that only those with truly superior sensitivity can fully appreciate art and that the average person mistakes some inferior product for authentic artistic expression. Thus, those who think of the theatre as an art form are often at odds with those who think of it as "show business."

If no definition of art is universally accepted, some of its distinguishing characteristics can be explored by comparing it with other approaches to experience. First and most broadly, art is one way whereby human beings seek to understand the world. In this repect, it may be compared with history, philosophy, or science, each of which strives to discover and record patterns in human experience. All of these approaches recognize that human experience is composed of innumerable happenings which have occurred to an infinite number of people through countless generations, and that each person's life is made up of a series of momentary occurrences, many seemingly coming about wholly by chance. One question

8

Beckett's *Waiting for Godot* unconventionally comments on the human experience. From the original New York production with Bert Lahr and E. G. Marshall. (Elliot Erwitt/Magnum)

they seek to answer is: What significant patterns can be perceived behind the apparent randomness? The search for meaning may take a different tack in each field, but it is always directed toward discovering those relationships that reveal order within what would otherwise seem to be chance events. Art, then, as one approach, shapes perceptions about human experience into forms (or patterned relationships) that help us order our views about mankind and the universe.

There are, however, significant differences in the methods used in various approaches to human experience. Historian, philosopher, and scientist do their research and then attempt to set down their conclusions in logical, expository prose: a point of view is expressed and proof marshaled to support that view and to gain its acceptance. They direct their appeal primarily to the intellect. The artist, on the other hand, works primarily from his own perceptions and seeks to involve the audience's emotions, imagination, and intellect directly. A play consequently shows events as though occurring at that moment before our eyes; we absorb them in the way we absorb life itself—through their direct operation on our senses. Art differs from life by stripping away irrelevant details and organizing events so that they compose a connected pattern. Thus, a play illuminates and comments (though sometimes indirectly) on human experience even as it creates it.

But, just as we do not mistake a statue for a real person, we do not mistake stage action for reality. Rather, we usually view a play with what Samuel Taylor Coleridge called a "willing suspension of disbelief." By this he meant that, while we know the events of a play are not real, we

9

agree for the moment not to disbelieve their reality. We are nevertheless not moved to immediate action by what we see on the stage as we would be by real-life events. We watch one man seemingly kill another, but make no attempt to rescue the victim or to call the police. This state in which we are sufficiently detached to view an artistic event semiobjectively is sometimes called *esthetic distance.* At the same time, the distance must not be so great as to induce indifference. Therefore, while a degree of detachment is necessary, involvement is of equal importance. This feeling of kinship is sometimes called *empathy.* Thus, we watch a play with a double sense of concern and detachment. It is both a removed and an intensified reaction of a kind seldom possible outside esthetic experience. Another way of putting this is that art lifts us above the everyday fray and gives us something like a "god's-eye" view of experience.

Some attributes of art, then, are these: It is one method available to all of us to discover and record patterns which provide insights, perceptions, and understanding about ourselves and our world. Art, thus, is one form of knowledge. In addition, it is an imaginative reshaping of experience which operates directly on our senses in a way that involves us both esthetically and empathically, allowing us to be simultaneously at a distance from and involved in the experience so that we participate in it emotionally even as we gain from it new intellectual insights. Art lays claim, then, to being serious (in the sense of having something important to communicate), but because its methods are so indirect (it presents experience but does not attempt to explain it fully) it is often ambiguous and therefore may easily be misunderstood.

SPECIAL QUALITIES OF THEATRICAL ART

But even within the fine arts theatre holds a special place; it is the art that comes closest to life as it is lived from day to day. Not only is human experience and action its subject, it uses live human beings (actors) as its primary means of communicating with an audience. Quite often the speech of the performers approximates that heard in real life and the actors may wear costumes that might be seen on the street; they may perform in settings that recall actual places. Not all theatre attempts to be so realistic and at times it may even approximate other performing arts (such as dance and music), but nevertheless it is the art most capable of recreating man's typical experiences.

Such lifelikeness is also one of the reasons theatre is often insufficiently valued; a play, a setting, the acting may so resemble what is familiar to spectators that they fail to recognize how difficult it is to produce this lifelikeness skillfully. To a certain degree all people are actors; they vary the roles they play (almost moment by moment) according to the people they encounter. In doing so, they utilize the same tools as the actor—voice, speech, movement, gesture, psychological motivation, and the like. Consequently, most persons do not fully recognize the problems faced by a skilled actor. Even those within the theatre often differ in their opinions about whether artistic excellence depends primarily on talent and instinct or on training and discipline.

The theatre further resembles life in being ephemeral. As in life, each episode is experienced and then immediately becomes part of the past. When the performance ends, its essence can never be fully recaptured, since—unlike a novel, painting, or statue, each of which remains relatively unchanged—a theatrical production when it is ended lives only in the play script, program, pictures, reviews, and memories of those who were present.

Theatre resembles life also in being the most objective of the arts, since characteristically it presents both outer and inner experience through speech and action. As in life, it is through listening and watching that we come to know characters both externally and internally. What we learn about their minds, personalities, and motivations comes from what

Arthur Miller's *Death of a Salesman* recreates significant human experiences. From the production starring George C. Scott. (Inge Morath/Magnum)

they say and do and from what others tell us about them. Thus we absorb a theatrical performance the way we do a scene from real life.

Additionally, the theatre can be said to resemble life because of the complexity of its means, for like a scene from life itself it is made up of intermingled sound, movement, place, dress, lighting, and so on. Another way of putting this is to say that theatre draws on all the other arts: literature in its script; painting, architecture, and sculpture (and sometimes dance) in its spectacle; and speech and music in its audible aspects. In some ways, then, theatre encompasses all the other arts.

Furthermore, theatre is psychologically the most immediate of the arts. Several contemporary critics have argued that the essence of the theatre (what distinguishes it from other dramatic media such as television and film) lies in the simultaneous presence of live actors and spectators in the same room, and that everything else is expendable.

On the surface, theatre may seem to have several drawbacks when compared with other media. For example, more people often see a filmed or televised show on a single evening than attend the live theatre during an entire year. In fact, the theatre may be likened to a handcrafted product in an age of mass production. Thousands of copies of a film may be printed and shown throughout the world simultaneously and year after year, and a televised program may be videotaped and repeated at will. These media, too, may make performers world-famous almost overnight, whereas the actor in the theatre may build up an international reputation only over a considerable period of time.

Nevertheless, the theatre has important attributes that television and film cannot duplicate. The most significant of these are the three-dimensionality of the theatrical experience and the special relationship between performers and spectators. In film and television, the camera is used to select what the audience can see and to insure that it will see nothing more; in the theatre, on the other hand, since the full acting area remains visible, the audience may choose what it will watch, even though the director may attempt to focus attention on some specific aspect of a scene. Perhaps most important, during a live performance there is continuous interaction between performer and spectator, permitting the audience a far more active role than is allowed by television and film. Ultimately, there is a fundamental difference in the psychological responses aroused by electronic media and theatre, because the former present pictures of events whereas the latter performs the actual events in what amounts to the same space as that occupied by the audience. This difference results in one unique characteristic of the theatre: its ability to offer intense sensory experience through the simultaneous presence of live actors and audience.

It is to these special qualities—lifelikeness, ephemerality, objectivity, complexity, and psychological immediacy—that we can relate many of both the theatre's weaknesses and strengths.

THE PROBLEM OF VALUE IN ART

Despite all that one can say about its nature and value, however, art is still not widely understood by the general public. In a society preoccupied with material success, as ours has been, art does not appear to be very useful, since it does not produce such obvious benefits as those of medicine or engineering. Even those artists (including performers) who are widely known and accepted are usually admired more for their commercial success than for their artistic talents, having shown that they can compete in the business world. Generally, careers in the arts are considered highly risky because they seldom offer financial security. Such attitudes about art have led to a situation in which children are systematically (although not necessarily intentionally) discouraged from developing their talents. By the time adulthood is reached, the average American has suppressed all artistic inclinations. Far too many adults are thus cut off from or are only partly aware of one of man's primary ways of knowing his world and understanding himself.

Ntozake Shange's *For Colored Girls Who Have Considered Suicide When the Rainbow is Enuf* uses music, dance, and poetry to appeal to the audience's common humanity. (Martha Swope)

13

Still, it is difficult to defend art on the basis of its immediate utility. Art ultimately must be valued because of its capacity to improve the quality of life—by increasing our sensitivity to others and our surroundings, by sharpening our perceptions, by reshaping our values so that moral and societal concerns take precedence over material well-being. Of all the arts, theatre has perhaps the greatest potential as a humanizing force, for at its best it asks us to enter imaginatively into the lives of others so we may understand their aspirations and motivations. Through role-playing (either in daily life or in the theatre) we come to understand who and what we are and to see ourselves in relation to others. Perhaps most important, in a world given increasingly to violence, the value of being able to understand and feel for others as human beings cannot be overestimated, because violence flourishes only when we so dehumanize others that we no longer think of their hopes, aims, and sufferings but treat them as objects to be manipulated or on whom to vent our frustrations. To know (emotionally, imaginatively, and intellectually) what it means to be human in the broadest sense ought to be one of the primary goals of both education and life, and for reaching that goal no approach has greater potential than theatre since man is its subject and human beings its primary medium.

But the theatre's great potential is not always or automatically fulfilled. Those working in theatre often are preoccupied with the immediate process or with egotistical goals, while audiences often concentrate only on surface qualities and students of theatre may fail to see anything in their study of the past that is pertinent to them. Furthermore, the skill and content of theatrical performances are not always of high quality. Naturally, if theatre is to realize its potential, all concerned must be willing to look beneath the surface and insist on excellence.

Unfortunately, quality—unlike quantity—is not measurable except subjectively. And subjectivity takes us into the realm of taste, judgment, and a host of variables about which agreement is seldom possible. There are many levels of taste, many degrees of complexity, and a wide range of quality. But, if we cannot expect ever to achieve complete agreement, we each can sharpen our own perceptions of the theatre and its processes. To do this, we need first to understand the theatre and how it works. Second, we need to develop some approach through which we can judge the relative merits of what is performed and how it is performed. Then, we should work to encourage those theatrical values that seem important to us. In this way we may acquire understanding and judgment—that is, we become critics of the theatre.

Under present conditions, most Americans come to adulthood having been denied extensive exposure to the arts, and especially to the theatre. Prior to entering college, few students have the opportunity to study and practice the art of the theatre in any systematic way. As an aid in compensating for this lack, the chapters that follow provide an overview of the theatre in its various aspects: how plays are structured; how the theatre has changed and developed through the ages; how it functions today; and how each theatre artist makes use of the materials available to him. Hopefully, taken all together, these discussions will lay the foundation for intelligent and sensitive reactions to the theatre.

THE CRITIC

In a sense each member of an audience is a critic, since he passes some kind of judgment, however fleeting, upon what he sees. The title of critic is usually reserved, however, for those persons who formulate their judgments for publication. Ideally, the critic should be an experienced and trained audience member who understands plays and theatrical practice well enough to assess effectiveness and his audience well enough to express evaluations in terms comprehensible to it.

Criticism should be illuminating to both the creators and the consumers of a theatre piece. In making explanations or in passing judgments, most critics refer to specific passages in a play, to characterization, structure, acting, or aspects of staging. In this way, they are of service to the theatre worker as well as to the public, for they point out the reasons for success or failure.

But a single piece of criticism will not serve the needs of all persons; the critic usually has a particular type of reader in mind. The reviews of plays published in the New York daily newspapers are addressed to a general public, and almost no background or knowledge is taken for granted. On the other hand, the criticism written for literary quarterlies is addressed to a better-informed and more select audience. Therefore, not all criticism can be read in the same way.

Even when the critic's assumptions are clear, there is often a wide range of response to his work. One reader will find a piece of criticism illuminating, while another will find nothing of value in it, for just as one is drawn to certain kinds of plays, one is also drawn to particular types of criticism.

THE MEANING AND PURPOSES OF CRITICISM

To many, criticism always implies adverse comments, but its true meaning is "the act of making judgments." Therefore, every evaluation should consider both excellence and failure—the effective and the ineffective—in a play and its production. Criticism may be used for three main purposes: exposition, appreciation or denunciation, and evaluation. A piece of criticism is seldom restricted to one of these purposes; usually all are found in conjunction.

For the critic, the curtain call is not the end of a play. (F.B. Grunzweig/Photo Researchers)

The purpose of expository criticism is to explain a play or production and the circumstances affecting it. The critic may write about the author, the period in which he lived, the production concept, and similar factors. Using this approach, a critic need make no judgment of worth. For example, he might explain how Shakespeare's *Richard III* is constructed or how the director has approached the script and, although his examination should lead to better understanding, it need not judge over-all effectiveness. Similarly, the reviewer may provide information about certain aspects of a production (the visual appearance of scenery and costumes, how this production differs from previous ones of the same play, and so on) without passing judgment on them. Eventually, he usually feels obliged to state his opinion of the production as a whole, but a large portion of his review may be purely expository.

Appreciative or denunciatory criticism is usually written by the critic who has already decided that a work is good or bad. His principal motive then is to make others feel the power or the lack of power in the play or production. He may proceed by describing his own responses and then attempt to evoke similar feelings in his readers. He may also analyze the script or production to show how structure, characterization, acting, or other elements bear out his judgment.

The evaluative critic may employ exposition, appreciation, or denunciation, but his principal aim is to judge effectiveness. As a rule, he begins by analyzing structure, characterization, ideas, acting, and visual elements. Upon this evidence, coupled with information drawn from other sources, he builds his evaluation of the script. If he is writing about a production, he may explain his understanding of the playwright's intentions and then go on to assess how effectively they have been realized on the stage; or he may concentrate on the acting and evaluate each performer's characterization. However he proceeds, his concern is to provide an evaluation of what he has seen and heard in the theatre.

THE BASIC PROBLEMS IN CRITICISM

The serious critic is concerned with three basic problems: understanding, assessing effectiveness, and judging ultimate worth.

In attempting to understand a play or performance, the critic must make sure that all of the important keys to its meaning have been explored. First, he may analyze the play, preferably through a study of the script. (See Chapter 2 for a discussion of dramatic structure.) Before he can fully understand the script, other explorations may be necessary. Sometimes a study of the author and his background is essential. If the play is a work from the past, it may be necessary to examine the dominant religious or psychological beliefs of that period, or the staging conventions in vogue when the play was written.

These methods used by the literary critic are also employed by theatre workers in their study of a script prior to its production. Unless the director, the actors, and the scenic artists understand a drama, it will be difficult for them to produce it satisfactorily. Although the literary critic and the theatre worker may arrive at the same conclusions in their studies, the theatre worker usually finds that his understanding of the play is modified during the rehearsal period. As the play takes shape on stage, he discovers qualities of which he was previously unaware, because plays do not reveal all of their potentialities on the printed page. Conversely, not all of the implications found in a script can be projected to an audience in a single production. Whenever possible a play should be studied both on the printed page and in performance.

Many reviewers write about plays they have not read and know only from a single viewing. Since understanding may be severely limited in such circumstances, most reviewers restrict themselves to reporting impressions without pretending to provide an extensive analysis of the play. Nevertheless, reviewers are sometimes guilty of damning a play rather than its inadequate production or a performance rather than its inadequate script, for it is difficult to sort out the sources of weaknesses or strengths on the basis of a single viewing.

After a play is understood, it may be judged in terms of how well it fulfills its intentions. Rarely does a playwright or director state his intentions directly. Rather, a play's intention must be determined through probing analysis. It is indicated by such elements as tone (a production may be humorous, satirical, serious, whimsical, and so on), ideas and their treatment, dialogue, characterization, conflicts, and spectacle. The critic comes to recognize whether the script is attempting to arouse indignation at some social injustice, deriding a political position, merely trying to offer an evening of entertainment, or seeking to accomplish some other purpose. Having decided upon the purpose, he can then assess how effectively this purpose has been realized.

Assessment of effectiveness can be based entirely upon a study of the script, but it is frequently helpful and always wise to note the response of audiences. It should be kept in mind, however, that while the response may be an accurate measure of the audience's enjoyment, it will not always give a true indication of the play's potential power. (For example, the play may not have been well performed.) Other factors — such as unfamiliar dramatic techniques or complex ideas — may be responsible for an audience's failure to appreciate a play's power. In such cases, the fault does not necessarily lie with the play, but may indicate shortcomings in the audience. But, if the play has been adequately performed and understood, then audience response is helpful in determining whether the intention of the playscript has been achieved. In making his judgment, the wise critic draws on all the resources available to him.

In seeking to assess the effectiveness of a production, the problems are much the same as in judging a script; however, rather than being concerned with the playwright's intention, the critic may focus on the director's concept, which may differ radically from what the script seems to demand. Of course, the critic may choose to assess how the director's conception is related to or differs from the playwright's script, but if he is concerned with the production as such (rather than as an attempt to embody a script faithfully), he must seek to assess how well the director has achieved what he set out to do. Although he may believe the director to be misguided in his conception, that belief is irrelevant in an assessment of whether or not the concept has been realized. Usually evidence as to the director's intention comes entirely from what the critic sees and hears during the performance, but often the director indicates what his intentions are through notes in the printed program, interviews given prior to the opening, or in publicity releases.

Even though a play or production is understood and judged successful in carrying out its intention, it may still be found unsatisfactory in relation to some larger system of value. Consequently, before passing final judgment, the critic may wish to ask whether the accomplishments are sufficiently significant to merit the highest commendation. It is in making this final judgment that he faces his greatest problem, for there are no universally accepted standards of worth, and none can be proven incontestably better than another.

To judge a play or performance, it must be surrounded by some larger context which places it in perspective. Disagreements about worth often stem from differences of opinion about the appropriate context. Some critics, for example, argue that the only meaningful context is other plays of the same type; other critics pay little attention to a play's dramatic form but view it within a context of philosophical concepts or of political, social, historical, or economic forces; still others are concerned with psychological forces, ritual elements, or communicative processes. A production may be valued for its novelty, its emotional power, its provocativeness, its relevance, its faithfulness to the script, or its entertainment. The contexts used by modern critics are numerous and varied.

Even though it is impossible to agree upon the single most appropriate context, judgments must be made. Therefore, since a critic cannot force anyone to accept his evaluation, he must rely upon persuasion. Perhaps his first problem is to recognize that his own ingrained convictions and prejudices play an important role in his critical judgments; consequently he should seek to clarify his standards both for himself and for his readers. If he first establishes the criteria by which he is judging a play and then states the evidence upon which he bases his judgment, he may persuade others that his is a dependable evaluation.

Because the theatre itself is a composite art and because each of us is subject to many influences, it is difficult to become a good theatre critic. The qualities for which the would-be critic must strive, however, are these: he must be sensitive to feelings, images, and ideas; he must become as well acquainted as possible with the theatre of all periods and of all types; he must be willing to explore plays until he understands them thoroughly; he must be tolerant of innovation; he must be aware of his own prejudices and values; he must be articulate and clear in expressing his judgments and their bases. Perhaps most important of all, he must be willing to alter his opinion when new experiences and evidence reveal inadequacies in his earlier judgment, for criticism is a continuing process rather than the dogmatic defense of a position. Ultimately, it is the purpose of this book to help those who read it to become informed and sensitive critics of plays both as scripts and as performances.

As a beginning on this path, let us look first at how plays are structured.

The Script: Dramatic Structure, Form, and Style

2

The play script is the typical starting point for the theatrical production. It is also the most common residue of production, since the script usually remains intact after its performance ends. Because the same script may serve as a basis for many different productions, it has greater permanence than its theatrical representations and therefore comes to be considered a literary work. Consequently, drama is often taught quite apart from theatre, and many people who read plays have never seen a live dramatic performance. Probably the majority of students get their first glimpse of theatre through reading plays in literature classes. But the script in itself may seem unsatisfactory or puzzling, for it is essentially a blueprint that demands from both reader and performer the imaginative recreation of much that is only implied on the printed page. Therefore, learning how to read, understand, and fill out the script (either in the mind or on the stage) is essential if the power of a play is to be fully realized.

ON READING A PLAY

There are no rules about how one should read a play. Nevertheless, some observations may be helpful to those for whom play reading is still a new experience. First, one must accept that the ability to read imaginatively and perceptively is a basic skill needed by all persons who seek to become educated, for without it much of human experience is forever lost, and intellectually we remain children suffering from historical and cultural amnesia.

Since all writers do not express themselves in the same form, all written works cannot be read in the same way. Each form has its own characteristics, and each makes distinctive demands on the reader. Thus, we cannot read a play in the same way we do an historical treatise, an essay, a biography, a novel, or a poem. To read a play adequately, we must first adjust our minds to the dramatic form so that its contents may be perceived. A play is distinctive in part because it is a form made up primarily of dialogue that must be constructed with great care in order to convey its

One way of approaching a play is for the actors to read and discuss it with the director. (Marion Bernstein/EPA)

intentions precisely while at the same time creating the sense of being the spontaneous oral utterances of characters involved in a developing action. Thus, it is at once a highly formal structure and a simulated spontaneous reflection of human experience.

Drama requires the reader to contribute more than any other form does. Not only must the reader see and understand what is explicitly said and done, but he must also be aware of all that is merely implied or left unsaid. While the dramatist may use stage directions to clarify setting, situation, or tone, for the most part he conveys his intentions through dialogue. Therefore, in reading a play we should assume that the writer has set down precisely what he wishes to say, but that, because he must convey his intentions through a likeness of conversation, we must be sensitive—as in real life—to the implications, unspoken feelings, and even deliberate deceptions typical of human interaction. Therefore, the reader must be alert to the nuances and shadings of each word and phrase. Although inwardly and imaginatively seeing and hearing a script is not a simple undertaking, it can be done adequately if we cultivate the imagination and develop the understanding appropriate to the task. Perhaps the best place to begin is with a look at how plays are constructed.

DRAMATIC ACTION

Broadly speaking, a play is a representation of "man in action." But action does not mean mere physical movement; it involves the psychological motivations that lie behind visible behavior. "Man in action" therefore includes the whole range of feelings, thoughts, and deeds that define what sort of creature man is—what he does and why he does what he does. Since this range is almost infinite, a single play can depict only a small part of a whole. Furthermore, because each playwright's vision differs, each drama is in some respect unique. Yet outstanding plays, no matter when or where they were written, tend to have qualities in common that permit us to draw conclusions about the characteristics of effective dramatic action.

Aristotle (the Greek philosopher of the fourth century B.C.) declares that a play should have a beginning, middle, and end. On the surface, this statement seems obvious, but it summarizes a fundamental principle. Basically, it means that a play should be *complete and self-contained,* that everything necessary for understanding it should be included within the play itself. If this principle is not observed, the action will probably be confusing or unsatisfying to audiences.

Dramatic action should be *purposeful,* organized to evoke a specific response such as pity, fear, laughter, or thoughtful contemplation. The purpose may be simple or complex, but the events, the characters, the mood should be shaped with some purpose in mind.

Dramatic action should be *varied* (in plot, characterization, ideas, mood, or spectacle) if monotony is to be avoided.

Dramatic action should *engage and maintain interest.* The characters must excite the audience's curiosity; the situation must be compelling enough to arouse interest, the issues vital enough to provoke concern, the visual or sound effects novel enough to attract attention.

Dramatic action should be *probable*—that is, all of the elements should be logically consistent. If they are, the play will seem believable even though it may not be true to real life and may deal with impossible events, as in fantasy.

METHODS OF ORGANIZING DRAMATIC ACTION

A play is composed of incidents organized to accomplish some purpose. Organization is primarily a matter of directing attention to relationships which create a meaningful pattern. The most common sources of unity are thought, character, and cause-to-effect arrangement of events.

Traditionally, the main organizational principle has been the *cause-to-effect arrangement of incidents.* Using this method, the playwright sets up in the opening scenes all of the necessary conditions—the situation, the desires and motivations of the characters—out of which later events develop. The goals of one character come into conflict with those of another, or two conflicting desires within the same character may lead to a crisis. Attempts to surmount the obstacles make up the substance of the play, each scene growing logically out of preceding ones.

Less often, a dramatist uses a *character* as the principal source of unity. Such a play may dramatize the life of a historical figure or a purely fictional one. An example would be Marlowe's *Doctor Faustus.*

A playwright may organize his material around a *basic idea,* with the scenes linked mainly because each concerns the main theme. This type of organization is used frequently by modern playwrights, especially those of the expressionistic, epic, and absurdist movements. For example, Brecht's *The Private Life of the Master Race* treats the rise of the Nazi party in a series of scenes that illustrate the inhumanity of Nazism. Many absurdist plays, such as Beckett's *Waiting for Godot,* do not develop a story so much as they embroider upon a central idea or mood.

Any organizational pattern other than cause-to-effect is apt to seem loose, often giving the effect of randomness. In analyzing a play, it is essential to pinpoint the source of unity, for only then will it appear to be a whole rather than a collection of unrelated happenings.

The structure of a play may also be approached through the parts of drama, which, in Aristotle's terms, are six: plot, character, thought, diction, music, and spectacle.

PLOT

Plot is often considered merely the summary of a play's incidents, but—though it includes the story line—it also refers to the organization of all the elements into a meaningful pattern. Plot is thus the over-all structure of a play.

The Beginning. The beginning of a play usually establishes the place, the occasion, the characters, the mood, the theme, and the type of probability. A play is somewhat like coming upon previously unknown places and persons. Initially, the novelty may excite interest, but, as the facts about the place and people are established, interest either wanes or increases. The playwright is faced with a double problem: he must give essential information but at the same time make the audience want to stay and see more.

The beginning of a play thus involves *exposition,* or the setting forth of information—about earlier events, the identity of the characters, and the present situation. While exposition is an unavoidable part of the opening scenes, it is not confined to them, for in most plays background information is only gradually revealed.

The amount of exposition required is partly determined by the *point of attack,* the moment at which the story is taken up. Shakespeare uses an early point of attack (that is, he begins the play near the beginning of the story and tells it chronologically). Thus he needs little exposition. Greek tragic dramatists, on the other hand, use later points, which require that many previous events be summarized for the audience's benefit. They thus actually show only the final parts of their stories.

Playwrights motivate giving exposition in many ways. For example, Ibsen most frequently introduces a character who has returned after a long absence. Answers to his questions about happenings while he was away supply the needed background information. On the other hand, in a nonrealistic play essential exposition may be given in a monologue. Many of Euripides' tragedies, for example, open with a monologue-prologue summarizing past events. In a musical play, exposition may be given in song and dance.

In most plays from the past, attention is usually focused early on a question, potential conflict, or theme. The beginning of such plays therefore includes what may be called an *inciting incident,* an occurrence that sets the main action in motion. In Sophocles' *Oedipus the King* a plague is destroying the city of Thebes; Oedipus has sought guidance from the oracle at Delphi, who declares that the murderer of King Laius must be found and punished before the plague can end. This is the event (introduced in the prologue) that sets the action in motion.

The inciting incident usually leads directly to a *major dramatic question* around which the play is organized, although this question may change as the play progresses. For example, the question first raised in nevertheless, frequently a theme or controlling idea around which the action is centered.

The Middle. The middle of a play is normally composed of a series of complications. A *complication* is any new element which changes the direction of the action—the discovery of new information, for example, or the arrival of a character. The substance of most complications is *discovery* (any occurrence of sufficient importance to alter the direction of action). Discoveries may involve objects (a wife discovers in her husband's pocket a weapon of the kind used in a murder), persons (a young man discovers that his rival in love is his brother), facts (a young man about to leave home discovers that his mother has cancer), values (a woman discovers that self-esteem is more important than marriage), or self (a man discovers that he has been acting from purely selfish motives when he thought he was acting out of love for his children). Each complication normally has a beginning, middle, and end—its own development, climax, and resolution—just as does the play as a whole. Usually the complications are overlapping rather than strung together in a series.

Means other than discoveries may be used to precipitate complications. Natural disasters (earthquakes, storms, shipwrecks, automobile accidents) are sometimes used. These are apt to seem especially contrived if they resolve the problem (for example, if the villain were to be killed in an automobile accident and as a result the struggle automatically ended).

The series of complications culminates in the *crisis,* or turning point of the action. For example, in *Oedipus the King* Oedipus sets out to discover the murderer of Laius; the crisis comes when Oedipus realizes that he himself is the guilty person. Not all plays have a clear-cut series of complications leading to a crisis. *Waiting for Godot,* for example, is less concerned with a progressing action than with a static condition. Nevertheless, interest is maintained by the frequent introduction of new elements.

The End. The final portion of a play, often called the *resolution* or *dénouement* (unraveling or untying), extends from the crisis to the final curtain. It varies in length. It serves to tie off the various strands of action and to answer the questions raised earlier. It brings the situation back to a state of balance and satisfies audience expectations.

Oedipus the King is: Will the murderer of Laius be found and the city saved? Later this question changes as interest shifts to the question of Oedipus' guilt.

Not all plays, especially recent ones, include inciting incidents or clearly identifiable major dramatic questions. All have focal points,

CHARACTER AND CHARACTERIZATION

Character is the primary material from which plots are created, for incidents are developed through the speech and behavior of dramatic personages. Characterization is the playwright's means of differentiating one personage from another.

The first level of characterization is *physical* and concerns such basic facts as sex, age, size, and color. Sometimes a dramatist does not supply all of this information, but it is present whenever the play is produced, since actors necessarily give concrete form to the characters.

The second level is *social.* It includes a character's economic status, profession or trade, religion, family relationships—all those factors that place him in his environment.

The third level is *psychological.* It reveals a character's habitual responses, desires, motivations, likes and dislikes—the inner workings of the mind. Since drama most often arises from conflicting desires, the psychological is the most essential level of characterization.

The fourth level is *moral.* It is most often used in serious plays, especially tragedies. Moral decisions differentiate characters more fully than any other type, since such decisions cause a character to examine his own motives, in the process of which his true nature is revealed both to himself and to the audience.

A playwright can emphasize one or more of these levels and may assign many or few traits, depending on *how the character functions in the play.* For example, the audience needs to know very little about a maid who appears only to announce dinner. The principal characters, on the other hand, should be drawn in considerable depth.

A character is revealed in several ways: through *descriptions in stage directions, prefaces, or other explanatory material* not part of the dialogue; through *what the character says;* through *what others say about him;* and, most important, through *what he does.*

Dramatic characters are usually both *typified* and *individualized.* If a character were totally unlike any person the spectators had ever known, they would be unable to understand him. But the audience may be dissatisfied unless the playwright goes beyond this typification and gives his characters individualizing traits. The best dramatic characters are usually easily recognizable types with some unusual or complex qualities.

The character of Dracula combines recognizable with bizarre qualities. From the Broadway production of *Dracula* with Frank Langella, 1978. (Martha Swope)

A playwright may be concerned with making his characters *sympathetic* or *unsympathetic*. Normally, sympathetic characters are given major virtues and lesser foibles, while the reverse is true of unsympathetic characters. The more a character is made either completely good or bad, the more he is apt to be unacceptable as a truthful reflection of human behavior. Acceptability varies with the type of play. Melodrama, for example, oversimplifies human psychology and clearly divides characters into good or evil. Tragedy, on the other hand, normally depicts more complex forces at work both within and without characters and requires greater depth of characterization.

THOUGHT

The third basic element of a play is *thought*. It includes the themes, arguments, and over-all meaning of the action. It is present in all plays, even the most light-hearted farce: a playwright cannot avoid expressing some ideas, since events and characterization always imply some view of human behavior. Thought is also one of the main sources of unity in drama; action—as in much recent drama—may be organized around a central idea, motif, or concern.

The significance or meaning of a play is normally implied rather than stated directly. It is to be discovered in the relationships among characters, the ideas associated with unsympathetic and sympathetic characters, the conflicts and their resolution, and such devices as spectacle, music, and song. Sometimes, however, the author's intention is clearly stated in the script, as when characters advocate a certain line of action, point of view, or specific social reform.

Dramatists in different periods have used various devices to project ideas. Greek playwrights made extensive use of the *chorus,* just as those of later periods employed such devices as *soliloquies, asides,* and other forms of *direct statement.* Still other tools for projecting meaning are *allegory* and *symbol.* In allegory, characters are personifications of abstract qualities (mercy, greed, and so on), as in the medieval play *Everyman.* A symbol is a concrete object or event which, while meaningful in itself, also suggests a concept or set of relationships. For example, in Ibsen's *The Wild Duck* the duck is both a real object and a symbol of a free, unhampered, but vulnerable creature. The symbol has been a favorite device with modern writers because it allows them to suggest deeper meanings even within a realistic framework.

DICTION

Plot, character, and thought are the basic ingredients of drama. To convey these to an audience, the playwright has at his disposal only two means—sound and spectacle. Sound includes language, music, and other aural effects; spectacle refers to all the visual elements of a production (physical movement and dance, costumes, scenery, properties, and lighting).

Language is the playwright's primary means of expression. When a play is performed, other expressive means (primarily music, sound effects, and spectacle) may be added, but to convey his intentions to others the dramatist depends almost entirely on dialogue and stage directions. Thus language (diction) is the playwright's primary tool.

Diction serves many purposes. It is used to *impart information,* to *characterize,* to *direct attention* to important plot elements, to *reveal the themes and ideas* of a play, to *establish tone or mood and level of probability,* and to *establish tempo and rhythm.*

The diction of every play, no matter how realistic, is more abstract and formal than that of normal conversation. A dramatist always selects, arranges, and heightens language more than anyone ever does in spontaneous speech. In a realistic play, although the dialogue is modeled after everyday usage and may retain its rhythms and basic vocabulary, the characters are usually more articulate and state their ideas and feelings more precisely than would their real-life counterparts.

The dialogue of nonrealistic plays may deviate markedly from normal speech. Sometimes (as in many of Ionesco's plays) the clichés of ordinary conversation are emphasized until they become ludicrous. More frequently, however, nonrealistic drama employs a larger vocabulary, abandons the rhythms of conversation, and makes considerable use of imagery and meter.

The basic criterion for judging diction is its *appropriateness* to the characters, the situation, the level of probability, and the type of play.

MUSIC

Music, as we ordinarily understand the term, does not occur in every play. But, if the term is extended to include all patterned sound, it is an important ingredient in every production, except those wholly silent.

Language has been described above as the playwright's principal means of expression. But a written script, like a musical score, is not fully realized until the performers—through the elements of pitch, stress, volume, tempo, duration, and quality—transform print into sound. It is through these elements that meaning is conveyed. Though the words of a sentence may remain constant, its meaning can be varied by manipulating emphasis or tone ("You say *he* told her?" contrasted with "You say he told *her*?," for example, or the difference between the tone of joy and that of sarcasm). Because written language is not always precise, actor and director can interpret a passage differently than the playwright intended.

The spoken aspect of language varies considerably in its formal qualities. In some plays, it simulates the loose rhythms of everyday speech, but in others, such as Shakespearean drama, it is shaped into highly formalized patterns. In delivery, the effective actor respects the pattern; it is one of the devices used by the playwright to define characters and their world.

In addition to the sound of the actors' voices, a play may also use music in the form of incidental songs or—as in musical comedy and opera—it may utilize song and instrumental accompaniment as integral structural means.

Music may serve many functions. It can *establish mood and enhance expectations,* it can *establish the level of probability,* it can *characterize,* it can *convey ideas,* it can *condense* by speeding up characterization and exposition, it can *lend variety,* and it can *be pleasurable in itself.*

SPECTACLE

Spectacle means simply all the visual elements of a production: the movement and spatial relations of characters, the lighting, settings, costumes, and properties. Since he normally depends upon others to supply these elements, the playwright does not have full control over them. Because he seldom describes the spectacle precisely, other theatre artists must discover his intentions by studying the plot, characters, thought, and dialogue. Similarly, the reader of a script must try to envision the spectacle or he may not grasp a play's full power.

Some texts give the reader more help than others. Many older plays contain almost no stage directions and all clues must be sought in the dialogue. Beginning in the nineteenth century, when the visual elements were given new prominence, stage directions became usual. Since that time the printed texts of plays commonly have included many aids designed to help the reader in visualizing the action.

Since Greek plays contain little or no stage direction, they are conducive to varying productions, as this one of Sophocles' *Oedipus* at the Darmstadt Theatre illustrates. (Courtesy German Information Center)

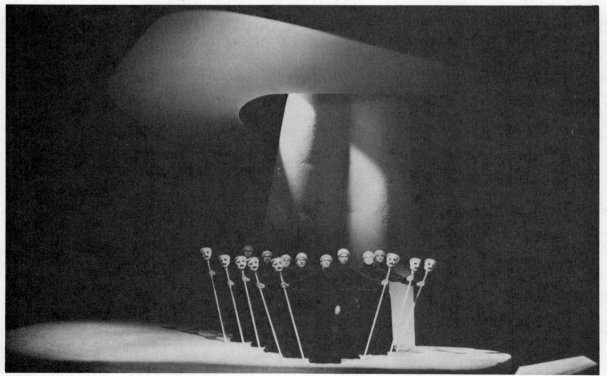

Spectacle has several functions. It *gives information* (establishing where and when the action occurs), it *aids characterization,* it *helps establish the level of probability* (an abstract setting suggests one level of reality, while a realistic one suggests another), and it *establishes mood and atmosphere.*

Spectacle, like the other elements of a play, should be *appropriate, expressive of the play's values, distinctive,* and *practicable.* (The process of transferring the written script to the stage is treated in Part Three.)

FORM IN DRAMA

These six parts—plot, character, thought, diction, music, and spectacle—make up every play, but they may be combined and varied in almost infinite ways. Certain basic patterns have nevertheless recurred often enough to permit us to divide plays into a limited number of dramatic forms. An almost endless number of forms and subforms has been suggested by critics, but all the labels they use can be related to one of three basic qualities: the serious, the comic, and the seriocomic. These three qualities are epitomized in three forms: tragedy, comedy, and melodrama.

Tragedy. A tragedy presents a genuinely serious action and maintains a serious mood throughout, although there may be moments of comic relief. It raises questions about the meaning of man's existence, his moral nature, and his social or psychological relationships.

Most tragedies written before the eighteenth century show the interaction between superhuman and human forces: a god, Providence, or some moral power independent of man usually affects the outcome of the action almost as much as do the human agents. Many tragedies (like *Oedipus the King*) imply that the protagonist has violated a moral order which must be vindicated and reestablished. Because superhuman forces are involved, the outcome often seems inevitable and predetermined.

In the eighteenth century, the supernatural element began to decline as social and psychological forces were given more emphasis and as human conflicts were emphasized. Eventually the action no longer involved man's will in conflict with divine laws but was restricted to conflict among human desires, laws, and institutions. Since strictly human problems may be more readily solved, happy resolutions became more probable. Because this later drama has often been concerned with everyday situations and seems less profound than earlier works, some critics have refused to call it tragedy and have substituted the term *drama.*

The protagonist or leading character of tragedy is usually a person who arouses our sympathy and admiration, but there are exceptions to this rule. Normally, the protagonist is ethically superior but sufficiently imperfect to be believably human. Often the tragic protagonist encounters disaster through his pursuit of some aim, worthy in itself, which conflicts with another claim. A recurring motif in serious drama is the imposition of a duty which, being performed, will lead to loss of life, love, or reputation. Hamlet is told to avenge his father's death, even though to do so means becoming a murderer or losing his own life. Another recurring motif in tragedy (seen in *King Lear*) is man's inability to control his destiny.

In most tragedies written before the eighteenth century the protagonists are members of the ruling class; since that time they have been increasingly drawn from the middle and lower classes. To assume that social class has any relation to nobility of character lacks reason, but most modern serious drama seems less powerful than the best tragedies of the Greeks and Elizabethans probably because of man's reduced estimate of his own importance in the whole scheme of being.

The emotional effect of tragedy is usually described as the "arousal of pity and fear," but these basic emotions include a wide range of other responses: compassion, admiration, foreboding, dread, awe, and terror. Pity and fear are rooted in two instinctive human reactions: fear out of the desire for self-preservation and pity out of concern for the welfare of others. Aristotle, in the *Poetics,* stated that pity is aroused by the apprehension of some pain or harm about to befall someone like ourselves, and that were we in the position of the endangered person we would feel fear. Thus pity and fear are complementary emotions.

In addition to arousing pity and fear, tragedy also calms or purges these emotions. Rather than leaving us emotionally unsettled, the ending of a tragedy releases the tensions that have been aroused and brings us back to a state of equilibrium. It not only resolves the situation which has aroused pity and fear, but it also leads us to recognize the inevitability of the outcome and to accept its implications.

Comedy. The action of comedy is based on some deviation from normality in action, character, thought, or speech. The deviation must not pose a serious threat and an "in fun" mood is usually maintained. There is no subject, however trivial or important, that cannot be treated in comedy provided it is placed in the right framework.

Comedy also demands that an audience view the character or situation objectively. Henri Bergson, in *Laughter,* states that comedy requires an "anesthesia of the heart," since it is difficult to laugh at anything about which we feel deeply. We might find it funny to see a man slip on a banana peel, but if we discover that he has just undergone a serious operation, our concern will destroy the laughter. Likewise, we may dislike some things so intensely that we cannot see their ridiculous qualities. Part of the pleasure of watching comedy comes from witnessing the triumph of normative behavior, characters, or ideas over a threat from the abnormal.

Because of its wide range, comedy is often divided into a number of subcategories. A *comedy of situation* shows the amusing consequences of putting characters in unusual circumstances. For example, several persons are planning to attend a masked ball but each, for his own reasons, tries to conceal his intentions. The devices for getting rid of each other, the attempts to elude discovery when all appear at the ball, the reactions upon being recognized, and the eventual reconciliation of the characters make up the comic action. In such a play, character and ideas are of minor importance.

Farce, sometimes considered a separate form, is basically a comedy of situation in which buffoonery, accident, and coincidence play an important part. Pies in the face, beatings, the naïve or mistaken views of characters, the ludicrous situation arising from coincidence exemplify the devices of farce. While farce seemingly has little purpose beyond entertainment, it has been a part of some of the world's finest comedies, including those of Shakespeare and Molière.

A *comedy of character* grows out of the eccentricities of the protagonist. For example, some of Molière's comedies are built around characters suffering from hypochondria, miserliness, or hypocrisy.

Romantic comedy usually treats the struggles, often centering around a love affair, of characters who are basically sympathetic. A comic response is aroused primarily because of the ludicrous devices the characters use in pursuing success and the misunderstandings or complications that result. Shakespeare's *Twelfth Night* and *As You Like It* are examples of the type.

A *comedy of ideas* has as its principal focus a conflict over a concept or a way of thought. It is exemplified in the plays of George Bernard Shaw and Aristophanes.

A *comedy of manners* shares some traits with the comedy of situation and of character. It shows the amusing results that come from adhering to a certain code of behavior at the expense of normal responses. Comedy of manners is often reserved as a label for plays about aristocratic and sophisticated characters who carry on witty and sparkling conversations; it is sometimes called *comedy of wit. The School for Scandal* is a good example of the type.

Almost all comedies have elements that relate them to more than one of these categories, and labels need to be used with some flexibility if they are to be helpful.

All comedy arouses emotions that lie in a range between joy and scorn. At one extreme, Shakespeare's romantic comedies produce a feeling of well-being, arousing smiles or quiet laughter but seldom boisterous laughter. On the other hand, Ben Jonson's *Volpone* at times becomes almost too painful to be amusing. These extremes of the gentlest and the bitterest ridicule mark the limits of comic response.

Unlike tragedy, comedy seldom raises deep moral questions. Rather, it builds on normative human responses and opposes deviations which threaten to destroy what is valuable. Since ideas about normal behavior vary from one period to another, so too the scope of comedy changes.

Melodrama. Although the term *melodrama* was not widely used until the nineteenth century, the type had existed since the fifth century B.C. In some periods it has been called *tragicomedy* and today it is often labeled *drama* because the term melodrama is in disrepute.

A melodrama deals with a serious action. Its seriousness, however, is often temporary and is usually caused by the maliciousness of an unsympathetic character. A happy resolution is achieved by destroying the power of the villain.

The characters in melodrama are usually divided into those who are almost completely sympathetic and those who are almost completely antipathetic. There may also be one or more simple-minded or uninhibited characters who provide comic relief.

The action of melodrama usually develops a powerful threat to the well-being of an innocent protagonist. It shows the character's entanglement in a web of circumstances and eventual rescue from death or ruin, usually at the last possible moment. (Most contemporary television series dealing with crime and danger are melodramas.)

Melodrama usually has a double ending, in which the good characters are rescued and rewarded and the evil are detected and punished. Thus it is related to tragedy through its serious action and to comedy through its happy ending. It has been a popular form throughout history, for it assures audiences that good triumphs over evil.

Mixed Forms. Although tragedy, comedy, and melodrama are the primary forms, many plays do not fit comfortably into any of these categories, since they mingle elements from two or all of them. This mixing of characteristics is most typical of modern times, when playwrights have often deliberately departed from the traditional forms. For example, Ionesco has labeled some of his works "tragic farces," while Harold Pinter called his early plays "comedies of menace." Such works are often now labeled "black comedy." Although these designations indicate significant departures from the conventional forms, they also suggest connections with them, and it can be illuminating to note in them the tendencies toward or departures from tragedy, comedy, or melodrama.

Ionesco labeled some of his works "tragic farces." This scene is from one of those, *The Chairs.* (Courtesy French Cultural Services)

STYLE

Even plays of the same type vary considerably. One cause of this variety is style. Like form, style is difficult to define because it has been used to designate many things. Basically, however, *style* is a quality that results from a characteristic mode of expression or method of presentation.

Style may stem from traits attributable to a period, a nation, a movement, or an author. In most periods, the drama of all Western nations has certain common qualities that are caused by prevailing religious, philosophical, and psychological concepts and by current theatrical conventions. Thus, we may speak of an eighteenth-century style. Within a period, however, there are national differences that permit us to distinguish a French from an English style. Furthermore, the dramas written by neoclassicists have qualities that distinguish them from those written by romantics, expressionists, or absurdists. Finally, the plays of individual authors have distinctive qualities that set them off from the work of all other writers. Thus, we may speak of Shakespeare's or Sophocles' style.

Style in theatre results from three basic influences. First, it is grounded upon assumptions about truth and reality. Dramatists of different movements or periods have sought to convey truthful pictures of humanity, but they have differed widely in their answers to these questions: What is ultimate truth? How can we perceive reality? Some persons have argued that surface appearances only disguise reality, which is to be found in some inner or spiritual realm. Others have maintained that truth can be discovered only by objective study of the things that can be felt, tasted, seen, heard, or smelled. To advocates of the latter view, observable details hold the key to truth, while to the former the same details only hide the truth. Although all writers attempt to depict the truth as they see it, the individual playwright's conception of truth is determined by his basic temperament and talents and by the philosophical, social, and psychological influences that have shaped him.

Second, style results from the manner in which the playwright manipulates his means of expression. All dramatists have at their disposal the same means — sound and spectacle. Nevertheless, the work of each playwright is distinctive, for each perceives the human condition from a somewhat different point of view. His perceptions are reflected in the situations, characters, and ideas he invents, in his manipulation of language, and in his suggestions for the use of spectacle.

In Beckett's *Endgame,* two characters perform entirely from inside trash cans. (Courtesy German Information Center)

Third, style results from the manner in which the play is presented in the theatre. The directing, acting, scenery, costumes, and lighting used to translate the play from the written script to the stage may each be manipulated to influence stylistic qualities. (Each of these elements is treated at length in Part Three.) Because so many people are involved in producing a play, it is not unusual to find conflicting or inconsistent styles in a single production. Normally, however, unity of style is a primary artistic goal. Each theatre artist seeks to create qualities similar to those found in the written text, and the director then coordinates all of the parts into a unified whole. Ultimately style results from the way in which means are adapted to ends. It contributes significantly to the sense of unity and wholeness which is a mark of effective drama.

Discussions of structure, form, and style remain abstract, however, until applied to specific examples. The chapters that follow show how these principles have been put into practice, both in the past and in our own time.

THE DEVELOPMENT OF THE THEATRE

PART **2**

The Theatre of Ancient Greece and Rome

3

No one really knows how the theatre began; it probably evolved from religious rituals, storytelling, and other activities of primitive man. There certainly were many semidramatic rituals in ancient Egypt and the Near East, but theatre as we know it seems to have emerged first in ancient Greece.

THE BEGINNINGS OF DRAMA IN GREECE

For several centuries, Greek drama was presented exclusively at festivals honoring Dionysus, the god of wine and fertility. Supposedly the son of Zeus (the greatest of Greek gods) and Semele (a mortal), Dionysus was killed, dismembered, and then resurrected. The myths that arose about him were closely related to the life cycle and to seasonal changes: birth, growth, decay, death, and rebirth; spring, summer, fall, and winter. His worship was designed in part to insure the return of spring and fertility, but as the god of wine he also represented many of the world's irrational forces, and his worship was a recognition of man's elemental passions.

The worship of Dionysus was introduced into Greece from Asia Minor around the thirteenth century B.C. By the seventh or eighth century contests of choral dancers were already being held at the festivals given in honor of Dionysus. These dances were accompanied by dithyrambs, or ecstatic hymns, in honor of the god. It is out of these hymns and dances that Aristotle says drama developed.

The Greeks did not observe a holy day comparable to the sabbath. Rather they had a series of religious festivals throughout the year honoring various gods. By the fifth century B.C. there were three festivals each year in honor of Dionysus at which plays were performed: the Rural Dionysia (in December); the Lenaia (in January); and the City (or Great) Dionysia (around the end of March). Drama was never a part of the festivals held in honor of other gods.

The first definite record of drama in Greece is found in 534 B.C., when the City Dionysia was reorganized and a contest for the best tragedy was instituted. The only dramatist of this period whose name has survived is Thespis, who won the first contest. Since he is also the first known actor, performers are still often called *thespians.*

The drama of Thespis was relatively simple, since it involved only one actor and a chorus. This does not mean that there was only one speaking character, but rather that all characters were played by the same actor. This single actor used masks in shifting his identity; when he left the stage to change roles, the chorus filled the intervals with singing and dancing. The chorus, therefore, was the principal unifying force in this early drama.

THE FIFTH CENTURY

Although drama was written and performed in Greece for many centuries, plays by only five writers — Aeschylus, Sophocles, Euripides, Aristophanes, and Menander — now exist. Out of the vast number of plays written, only forty-five survive — thirty-two tragedies, twelve comedies, and one satyr play. All but four of these plays were written during the fifth century.

Aeschylus (525–456 B.C.) is the earliest dramatist whose plays have survived. The titles of seventy-nine of his plays have come down to us but only seven works remain: *The Persians* (472), *Seven against Thebes* (467), the *Oresteia* — a trilogy of plays made up of *Agamemnon, Choephoroe,* and *Eumenides* (458), *The Suppliants,* and *Prometheus Bound* (exact dates unknown).

Aeschylus' major innovation was the introduction of a second actor, which allowed face-to-face conflict for the first time. The subsequent increase in emphasis on the actor reduced the importance of the chorus, though it remained a dominant force. The power of Aeschylus' drama can best be appreciated through the *Oresteia,* one of the great monuments of dramatic literature. This trilogy demonstrates his interests well, for here he deals with growth in the concept of justice. In the first two plays the characters conceive of justice as personal revenge, but in the final play private justice is replaced by the impartial power of the state. This evolutionary process is demonstrated through a powerful story of murder, reprisal, and remorse.

Sophocles (496–406) is frequently called the greatest of the Greek tragedians. He is credited with over a hundred plays, of which only seven now exist: *Ajax* (dated variously from 450 to 440), *Antigone* (around 440), *Oedipus the King* (approximately 430 to 425), *Philoctetes* (409), *Electra* and *Trachiniae* (dates unknown, though considered to be late plays), and *Oedipus at Colonus* (written shortly before Sophocles' death). In addition, a substantial part of *The Trackers,* a satyr play, is extant. Sophocles' introduction of a third actor encouraged greater dramatic complexity than had been possible with two actors. He was much more concerned with human relationships than with the religious and philosophical issues which had interested Aeschylus. Furthermore, his dramas place more emphasis upon building skillful climaxes and well-developed episodes than those of Aeschylus. (The qualities of Sophocles' drama will be explored at greater length in the detailed examination of *Oedipus the King.*)

Euripides (480–406) was the last of the great Greek tragedians. He is said to have written ninety-two plays, of which seventeen tragedies have survived. Among these the most famous are: *Alcestis* (438), *Medea* (431), *Hippolytus* (428), *Ion* and *Electra* (dates unknown), *The Trojan Women* (415), and *The Bacchae* (produced after his death). In addition, *The Cyclops* is the only complete satyr play that now exists. Although Euripides achieved great popularity in later times, he was not widely appreciated in his own day.

Euripides reduced the role of the chorus until its connection with the rest of the play was often vague. He was a skeptic who questioned many Athenian ideals; even the gods did not escape examination, and in his plays they were frequently made to appear petty and ineffectual; he probed the motives of his characters and found little to admire. He also turned toward melodrama and frequently resorted to contrived endings. Thus he has been admired for his ideas and his psychological realism, but has been criticized for faulty dramatic structure. With his death, the great era of Greek tragedy came to an end.

The characteristics of Greek tragedy can best be appreciated through an examination of a representative example. Here, *Oedipus the King* will be used. Since information about the theatrical conventions for which it was written will contribute much to our understanding of the play, it will be helpful first to explore the practices that prevailed in 430 B.C., the approximate time when Sophocles' play was first performed.

PLAY PRODUCTION IN GREECE

It was at the City Dionysia, one of the great religious and civic occasions of the Athenian year, that *Oedipus the King* was first presented. If a tragic dramatist wished to enter plays at the City Dionysia, he applied to the principal civic magistrate (the *archon eponymous*) for a chorus. It is not known how this official decided among the applicants, but three tragic writers were granted choruses at each City Dionysia.

The magistrate also appointed the *choregoi,* wealthy citizens who bore the expense of the choruses. One *choregus* was appointed for each dramatist, and the *choregoi* and playwrights were then matched by lot. The *choregus* paid for the training of the chorus, its costumes, the musicians, the supernumerary actors and their costumes, and perhaps for the scenery. In other words, he was responsible for everything except the theatre and the speaking actors.

Each playwright granted a chorus for the City Dionysia supplied three tragedies and a satyr play. Usually the playwright directed his own works and was in charge of the production as a whole. Until the time of Sophocles the playwright acted in his own plays as well. For his efforts, the playwright was no doubt given some financial remuneration by the state and there was a prize for the winner of the contest, but the amount of money a playwright might have received for his work is unknown.

The state paid the actors, supplied their costumes, and furnished the theatre in which the plays were performed. Dramatic production in the fifth century was thus financed either by wealthy citizens or by the government and was looked upon as a religious and civic function of such importance that during it no legal proceedings were allowed and prisoners were released. At the festival one day was devoted to a contest for comedies; this was followed by three days on each of which three tragedies and a satyr play were performed.

To this civic and religious celebration everyone was welcome. Originally, admission was probably free but was later set at the small sum of two *obols,* and even then a public fund was established to provide tickets for those who could not afford the price of admission. The theatre was considered to be the right of everyone rather than a function for the few. In the fifth century, prizes were awarded at each City Dionysia for the best plays (there was a prize for the best comedy and for the best group of tragedies, the honor being shared by the playwright and the *choregus*) and to the best tragic actor. The state supervised the judging, and elaborate precautions were taken to insure the secrecy of voting.

THE THEATRE OF DIONYSUS

Plays were presented in the Theatre of Dionysus situated on the slope of the Acropolis above the Temple of Dionysus. This theatre underwent many changes. In the sixth century it consisted of the hillside on which the spectators stood or sat, and a flat terrace at the foot of the hill for the performers. In the middle of this terrace or *orchestra* (the "dancing place") was an altar (or *thymele*). There probably was no scenic background. Seats, forming an auditorium or *theatron* (the "seeing place"), were gradually added for spectators.

During the fifth and fourth centuries this basic structure was elaborated: a scene house was added and the whole theatre was reconstructed in stone, although this process was not completed until well into the fourth century. The auditorium was the first part of the theatre to assume permanent form, when stadiumlike seating was provided by setting stones into the hillside. The semicircular auditorium, which seated about fourteen thousand persons, curved around the circular orchestra, which measured about sixty-five feet in diameter.

The stage house (or *skene*) was the last part to be constructed in stone, and was remodeled many times after that. For these reasons, it is difficult to get a clear impression of the scenic background of plays in the fifth century. The *skene* was originally merely a place where actors might retire to change costumes. Gradually this house came to be used as a background for the action of the play. At the time *Oedipus the King* was first performed the *skene* was probably a long building which, with its projecting side wings (called *paraskenia*), formed a rectangular background opposite the spectators. It was not joined to the auditorium, and the space on each side between the *paraskenia* and the auditorium provided entrances into the orchestra. These entrances were called *parodoi*. (For a plan of the theatre as a whole see the illustration on page 46.)

Most scholars believe that the same formalized background was used for all plays. Others, however, argue that, since it was not entirely permanent, the appearance of the *skene* could have been changed from year to year or from play to play. It is impossible to know the truth, but, considering the lack of realistic detail in the plays, it seems unlikely that the Greeks ever attempted to create the illusion of a real place in their theatre.

It is unclear whether there was a raised stage in the theatre of the

45

The ruins of the Theatre of Dionysus
at Athens today. Evidences of the
remodeling of c. A.D. 270 remain.
(From Ernest Fiechter, *Antike
Griechische Theaterbauten,*
courtesy Dr. Charlotte Fiechter.
Right: Ground plan of the precinct of
Dionysus at Athens showing the
Theatre and the Temple of Dionysus.
(From Dorpfeld-Reisch, *Das
Griechische Theater,* 1896)

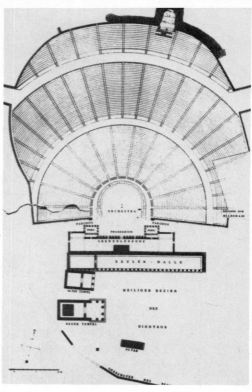

fifth century. Since the plays seem to require that the actors and the chorus mingle freely, if a platform was used it was probably low enough to allow free access between stage and orchestra. If there was no stage, both the chorus and actors would have used the acting area composed of the orchestra and the rectangular space formed by the scene house. The roof of the stage house also could be used as an acting area.

When the available information about the Greek theatre is assembled, a fairly clear picture of its basic structure emerges, but the details of the scenic background remain unclear. (A number of reconstructions of the *skene,* showing variations on many possible features, may be seen on page 48.)

While most of the action of Greek plays takes place out of doors, occasionally interiors are indicated. For example, most deaths occur offstage, but the bodies are frequently displayed afterward. For this purpose the large central doorway seems to have been opened and a wheeled platform moved forward. This device is called an *eccyclema* or *exaustra.*

Another effect frequently demanded in Greek plays is the appearance of gods. These characters may descend to the orchestra level or be lifted up from the orchestra to the roof of the stage house. For this purpose, a cranelike device called the *machina* was used. The overuse of gods to resolve difficult dramatic situations led to the Latin phrase *deus ex machina* to describe any contrived ending.

It is possible that *periaktoi* were also in use, although these may belong to a later period. *Periaktoi* are constructed of three flats put together to form a triangle; the triangle is then mounted on a central pivot. Since each surface can be exposed or concealed as desired, it may be used for sudden revelations or for changes in the background.

THE ACTOR

From the time of Sophocles onward, the number of speaking actors in Greek tragedy seems to have been restricted to three. Although there might be *extras,* these were not considered actors. In the second half of the fifth century the state supplied three speaking actors for each tragic playwright competing in the contests. A principal actor was assigned to each playwright by lot. The playwright and his leading actor probably chose the other two actors. All were male and all acted in each of the four plays presented by the same dramatist. Since there were only three actors, each might be asked to play a number of roles.

The style of acting is uncertain. The plays themselves call for simple realistic actions (such as weeping, running, and falling to the ground). On the other hand, many elements argue against any marked realism. The fact that the same actor played many roles and that men assumed women's parts suggests that performances could never have been very

Drawings by Ernst Fiechter of varying conceptions of the stage house for the Theatre of Dionysus in the fifth century B.C. (From Fiechter, *Antike Griechische Theaterbauten,* courtesy Verlag W. Kohlhammer GmbH, Stuttgart.)

close to real life. Furthermore, some plays could be performed by three actors only if the same role were played by a different actor in different scenes of the play. The large musical element, the use of dance, and the rather abstract treatment of the story also argue against a realistic style of acting. Nevertheless, the performances should not be thought of as devoid of clearly identifiable human actions. The style suggested by the scripts may be characterized as simple, expressive, and idealized.

MASKS AND COSTUMES

All the actors in Greek tragedy wore masks constructed of lightweight linen, cork, or wood. There were several reasons for this practice: each actor played a number of roles; all the actors were male though many of the characters were female; the range of age and character types played

An ivory statuette of a tragic actor, probably Roman, although the Greek tragic actor of the Hellenistic period probably wore similar costumes and masks. Note the high headdress, distorted features of the mask, and thick-soled boots concealed beneath the robe. The statuette stands on two pegs by which it was attached to a base, now missing. (Reprinted from *Monumenti Inediti,* Vol. XI, 1879.)

by a single actor was great. Although the mouths were open, the features were not exaggerated to any marked degree. Headdresses seem to have followed relatively closely those normally worn during the period.

A variety of clothing was used for stage purposes. A long-sleeved, ankle-length, heavily embroidered tunic, or *chiton,* was worn by certain characters, and some historians have argued that it was used for all the principal roles of tragedy. Since some plays contain references to mourning dress, to ragged garments, and to distinctions in clothing between Greeks and foreigners, however, it seems likely that costumes varied considerably. It may be that the sleeved, embroidered tunic (which was not worn in Greek daily life), was reserved for supernatural and non-Greek characters, while native dress was used for others. An ankle-length or knee-length *chiton* was the usual daily dress in Greece. The selection of the costume was probably determined at least in part by its appropriateness to the role. As for footwear, the tragic actor usually wore a soft, flexible, high-topped boot in common use at that time.

THE CHORUS, MUSIC, AND DANCE

It is generally assumed that during Sophocles' lifetime the chorus was composed of fifteen persons. Usually the members performed in unison, but at times they were divided into two semichoruses of seven members, which might perform in turn or which might exchange or divide speeches. The chorus leader sometimes had solo lines, but the chorus probably spoke and sang as a group (though some modern editions of the plays divide the speeches and assign them to individual chorus members).

The chorus usually makes its entrance after the prologue (or opening scene) and except in rare cases remains until the end of the play. It serves many functions. First, it is an actor who expresses opinions, gives advice, and sometimes threatens to interfere in the events of the play. Second, it may express the author's views and set up a standard against which the actions of the characters can be judged. Third, it is frequently the ideal spectator, reacting to the events and characters as the author would like his audience to respond. Fourth, it helps to set the mood of the play and to heighten dramatic effects. Fifth, the chorus adds color, movement, and spectacle. In the fifth century, all the choral interludes were accompanied by music and were both sung and danced.

The exact nature of Greek music and dance is unknown. Only a few fragments of music have survived, but we do know that the Greeks believed that both music and dance had ethical content. It is therefore reasonable to assume that in most tragedies the music and dance displayed the qualities that the Greeks associated with stateliness and moral uprightness.

OEDIPUS THE KING

With this background in mind, we may now proceed to examine Sophocles' *Oedipus the King* as an example of Greek tragedy.

Themes and Ideas. As in all great plays, there are a number of important themes in *Oedipus the King*. One concerns the fall of Oedipus from the place of highest honor to that of an outcast and demonstrates the uncertainty of human destiny. A second theme is man's limitation in controlling his fate. Oedipus is a man who attempts to do his best at all times; he has done what he considers necessary to avoid the terrible fate predicted by the oracle (that he will kill his father and marry his mother). But he cannot foresee what is in store for him. The contrast, then, between man seeking to control his destiny and fate determining destiny is clearly depicted.

It is significant that no attempt is made to explain why destruction comes to Oedipus. It is implied that man must submit to fate and that in struggling to avoid it he only becomes more entangled. There is then an

Oedipus the King as presented by the Greek National Theatre at Epidaurus in 1960. (Courtesy of the Greek National Theatre.)

irrational, or at least an unknowable, force at work. No one asks why the gods have decreed Oedipus' fate. The truth of the oracles is established, but the purpose is unclear. The Greek concept of the gods did not assume that all the gods were benevolent—all forces were deified, whether good or evil.

It is also possible to interpret this play as suggesting that the gods, rather than having decreed the characters' fates, have merely foreseen and foretold what they will do when confronted with certain problems. Such an interpretation, while it shifts the emphasis somewhat, does not contradict the picture of man as a victim of forces beyond his control, no matter by what name we call them.

Another theme, which may not have been a conscious one with Sophocles, is that of Oedipus as scapegoat. The city of Thebes will be saved if the one guilty man can be found and punished. Oedipus in a sense, then, takes the sins of the city upon himself, and in his punishment lies the salvation of others.

Another motif—blindness versus sight—is emphasized in poetic images and in various comparisons. A contrast is repeatedly drawn between physical sight and the inner sight of understanding. For example, Tiresias, though blind, can see the truth which escapes Oedipus, while Oedipus, who has penetrated the riddle of the Sphinx, cannot solve the puzzle of his own life. When it is revealed to him, he blinds himself in an act of retribution.

Plot and Structure. The skill with which *Oedipus the King* is constructed can be appreciated if we compare the complex story (which actually begins with a prophecy prior to the birth of Oedipus) with Sophocles' ordering of the events. In the play there is a simultaneous movement backward and forward in time as the revelation of the past moves Oedipus ever nearer to his doom in the present.

The division of the play into a prologue and five episodes separated by choral passages is typical of Greek tragedy. The prologue is devoted principally to exposition: a plague is destroying the city of Thebes; Creon returns from Delphi with a command from the Oracle to find and punish the murderer of Laius; Oedipus promises to obey the command. Thus, all of the necessary information is given in a very brief scene, and the first important question (Who is the murderer of Laius?) is raised. The prologue is followed by the *parodos,* or entry of the chorus, and the first choral song, which offers prayers to the gods for deliverance.

The first episode begins with Oedipus' proclamation and his curse upon the murderer. This proclamation has great dramatic power because Oedipus is unknowingly pronouncing a curse upon himself. Then Tiresias, the seer, enters. His refusal to answer questions provokes Oedipus' anger, the first display of a response which is developed forcefully throughout the first four episodes. It is his quick temper, we later discover, that caused Oedipus to kill Laius. By the time Tiresias has been driven to answer, Oedipus suspects some trickery. The scene ends in a stalemate of accusations.

It is interesting to note that while all of the first four episodes move forward in the present, they go successively further backward in time. This first episode reveals only that part of the past immediately preceding Oedipus' arrival at Thebes.

The choral passage which follows the first episode reflects upon the previous scene, stating the confusion which Sophocles wishes the audience to feel.

The second episode builds logically upon the first. Creon comes to defend himself from the accusations of conspiracy with Tiresias. Jocasta is drawn to the scene by the quarrel and she and the chorus persuade Oedipus to abate his anger. This quarrel illustrates Oedipus' complete faith in his own righteousness. In spite of Tiresias' accusation, no suspicion of his own guilt has entered his mind. Ironically, it is Jocasta's attempt to placate Oedipus that leads to his first suspicion about himself. She tells him that oracles are not to be believed and as evidence points to Laius' death, which did not come in the manner prophesied. But her description recalls to Oedipus the circumstances under which he has killed a man. He insists that Jocasta send for the one survivor of Laius' party. This scene continues the backward exploration of the past, for Oedipus tells of his life in Corinth, his visit to the Oracle of Delphi, and the murder of the man who is later discovered to have been Laius.

The choral song which follows is concerned with the questions Jocasta has raised about oracles. The chorus concludes that if oracles are proven untrue, then the gods themselves are to be doubted.

Though Jocasta has called oracles into question, she obviously does not disbelieve in the gods themselves, for at the beginning of the third episode she makes offerings to them. She is interrupted by the entrance of the Messenger from Corinth, who brings news of the death of Oedipus' supposed father, Polybus. But this news, rather than arousing grief, as one would expect, is greeted with rejoicing, for it seems to disprove the oracle which had predicted that Oedipus would kill his father. This seeming reversal only serves to heighten the effect of the following events. Oedipus still fears returning to Corinth because the oracle also has prophesied that he will marry his own mother. Thinking that he will set Oedipus' mind at ease, the Messenger reveals that he himself brought Oedipus as an infant to Polybus. The circumstances under which the Messenger acquired the child bring home the truth to Jocasta. This discovery leads to a complete reversal for Jocasta, for the oracles she has cast doubt upon in the preceding scene have suddenly been vindicated. She strives to stop Oedipus from making further inquiries, but he interprets her entreaties as fear that he may be of humble birth. Jocasta goes into the palace; it is the last we see of her.

This scene not only has revealed the truth to Jocasta, it has diverted attention from the murder of Laius to the birth of Oedipus. It goes backward in time to the infancy of Oedipus. The choral song which follows is filled with romantic hopes, as the chorus speculates on Oedipus' parentage and suggests such possibilities as Apollo and the nymphs. The truth is deliberately kept at a distance here in order to make the following scene more powerful.

This choral song is followed by the entry of the Herdsman (the sole survivor of Laius' party at the time of the murder and the person from whom the Corinthian Messenger had acquired the infant Oedipus). The Herdsman does not wish to speak, but he is tortured by Oedipus' servants into doing so. In this very rapid scene everything that has gone before is brought to a climax. We are taken back to the beginning of the story (Oedipus' birth), we learn the secret of his parentage, we find out who murdered Laius, we discover that Oedipus is married to his mother. The climax is reached in Oedipus' cry of despair and disgust as he rushes into the palace. The brief choral song which follows comments upon the fickleness of fate and points to Oedipus' life as an example.

The final episode is divided into two parts. A messenger enters and describes what has happened offstage. The "messenger scene" is a standard part of Greek drama, since Greek sensibilities dictated that scenes of extreme violence take place offstage, although the results of the violence (the bodies of the dead, or in this case Oedipus' blindness) might be shown. Following the messenger scene, Oedipus returns to the stage and seeks to prepare himself for the future.

Oedipus the King is structurally unusual, for the resolution scene is the longest in the play. Obviously, Sophocles was not primarily concerned with discovering the murderer of Laius, for the interest in this lengthy final scene is shifted to the question: What will Oedipus do now that he knows the truth?

Up to this scene the play has concentrated upon Oedipus as the ruler of Thebes, but in the resolution Oedipus as a man and a father becomes the center of interest. By this point he has ceased to be the ruler of Thebes and has become the lowest of its citizens, and much of the intense pathos is due to this change. An audience may feel for Oedipus the outcast as it never could feel for the self-righteous ruler shown in the prologue.

Oedipus' act of blinding himself grows believably out of his character, for it is his very uprightness and deep sense of moral outrage that causes him to punish himself so terribly. Although he is innocent of intentional sin, he considers the deeds themselves (murder of a blood relative and incest) to be so horrible that ignorance cannot wipe away the moral stigma. Part of the play's power resides in the revulsion with which people in all ages have viewed patricide and incest. That they are committed by an essentially good man only makes them more terrible.

Characters and Acting. Sophocles pays little attention to the physiological level of characterization. The principal characters—Oedipus, Creon, and Jocasta—are mature persons, but Sophocles has said almost nothing about their age or appearance. One factor that is apt to distract modern readers—the relative ages of Jocasta and Oedipus—is not even mentioned by Sophocles. When Oedipus answered the riddle of the Sphinx, his reward, being made king, carried with it the stipulation that he marry the queen, Jocasta. Sophocles, it should be noted, never questions the suitability of the marriage on the grounds of disparity in age.

Sophocles does give brief indications of age for other roles. The Priest of the prologue is spoken of as being old; the chorus is made up of Theban elders; Tiresias is old and blind; the Herdsman is an old man. In almost every case, age is associated with wisdom and experience. On the other hand, there are a number of young characters, none of whom speaks: the band of suppliants in the prologue includes children, and Antigone and Ismene are very young. Here, the innocence of childhood is used to arouse pity.

On the sociological level of characterization, Sophocles again indicates little. Oedipus, Creon, and Jocasta hold joint authority in Thebes, although the power has been delegated to Oedipus. Vocational designations—a priest, a seer, a herdsman, servants—are used for some of the characters.

Sophocles is principally concerned with psychological and ethical characteristics. For example, Oedipus' moral uprightness, his reputation for wisdom, his quick temper, his insistence on discovering truth, his suspicion, his love for his children, his strength in the face of disaster are emphasized. It is these qualities that make us understand Oedipus. But even here, a very limited number of traits is shown.

Creon is given even fewer characteristics. He has been Oedipus' trusted friend and brother-in-law. He is quick to defend his honor, and is a man of common sense and uprightness who acts as honorably and compassionately as he can when the truth is discovered. Jocasta is similarly restricted. She strives to make life run smoothly for Oedipus, she tries to comfort him, to mediate between him and Creon, to stop Oedipus in his quest; she commits suicide when the truth becomes clear. We know nothing of her as a mother, and the very existence of the children is not mentioned until after her death.

In the first production of *Oedipus the King,* all of the speaking roles would have been taken by three actors. The most likely casting would have been as follows: the first actor would play Oedipus throughout, since he is present in every scene; the second actor would play Creon and the Messenger from Corinth; the third actor would play the Priest, Tiresias, Jocasta, the Herdsman, and the second Messenger. The greatest range is required of the third actor, while the greatest individual power is required of the first.

The demands made on the third actor raises questions about the degree to which he differentiated between characters and the importance masks and costumes played in keeping characters separated for the audience. One should remember, however, that no two of the roles played by the third actor closely resemble each other and that the separation in terms of type might make his task simpler than it at first appears.

In addition to the three speaking actors, a large number of supernumeraries is required, many of whom no doubt appeared in more than one scene. For example, the band of suppliants in the prologue includes children, two of whom could later appear as Antigone and Ismene. Some who portrayed suppliants probably also later appeared as servants and attendants. To the actors must be added the chorus of fifteen members. Therefore, the total number in the cast was probably not less than thirty-five.

The use of masks, the doubling of roles, the fact that Jocasta was played by a man, the relatively small range of action—all these factors suggest that, while the aim was to create moving representations of human actions, the over-all effect would be considerably more abstract than the acting normally seen in the modern theatre.

Setting, Spectacle, Music, and Dance. The reader used to all the stage directions given in modern scripts may find a Greek tragedy lacking in spectacle upon first reading. If he tries to envision the action as it unfolds moment by moment, however, quite a different impression results.

First of all, the Greek theatre had no curtain. The play begins, therefore, with the procession of the suppliants through one of the *parodoi.* Oedipus arrives to hear their pleas; then Creon enters. Later the suppliants leave, and immediately the chorus enters with a song which is accompanied by music and dance. The spectacle is equally complex throughout the play.

The setting of *Oedipus the King* is simple. The stage house represents a palace; no changes are made and no machinery is needed. There would be an altar in the middle of the orchestra and others near the stage house, upon which Jocasta could place her offerings. Since the play was performed out of doors in daylight, no artificial illumination was necessary.

Costumes also would add to the spectacle. Since most of the characters, including the chorus, are dignified Greek citizens, they probably wore long *chitons.* But there would also be many distinctions among the characters. Suppliants would carry branches as symbols; the Priest, Tiresias, and the Herdsman would wear garments indicative of their occupations. The rich costumes of Oedipus, Jocasta, and Creon would contrast effectively with the simpler garments of the servants. Each actor would wear a mask indicative of his age and character. Choral dancing is also an important element of the spectacle.

The aural appeals were several: instrumental music, singing, and the speech of actors. The Greeks placed great emphasis on effective oral reading. The actors' voices, therefore, must have been well trained. Occasionally, music may have been used during the episodes, but normally it would be reserved for choral passages, all of which were sung and danced to flute music. Movement, music, and song combined to make the choral interludes among the most striking and effective features of Greek tragedy.

When the dramatic, visual, and musical appeals of Greek drama are considered, it becomes easier to understand why these plays, even after the passage of twenty-five hundred years, are still powerful.

THE SATYR PLAY

During the fifth century B.C., each writer of tragedy was required to present a satyr play whenever he competed in the festivals. A satyr play was comic in tone (usually burlesquing a Greek myth) and used a chorus of satyrs. Following the three tragedies, it formed a kind of afterpiece, for it was short and sent the audience home in a happy frame of mind. Since the actors and choruses were the same for both tragedies and satyr play, the conventions of acting, costuming, and scenery were probably similar for both forms, although they were given a marked satirical turn in the satyr plays.

Only one complete satyr play—the *Cyclops* by Euripides—still exists.

Actors of a satyr play. From a vase of the late fifth century, B.C. Note the masks and the various kinds of costume. (From Baumeister, *Denkmaler des Klassichens Altertums,* 1888.)

It is a parody of a serious story — found in the *Odyssey* — of Odysseus' encounter with the Cyclops. A substantial part of one other satyr play — *The Trackers* by Sophocles — is also extant. It deals with Apollo's attempts to recover a herd of cattle stolen from him by Hermes.

COMEDY

Greek comedy developed later than did tragedy. It was not officially recognized as a part of the festivals — that is, it was not granted a chorus — until about 487 B.C., when it became a regular feature of the City Dionysia in Athens. After 487, one day of each festival was devoted to the presentation of five comedies. At the City Dionysia, however, comedy was always considered inferior to tragedy; it was to find its true home at the Lenaia — another of the Dionysian festivals — at which it was given official state support beginning around 442 B.C. At the same time, contests for both comic poets and comic actors were inaugurated there. The festival arrangement and the production procedures were similar to those for the City Dionysia, though the Lenaia festival was less elaborate. Five comic poets competed at the Lenaia, as at the City Dionysia. After 432, two tragic dramatists provided two tragedies each year as well. Satyr plays were never presented at the Lenaia.

Comedy used a chorus of twenty-four members — which, like the tragic chorus, might be divided into two semichoruses. The chorus also sang and danced and served the same functions as the tragic chorus, but its music and dance were directed, as a rule, toward creating comic effects, although Aristophanes frequently inserted beautiful lyrical choruses into his comedies.

There were fewer restrictions on the number of actors in comedy than in tragedy. Although most comedies could be performed by three actors, occasionally as many as five were required. The acting style was probably based upon everyday behavior but exaggerated for comic effect.

The costume was usually a very tight, too-short *chiton* worn over flesh-colored tights, which created a ludicrous effect of partial nakedness. This effect was further emphasized by the *phallus,* which was attached to the costumes of most male characters. The phallus was both a source of ribald humor and a constant reminder of the Dionysian purpose of the festival. Masks also were used to emphasize the ridiculous appearance of the characters. (See the illustration on page 59 and the somewhat similar satyr-play dress on page 57.) In addition, masks and costumes created appropriate likenesses for the nonhuman choruses — of birds, frogs, clouds, wasps, and so on — that abound in Old Comedy.

Principally, however, comedy differed from tragedy in its subject matter. Most typically it was concerned with contemporary matters of

A painting on a Greek vase of Dionysus and a comic actor. (Trustees of the British Museum)

politics or art, with questions of peace or war, with persons or practices disliked by the comic writer. Occasionally the playwright used mythological material as a framework for his satire, but usually he invented his own plots and often referred to contemporary persons or situations. The allusions were no doubt a source of considerable pleasure to the audiences of the day, but are often obscure to a modern reader.

Numerous authors wrote Old Comedy, as the plays prior to 400 B.C. are called, but works by only one—Aristophanes (c. 448–380)—have survived. Aristophanes wrote about forty plays, of which eleven are extant: *The Acharnians* (425), *The Knights* (424), *The Clouds* (423), *The Wasps* (422), *Peace* (421), *The Birds* (414), *Lysistrata* (411), *Thesmophoriazusae* (411), *The Frogs* (405), *Ecclesiazusae* (392 or 391), and *Plutus* (388). These plays mingle farce, personal abuse, fantasy, beautiful lyric poetry, literary and musical parody, and serious commentary on contemporary affairs.

The plot of an Old Comedy usually revolves around a "happy idea" and the results of putting it into practice. In *Lysistrata,* for example, the women of Greece decide that they will bring a war to its end by going on a sex strike and eventually succeed. Structurally, Old Comedy has several typical features: a *prologue,* during which the happy idea is conceived; the *parodos,* or entry of the chorus; the *agon,* or debate over the merits of the idea, ending in its adoption; the *parabasis,* a choral passage addressed to the audience and most frequently filled with advice on civic or other contemporary problems; a series of *episodes* showing the happy idea in practice; and the *komos,* or exit to feasting and general revelry. The unity of Old Comedy, then, is to be found in its ruling idea rather than in a sequence of causally related events. Sometimes hours or days are assumed to have passed during one or two speeches, and place may change often. Furthermore, stage illusion is broken frequently as characters make comments about or to the audience.

The characters are usually well-to-do landowners or slaves, but occasionally heroes or gods appear, though they are always brought down to the level of ordinary humanity. The physical and ridiculous details of everyday life are emphasized throughout. For example, at the opening of *The Clouds,* the principal character, wrapped in blankets, is snoring; later he goes over his account books, catches bedbugs, and climbs onto the roof.

As in tragedy, the visual background for Old Comedy was the scene house, though each door often represented a different place. The *eccyclema* and the *machina* were also frequently used for comic effects. For example, in *Peace,* one of the characters flies off on the back of a dung beetle to consult the gods.

Overall, Old Comedy, with its rich mixture of farce, fantasy and poetry, music and dance was extremely varied in its appeal.

LATE GREEK DRAMA

After the fifth century, Greek drama declined markedly in quality, if not in quantity. Nevertheless, the theatre continued to expand, both in geographical distribution and in popularity.

In the fourth century, the Macedonians under Alexander the Great overran Greece and went on to conquer Asia Minor and northern Africa. Since the Greeks had already established colonies in Southern Italy and Sicily, by the end of the fourth century almost all of the Mediterranean area had been Hellenized. Wherever the Greek influence was felt theatres were built.

Although the taste for tragedy continued, comedy was the preferred form. The New Comedy (as it is usually called) is most intimately associated with Menander (c. 342–292 B.C.), a native of Athens, who is said to have written over one hundred comedies—of which only one, *The Grouch,* remains in its entirety.

New Comedy was divided into five parts by four choral interludes. By this time, however, the chorus was of little importance and served merely to break the play into scenes. But the major change was in subject matter, which was now drawn from the everyday life of middle-class Athenians. The plays were light in tone and typically showed a son's attempt to marry in spite of his father's opposition. The son was usually aided by a clever slave, who was the major source of humor. Eventually the father was reconciled to the son's choice, frequently because the girl was discovered to be the long-lost child of a friend.

New Comedy used costumes which were reasonably close copies of everyday garments and masks which depicted basic character types of the period. Altogether, it marked a movement toward realism in staging and toward conventionalization in depicting human behavior.

At the same time, the staging of tragedy moved further away from realism. It is to this period (usually called the Hellenistic age) that the distorted masks, high headdresses, thick-soled boots, and padded bodies of tragic actors belong. New theatres were built, with stages raised from eight to thirteen feet above the level of the orchestra. The actor became increasingly the center of interest as he performed on this new stage high above the orchestra.

THE RISE OF ROME

In the third century B.C. Rome began to expand as a power and soon came into contact with the Greek theatre for the first time. As it absorbed the Hellenic world, it also took over the theatre and transformed it. By the second century B.C. the distinctively Greek theatre had almost entirely disappeared and from then until the sixth century A.D. the theatre was to be principally Roman.

Although some kind of theatrical performances were probably given in Rome at an earlier date, the first regular dramas were performed there in 240 B.C., having been imported from the Greek colonies in Sicily and southern Italy. These plays were by Livius Andronicus, who is often considered the originator of Roman literature. Thereafter drama was a recognized part of Roman life.

Unfortunately, out of the vast number of Roman plays written, works by only three dramatists survive: twenty-one comedies by Plautus, six comedies by Terence, and nine tragedies by Seneca. The comedies of Plautus and Terence date from about 205 to 160 B.C., the tragedies of Seneca from the first century A.D.

ROMAN FESTIVALS

The *ludi,* or festivals, in Rome at which plays were performed were not associated with the worship of Dionysus, but were of various types. Most were official religious celebrations, but some were financed by wealthy citizens for special occasions, such as the funeral of a distinguished figure or the triumphal entry of a victorious army. Originally (in 240 B.C.), drama was given only at the *ludi Romani,* or Roman Games, and was probably restricted to a single day. But the popularity of dramatic entertainments insured their gradual expansion, and as the number of Roman festivals was increased so were the occasions for presenting plays. By A.D. 354, there were 175 public festival days, of which 101 were devoted to theatrical spectacles.

As in Greece, production expenses were assumed by the state or by wealthy citizens. The Senate made an appropriation for each festival as a whole, and frequently the officials in charge contributed additional funds. These officials normally contracted for productions with the managers of theatrical companies, who then were responsible for all details of production: finding scripts, providing actors, musicians, costumes, and so on. Although each manager was assured of a certain sum of money, special incentives were provided in the form of prizes for the most successful troupes. The manager probably bought the play script outright from the author; it then remained the manager's property and might be played as often as he wished or as audiences demanded.

Admission was free to everyone, seats were not reserved, and audiences were unruly. The programs were lengthy, being composed of a series of plays; and, since the plays often had to compete with rival attractions, the troupes were forced to provide a kind of entertainment that would satisfy a mass audience.

THE THEATRE AND STAGE IN THE TIME OF PLAUTUS AND TERENCE

Besides paying basic production expenses, the state supplied the theatre in which plays were presented. In the time of Plautus and Terence, it was a temporary one, for no permanent theatre was built in Rome until 55 B.C.

The theatre of Plautus and Terence probably included temporary scaffolds (outlining a semicircular orchestra), which provided seating for the spectators, and a long narrow stage rising about five feet above the orchestra level (the later stages were over one hundred feet long), which was bounded by the stage house at the back and ends.

The appearance of the stage background, called the *scaenae frons,* is disputed. Some think that it was a flat wall upon which columns, statues, or other details were painted. Others believe that there were three-dimensional niches and porticos. The back wall of the stage probably contained three openings, each of which might be treated, in comedy, as the entrance to a house. The stage then became a street, and the entrances at either end of the stage were assumed to be continuations of that street. Since windows and a second story are also required by some plays, the background must have provided these as well.

COSTUMES AND MASKS

Costumes in the Roman theatre varied with the type of play. The works of Plautus and Terence were adapted from Greek New Comedy and retained the Greek setting and garments. Other playwrights, however, wrote of Roman characters, and the costumes varied accordingly. In either case, the costumes were similar to those of daily life, although those of the more ludicrous comic characters were perhaps exaggerated.

Since most of the characters in Roman comedy were "types," the costumes also became standardized. There is evidence to suggest that certain colors were associated with particular groups, such as yellow with courtesans and red with slaves. This conventional use of color extended to wigs as well. All of the actors wore masks, which made the doubling of parts much easier and simplified the casting of such roles as the identical twins in *The Menaechmi*. Each actor in comedy also wore a thin sandal or slipper called a *soccus*.

A scene from Greek New Comedy. Drawing of a bas-relief from the Palais Farnese. (From Pougin's *Dictionnaire*, 1885)

63

COMIC PLAYWRIGHTS AND CONVENTIONS

Although there were numerous comic writers in Rome, works by only two — Plautus and Terence — have survived. Titus Maccius Plautus (c. 254–184 B.C.) is the earliest Roman playwright whose works still exist. Innumerable plays have been attributed to him, but the titles of only twenty-one have been agreed upon, all of which survive. The oldest dates from about 205 and the last from about the time of Plautus' death. Some of his most famous works are: *Amphitryon, The Pot of Gold, The Captives, The Braggart Warrior,* and *The Twin Menaechmi.*

Publius Terentius Afer, commonly called Terence, was born in 195 (some accounts say 185) and died in 159 B.C. A native of North Africa, he was brought to Rome as a slave, was later freed, and became the friend of many of the great men of his day. He wrote only six plays, all of which still exist: *The Woman of Andros, The Self-Tormenter, The Eunuch, Phormio, The Mother-in-Law,* and *The Brothers.*

All existing Roman comedy is based on Greek New Comedy, although significant changes have been made in the process of adaptation. First, the chorus has been abandoned, doing away with the division into acts or scenes. (The divisions found in most modern editions were made in later times.) Second, the musical elements formerly associated with the chorus have been scattered throughout the plays. In some respects a Roman comedy resembled a modern musical, for certain scenes were spoken, others recited to musical accompaniment, and there might be a number of songs. In Plautus' plays about two-thirds of the lines were accompanied by music, and the average number of songs were three. Although Terence did not use songs, music accompanied approximately half of his dialogue.

Roman comedy, like Greek New Comedy, does not deal with political and social problems but with everyday domestic affairs. Almost invariably the plots turn on misunderstandings of one sort or another: mistaken identity (frequently involving long-lost children), misunderstood motives, or deliberate deception. All action takes place in the street. This often leads to the necessity of staging scenes out of doors that would more logically occur inside, and characters must frequently explain what has happened indoors.

Roman comedy deals with the affairs of the well-to-do middle class, and the characters fall into clearly defined types: the older man who is concerned about his wealth or children, the young man who rebels against authority, the clever slave, the parasite, the courtesan, the slave dealer, and the cowardly soldier. Of all the characters, the most famous is perhaps the slave, who, to help his master, devises all sorts of schemes, most of which go awry and lead to further complications. Very few respectable women appear in Roman comedy, and while love affairs may

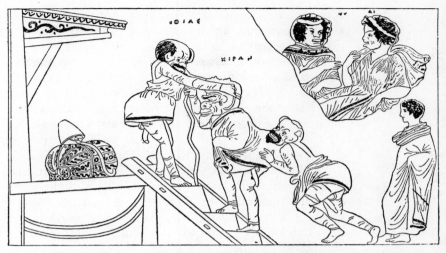

The *fabula Atellana* and mime were probably influenced by the *phlyax* of Sicily and southern Italy. *Phlyax* (a form of mime) dealt primarily with mythological travesty and farcical situations; it flourished c. 400-200 B.C. As this redrawn vase painting shows, the costumes were similar to those of Greek Old Comedy. Note also the stage with steps leading up to it. (From Baumeister, *Denkmaler des Klassischen Altertums,* 1889)

be the source of a play's misunderstandings, the women involved are often kept offstage.

The Menaechmi, probably the most popular of Plautus' plays, will be examined here as an example of Roman comedy. In it, the comic possibilities of mistaken identity involving identical twins are handled with great effectiveness.

THE MENAECHMI

Plot and Structure. As in most of Plautus' plays, *The Menaechmi* begins with a prologue which clarifies the backgrounds of the dramatic action. All important information is repeated more than once. At the same time, Plautus works in several jokes about the theatre to put the audience in a comic frame of mind.

Following the prologue, the introductory scenes of the play establish the present conditions out of which the comedy will grow: the dispute between Menaechmus I and his wife; the visit of Menaechmus I to the courtesan Erotium, his gift to her of a dress stolen from his wife, their plans for a banquet later in the day, and the departure of Menaechmus I to the Forum; the entrance of Menaechmus II and his slave, Messenio. The remainder of the play presents a series of scenes in which the two

Menaechmi are in turn mistaken for each other and accused of acts about which they know nothing. Eventually they meet and the complications are resolved.

Plautus subordinates everything to his main purpose—to entertain—and develops his material with great economy. Not only has he eliminated everything that does not contribute to his principal aim, he also has made effective use of such devices as the stolen dress, which becomes a source of unity since it passes through the hands of practically all the characters and is used as evidence to support almost all the charges brought against the two Menaechmi.

Although Plautus' comic sense is everywhere evident, it may be seen at work especially in the reunion, which might have concluded the play on a sentimental note. Instead, the final lines give the story a twist in keeping with the sophisticated tone of earlier scenes: Menaechmus I offers all of his goods for sale—including his wife, if anyone is foolish enough to buy her.

Characters and Acting. The characters of *The Menaechmi* are motivated principally by selfish and material interests. With the possible exceptions of Messenio and the father, none of the characters may be considered admirable. Plautus has little interest in social satire. He concentrates on the ridiculous situation without exploring its significance. Consequently, when his characters indulge in adultery, stealing, or deception, they merely contribute to the overall-tone of good-humored cynicism.

As in most Roman comedy, the characters in *The Menaechmi* are types rather than individuals. Some roles are summed up in their names: Peniculus (or "Brush") suggests the parasite's ability to sweep the table clean; the cook is called Cylindrus (or "Roller"); and the courtesan is named Erotium (or "Lovey"). Each character has a restricted number of motivations: the twins wish to satisfy their physical desires; the wife wants to reform her husband; the father desires to keep peace in the family; and the quack doctor is seeking a patient upon whom he can practice a lengthy and costly treatment. In spite of the restricted number of traits, however, each character is sufficiently delineated for its function in the play.

The ten speaking roles of *The Menaechmi* could easily be performed by a company of six actors. In the Roman theatre, all parts were played by men. Extras (used in nonspeaking roles) were employed as needed. The play does not require actors who are skilled in the subtle portrayal of a wide range of emotions; rather, they must have that highly developed comic technique that produces precision in the timing of business and dialogue. The scenes of quarreling, drunkenness, and madness indicate that physical nimbleness is essential.

Scenery and Music. Since *The Menaechmi* is set in a street before two houses, the stage and its architectural background would be sufficient to meet the scenic demands.

The costumes were based on those of everyday Greek life, but were conventionalized according to social class, occupation, age, and sex. Each of the characters also wore a mask and wig. Since the performances took place in unroofed theatres and during the day, no artificial illumination was required.

Because the music is now lost, it is sometimes difficult for the modern reader to remember that music played an important role in the original productions of all Roman comedies. It was performed on a "flute" with two pipes, each about twenty inches long, which was bound to the performer's head so as to leave his hands free to play the notes. The flute player was on stage throughout the performance. Well over half of the dialogue in *The Menaechmi* was accompanied by music, and a number of the characters probably had "entering" songs on their first appearance. The total effect must have been comparable to that of present-day musical comedy.

Thus, *The Menaechmi* is a farcical comedy designed primarily to divert an audience, an aim in which it is very successful.

OTHER ROMAN DRAMA

The Roman comedy that has survived is of the type called *fabula palliata* (*fabula* means play, and *palliata* designates a Greek garment worn by the characters). There were, however, several other kinds of Roman drama. The *fabula togata,* or comedy on Roman themes, drew its material from native life.

Tragedy also had an important place in the Roman theatre. As with comedy, Greece provided the models upon which the Roman playwrights built. Also like comedy, tragedy is usually divided into two types according to whether it used Greek or Roman themes. The former is called *fabula crepidata* and the latter *fabula praetexta*. Both types featured horrifying plots, totally good or totally depraved characters, melodramatic effects, and bombastic speeches.

The Roman tragedies that have survived are based on Greek themes and are the work of Lucius Annaeus Seneca (4 B.C. – A.D. 65), one of the emperor Nero's principal advisers. Nine of his tragedies are extant, of which five are adapted from plays by Euripides. (A tenth play is sometimes attributed to Seneca, but is undoubtedly the work of a later unknown author.)

Seneca was not a professional dramatist and his plays probably were not staged. Nevertheless, since he was a major influence on Renaissance tragedy, the characteristics of his work are important. First, Seneca's plays are divided into five acts by choral interludes. Although Renaissance dramatists seldom used a chorus, they did adopt Seneca's five-act structure. Second, the elaborately constructed speeches resembling forensic addresses found in Senecan drama became features of Elizabethan tragedy. Third, Seneca's fondness for *sententiae* (brief moral conclusions about human behavior, resembling proverbs) influenced Shakespeare and later writers. Other features of Senecan drama which recur in the Renaissance are violent actions onstage, a preoccupation with magic and death, and characters dominated by a single motive which drives them to their doom.

In addition to comedy and tragedy, a number of minor dramatic types were performed in the Roman theatre. After the first century B.C. regular comedy or tragedy declined and the stage was taken over by minor dramatic forms, especially *fabula Atellana,* mime, and pantomime.

The *fabula Attelana,* a short farce, was one of the oldest of Roman theatrical forms, having been imported from Atella, an area near Naples. It employed a set of stock characters: Maccus, a fool or stupid clown; Bucco, a glutton or braggart; Pappus, a foolish old man who was easily deceived; and Dossenus, a cunning swindler and glutton, who was probably hunchbacked. Originally the dialogue was improvised, and the plots revolved around various forms of trickery, cheating, and general buffoonery in a rural setting. Music and dance also played an important part. After the *fabula Atellana* was converted into a literary form in the first century B.C., the short farce became the most popular of all dramatic types.

The mime may be traced back to the sixth century B.C. in Greece, but the earliest record of its appearance in Rome is found in 211 B.C. Many mime troupes traveled widely and performed on makeshift stages. Their plays were short, topical, farcical, and, in the beginning, improvised. While the mime had certain features in common with the *fabula Atellana,* there were also important differences: the female roles were played by women (thus the mime was the first form to make use of actresses), the actors did not usually wear masks, and its subjects were primarily drawn from urban life.

Like the Atellan farce, the mime became a literary form in the first century B.C. The subjects of the later mime were often adultery and unnatural vices, and the language was frequently indecent. These characteristics set the rising Christian religion against the mime troupes, who retaliated by ridiculing the sacraments and beliefs of the church. Thus, the mime was more responsible than any other form for the opposition of Christians to the theatre.

One other dramatic type, the pantomime, was also popular in late

Rome. This silent interpretive dance was performed by a single actor who played many roles, each of which was indicated by a mask with a closed mouth. A chorus narrated the story, which was usually serious and drawn from mythology, while the action was accompanied by music, played by an orchestra composed of flutes, pipes, and cymbals and other percussion instruments. In late Rome, pantomime largely replaced tragedy, and was especially popular with the ruling classes.

The degeneration of the theatre under the Roman Empire—which superseded the Republic in 27 B.C.—is further illustrated by the fact that gladiatorial contents were sometimes held in the orchestras and on the stages of theatres. Furthermore, in many theatres the orchestras could be flooded for water ballets or sea battles (called *naumachia*). Thus spectacular, sensational, indecent, and exotic elements increased steadily in im-

A somewhat fanciful reconstruction of a naumachia. (From Laumann, *La Machinerie au Théâtre,* 1897)

portance after the first century A.D. Comedies were occasionally staged, but during the Empire the usual fare was mime, pantomime, and nondramatic spectacle.

THE THEATRE BUILDING OF THE ROMAN EMPIRE

The first permanent theatre on the Roman plan was built at Pompeii about 75 B.C.; Rome itself did not have a permanent theatre until 55 B.C.

A Roman theatre built on the seashore at Leptis Magna, Libya. (Georg Gerster/Rapho, Photo Researchers)

After this time new theatres were built wherever Rome's dominance extended, and most of the existing Greek theatres were remodeled along Roman lines. The latter structures are often called Greco-Roman theatres, since they display characteristics of both types.

The typical Roman theatre was constructed on level ground—unlike the Greek, which used a hillside to support its seats. The stage house and the auditorium were of the same height and formed a single architectural unit. (In a Greek theatre, the scene building and the auditorium were not joined and were, in effect, two separate structures.) The orchestra of a Roman theatre was a half-circle with the front of the stage set on its diameter. The auditorium typically seated between ten thousand and fifteen thousand spectators, although some are said to have accommodated as many as forty thousand.

The stage itself was raised about five feet above the level of the orchestra, and measured one hundred to three hundred feet in length and twenty to forty feet in depth. It had a permanent architectural background (called the *scaenae frons*) with a minimum of three doors in the rear wall (though frequently there were more), and at least one at either end of the stage. The *scaenae frons* was two or three stories high, decorated with columns, niches, statues, and porticos, and was in some cases gilded or painted.

Two other features distinguish the Roman from the Greek stage. First, sometime between 133 and 56 B.C., a curtain was introduced in the Roman theatre. It was dropped into a slot at the front of the stage at the beginning of a performance and raised at the end. Second, the Roman stage had a roof, which served at least two functions: it protected the elaborate *scaenae frons* from the weather and it improved the acoustics.

THE END OF DRAMA IN THE CLASSICAL WORLD

The immorality and decadence of the Roman theatre alienated the early Christians. At first Christianity was of little importance, but after it was recognized as the semiofficial religion of Rome by the Emperor Constantine, who ruled from A.D. 312 to 337, the theatre encountered increasing difficulties. Despite restrictions, however, performances continued to be popular and their eventual abandonment seems to have been a result more of invasions from northern tribes than of the moral scruples of Romans. By 476, Rome itself had twice been sacked. Although festivals were revived for a time, the last recorded performance is found in A.D. 533.

The accomplishment of the Roman theatre is not great when compared with the Greek, but it did produce three playwrights of importance — Plautus, Terence, and Seneca. Furthermore, its drama and theatre were to be major influences on Renaissance writers and theatre artists, and consequently helped to shape the European theatre of later times.

Together, the Greek and Roman theatres lasted for more than a thousand years. They represent the first great flowering of drama and set a standard seldom matched since.

Medieval
Theatre
and Drama

4

Although it is sometimes claimed that theatrical activities were completely suppressed during the centuries that followed the fall of Rome, numerous contemporary documents attest to the continued presence of *mimes, histriones,* and *ioculatores* (Latin terms for actors). Little is known about these performers, however, for the opposition of the church made it difficult for them to entertain openly.

Regardless of the type and extent of these entertainments, the theatre could not expand extensively until the church began to make use of dramatic interludes in its own services. These innovations, begun in the tenth century, were the first step in restoring the theatre to a respected place in society after a lapse of four hundred years.

DRAMA IN THE CHURCH

It is not clear why the church began to use dramatized episodes, but the most likely answer is that it wished to make its lessons more graphic. Furthermore, since the majority of persons could not understand Latin (the language of the church), spectacle had long been an important means of vivifying church doctrine, and dramatic interludes were merely a further development of this tendency.

The organization of the church year around the principal events of the Old and New Testaments also encouraged the development of drama appropriate to each season. Easter was the first event to be given dramatic treatment in church services, but others were dramatized later, although the majority of church plays always centered around Christmas and Easter. The earliest extant playlet, a four-line dramatization of the resurrection with directions for its performance, is found in the *Regularis Concordia* (or *Monastic Agreement*) compiled between 965 and 975 by Ethelwold, Bishop of Winchester (England). By the end of the tenth century, such plays were common in many parts of Europe.

The length and complexity of the plays differed considerably, some

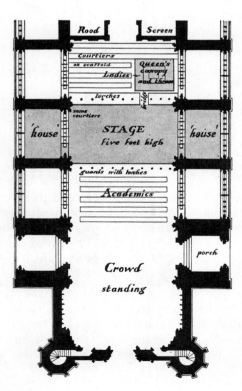

The floor plan for the Outer Chapel at King's College (Cambridge, England) as it was prepared for plays performed for Queen Elizabeth in 1564. (The New York Public Library)

being only a few lines long and dealing with a single episode, others much longer and including a number of related events. Next in number to the plays dealing with the Easter season were those treating events associated with Christmas and Twelfth Night, but numerous other Biblical subjects were also dramatized.

Drama was not produced in all churches of the period but was confined as a rule to cathedrals and monasteries—in other words, to churches that had enough clergy to present plays. In the church evolved a number of staging conventions that were to remain in use throughout the Middle Ages. The acting space was divided into two parts: the *mansions* and the *platea*. The mansions were simple scenic devices for indicating the location of incidents. For example, a throne might be used to suggest the residence of Pilate. Each place was represented by a different mansion, and all remained in view throughout the play. Since the action could not be performed in the limited space provided by the typical mansion, the actors used as much of the adjacent floor area as they needed. Often the same space was used in many different scenes. This generalized acting area was called the *platea*. Thus, a series of mansions was arranged around a common playing space, and the performers moved from one mansion to another as the action demanded.

For two hundred years religious plays were to remain within the church; not until after 1200 did they begin to be performed outside.

DRAMA OUTSIDE THE CHURCH

It is difficult to determine why performances began to be given out of doors. It has been suggested that the plays had begun to interfere with the liturgy and that drama had developed as far as it could within the restricted confines of church services. Regardless of the motives, around 1200 plays began to be performed outside as well as inside churches.

We know little about outdoor performances between 1200 and 1350, perhaps because the productions were no longer integral parts of church services but had not yet been taken over by secular organizations. During the fourteenth century, when lengthy vernacular religious plays appeared, information becomes much more plentiful. A number of significant changes had occurred in religious drama by 1400. Outdoor plays had come to be staged primarily during the spring and summer months, in large part because of favorable weather. The most usual time was Corpus Christi (the date of which may vary from May 23 to June 24), but other popular times were Easter, Whitsunday, or the feast day of a city's patron saint. Another important change was the abandonment of Latin in favor of the vernacular tongues. This change not only led to the substitution of spoken for chanted dialogue, it also made possible the use of laymen as actors.

75

With the vernacular drama came secular control over most aspects of production. In some areas, trade guilds became the principal producers of plays; in others, municipal authorities assumed control; in still others, special societies were formed to present religious dramas. While the church participated less and less in the actual process of production, its approval nevertheless continued to be necessary.

Under this arrangement, the medieval theatre flourished. From about 1350 to 1550 it steadily grew in complexity and technical proficiency.

STAGING TECHNIQUES

The stages on which the vernacular plays were performed might be either fixed or movable. The placement of the fixed stages varied considerably, but most typically they were set against buildings on one side of a town square. They might also extend down the middle of a square (and be viewed from three sides), or they might be set up in an ancient Roman amphitheatre or other circular place (and be viewed in the round). The movable stage was usually a wagon on which mansions were mounted and moved from one location to another. The movable stage was exploited most fully in England and Spain, but either type of stage might be found throughout Europe.

Regardless of the type of stage, the basic approach to production was the same everywhere. First, the scenic conventions were those inherited from the church—a series of mansions abutting on a generalized acting area (the *platea*). Second, the script was composed of a series of playlets, each more or less complete in itself and connected with the others only because all were taken from the Bible or some other religious source; the order in which the playlets were performed was determined by the original source rather than by any causal relationship among them. Third, almost every production involved three planes of being—Heaven, Earth, and Hell—and all were frequently represented scenically. The typical platform stage used a horizontal placement, with Heaven always on the right and Hell on the left (as one faced the audience). The earthly scenes were staged between these two points. On the wagons Heaven, Earth, and Hell were often arranged vertically, although a single wagon seldom depicted all three levels. Fourth, the greatest attention was devoted to special effects, which were made convincingly realistic, perhaps out of fear of raising doubts about the miraculous events described in the Bible. Medieval producers welcomed the challenge posed by such episodes as Christ walking on the water and being lifted up to the top of a temple. Special pains were also taken in the depiction of Hell and its horrors. The entrance to Hell was often represented as the mouth of a fire-breathing monster (hence the name *hell mouth*).

Hofmannsthal's *The Great Theatre of the World,* a play which adapts Medieval conventions, is performed in a cathedral at Salzburg, Austria. (Courtesy German Information Center)

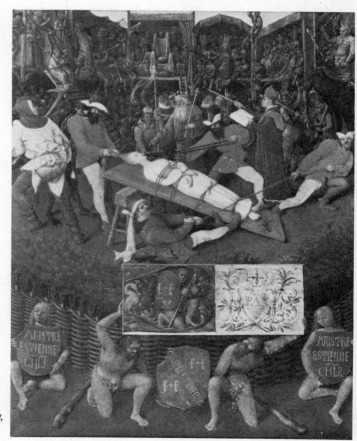

A performance of *The Martyrdom of St. Apollonia,* a mystery play, from a miniature by Jean Fouquet in *Les Heures d'Etienne Chevalier,* c. 1460. (Musée Condé de Chantilly, photo Giraudon)

To achieve these special effects, a considerable amount of stage machinery (called *secrets*) was invented. Much of it was operated from beneath the stage, and the numerous trap doors also permitted the appearance and disappearance of persons and objects. For the scenes which required "flying," pulleys and ropes were attached to adjoining buildings. Such machinery demanded considerable skill. For a play staged at Mons (in Belgium) in 1501, seventeen people were needed to operate the Hell machinery alone.

Obviously, special effects could be more extensive on a fixed than on a movable stage. It is not surprising, therefore, that the stationary stages had more elaborate stage machinery than did the pageant wagons.

It was not, however, the sole aim of the medieval stage to produce convincing special effects, for these realistic features were coupled with fragmentary scenery and symbolic devices. No place was depicted in its entirety: a small building might represent Jerusalem; a chair under a portico might become the palace of Herod. Moreover, all of the places needed for the play were present simultaneously, thus further preventing the illusion of a real place. Typically, even the wagon stages carried more than one mansion.

Costumes had to distinguish between the inhabitants of Heaven, Earth, and Hell. God, the angels, the saints, and certain biblical characters wore church garments, often with added accessories. (For example, angels wore church robes with wings attached, while God was dressed as a high church official.) Each of the saints and important biblical personages was also associated with a specific symbol. (For example, St. Peter was identified by his keys to the Kingdom of Heaven.) Since the audience was familiar with such visual symbolism, the mere display of an emblem served to identify the character. Secular, earthly characters wore the contemporary medieval garments appropriate to their ranks, for there was no attempt to achieve historical accuracy. The greatest imagination went into costuming the devils, who were usually fancifully conceived with wings, claws, beaks, horns, or tails.

CONVENTIONS OF THOUGHT AFFECTING MEDIEVAL DRAMA

Since we no longer think in medieval terms, some attempt to recapture the outlook of that time is essential, for otherwise its drama is apt to seem childish or naïve. In that period, man was said to participate in two kinds of time: eternal and temporal. God, the Devil, and man's immortal soul exist in eternity—which, unlike man's physical existence, has neither beginning nor end. If man considers only his earthly life, therefore, time may appear to be limited, but if he contemplates God, he sees that life is merely a preparation for eternity, in which his immortal soul participates. When he leaves his earthly existence, he enters into either eternal salvation or damnation. Thus temporal existence is a short preface to the ultimate reality, eternity. The central part of the stage, then—the earthly and temporal realm—was framed by Heaven and Hell, the eternal realms, one of which man must choose.

For the medieval mind, earthly time and place were relatively unimportant. The historical period or geographical location of an event was insignificant when set against the framework of eternity. Consequently, no sense of history is found in medieval plays. Audiences were not offended when ancient Israelites were dressed in medieval garments, or when Old Testament characters referred to Christian saints.

The fluidity of time is also reflected in the structure of medieval cycles, in which a series of short plays dramatized biblical material, beginning with Creation and concluding with the Last Judgment. Seldom was any causal relationship established among plays or even among the incidents of a single play. For the medieval mind, Providence played a large part in human affairs, and events were thought to happen simply because God willed them.

Another factor which sometimes puzzles the modern reader is the presence of comic elements in religious plays. Our austere view of religion, however, dates only from the sixteenth century. Prior to that time, the church permitted many satirical elements in its festivals. The Feast of Fools, for example, was a kind of New Year's rite during which the minor clergy were allowed to ridicule the mass and the church officials. It is not surprising, then, that comic elements were included in plays. Usually, however, the comic was restricted to devils, evil persons, or nonbiblical, lower-class characters.

THE MYSTERY PLAY

The mystery play, which drew its subjects from scripture, was the major form of medieval drama. Its name is probably derived from *mystère*, the French word used in the Middle Ages to designate any trade or craft. Thus, "mystery" came to mean those plays produced by the trade guilds.

The dramas most readily available for study are those written in English. Most of the extant English plays are from four cycles: the York, containing forty-eight plays; the Chester, containing twenty-four; the Townley manuscript plays, or Wakefield cycle, containing thirty-two plays; and the Ludus Coventriae or N_____Town cycle containing forty-two plays. (The blank was filled in with the name of the town where the cycle was to be performed.)

STAGING OF CYCLE PLAYS IN ENGLAND DURING THE FIFTEENTH CENTURY

English plays were usually staged as a part of the Corpus Christi festival, the essential feature of which was a procession through the town with the consecrated bread and wine (or host). This may explain why several towns in northern England adopted the processional form of staging—that is, the mounting of plays on wagons and the movement of these wagons to a series of places throughout the town.

Although plays were not given each year, they were presented at reasonably regular intervals. The town council decided whether the plays were to be included, and the guilds assumed primary responsibility for producing them.

Each trade guild was assigned one play, or, in the case of small guilds, two or more might produce a play together. The master copy of the cycle, which had the approval of the church, was retained by the town council, and each guild was cautioned to stage its play with care and to remain faithful to the text. A fine was imposed if a guild was proved negligent.

No adequate description of the pageant wagons has been preserved. They were probably as large as the narrow city streets would permit and were designed to meet the requirements of specific plays. A wagon almost always had to carry two or more mansions, and might need machinery for special effects as well.

There is much disagreement as to where the acting took place. Some argue that it occurred only on the wagon; others believe that the actors used both the wagon and the street; and still others state that the wagons were pulled up alongside a platform which served as the acting area, or *platea,* while the wagon provided the mansions. It is possible that the wagon, a platform, and the street were all used as acting areas.

The actors were primarily amateurs. A few were paid large sums, however, and it is likely that these were skilled performers who played the leading roles, helped with the staging, and coached the other actors.

Each guild presented its play at several places. Thus, audiences gathered at a number of points and the plays were brought to them in a manner that combined a parade and dramatic entertainment.

THE SECOND SHEPHERDS' PLAY

The Second Shepherds' Play is probably the best known of the English cycle plays. It is the thirteenth part of the Wakefield cycle, from which thirty-two plays—ranging from Creation to the Last Judgment—have survived. It is called *The "Second" Shepherds' Play* because the surviving manuscript includes two plays (of which this is the later) on the same subject.

Plot and Structure. The majority of *The Second Shepherds' Play* is an elaboration of a single sentence from the New Testament (Luke 2:8): "And there were in the same country shepherds abiding in the field, keeping watch over their flock by night." The number of Shepherds is not specified in the Bible, but three are used in the play, probably to suggest a parallel with the three Wise Men.

Like most medieval dramas, *The Second Shepherds' Play* has an early point of attack. It introduces in leisurely fashion the characters and situation as each shepherd in turn complains about a different problem. The opening is made even more casual by the inclusion of a song.

Yet this simple beginning serves several purposes that may not be readily apparent. First, through the various complaints, it depicts a world in need of Christ's coming. Second, it relates the biblical story to the contemporary scene and thereby to the audience. Third, the introduction prepares for an unusual occurrence by the third Shepherd's recital of abnormal conditions. There is little forward movement in the story, however, until Mak appears.

Mak's reputation as a trickster is established immediately by the Shepherds' concern for their sheep. Soon, however, they all lie down for the night. When the Shepherds are safely asleep, Mak steals a sheep and carries it home to his wife, Gill. As a precaution against discovery, she suggests that they place the sheep in a cradle and pretend that it is a newborn baby. Mak then goes back to the fields and lies down as before.

The Shepherds awake and, with difficulty, arouse Mak, who has been feigning sleep. After Mak takes his leave, the Shepherds discover that a sheep is missing and they immediately suspect Mak. While the Shepherds search the house, Mak protests his innocence and Gill counterfeits post-childbirth pains. As they are leaving, one of the Shepherds remembers the child and insists upon presenting a gift to it; the sheep is discovered and Mak is tossed in a blanket as punishment. This portion of the play is closely related to the medieval farce (to be discussed later). It also shows much greater skill in writing than other parts of the play.

After recovering their sheep, the Shepherds return to the field. A marked change now takes place as the tone of the play becomes serious and devotional. An Angel appears and announces the birth of Christ; the Shepherds go to Bethlehem, worship the child, and present their gifts. Christ has appeared within a familiar scene; His promise is not to some forgotten past but to the immediate present.

Themes and Ideas. *The Second Shepherds' Play* has frequently been viewed as a work composed of two unrelated stories of sharply contrasting tone. A close examination of the work, however, reveals that it is unified through its themes and ideas.

There are many parallels between the two stories. In both there is a father, mother, and child; the child is in a cradle; one "child" is a lamb, and the other is Christ, the "Lamb of God"; the Shepherds present gifts to both. The difference between the two stories is to be found in the significance of the events: one shows a world in need of Christ, and other portrays his arrival.

Characterization and Acting. There are seven roles—not counting the infant. All parts were played by men, and the same actor could have played both Gill and Mary.

Little is indicated about the physical appearance of the characters. All are adults of unspecified age except the third Shepherd—a boy—and the Christ child—probably represented by a doll. The sociological traits are also limited. The Shepherds, Mak, and Gill are peasants; it is implied that Mak lives by stealing.

Psychological characterization is slight but effectively drawn. The three Shepherds are differentiated primarily through their opening monologues. All are generous, as may be seen from their reactions to the supposed child of Gill and to the Christ child, and from their decision not to prosecute Mak. (In medieval times, stealing was a hanging offense.) A good impulse, the desire to give the "child" a gift, leads to the uncovering of Mak's guilt. Mak is a clever knave who is somewhat henpecked and cowardly. Gill is shrewish and clever; it is her idea to put the lamb in the cradle and pass it off as a child.

There is a considerable amount of physical action in the play and, with the exception of the Angel's appearance, all of it is reasonably realistic. Transitional action, however, is indicated only sketchily. For example, the Shepherds lie down and appear to fall asleep instantly. The actors therefore must supply many details or the action will seem abrupt. Because they each have only one speech, Mary and the Angel are characterized least and seem especially stiff and stereotyped when compared to the other characters.

Most of the actors must sing. The Shepherds have a song in the introductory scene and another at the end of the play. Mak sings a lullaby to his stolen sheep, and the Angel sings *Gloria in excelsis*.

Spectacle. *The Second Shepherds' Play* calls for three locales—the fields, Mak's house, and the stable at Bethlehem. One mansion might be sufficient, however, since the fields really require no background, and the other two are so similar in scenic demands that the same mansion could be used in both.

No doubt the mansion used for Mak's house and the stable was equipped with a curtain which could be drawn to reveal the interior.

Mak's house must have a door (at which he knocks), a cradle, and a bed. All of these would be appropriate items for the stable (the bed for Mak's house need only be made of straw).

It is difficult to imagine this play being performed on a wagon —which would, at the very least, have to be divided into two parts. It is more logical to suppose that the wagon carried only the necessary scenic background and could be pulled up alongside another platform which would serve as the *platea,* or generalized acting area.

The costume demands for the play are simple: for the Shepherds, Mak, and Gill, the everyday contemporary dress of the lower classes; for the Angel, an ecclesiastical garment with wings added; for Mary, an upper-class medieval garment (the traditional way of representing her in art by this time) and the symbols associated with her.

Although the staging demands are simple, *The Second Shepherds' Play* has a considerable range of appeals. Its variety makes it an excellent example of that combination of teaching and entertainment which was typical of medieval drama.

PRODUCTION ON FIXED STAGES

The staging of *The Second Shepherds' Play* is relatively simple in comparison with productions given on fixed stages, where all the parts of a cycle were performed on a single platform. The latter arrangement made the whole process far more complex than in the former, where responsibility for each part of a cycle was assumed by a different guild, each of which worked more or less independently. When wagons were used, the actual performance required virtually no coordination beyond arranging the wagons in proper sequence. But for productions on fixed stages, coordination at every step was crucial. Not only did this involve finances, it extended as well to casting, rehearsals, the acquisition of scenery, and the perfection of special effects. Furthermore, a place capable of holding the entire audience at once had to be found. Because of all these problems, the responsibility for an entire production was usually assumed by a committee, although it often delegated the actual work of staging to a small group or even to one person.

But if the managerial problems of the fixed stage were great, so were its potentials for scope and spectacle. *The Acts of the Apostles,* presented at Bourges (France) in 1536, for example, had a cast of three hundred and required forty days to perform; the passion play staged at Valenciennes (France) in 1547 extended over twenty-five days. Fixed stages were sometimes as much as two hundred feet long and sixty feet deep, and on them were present simultaneously all of the mansions (sometimes as many as twenty) needed for a full day of playing. Furthermore, much more spectacular special effects could be arranged on fixed than on movable stages. At Valenciennes, for example, such scenes as Christ being lifted up some forty feet to the top of a temple and the storm at sea with Christ walking on the water were shown; in another play, St. Paul's decapitated head bounced three times and at each spot a spring flowed, one of milk, one of blood, and one of water. Unified control over production also facilitated double casting and the liberal use of crowd scenes. Considering all of these factors, it seems certain that the productions given on fixed stages were far more impressive visually than were those mounted on wagons.

OTHER RELIGIOUS DRAMATIC FORMS

Thus far, only church drama (often called *liturgical* drama) and cycle (or *mystery*) plays have been discussed. Actually, however, there are many kinds of medieval drama.

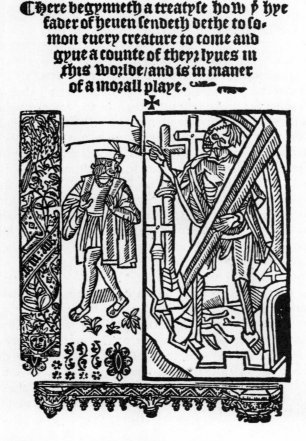

Frontispiece to the edition of *Everyman* published by John Sklot, c. 1530.

A scene from *Everyman* performed at the Salzburg Festival in 1962. (Courtesy Austrian Information Service)

Morality plays flourished between 1400 and 1550. They are historically significant, since they dramatize the spiritual trials of the average man, whereas mystery plays treat biblical or saintly characters. Thus, they form a bridge between religious and secular drama. Examples of the morality play include: *Pride of Life* (about 1410), *The Castle of Perseverance* (about 1425), *Mankind* (about 1475), and *Everyman* (about 1500).

The plays are allegories about the moral temptations that beset all men. The protagonist (usually called Mankind or Everyman) is advised and cajoled by personifications of good and evil (such as good and bad angels, the seven virtues, and the seven deadly sins), and is surrounded by such characters as Mercy, Good Deeds, Knowledge, Mischief, and Death.

The most famous morality play is *Everyman.* Whereas many morality plays cover man's entire life, *Everyman* deals only with his preparation for death. Everyman searches to find one among his former companions (Kindred, Goods, Beauty, Strength, Discretion, Five Wits) who will accompany him to the grave; eventually only Good Deeds goes with him. In his search, Everyman comes to understand his past life and its relation to his salvation.

During the sixteenth century the morality play was gradually secularized, and its former subjects were replaced by such new ones as the proper training of rulers and the content of good education. Then, at the time of the religious reformation in England, it became a vehicle for controversy. For example, John Bale (1495–1563) mixed abstract figures with historical personages in *King John* to denounce the papacy. Such changes moved the morality play increasingly toward a drama with completely secular subject matter and human characters. Since morality plays came to be performed by small professional troupes, they pointed toward the establishment of a secular and professional stage.

SECULAR DRAMATIC FORMS

In addition to religious and didactic plays, there were a number of secular dramatic forms in the Middle Ages, of which the *farce* is probably the most interesting and important. It was especially well developed in France, although it also had important exponents in England. The farce is lacking in religious or didactic elements, and shows, rather, the ridiculous depravity of man.

A scene from *Pierre Patelin* from a woodcut illustration made in 1489. (Courtesy French Cultural Services)

Folk play performed in the banqueting hall of Haddon Hall, Derbyshire. (From Joseph Nash, *The Mansion of England in Olden Times,* Vol. I., 1869)

Probably the best example of medieval farce is *Pierre Patelin,* an anonymous French play of the fifteenth century. Patelin, a lawyer, is near financial ruin. He nevertheless persuades a merchant to let him have a fine piece of cloth. The merchant agrees to come to Patelin's house to collect his money and to have dinner. When the merchant arrives, Patelin is in bed, and his wife swears that he has not been out of the house. Patelin pretends madness, beats the merchant, and drives him away. This part of the plot is rather loosely joined to a second one. Patelin meets a shepherd and agrees to defend him in court against a charge of sheep-stealing. He cautions the shepherd to answer only with a "baa" no matter what anyone says to him. In court, the accuser turns out to be the cloth merchant, who creates such bewilderment with his alternating charges against Patelin and the shepherd that the judge (in view of the confusion and the shepherd's seeming feeblemindedness) dismisses the case. When Patelin tries to collect his fee, however, the shepherd runs away, calling "baa." The story shows a series of clever knaves outwitting each other. The final comic twist comes when the master knave is outwitted by an apparent simpleton.

Another dramatic form is the *secular interlude,* a nonreligious serious or comic play. It began to appear near the end of the fifteenth century, and was performed by traveling players or by troupes employed by noblemen. Such plays were probably called interludes because they were performed between the parts of a celebration (for example, the courses of a banquet). In the sixteenth century, the secular interlude was not always distinguishable from the morality play or the farce. All eventually merged in Renaissance drama.

DECLINE AND TRANSITION

Many factors account for the decline of medieval drama. First, the increasing interest in classical learning (to be discussed in the next chapter) introduced many new concepts which affected the writing and staging of plays. Second, changes in the social structure gradually destroyed the feudal and corporate life which had encouraged such community projects as the presentation of cycle plays. Third, and perhaps most decisive, dissension within the church led to the prohibition of religious plays both in England and on the Continent. Religious strife caused Elizabeth I to forbid religious plays when she came to the throne in 1558, and after this date they were gradually suppressed. As a result, the drama of the Middle Ages had by the late sixteenth century ceased to be a vital force.

In the long run, perhaps the most significant change is to be seen in the relationship between the theatre and society. In Greece, Rome, and Medieval Europe the theatre enjoyed the active support of governmental and religious groups. Essentially it had been a community offering used to celebrate special events considered significant to all. Beginning in the sixteenth century, however, the theatre ceased to have a religious and civic function, and henceforth it had to justify itself on purely commercial or artistic grounds. Thus, at the end of the medieval period, the theatre began a new phase of its existence.

Elizabethan England

5

$\mathbf{E}$ven before the medieval theatre had ceased to be productive, the impact of the Renaissance had begun to transform dramatic practice in Western Europe. Although the Renaissance was felt earliest and most fully in Italy, developments in England will be treated first because the English theatre between 1550 and 1650 drew more extensively on the medieval than on the Renaissance heritage and consequently marks a transition away from rather than—as in Italy—a sharp break with the past. During this time, England reached a peak of creativity unmatched in the history of the theatre.

EMERGENCE OF THE PROFESSIONAL ACTING COMPANY

Although by the fifteenth century there were wandering players in England, actors (if they had no other profession) were, according to the

89

laws of the time, vagrants and rogues. Those troupes attached to the households of nobles were exempted from this category because they were classified as servants rather than actors.

Acting was first recognized as a legal profession in England in the 1570s when the Master of Revels (a court official) was assigned the duties of examining all plays and licensing all acting companies, thus placing the English theatre directly under the control of the central government. To receive a license under this arrangement, a troupe had to be under the patronage of a nobleman; equipped with this protection and a license from the Master of Revels, a company had a clear legal right to perform.

Unlike the aristocracy, who encouraged it, the merchant class viewed the theatre with distrust. Many believed that it took people away from their jobs and thereby interfered with honest pursuits and that plays encouraged immorality. The powerful town councils, largely composed of middle-class tradesmen, were for the most part opposed to professional theatrical activities of any kind. It was in London, where the theatre was centered, that local officials raised the most strenuous objections. Consequently, when theatres were built (the first in 1576), their owners located them just outside the city limits in order to escape the jurisdiction of the London council. Despite all opposition, by the 1580s there were always at least two companies playing in or around London and frequently more.

INFLUENCES ON THE DEVELOPMENT OF ELIZABETHAN DRAMA

The drama that emerged in the late 1580s may be traced to many influences, among them schools and universities, the Inns of Court, and the popular theatre.

The revival of interest in classical learning that had begun in Italy in the fifteenth century soon reached England, where by the early sixteenth century plays were being studied and produced in schools and universities. Some of the best early plays of the English Renaissance were written and produced in the schools. *Ralph Roister Doister* by Nicholas Udall (1505–1556) was probably performed at Eton while Udall was headmaster there between 1534 and 1541. It shows the foolish posturings of a boastful coward and his discomfiture. *Gammer Gurton's Needle* was acted at Cambridge University sometime between 1552 and 1563. It develops a series of misunderstandings between two neighboring households over the loss of a needle. Both plays show clearly the influence of Roman comedy.

The Inns of Court—combined residences and training centers for lawyers—were a second influence on the development of Elizabethan drama. Like the schools, the Inns of Court produced plays for themselves and important guests. The first regular English tragedy, *Gorboduc* by Thomas Sackville and Thomas Norton, was produced at one of these Inns in 1561 with Queen Elizabeth in attendance.

But Elizabethan drama probably owes its greatest debt to medieval drama and to the interludes produced by professional troupes in the sixteenth century. The latter plays were a bizarre mixture of elements drawn from earlier native drama and often from the new classical learning as well. It was out of these combined influences that a new drama emerged between 1585 and 1642.

THE ELIZABETHAN THEATRE STRUCTURE

Before considering how the dramatists of Shakespeare's age built on the work of their predecessors, it will be helpful to examine the physical theatre and staging conventions in use between 1585 and 1642.

Two kinds of theatre buildings—open-air structures and indoor halls—were in use during Shakespeare's career. The former are often referred to as "public" and the latter as "private." In actuality, both were public in the sense that they were open to anyone willing to pay admission, but "private" theatres were smaller, charged higher admission fees, and played to a more select audience.

A drawing of the Globe Theatre made during Shakespeare's time. (New York Public Library)

At least nine public playhouses, not counting remodelings and reconstructions, were built before 1615. Of these, the most important were The Theatre (1576), The Globe (1599), and The Fortune (1600). All were built outside the city limits, either in the northern suburbs or on the south bank of the Thames River. The theatres varied in size, but the most elaborate seated from two to three thousand spectators. They were of differing shapes: round, square, octagonal. Typically, they were laid out in this manner: a large central unroofed space, called the *pit* or *yard,* was enclosed by three tiers of roofed galleries. At the entrance to the theatre each person paid the same admission price. This entitled him to stand in the yard; if he wished to sit, he paid an additional fee and was admitted to the galleries. At least one gallery had some private boxes, or "Lords' rooms," the use of which required still another fee.

A raised stage (from four to six feet high) extended to the center of the yard. This large platform was the principal acting area. Spectators could stand around three sides, and the galleries also commanded a view from at least three sides. At the rear of the stage, there was a multi-leveled façade. On the stage level, two large doors served as entrances and exits for actors and as passageways through which heavy properties and set pieces could be moved.

The greatest disagreement about the Elizabethan theatre concerns the discovery space (sometimes called the "inner below"). It is generally agreed that there was an area at the rear of the main stage where characters or objects might be concealed or revealed. Its size and location, however, are disputed. The two major answers have been: (1) that this area was recessed into the back wall with a curtain across the front; and (2) that it jutted onto the forestage like a pavilion and thus had curtains around three sides. Recently it has been suggested that there was no separate discovery space and that the area immediately behind the two doors was used for this purpose.

The second level of the façade also could be used as an acting area. Conclusions about this upper stage tend to be based on those about the discovery space. Those scholars who believe that there was an "inner below" state that there was a similar recessed space on the second level called the "inner above," while those who prefer the "pavilion" argue that there was an acting area on top of this forward projection. In any case, this second level was probably used to represent balconies, battlements, upper-story windows, and other high places. The façade may also have had a third level, often called the "musicians' gallery" because of its supposed primary use.

The basic outlines of the stage, then, are simple: (1) a large platform (at the Fortune Theatre it was approximately forty-three feet wide by twenty-seven-and-a-half feet deep) jutting to the middle of the theatre structure; (2) a door on each side at the rear of this stage; (3) one or

An English inn yard, a possible forerunner of playhouses. (From the Folger Shakespeare Library Prints)

more discovery spaces; (4) an acting area on the second level; and (5) possibly a third level.

This stage encouraged a continuous flow of dramatic action. As the actors left the forestage by one door at the end of a scene, another group might enter at the other door to begin the next scene; or the discovery space might be opened and the stage would become a new place; or a scene on the forestage might be followed by one on the upper level; or more than one level might be used at the same time.

It is usual today to assume that no scenery was used in the Elizabethan theatre, but the records kept by Philip Henslowe (a businessman associated with the Admiral's Men) list such items as rocks, trees, beds, a hell mouth, and a cloth representing the "city of Rome." It is possible, therefore, that set pieces were put up occasionally as on the medieval stage. It seems unlikely, however, that very much scenery was used, as it would have seriously interrupted the flow of scenes.

Machinery was housed both below and above the stage. Trap doors in the floor allowed for grave scenes, for the appearances of ghosts and devils, for fire and smoke, and for other special effects. Typically, a roof

Johannes de Witt of the Netherlands visited London in 1596 and made a sketch of The Swan Theatre. De Witt's friend, Arend van Buchell, made a copy of the sketch, which is reproduced here. De Witt's own drawing has not survived. Since this sketch is the primary contemporary pictorial evidence, it influences attempts to reconstruct the Elizabethan theatre. (From Bapst's *Essai sur l'Histoire du Théâtre,* Paris, 1893)

(supported by posts at the front of the stage) extended over the stage. Cranes, ropes, and pulleys for raising and lowering objects were housed there.

The first private theatre was opened in 1576 in Blackfriars, a fashionable residential area which had formerly been a monastery. Remodeled from a large room in one of the monastic buildings, it was used by boys' companies until closed in 1584. The second Blackfriars Theatre was built by James Burbage in 1596, perhaps in anticipation of moving there when his lease on the theatre's site expired in 1597. The opposition of local residents put an end to his plans, however, and in 1600 the theatre was leased to another boys' company, which was extremely successful until 1608 when it was silenced for violations of censorship.

When the boys' company was forbidden, the Burbages resumed posession of the Blackfriars Theatre, which became the winter home of the King's Men after 1610. The success of this innovation led other adult troupes to open private theatres, of which there had been at least six in London by 1642. In 1629–30 a cockfighting ring was converted into a private theatre (the Cockpit at Court) to provide a suitable space for performances by professional companies at the court of Charles I. Between 1610 and 1642 private theatres surpassed public theatres in prestige, and the open-air structures came to be used only during the five warm-weather months.

In basic features, the private theatres differ little from the public ones. Roofed and restricted in size, their seating capacities were only about one-fourth to one-half of that of the outdoor theatres. All spectators were seated — in the pit, galleries (of which there were from one to three), or in private boxes. The stage and the background were similar to those in the public theatres. Since companies moved freely from public to private theatres, staging conventions must have been similar at both.

LIGHTING AND COSTUMES

In the public theatres no artificial illumination was required, since the performances occurred out of doors and in the afternoon. The private theatres probably used candlelight, but little is known of stage-lighting practices.

While little scenery was used, the Elizabethan stage was certainly not devoid of color and pageantry. Banners and other devices were employed to distinguish between armies or factions; there were many battles, processions, and dances. Most important, costumes were an ever-present source of visual pleasure.

The costumes were of two basic kinds, contemporary clothing and conventional dress. By far the majority of roles were costumed in Elizabethan garments appropriate to the rank or profession of each character. Like the medieval, the Elizabethan mind had little sense of history,

A woodcut of William Kemp, an Elizabethan comic actor, c. 1600. (Folger Shakespeare Library)

95

and characters from almost any place or time could be dressed as Elizabethans would.

On the other hand, certain stereotypes of the period made it necessary to set off some roles by conventionalized costumes: (1) special foreign groups, such as Romans, Turks, or Spaniards, (2) supernatural beings, such as fairies, classical gods, ghosts, and witches, (3) certain professional types, such as clerics, senators, and clowns, and (4) animals.

In spite of this apparent complexity, the majority of costumes were basically Elizabethan garments, and most of the conventionalized costumes were created by superimposing a few simple elements on contemporary dress. For example, Roman characters were identified by the addition of drapery to Elizabethan clothing.

THE ACTING TROUPES

Adult acting companies included from ten to twenty members, of whom approximately ten were shareholders (that is, partners in the management) and the rest hired men. The latter (who included extras, doorkeepers, musicians, and stagehands) were paid a set wage comparable to that received by skilled laborers in other trades. The shareholders divided the money left after all expenses were paid. Besides the adult actors, each company included apprentices (from three to five boys) who performed child and female roles.

In addition to being a shareholder, an actor might also be a "householder," or part owner of the theatre building in which the company performed. If the company did not have the capital needed to build a theatre or to buy costumes and equipment, it had to enter into agreements with others, who then usually became householders. For their investment, the householders received half of the gallery receipts, while the acting company retained the other half and all of the general admission fees.

The adult acting companies performed a large repertory, changing the bill almost daily. A play was repeated several times during a season if there was sufficient demand; when no longer popular it was dropped and a new work was added.

The children's companies were composed of choirboys from court chapels or cathedrals. Under the guise of training, the choirmasters exploited their students' talents by staging plays for which they charged admission. In the children's companies, the masters were completely in charge and reaped the profits.

Performances were given regularly except during plagues, certain religious seasons, or upon the death or severe illness of a ruler or important public official. The audience was composed of all sorts of persons:

noblemen, merchants, workmen, and women. Some playwrights wrote disparagingly of them, especially the "groundlings" who stood in the yard, while others praised their perceptiveness.

PRINCIPAL DRAMATISTS PRIOR TO SHAKESPEARE

By the time Shakespeare began to write for the stage around 1590, several competent and successful dramatists had appeared. Thomas Kyd (1558–1594), after studying Roman drama as a student, won unprecedented fame with *The Spanish Tragedy* (c. 1587), the most popular play of the age. Kyd's drama shows the influence of Seneca in its sensational subject, the motive of revenge, and the use of ghosts. It is an outstanding example of the "revenge" play (of which *Hamlet* is also an example). Perhaps most important, Kyd showed his successors how to construct striking situations, startling reversals, and suspenseful plots.

Christopher Marlowe (1564–1593), educated at Cambridge University, is noted especially for *Doctor Faustus* and *Edward II*. His principal contributions to Elizabethan playwriting are the perfection of blank verse and the organization of plays around one strong character whose

An illustration from the title page of Thomas Kyd's *The Spanish Tragedy*, dated 1615.

A woodcut of Faustus and Mephistopheles, from the 1631 edition of Marlowe's *Faustus*. (New York Public Library)

motives are explored thoroughly. Marlowe also helped to develop the history play.

John Lyly (c. 1554–1606) is noted principally for his prose comedies, written in an elegant and sophisticated style on themes taken from mythology. The plays have pastoral settings—a kind of "never-never land" where everything is delicate and graceful. Widely admired, they influenced Shakespeare's *A Midsummer Night's Dream, As You Like It,* and *Twelfth Night.*

SHAKESPEARE

William Shakespeare (1564–1616) is generally conceded to be the greatest of Elizabethan dramatists. Little is known of his early life, but by 1590 he seems to have been established in London, and by 1595 was a shareholder and actor in the Lord Chamberlain's company (later the King's Men). After 1599, he was a householder in The Globe theatre as well. As householder, actor, director, and playwright, he was the most versatile theatrical figure of his age.

Shakespeare began writing plays around 1590 and completed about thirty-eight. Like most of his contemporaries, Shakespeare borrowed much from novels, older plays, history, mythology, and other sources. His plays have been divided into three groups: histories, comedies, and tragedies. In the first he dealt with the English past, especially the period of the Wars of the Roses. The histories (*Richard II, Henry IV,* Parts I and II, *Henry V,* and *Richard III*), show his skill at reducing large masses of material to the demands of the stage. His comedies represent a wide range of types. *The Comedy of Errors* (based on Plautus' *Menaechmi*), *The Taming of the Shrew,* and *The Merry Wives of Windsor* emphasize farce; *A Midsummer Night's Dream, As You Like It,* and *Twelfth Night* are romantic comedies; *All's Well That Ends Well, Measure for Measure,* and *Troilus and Cressida* are plays so nearly serious that they are frequently termed *dark* comedies.

But it was in tragedy that Shakespeare displayed his greatest genius. *Romeo and Juliet, Hamlet, Macbeth, Othello,* and *King Lear* must be ranked among the greatest tragedies ever written. Since it is impossible to discuss all of Shakespeare's plays, a single work, *King Lear,* will be examined in detail.

A reconstruction of an Elizabethan presentation of *A Midsummer Night's Dream.* (New York Public Library)

KING LEAR

Themes and Ideas. One theme is appearance versus truth. Both Lear and Gloucester are deceived (on very little evidence) by an appearance of treachery in children who are actually loyal and true, and both accept as truth the lies told by their false children. As in *Oedipus the King,* a contrast is drawn between physical sight and spiritual blindness. Gloucester says, after his eyes have been put out, "I stumbled when I saw." In Lear's case, madness is substituted for blindness, but in this state he grasps the truth more firmly than when he was sane.

Another theme concerns the degree to which man's fate is determined by forces outside himself. For instance, Gloucester says: "As flies to wanton boys are we to th'gods;/They kill us for their sport." On the other hand, there are numerous suggestions in the play that man's fate is determined by his own decisions. It is Lear's first choice that makes all of the later events possible; similarly, it is Gloucester's hasty belief in Edmund's lies that leads to his downfall. Thus, in the final scene, Edgar states: "The gods are just, and of our pleasant vices/Make instruments to plague us."

These opposing views of human destiny are partially explained by the Renaissance conception of the universe. Man, as the final creation of God, was thought to be the center of God's concern, since God had created the earth for man's use. Furthermore, at this time it was still believed that the entire universe revolved around the immobile earth. The planets were said to move in concentric spheres, one inside the other. Because all parts of the universe were connected like the cogs of a machine, the well-being of the whole was affected by each part and chaotic conditions in any part were felt throughout the universe. This explains why physical manifestations of disorder play such a large part in Shakespeare's tragedies. The storm in *King Lear,* for example, is a metaphorical indication of the disruption of order.

To Shakespeare, man is not a mere puppet but an intelligent being free to choose his own path. Consequently, he frequently violates the divine order, and, when he does, he suffers accordingly.

Plot and Structure. Shakespeare's skill in play construction may be seen by examining the over-all movement of the main plot. The opening scene establishes Lear's position as an absolute monarch. He disposes of the kingdom as though it were his own private property and passes sentence on his daughters and subjects without consulting anyone. In this scene Lear's character is established. Furthermore, without this scene it would be impossible to appreciate the extent of Lear's fall. The opening also prepares for later events by revealing the true motives of Goneril, Regan, Cordelia, and Kent.

Between this beginning and Lear's reunion with Cordelia near the play's close comes a series of humiliations for Lear which, though mild at first, culminate in his madness. Although Lear's downfall is not undeserved, the undisguised evil of Goneril and Regan arouse our indignation at his treatment and create constantly increasing sympathy for him. In the storm scene he is completely stripped of authority and is forced to face himself as a man, alone, at the mercy of both inward and outward torments. The scenes that follow the storm show Lear's attempts to reorient himself. In his powerless state he comes to know the difference between freely offered devotion and what is pretended for the sake of reward. But the evil forces Lear has unleashed through Goneril and Regan prevent him from rebuilding a life based on his newfound wisdom.

Much the same progression is found in the subplot. Like Lear, Gloucester is forced to reexamine himself and he too experiences a spiritual rebirth. Perhaps Shakespeare's structural skill can be seen most clearly in the intertwining of the two plots and in the way the resolutions of the two stories are essentially one.

Characterization and Acting. The role of Lear is far more complex than any other in the play. It is sometimes difficult to distinguish between such characters as Goneril and Regan because of the few traits assigned each; both have the same motives, and the over-all impression is simply that each is completely depraved. Cordelia, on the other hand, has as little trace of evil as her sisters have of good.

Shakespeare gives scant information about the physical and social attributes of his characters and emphasizes psychological motives instead. Each of the secondary personages has one dominant drive that is placed in opposition to that of another character. Thus, Cordelia is contrasted with her sisters, Edgar with Edmund, Cornwall with Albany, Kent with Oswald, and France with Burgundy.

Gloucester comes near to being a copy of Lear. Both are old men, easily deceived, and they undergo many of the same experiences. Lear's role, however, is developed at much greater length and in more depth than is Gloucester's.

Lear is a difficult role for an actor because the part encompasses a wide range of action, emotion, and psychological change. In the opening scene, Lear is in complete command; he is easily angered and insists upon having his every wish satisfied. This habitual, and somewhat childish, behavior defeats him when he no longer has the power to enforce his desires. Impotence commences during his first clash with Goneril, and his sense of frustration grows until it leads to madness. From madness, Lear gradually begins a spiritual ascent, though he never regains his physical vigor.

Throughout the play, Shakespeare includes details that humanize Lear. Perhaps the most obvious of these comes in one of the final speeches, into which Lear injects, "Pray you, undo this button." Here, a figure fighting with overwhelming emotions is suddenly reduced to the level of common humanity. It is a simple touch, but one that arouses pathos more effectively than any description of Lear's feelings could.

Language. Shakespeare's dramatic poetry is generally conceded to be the greatest in the English language. The basic medium is blank verse, which retains much of the flexibility of ordinary speech while elevating and formalizing it. There are as well many passages in prose, which typically are spoken by lower-class characters. In *King Lear,* both Edgar and Lear turn to prose in the mad scenes, for though they do not change rank in actuality, they look at life from the standpoint of the simple mind.

Probably the most important element in Shakespeare's dialogue is figurative language. The principal purpose of a figure of speech in dramatic poetry is to set up either direct or indirect comparisons. Shakespeare's superiority over other writers of dramatic poetry lies in his use of comparisons which enlarge the significance without distracting attention from the dramatic situation. His poetic devices partially fulfill the same function as the constant visual representation of heaven and hell on the medieval stage. They relate human actions to the divine and demonic forces of the universe and treat man's affairs as significant to all creation.

Shakespeare's language makes special demands on the actor. Figures of speech are apt to seem contrived and bombastic if the actor does not appear to be experiencing feelings sufficient to call forth such language spontaneously. All too frequently, Shakespeare's plays are damaged in performance when actors do not rise to the emotional demands of the poetry. Therefore, the very richness of expression can be a stumbling block for both performer and reader.

Spectacle and Sound. There are many opportunities for visual splendor in *King Lear.* The action occurs in a large number of places, and if all were depicted realistically the stage would present a constantly changing aspect. Our knowledge of the Elizabethan stage, however, suggests that Shakespeare envisioned the spectacle in terms of stage properties, costumes, and the movement of actors.

Although scenery is not important, the frequent change of stage place is. The forestage, discovery space, and upper stage would allow the necessary flow of one scene into the next. For example, the storm scene, which is set consecutively in an open space, before a hovel, and inside a farmhouse, would require utilization of only the forestage and the discovery space.

King Lear in the heath scene with The Fool and Edgar. (Courtesy German Information Center)

The relatively bare stage is enlivened by processions, numerous attendants, and constant physical movement. The opening scene, for example, is an important state occasion which would demand an elaborate procession of officials and courtiers, all of whom would be dressed in their finest garments. In later scenes, banners and heraldic devices would be used to distinguish Albany's and Cornwall's forces from those of the French.

The actors' stage business also creates spectacle. Gloucester's eyes are put out, Kent is seized and placed in the stocks, Edgar and Edmund fight a duel, Lear dies. Nearly every scene offers physical action of this sort. (A comparison of the onstage action of *King Lear* with that of *Oedipus the King* helps to define a principal difference between Elizabethan and Greek tragedy.)

The costumes are an important visual element. In Shakespeare's day, most characters probably wore contemporary garments, but the com-

103

pany's large wardrobe would provide much variety in color and line and make frequent costume changes possible.

Such sound effects as the storm, offstage fighting, and trumpet flourishes are important in *King Lear*. Music is used in a number of scenes. But most important is the sound of the actors' voices speaking Shakespeare's poetry.

King Lear, because of its combination of universal themes, a compelling story, powerful characters, great poetry, and interesting visual and aural effects, is one of the world's greatest plays. Although it embodies the values of its own period, it is timeless in appeal and transcends the limitations of a particular era. Thus, it continues to move audiences today as it has since its first presentation.

SHAKESPEARE'S CONTEMPORARIES AND SUCCESSORS

Shakespeare's greatness often diverts attention from his contemporaries and successors, many of whom are also among the world's finest dramatists. Of Shakespeare's contemporaries, Ben Jonson (1572–1637) was the most important. He began his career in the theatre as an actor (around 1597), but did not continue long in that profession. In 1598 he wrote *Every Man in His Humour* (in which Shakespeare acted), and soon became one of the most controversial authors of the day. Of all the authors of the period, Jonson was most attuned to classical ideas, and his work as a poet, playwright, and critic influenced many younger men to move in the direction of neoclassicism.

His most famous plays are *Volpone* (1606), *The Silent Woman* (1609), and *The Alchemist* (1610) — all comedies. His tragedies were not well received. Jonson also wrote most of the masques (to be discussed later) presented at the courts of James I and Charles I.

Jonson's most widely admired play is *Volpone*. The main character, Volpone, pretends to be rich and without heirs. Each of several persons is led to believe that he will inherit the fortune if he can stay in favor with Volpone. Consequently, each showers him with expensive gifts. At last, Volpone tires of his deception, makes a will leaving all his wealth to his servant, Mosca, and pretends to die. Later, when he tries to reclaim his property, Mosca refuses to give it up. Eventually Volpone, Mosca, and the would-be heirs are exposed and punished.

Francis Beaumont (c. 1584–1616) and John Fletcher (1579–1625), who wrote a number of plays in collaboration, were principally responsible for establishing the vogue for tragicomedy and romantic tragedy with *Philaster, The Maid's Tragedy, A King and No King,* and *The Scornful Lady,* all written between 1608 and 1613. The subjects of Beaumont and

Fletcher's plays were usually sensational. For example, in *The Maid's Tragedy* a wife tells her husband on their wedding night that she is the King's mistress and that she has married him only as a means of continuing her affair. The rest of the play develops from this sensational revelation. Both playwrights were particularly skilled in dramatic construction. They built complications to startling climaxes, alternated quiet and tumultuous episodes, and condensed complex material into far fewer scenes than Shakespeare employed. Their plays show more technical proficiency than Shakespeare's, but their subjects emphasized the shocking rather than the significant.

The work of Beaumont and Fletcher set the standard for the period between 1610 and 1642. Important writers of tragedy during these years include John Webster (?–c. 1630), with *The White Devil* (1612) and *The Duchess of Malfi* (1614), and John Ford (1586–1639), best known for *'Tis Pity She's a Whore* (c. 1625–1633), in which a brother and sister are lovers. Other noteworthy playwrights of the time were Thomas Middleton (1580–1627), Philip Massinger (1583–1640), Thomas Heywood (c. 1574–1641), Thomas Dekker (c. 1572–c. 1632), and James Shirley (1596–1666).

THE COURT MASQUE

When James I came to the English throne in 1603, he brought with him a taste for elaborate theatrical entertainment. He became the patron of Shakespeare's company, which was renamed the King's Men, and all other troupes were placed under the patronage of members of the royal family.

Unlike Elizabeth, who usually contented herself with performances by the public troupes, James and his son, Charles I, also financed private court entertainments, called *masques*, which were performed on special occasions, such as weddings, births, and visits from foreign dignitaries. The English masque was similar in all important respects to the Italian *intermezzo* (to be discussed in the next chapter) and utilized Italian staging methods. The scripts for most of the masques were by Ben Jonson, while the settings and costumes were, with a few exceptions, designed by Inigo Jones (1573–1652), the court architect. Jones had studied in Italy, and it was he who introduced Italian staging methods into England.

The masque featured allegorical stories designed to honor a person or occasion through a fanciful comparison with mythological or historical characters or situations. The speaking and singing roles were assumed by professional court musicians, while comic roles were played by profes-

A drawing by Inigo Jones for William Davenant's masque *Salmacida Spolia* . (Devonshire Collection, Chatsworth Library, Derbyshire, England)

sional actors. The major emphasis, however, was upon the courtier-dancers. Above all, the masque provided ample opportunity for elaborate spectacle and scenic display, and by 1640, when the last court masque was staged, Jones had introduced almost all of the scenic devices that had been popularized in Italy.

The influence of the masque was soon felt in the public theatres, where processions, music, allegorical scenes, and dances were employed with increasing frequency. But the influence of the masque on scenery in the public theatre was not great until after 1660, when the proscenium arch and perspective settings became standard.

CLOSING OF THE ENGLISH THEATRES

Although the theatre was a thriving institution and was encouraged by the royal family, Puritan opposition to it grew throughout the first part of the seventeenth century. In 1642, civil war was used as an excuse for

Costume by Inigo Jones for Tethys or a Nymph in Daniel's *Tethys Festival* (1610). (Devonshire Collection, Chatsworth Library, Derbyshire, England)

Costumes by Inigo Jones for antimasque characters in Jonson's *Chloridia* (1631). (Devonshire Collection, Chatsworth Library, Derbyshire, England)

closing all theatres. They were not to be reopened until Charles II was restored to the throne in 1660. Although there were surreptitious performances during the Commonwealth, the English theatre was virtually nonexistent during these years. When it was revived in 1660, it bore little resemblance to the theatre of Shakespeare, for it then embraced Italian staging ideals and the neoclassical mode.

From the Renaissance to Neoclassicism in Italy and France

6

During the fifteenth and sixteenth centuries, Italy made a sharp break with medieval dramatic practices. Out of its new concerns were to come the proscenium-arch stage, perspective scenery, new conceptions of dramatic form, and many practices that would dominate the theatre until the twentieth century. Although most significant innovations began in Italy, they were perfected in France, which by the late seventeenth century had become the cultural leader of Western Europe.

BACKGROUND

Many forces helped to create the Renaissance. Probably the most important was the general secularization of thought, as men ceased to be overwhelmingly preoccupied with the problem of salvation and devoted

The "Terence stage" as depicted in the edition of Terence's plays published in Lyon in 1493. Here is shown a scene from *Adelphi*. Note the several doors, each with a name above to identify it as the house of a character.

more attention to problems of daily life. In pursuing these interests, scholars turned once more to the classical world, especially to Rome, since Latin was the language of educated persons and Greek was little known until the sixteenth century.

Interest in classical learning soon extended to plays, especially those by Plautus, Terence, and Seneca. After 1453, however, when Constantinople fell to the Turks and many scholars fled to the West with valuable manuscripts, Greek dramas also began to be known once more. Soon afterward, the introduction of the recently invented printing press into Italy (in 1465) made it possible to publish and disseminate widely texts that had previously been available only to the few in hand-copied manuscripts.

Interest in classical drama soon led to a desire to see these works staged, and by the 1470s productions at the courts of rulers or at academies were beginning to be given. At this time Italy was made up of independent states each ruled by a duke or prince, and the maintenance of a sumptuous court at which the arts were patronized had become a common means of demonstrating the cultural superiority of one ruler over another. It was in the court theatres that those scenic conventions destined to dominate the Western stage until the modern era first were introduced.

Academies also contributed significantly to this development. An academy was a clublike organization formed for the purpose of studying a specific subject. Some were devoted to classical architecture; these took their inspiration from *De Architectura* (written by the Roman architect Vitruvius in the first century B.C.), which was to be the major influence on theatre architecture in the Renaissance. Others studied literary theory, especially as found in the works of Aristotle and Horace.

The personnel of theatres both at court and academies was essentially amateur, for the actors were usually courtiers or students, the plays were normally written by authors under royal patronage, and the scenery was most often designed by court architects or members of academies. Furthermore, performances were open only to select audiences and were given only on special occasions such as royal weddings, the birthdays of rulers, or visits by important foreigners.

ITALIAN DRAMA OF THE RENAISSANCE

Since medieval drama was scorned as formless and old-fashioned, the works staged by courts and academies were either Roman plays or close imitations of them. The first comedy written in Italian was Lodovico Ariosto's (1474–1533) *La Cassaria (The Casket)*, staged at the court of Ferrara in 1508. In it, a favorite Roman plot (in which lovers are united following the discovery that the girl is the long-lost child of a rich father) is placed in a contemporary Italian setting. The play with the greatest appeal today is *Mandragola* (c. 1513–1520) by Niccolo Machiavelli (1469–1527). It showed how a jealous old man is tricked into approving of an adulterous relation between his wife and a young man. It combines classical form with the subject matter of typical medieval farce. By 1540, native comedy was well established in Italy.

The first important tragedies written in Italian were *Sofonisba* (1515) by Giangiorgio Trissino (1478–1550) and *Orbecche* (1541) by Giambattista Giraldi Cinthio. They did much to reestablish the tragic mode which had lain fallow since Roman times.

A third form, the *pastoral,* also came into prominence in the sixteenth century. Its emphasis was on fine sentiments, delicate emotions, and romantic love stories. The most popular of the pastoral plays was *The Faithful Shepherd* (c. 1590) by Giambattista Guarini (1538–1612).

111

INTERMEZZI AND OPERA

Since the love for spectacle could not always be satisfied by this classically inspired drama, most of which required only a single setting, it had to be met in other ways. From the late fifteenth century until about 1600, the principal spectacular pieces were *intermezzi,* presented between the acts of regular dramas. Typically the subjects for intermezzi were drawn from Greek and Roman mythology, especially those stories that allowed the use of elaborate special effects, such as Perseus on his flying horse fighting a sea monster. Each character and event was given an allegorical interpretation that related it to the royal patron, his enemies, or friends. Music and dance also were emphasized. By the 1580s intermezzi were more popular than the regular drama.

The appeal of intermezzi was undermined by the rise of opera, which received its first impetus from the Camerata Academy in Florence, a group especially interested in Greek music and its relation to drama. The members of the Camerata knew that Greek tragedy had had a chorus, that it had included music and dance, that at least part of the dialogue had been sung or chanted, and that the plots had been drawn from Greek mythology. Out of their efforts to write plays of this kind, opera took shape in the 1590s. By 1650 the new form was popular throughout Italy and was rapidly spreading to all of Europe. After 1600 opera was increasingly important in stimulating experiments with scenery and special effects. It was also with opera that Italian theatrical practices were first imported into most European countries.

DEVELOPMENT OF THE ITALIAN STAGE

From the very beginning, two influences on staging were at work: one that stemmed from the architectural treatise of Vitruvius, and another derived from the contemporary interest in perspective. Attempts to combine these two forces led eventually to the picture-frame stage.

It is difficult today to appreciate the reaction of the Renaissance mind to perspective, which was sometimes viewed as a form of magic, since through its use the artist created the illusion of space and distance where they did not actually exist. Perspective gave the artist a power he had not previously possessed, and he applied it in all possible ways. It is not surprising, then, that he recognized its possibilities for stage scenery. Although perspective settings may have been used as early as the 1480s, the first certain example is that for Ariosto's *La Cassaria* in 1508.

The joint influence of Vitruvius' work and of perspective are evident in the first treatise on staging in the Renaissance: a portion of *Architettura* (1545) by Sebastiano Serlio (1475–1554). In his book Serlio shows

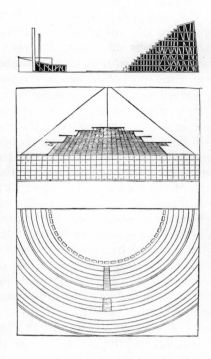

Above: left, a cross section of Serlio's theatre above his ground plan for a theatre; right, Serlio's design for the comic scene. (From Sebastiano Serlio's *Architettura,* 1545) Below: left, Serlio's tragic scene; right, his pastoral scene. (From Sebastiano Serlio's *Architettura,* Book 2, 1569 ed.)

how a theatre is to be laid out, how the stage is to be erected, and how scenery is to be arranged; he outlines the rules of perspective and discusses a number of additional topics. Since, like most of his contemporaries, Serlio assumed that theatres would be set up in already-existing halls, his plan is an adaptation of Vitruvius' description of the Roman theatre to an indoor, rectangular space. (See the illustrations on page 113.) The stage floor is sloped upward toward the back and is painted in squares, the lines of which diminish in size and converge toward the center back to create a sense of distance in a very limited space. Houses constructed of canvas stretched over wooden frames are set up on both sides of the stage. The plan is completed by a backcloth hung at the rear of the stage. To give the illusion of diminishing size and distance as they near the back wall of the stage, the tops of the flats are shaped to slope downward just as the floor slopes upward toward the back.

Serlio envisioned the need for only three settings — one for tragedy, one for comedy, and one for pastoral. His engravings illustrating these settings were widely reprinted and were imitated by other designers all over Europe. Serlio's scenes for comedy and tragedy are essentially the street scenes of the Roman theatre translated into perspective settings.

As the theatre gained a more solid foothold, the need for permanent theatres was felt. The oldest surviving Renaissance theatre is the Teatro Olimpico, built by the Olympic Academy of Vicenza. First used in 1585, it still stands. The stage, the stage background, and the auditorium of the Teatro Olimpico more nearly follow Vitruvius' plan of a Roman theatre than any other edifice of the period. But even here the influence of perspective scenery is felt, for the floor was raked upward behind the façade doors and a street in perspective was set up behind each. (See photograph below and plan, page 115.) The street scenes were entirely fixed and could not be shifted. The Teatro Olimpico, therefore, was not in line with the growing demand for more spectacle.

The form the theatre was ultimately to take can be seen clearly for the first time in the Teatro Farnese, built in the ducal palace at Parma in 1618. It is the first theatre known to have been constructed with a permanent proscenium arch.

The origin of the proscenium arch is a much-debated question. Some scholars argue that it comes from the enlargement of the central doorway of the Roman stage façade. Others contend that it is indebted to paintings in which buildings and other objects are used to frame the perspective picture. Regardless of its origin, however, the proscenium arch serves two basic functions. First, if perspective is to be effective there must be some means of restricting the view of the audience if the illusion of place and of distance is not to be destroyed. Second, if scenery is to be shifted (and by the seventeenth century there was a growing demand for more spectacle) some framework to hide the

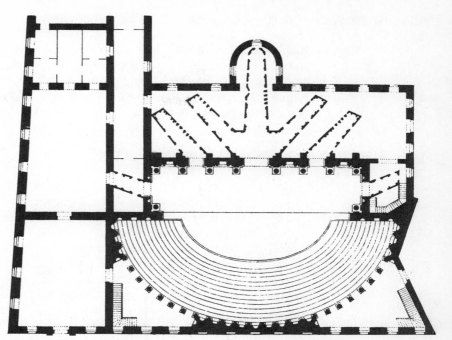

Top: A ground plan for the
Teatro Olimpico at Vicenza.
(From A. Streit's *Das Theater*,
Vienna, 1903)
Bottom: Teatro Olimpico,
Vicenza. Built between 1580
and 1584 by Italian architect
Vincenzo Scamozzi from the
basic design by Andrea
Palladio. (Inigo Jones later
imported Palladio's classical
style into England where
Palladian motifs became
popular.)

machinery and the offstage spaces is desirable. The proscenium helps to maintain the magic of the theatre by concealing the mechanics by which that magic is created. The Farnese put into permanent form a device which had been evolving over a number of years and thereby became the prototype of theatres up to modern times.

MAIN FEATURES OF THE ITALIAN THEATRE

Although the stage of the Teatro Farnese was the prototype of those that followed, its auditorium was still that of a conventional court theatre. To discover the prototype of future auditoriums, one must turn to the public opera houses, the first of which was opened in Venice in 1637. Although their features were never completely standardized, public theatres characteristically were to have auditoriums arranged in the following manner. Overall, the auditorium was usually shaped like an elongated U. Around the walls, boxes were set in tiers one above the other. The number of tiers varied from one theatre to another, but there were usually two or more. Boxes were valued for their relative privacy and were especially popular with well-to-do and socially prominent persons. Above the top row of boxes there was often an undivided gallery, normally occupied by servants or members of the lower classes. The central floor space (the orchestra or pit) was not popular with the elite until the late nineteenth century. Except in England, there were no seats in the pit until near the end of the eighteenth century, and consequently the spectators stood and moved about freely. This area was usually occupied by fashionable young gentlemen and would-be critics. The price of admission to this part of the house was less than that charged for boxes, but more than that charged for the gallery.

Since these were indoor theatres, they required artificial lighting. Candles and oil lamps were the standard illuminants. Chandeliers often hung in the auditorium and sometimes over the stage itself. Lights were mounted behind the proscenium arch (both at the sides and above), footlights were used at the front edge of the stage, and lights might be mounted on vertical poles behind each set of wings. Although the stage was sometimes darkened by the use of stovepipelike devices lowered around the lights, for the most part there was little effective control over intensity, color, or distribution.

Another important feature of this theatre was its scene-shifting devices. Because the Serlian settings, with their three-dimensional details, were difficult to shift, the intermezzi were staged at first by drawing pageant wagons into the space forward of the stage or by carrying portable set pieces onto the platform. But around 1550, *periaktoi* began to be used for changing the wings, and by 1638 Nicola Sabbattini (1574–1654), in his *Manual for Constructing Theatrical Scenes and Ma-*

116

The painting on this vase depicts part of Euripides' story of *Medea*. Medea's husband Jason left her to marry King Creon's daughter. Enraged, Medea poisoned a robe and sent it to her rival. After touching the robe, King Creon and his daughter die (top center). A serpent-drawn chariot arrives to carry Medea to asylum in Athens (lower center). (Glyptothek, Munich; photo, American Heritage)

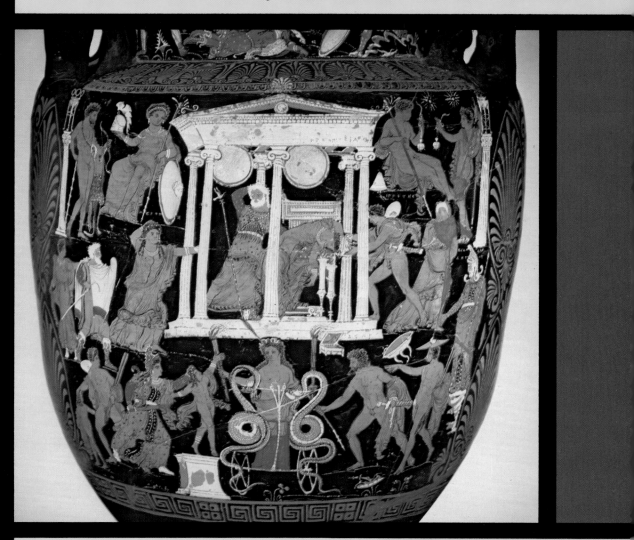

Often in Roman theatre, masks such as those shown in this mosaic were used to create the characters. (Museo Gregoriano, Vatican; photo, Scala/EPA)

Medieval dancers and musicians on a simple platform. Note the entrance at left. From a Latin manuscript in the Casanatense Library, Rome, late fourteenth century. (photo, Scala/EPA)

In this composite of actors who performed at the Théâtre Royale in Paris during the seventeenth century is Molière (far left). Note the commedia dell'arte style of costumes. French and Italian theatre strongly influenced each other during this time. (Comédie Française)

A street scene of commedia dell'arte players. These plays were often improvised from set situations and stock characters. The actors were recognized by their costumes and often played the same roles. Note the masks on several of the actors. From an anonymous painting. (Museo del Burkardo, Rome; photo, Photo Researchers)

The interior of the Theatre Royal, Turin, Italy, in 1740 from a painting by Pietro Domenico Olivero. On stage is the final scene from the opera, *Arsace* by F. Fee, which opened the theatre. Giuseppe Bibiena, a member of the family known for settings conceived on an enormous scale and with excessive ornamentation, designed the scenery. The proscenium arch of the theatre is so deep that it contains a set of boxes on each of five levels. Note the actors' costumes, the fruit and drink vendors, and the soldier at the front of the auditorium posted to keep order. (Courtesy Civic Museum, Turin)

The interior of Park Theatre in New York in November 1822. The theatre was rebuilt in 1821 after a fire. On stage is a performance of *Monsieur Tonson,* a farce by the English dramatist William T. Moncrieff. This watercolor by John Searle was commissioned by William Bayard and the faces in the audience were all portraits including that of the artist (center front orchestra). (New York Historical Society)

chines (a major source of information about seventeenth-century practices), could list four methods of shifting scenery. The one that eventually triumphed required that angled wings be replaced by flat wings. The first clear record of a setting composed entirely of flat wings is found in 1606, but by 1650 this arrangement, probably because of its greater mobility, had virtually replaced all others. Using it, wings were set up parallel to the front of the stage in a series from front to back. At each wing position as many different flats were put up (one immediately back of another) as there were scenes to be depicted during the performance. To change from one scene to the next, the visible wings were pulled offstage, revealing others upon which was painted the new scene. The set was enclosed at the back by painted flats which met at the center of the stage. Several back-scenes could be set up, and shifted in the same way as the side wings.

Borders (two-dimensional cloths) hung above each set of wings and continued the scene overhead. Not only did they block the audience's view of the overhead area, but space between them permitted lighting and special effects to operate from above.

Borders, side wings, and back-scenes were the three basic elements of every set. To shift them simultaneously and instantaneously was the ideal. At first many stagehands were used to make quick changes, but the results were not always satisfactory since it was difficult to synchronize their movements. The final solution, eventually adopted throughout Europe with the exception of England, was the *chariot-and-pole* system. At each wing and back-scene position, slots were cut in the stage floor parallel to the front of the stage. At corresponding positions under the stage, tracks were set up. Frames on casters (chariots) were placed in these tracks, and to each chariot were attached poles which extended upward through the slots in the floor. In turn, the wings and back-scenes were attached to these poles. Moving the chariots toward the center of the stage thrust a set onstage, while the reverse process moved it offstage.

This basic arrangement was further mechanized by a system of ropes and windlasses. Any chariot or border could be attached by rope to a windlass. When the wings, borders, and back-scene of a single setting were attached to the same windlass, one man could change the entire set by turning a single crank. The change could be accomplished instantly and all of the pieces of the set moved in unison. The chariot-and-pole system was perfected by Giacomo Torelli (1608–1678) in the 1640s at first in Venice and then in Paris.

The *groove* system, used in England after 1640, was less complicated. Pieces of wood were attached overhead and to the stage floor to make grooves in which the flats could slide on and off the stage. Both systems fulfill the same function and were used as long as the *wing-and-drop* setting dominated the stage.

117

A design by Torelli for *Bellerophon* (Venice, 1642). (Courtesy French Cultural Services)

Machinery for special effects was also important in the Italian theatre. The stage floor had a number of trap doors through which could be manipulated such special effects as flames and smoke; the appearance or disappearance of buildings, trees, or persons; and earthquakes or seemingly magical occurrences. Other devices were operated from overhead. A favorite effect was the appearance of supernatural beings in clouds, astride mythical animals, or in chariots. These machines, sometimes called *glories,* were usually wooden platforms concealed by painted clouds and suspended by ropes, pulleys, and cranes.

To heighten surprise, the front curtain was used only to keep the stage hidden until the play was ready to begin. Thereafter, the changing of the scenery was part of the performance and was considered in itself to be a special effect.

By the mid-seventeenth century all elements of the picture-frame stage had developed in Italy. From there it had spread to all of Europe before 1700 and remained relatively unchanged until the late nineteenth century. Many of its elements still dominate theatre architecture and staging practices.

COMMEDIA DELL'ARTE

Alongside the drama of the court and academy there grew up another quite different form, *commedia dell'arte*. (*Arte* signified that the actors were artists or professionals in contrast to the amateurs who performed the *erudita* or learned drama.) It was actor-centered, improvised, and adaptable to almost any playing condition.

In commedia dell'arte, the same set of stock characters always appear. This scene is from a twentieth-century commedia script, *The Strolling Players* by Darwin Reid Payne and Christian Moe, presented by the Theatre London's Young Company (Canada). (Carolyn A. McKeone/FPG)

The actor was the heart of commedia dell'arte and almost the only essential element. The script was a scenario which merely outlined the principal action and its outcome. The actors improvised the dialogue and developed the complications as the situation seemed to demand.

The same set of stock characters appeared in all the plays performed by a single troupe, and the same actor always played the same role. The typical characters may be divided into three categories: lovers, professionals, and servants.

The performers of the lovers' roles did not wear masks and were expected to be handsome and sympathetic. There was always one male and one female lover, and often there was an additional pair. Although the plot often centered around some obstacle to their marriage, the lovers were not usually the center of interest. They provided an excuse for the plot and served as the norm against which other characters could be judged; they were dressed fashionably and frequently spoke elegantly and poetically.

Three professional types appeared most frequently: Pantalone, an old merchant, miser, and often the father or suitor of one of the young women; Dottore, a pedantic lawyer, and frequently the father of one of the young men or a suitor of one of the young women; the Capitano, a soldier who boasted of his prowess in love and war but invariably proved to be a coward. Each of these characters had his own distinctive mask and costume which he wore in all plays.

The principal comic roles were those of the servants, or *zanni,* who resorted to all sort of machinations in helping or thwarting the lovers or professional types. They varied from the stupid to the clever and might have marked physical characteristics, such as a large nose or a humped back. Each had his own mask, costume, and fixed characterization. The most famous of the zanni were Harlequin, Pulcinello, Brighella, and Scaramouche. There were also one or two female servants who frequently carried on love affairs with the male servants. All female roles were played by women.

While each play was improvised, the actors, after a time, developed a set of speeches, well-polished comic routines, and other dependable aids in holding attention. Each troupe had a number of proven *lazzi,* or extended bits of comic business which could be utilized when appropriate or when audience attention wandered.

Commedia came into prominence shortly after 1550; soon it was popular throughout Italy, and before the end of the century troupes were playing in France and elsewhere. In the seventeenth century the commedia spread to all of Europe. It declined after 1750 and was virtually dead by 1800.

The commedia actors played for all types of audiences and produced a genuinely popular theatre movement. They were equally at home in the market place, at fairs, or at courts. After public theatres began to be built in Italy in the seventeenth century, the troupes made use of proscenium theatres, and scenarios were written to take advantage of new scenic possibilities and special effects.

Almost eight hundred commedia dell'arte scenarios still exist. Since they only outline the action, however, it is difficult to get a clear picture of the actual quality of a commedia performance, although all accounts testify to the great skill of the actors.

THE FRENCH RENAISSANCE

The Renaissance was late in coming to France, where it made no marked impact until around 1550. The first plays in the classical manner written in French were produced in 1552, but before the new mode could

The court of France sponsored many spectacles similar to those of Italy. This illustration depicts *Circe* by Beaujoyeulx in 1581. The settings are by Jacques Patin. Note the galleries for spectators and the mansionlike arrangement of the scenery. The theatre was a hall in the Petit Bourbon and was later converted to the Italian ideal by Torelli in 1645. Molière's company used the Petit Bourbon from 1658 to 1660, when the building was demolished. (From Germain Bapst's *Essai sur l'Histoire du Théâtre,* Paris, 1893) (Courtesy French Cultural Services)

become fully established it was interrupted by civil war that kept France in turmoil off and on until the 1620s.

Another obstacle to the adoption of Italian conventions was the Confrèrie de la Passion, which had held a monopoly on play production in Paris since the early fifteenth century, when it was organized to present religious dramas. In 1548 this group began building a new theatre, the Hôtel de Bourgogne, but before it was completed religious plays were forbidden. Nevertheless, the Confrèrie's monopoly was reconfirmed. Soon it gave up producing plays and thereafter rented its theatre to visiting companies and demanded fees from any group that wished to perform in Paris. Because of this monopoly and the civil war, performances in Paris were sporadic until the troupe headed by Valleran-Lecomte leased the Hôtel de Bourgogne in 1598. After Valleran's death around 1612, the Parisian stage was dominated until about 1625 by the farce actors Turlupin, Gaultier-Garguille, and Gros-Guillaume. The principal playwright of this period was Alexandre Hardy (c. 1572–1632), author of about five hundred works (mostly episodic tragicomedies), and probably the first French author to make a living from writing for the stage.

Between 1550 and 1640 the staging of plays at the Hôtel de Bourgogne deviated markedly from Italian practices, for medieval mansions were still in use. But, since the visible stage space was only about twenty-five feet wide, the mansions were set up along the sides (one behind the other from front to back) and across the rear of the stage. The space in the middle served as a *platea*. A number of designs for

La Troupe Royale from the Hôtel de Bourgogne, c. 1625. Note the commedia-like characters. (Courtesy French Cultural Services)

Mahelot's design for *La Prise de Marsilly* at the Hôtel de Bourgogne in the 1630s. Note the simultaneous representation of a number of locales. (Courtesy Bibliothèque Nationale, Paris)

these simultaneous settings still exist. (See the illustration above.) Not until about 1640 did the new Italian mode significantly begin to alter French theatrical practices, which until that time continued to be essentially medieval.

CHANGES IN FRENCH THEATRE, 1625–1650

The period from 1625 to 1650 brought sweeping changes to France. After Cardinal Richelieu became chief minister around 1625, the political situation stabilized. Whereas before this time the professional theatre had maintained only a precarious foothold, after 1629 there were always at least two professional companies performing in Paris and often there were more. Richelieu also encouraged the importation of Italian practices, and in 1641 he built in his palace a theatre which included the first proscenium arch in France. After Richelieu's death, his successor, Cardinal Mazarin, promoted Italian opera and in 1645 imported Torelli from Italy to design settings. Torelli remodeled the existing court theatres to include the chariot-and-pole scene-shifting devices. Soon afterward, Italian practices were adopted by the public theatres of Paris as well. Thus, by 1650 the Italian mode had triumphed in France.

Richelieu also strongly supported the French Academy (modeled after the academies of Italy), which took as its province the principles and practice of literary composition and the rules of the French language. This group, whose membership is restricted to the forty supposedly most eminent literary figures of the day, was granted a royal charter in 1636 and still exists.

THE BASIC PRINCIPLES OF NEOCLASSICISM

The French Academy inherited its standards of drama primarily from Italian critics. Since these standards undergird neoclassicism, the dominant artistic mode of the seventeenth and eighteenth centuries, they are important to any study of theatre and drama in that era.

The neoclassicists were primarily concerned with a number of basic issues: verisimilitude; purity of dramatic types; the five-act form; decorum; the purposes of drama; and the three unities.

Verisimilitude, or "the appearance of truth," is a complex concept with three basic aspects: reality, morality, and generality or abstraction. The desire for "reality" required the playwright to rule out those things that could not actually happen in real life. Thus, it eliminated fantasy and the supernatural unless they were an accepted part of a story (as in Greek myths or biblical material). Such conventions as the soliloquy and chorus were discouraged on the grounds that it is unnatural for characters to speak aloud while alone or to discuss private matters in the presence of a group. To replace these devices, each main character came to be given a trusted companion, or *confidant,* to whom he could reveal his innermost secrets. Violence was placed offstage because of the difficulty of making it convincing.

This demand for faithfulness to reality was considerably modified by the insistence that drama teach moral lessons. The dramatist was asked not merely to copy life but to reveal its ideal moral patterns. Since God was thought to be both omnipotent and just, a play was expected to show wickedness punished and goodness rewarded. Those instances in which injustice seems to prevail were explained as a part of God's plan, which is often beyond human comprehension but inevitably just. Therefore, such apparent aberrations were considered unsuitable subjects for drama, for playwrights should depict that ultimate truth which is inseparable from morality and justice.

Both reality and morality were further modified by the principle of abstraction or generality. Rather than seek truth in a welter of details, the neoclassicist sought it in those attributes that are shared by all things in the same category. Those characteristics that are variable were considered to be accidental and therefore no essential part of truth. Thus, the truth was defined as norms that are discoverable through rational and systematic examination. Since these norms were considered the highest form of truth, which remains unchanged regardless of the time and place, rational men were expected to accept them as the basis for literary creation and critical judgment.

The idea that truth is to be found in "norms" was extended to every aspect of dramatic composition. Drama itself was reduced to two basic types, tragedy and comedy, with others labeled inferior because they were *mixed forms*. According to the accepted theory, tragedy draws its characters from rulers or the nobility; its stories deal with affairs of state, the downfall of rulers, and similar events; its endings are always unhappy; and its style is lofty and poetic. Comedy, on the other hand, draws its characters from the middle or lower classes; its stories deal with domestic and private affairs; its endings are always happy; and its style is characterized by the use of ordinary speech. Such distinctions meant, among other things, that tragedy could not be written about the common man and that comedy could not be written about the nobility. In actual practice there were many other dramatic types. The usual explanation of such deviations was that these forms, as products of poorly educated or tasteless writers, were unworthy of critical consideration.

Deviant plays also usually violated the precept that all regular drama be divided into five acts. Horace had first stated this demand in Roman times (without offering any justification for it), and neoclassic critics adopted it. Failure to observe the five-act rule was sufficient to mark any play as "illegitimate."

Perhaps most important to the dramatist was the belief that human nature has its own governing patterns that are the same in all places and in all periods. The dramatist, therefore, was expected to confine himself to writing about the permanent aspects of humanity. This meant cutting away all qualities attributed to a particular time, place, or personal peculiarity. In neoclassical plays, consequently, there is little concern with individualizing details and great emphasis on the universal aspects of character and situation.

These criteria are most easily seen at work in characterization. Each age group, rank, profession, and sex was thought to have its own essence, and the dramatist was expected to remain true to these norms in creating each of his characters. This principle of character portrayal was called *decorum*.

The humanist movement in the Renaissance, seeking to justify literature as a legitimate study, emphasized the usefulness of drama for teaching moral lessons, and this was the line taken by almost all theorists between 1500 and 1800. Most argued that the purpose of drama is twofold—to teach and to please. If the teaching were to be clear, the plays should show characters being punished or rewarded for their behavior. (The term *poetic justice* was coined in the seventeenth century to indicate this meting out of justified rewards and punishments.) Consequently, comedy was expected to ridicule behavior that should be avoided, and tragedy to show the horrible results of mistakes and misdeeds.

Verisimilitude was also said to dictate adherence to the unities of action, time, and place. While unity of action has been demanded in almost every age, critics in the neoclassical period normally interpreted the rule to mean that a play should have only one action, and that there should be no subplots. Neoclassical theorists are the only ones who have placed great emphasis upon the unities of time and place. Castelvetro, writing in Italy around 1570, argued that since an audience knows that it has been in the theatre for only a few hours, an author cannot convince it that several days or years have passed. Thereafter most critics argued that the time of the action should not exceed twenty-four hours. Castelvetro also argued that the audience knows that it has only been in one place and, therefore, it cannot be expected to accept a change in a play's locale from Rome to Athens, or to other widely separated places. The demand for unity of place was sometimes broadened by other critics to allow more than one location if all could be reached easily within the twenty-four-hour time limit.

These, then, are the basic principles of neoclassicism. They may seem artificial and arbitrary today, but in the seventeenth and eighteenth centuries they were meaningful concepts that seriously affected the writing and staging of plays.

CORNEILLE AND RACINE

The writer most closely associated with the transition to classicism in France is Pierre Corneille (1606–1684), who began writing plays in the late 1620s, but did not win great success until 1636, with *The Cid*. The production of this play set off a controversy, for in many ways it adhered to neoclassical demands, but it raised serious questions about the validity of verisimilitude, decorum, and the unities.

The Cid is essentially a tragicomedy centering around the rival demands of love and honor. The unities are for the most part observed—the action is completed within twenty-four hours, the place is confined to the city of Seville, and there are no important subplots. But so many things happen in twenty-four hours that verisimilitude is strained. Furthermore, at the end of the play Chimène, the play's heroine, has agreed to marry Roderigue, who has killed Chimène's father in a duel less than twenty-four hours earlier. This ending both strains decorum and (since it is a happy one for the main characters) puts *The Cid* outside the neoclassical conception of tragedy.

The play was a great success in the theatre, nevertheless, and was both denounced and extravagantly praised. The newly formed French Academy was asked to arbitrate the dispute. It declared that *The Cid* was not a tragedy, and that, while it had many things to recommend it, verisimilitude and decorum (the most important requirements) had been violated. The whole controversy seems somewhat ridiculous today, but at the time it served to make the public conscious of the neoclassical ideals. Corneille eventually accepted the judgment passed on *The Cid* and in his subsequent plays adhered to the new demands and helped to establish French classicism.

The work of Jean Racine (1639–1699) marks the peak of French classical tragedy. Among his most famous works are *Andromaque* (1667), *Bérénice* (1670), and *Phaedra* (1677). The essential qualities of Racine's plays may best be seen by examining *Phaedra,* usually considered the greatest of French tragedies.

PHAEDRA

Against her will, Phaedra loves her stepson, Hippolytus. Although she is fully aware that this love is wrong, she is powerless to resist it. Racine concentrates principally upon depicting this conflict within Phaedra.

Most plays concerned with the conflict of good and evil have shown goodness threatened by some external evil or forces set in motion by an ill-advised decision. In *Phaedra,* good and evil are bound up in the same personality. Herein lies the power of the play, for it shows a person who is thoroughly moral in her convictions but whose willpower has been sapped by irrational emotional drives. Since the conflict is primarily an internal one, Racine needs little external action.

The opening act of the play reveals that Phaedra has been in love with Hippolytus for a long time and that her inner torment has at last driven her to the verge of suicide. She is prevented from carrying out her decision by the news that her husband, Theseus, has died. Oenone, Phaedra's nurse and *confidante,* convinces Phaedra that it is now no longer shameful for her to love Hippolytus.

Phaedra declares her love to Hippolytus, who reacts with disgust. Then the news comes that Theseus is not only alive but has also arrived in the city. When Theseus enters with Hippolytus, Phaedra is faced with a dilemma: How can she greet her husband in the presence of his son, to whom she had just declared her love? Her hasty departure arouses Theseus' suspicion, and Oenone, to save her mistress, accuses Hippolytus of having made advances to Phaedra. Theseus calls down a terrible curse upon Hippolytus and banishes him.

Phaedra is on the verge of telling Theseus the truth when he unwittingly reveals that Hippolytus is in love with someone else. Her jealousy

A scene from *Phaedra* by Racine, performed by the Comédie Française. Seen here are Phaedra and Hippolytus. (Courtesy French Cultural Services)

aroused, she refrains from making the revelation that could save Hippolytus' life.

As Hippolytus leaves Troezen his horses bolt and drag him to his death. Oenone commits suicide and Phaedra, driven by remorse, takes poison. Before she dies, however, she confesses her guilt to Theseus.

As this brief outline shows, the character relationships in *Phaedra* are complex, while the external action is simple. The complications are important only because of the emotional reactions they arouse in the characters. The crucial factor at almost every point is Phaedra's uncontrollable passion for Hippolytus; it is this passion that brings misery to everyone.

Racine adheres to the neoclassical ideals of drama almost completely. The unity of time is clearly observed; a few hours at the most elapse during the course of the play. The place is unspecified but is in and around the palace.

Racine based his play on Euripides' *Hippolytus,* but made many significant changes. In Euripides' drama the emphasis is on Hippolytus' self-righteous vow to remain chaste throughout his life. To punish him for denying her power, Aphrodite sets Phaedra's love in motion. The results are much the same as in Racine's play, but the causes and the implications are entirely different.

Racine eliminated the gods as characters in his play and brought events into the realm of verisimilitude by showing only those occurrences that could happen in real life. *Phaedra* also departs obviously from its Greek model in eliminating the chorus and substituting *confidants* for it.

While Phaedra is the center of concern, each of the other principal characters is also confronted with a psychological conflict of his own. All desire to act rationally, but each is swayed by irrational forces. Phaedra's is merely the most extreme of the cases.

Almost nothing is said about the age or physical appearance of the characters. The emphasis is entirely upon their psychological and moral states. Decorum of character is observed for the most part, and it is the departure from decorous behavior that brings doom. Broad strokes rather than small details have been used. The play aims at the universal rather than the particulars of time, place, and character.

PLAY PRODUCTION IN FRANCE, 1650–1675

The Parisian acting troupes in the mid-seventeenth century were organized on a sharing plan similar to that used by Shakespeare's company. They also included women, who had equal rights with the men and received comparable pay. A French company was usually composed of from ten to fifteen members, but a number of other persons were employed as supernumerary actors, musicians, scene painters, stage hands, and so on.

At the end of each performance the costs of production were deducted from the receipts and the remainder divided among the shareholders. Thus each actor's income depended upon the success of the company rather than upon a fixed salary. All of the leading groups in Paris at the time, however, received some money yearly from the crown, although the sum was not large enough to guarantee them against loss.

Plays were selected by a vote of the troupe after hearing a reading of the work by its author. A play might be bought outright, but a more usual practice was to give the author a percentage of the receipts for a limited number of performances, after which the play belonged solely to the troupe. Companies usually had fifty or more plays in their active repertory.

Casting was simplified because each actor normally played a limited range of roles. When a new actor came into a troupe he learned his roles from the person he was replacing, or from someone else in the company who was acquainted with the way in which the parts had been played

The tragic hero's costume as it developed during the seventeenth ceutury and persisted through most of the eighteenth. An engraving after a painting by Watteau. (From Gillaumont's *Costumes de la Comédie Française,* 1884)

before. Roles came to be played in a traditional manner passed on from one actor to another. One additional convention should be noted: ridiculous old women were usually played by men.

Actors were expected to furnish their own costumes. Generally, costumes were contemporary garments, but, as on the Elizabethan stage, there were a number of conventionalized costumes. Classical, Near Eastern, and Indian characters were usually played in elaborate and costly costumes quite unlike those worn in daily life. The typical dress of classical heroes was the *habit à la romaine,* an adaptation of Roman armor, tunic, and boots, surmounted by a full-bottomed wig and plumed headdress. (See the illustration above.)

The scenic demands were simple. Ordinarily, the setting represented a single place and even that was not indicated in detail because of the neoclassical quest for generality. Therefore, the same set (done in the Italian manner with wings, borders, and back-scenes) could be used for a number of different plays. Furthermore, some spectators were seated on the stage itself (on chairs or benches at either side), leaving an acting area only about fifteen feet wide. The actor, therefore, performed in the midst of spectators and in a very confined space. As a result, the majority of plays did not call for very much physical action, and little attention was paid to creating the illusion of a specific place.

Molière is known today principally for his comedies. (Courtesy French Cultural Services)

MOLIÈRE

The greatest French writer of comedy in the seventeenth century was Jean-Baptiste Poquelin (1622–1673), who assumed the name Molière. He is noted today principally for his comedies of character and ideas, but he wrote many other kinds of plays. Greatly influenced by commedia dell'arte, many of his plays are farces featuring commedia character types. He borrowed freely from Plautus and Terence and from Spanish and Italian sources. It was almost solely through his efforts that French classical comedy came to equal French tragedy. His plays are still performed in almost every country of the world.

Molière's most famous works are: *The School for Wives* (1662), *Tartuffe* (1664), *The Miser* (1668), *The Doctor in Spite of Himself* (1666), *The Misanthrope* (1666), and *The Imaginary Invalid* (1673). *Tartuffe* will be examined here as an example of his comedy.

TARTUFFE

Tartuffe was produced in a three-act version in 1664, in an altered form in 1667, and in its present five-act form in 1669. It has remained in the repertory almost continuously and has been performed more often than any other play by Molière.

Themes and Ideas. *Tartuffe* is obviously concerned with religious hypocrisy. The most likely target of Molière's satire is the Company of the Holy Sacrament, a secret society of the time, one of whose purposes was the improvement of morals through "spiritual police" who spied on

131

The frontispiece from the original
edition of *Tartuffe*, 1669. (Courtesy
French Cultural Services)

the private lives of others. Molière read *Tartuffe* to several persons
before it was first produced in 1664, and the Company immediately
organized an attack upon it. The controversy became so heated that
Louis XIV forbade further performances. Molière revised the play in
1667, only to have it withdrawn again. By 1669 the opposition was
largely gone.

Whether or not Molière had the Company in mind, it is clear that he
was thinking of groups like the Company, who feel that they alone can tell
true piety from false and who create conditions under which hypocrites
can flourish.

As in all of Molière's works, the balanced view of life is upheld in
Tartuffe. To Molière, true piety does not demand the abandonment of
pleasure but the right use of it. The truly devout try to reform the world
by actions that set a good example rather than by pious speeches.

Plot, Structure, and Characterizations. The plot of *Tartuffe* can be
divided into five stages: the demonstration of Tartuffe's complete hold
over Orgon; the unmasking of Tartuffe; Tartuffe's attempted revenge;
the foiling of Tartuffe's plan; and the happy resolution. There are three
important reversals. The first (the unmasking of Tartuffe) brings all of
the characters to an awareness of the true situation. The resulting happiness is quickly dispelled, however, when Orgon is shown to be at the
mercy of Tartuffe.

The first two reversals (turning the tables on Tartuffe; Tartuffe

132

turning the tables on Orgon) have been carefully foreshadowed, but the final one and the play's resolution have not. The contrived ending (in which Tartuffe is discovered to be a notorious criminal) is emotionally satisfying in the sense that justice triumphs, but the contrivance cannot be explained away by accepted criteria of good dramatic construction.

To prevent any confusion about Tartuffe's true nature, Molière uses two acts to prepare for his entrance. The first act also includes a lengthy argument by Cleante, the character who most nearly represents Molière's point of view, in which true piety is distinguished from false.

The structure of *Tartuffe* may also be clarified by examining the use made of various characters. Cleante appears in Act I, where he performs his principal function—to present the commonsense point of view. He does not appear again until Act IV; in that act and in Act V he merely reinforces the ideas he has set forth in Act I. He does not influence the action at all; he merely points up the theme.

While Dorine, the maid, appears in each act, her role is virtually completed after the beginning of Act III, even though she has been a major character up to that point. Her frankness and openness are used as a foil to show off Orgon's credulity, the lovers' petulance, and Tartuffe's false piety. It is she, with her wit and common sense, who sets their exaggerated behavior in proper perspective.

Even Tartuffe is given rather strange treatment when he finally makes his appearance after two acts of preparation. The majority of his role is given over to his two "love scenes" with Elmire. Molière seems to take it for granted that the audience will accept the picture of Tartuffe painted by the other characters and that the play need only emphasize one aspect of his hypocrisy.

Tartuffe displays another side of his character when he is denounced by Damis. Rather than defend himself, he appears to accept the accusations with humility. This scene more than any other shows why Orgon has been taken in by Tartuffe.

The lovers, Valère and Mariane, appear in Act II and are unimportant thereafter. They serve merely to show how far Orgon has been influenced by Tartuffe, since Orgon is planning to marry his daughter Mariane to Tartuffe. The lovers' quarrel is a source of amusement but is largely unrelated to the rest of the play.

Elmire appears in Act III (in which Tartuffe tries to seduce her), but she has only a few lines and most of these treat Tartuffe's suggestions with an air of frivolity. The bulk of her lines comes in Act IV, where she serves as the instrument for unmasking Tartuffe. This uneven distribution of the role has led some critics to argue that her moral character is questionable. It seems clear, however, that Molière had in mind a reasonably worldly but upright woman.

It is Orgon's role, however, that is most evenly distributed throughout the play. While the Tartuffes of the world are dangerous, they can exist only because of the Orgons, since the success of the wicked depends on the gullibility of the foolish. Just as Molière emphasizes Tartuffe's calculated piety, so too he emphasizes Orgon's impulsiveness and stubbornness. Orgon errs largely because he acts without considering sufficient aspects of a question. When Tartuffe is finally unmasked, Orgon's character remains consistent; failing to see the difference between hypocrisy and piety, he says: "I give up all pious people. From now on I will hold them in utter contempt." Thus, instead of returning to middle ground he assumes an equally exaggerated, though opposite, position.

Little indication is given of the age or physical appearance of the characters. Since Moliere wrote with his own company in mind and directed the play, he did not need to specify every detail in his script. The role of Tartuffe was written for DuCroisy, a large man with a ruddy complexion. This, no doubt, was one of the sources of humor. All of Tartuffe's talk about scourges and fasting was contradicted by his obvious plumpness and lecherousness. Orgon was played by Molière, noted for his expressive face and body, while Elmire was acted by Molière's wife, who was twenty-seven in 1669. Since Mme. Pernell was played by a man, the character was no doubt intended to be ridiculous in her denunciation of pleasure. All of the characters are drawn from the middle or lower classes (in accordance with neoclassical theories of comedy).

The unities of time and place are strictly observed. Only a single room is required and even that need have only a table, under which Orgon can be concealed, and a closet (in which Damis can hide) since no specific use is made of the setting except in these two instances. The action is continuous, or nearly so, and occurs in a single day. All of the episodes, with the possible exception of the lovers' quarrel, are directly related to the main theme of the play. *Tartuffe* is clearly within the classical tradition.

THE THEATRE AFTER MOLIÈRE'S DEATH

Molière died in 1673. His life and death illustrate the status of the actor in France at that time, for, while he was highly admired as an author, his acting made him ineligible for many honors, such as membership in the French Academy, and upon his death he was forbidden a Christian burial, since the church's strictures against actors, issued in late Roman times, were still in effect. Most actors renounced their professions when death approached so that they might be accepted back into the church, but Molière died suddenly, having been taken ill during a performance. Thus, while the actor's legal and economic status had improved by 1673, he was still in some senses an outcast.

Following Molière's death, French drama rapidly declined. Corneille

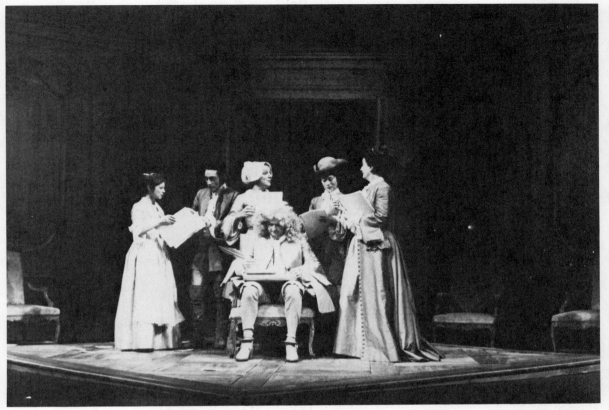

The Comédie Française, the first national theatre in the world, more nearly embodies a continuous theatrical tradition than any other single theatre. Shown here is a recent production. (Courtesy French Cultural Services)

gave up writing after 1674 and Racine wrote no plays for the public stage after 1677. The great age of French playwriting was over by 1680.

The number of theatres also shrank steadily after 1673. At the time of Molière's death, five theatrical companies were playing in Paris: Molière's, the companies at the Hôtel de Bourgogne and the Marais, a company of Italian actors, and an opera troupe. In 1673, the director of the opera, Jean-Baptiste Lully, gained control of Molière's theatre and forced the company to move. Soon afterward Molière's company merged with the one at the Marais theatre and, in 1680, this combined company was ordered to merge with the Hôtel de Bourgogne troupe.

This final merger is one of the most important events in French theatrical history, for the combined group formed the Comédie Française, the first national theatre in the world. This organization is still in existence, and more nearly embodies a continuous theatrical tradition than any other single theatre.

The order that created the Comédie Française also laid down the rules under which it was to operate. Like its predecessors, it was to be a shareholding company governed democratically by its members. Procedures were established for the admission and retirement of actors, for paying pensions, and for numerous other matters. A yearly subsidy was provided by the state.

After 1680, there were for some time three troupes in Paris (the Comédie Française, the Opéra, and an Italian commedia dell'arte company) and when the Italian troupe left in 1697 the number was reduced to two.

In 1672, the Opéra had been awarded a monopoly on musical drama. After the expulsion of the Italians, the Comédie Française achieved a similar monopoly on spoken drama. Thus, by the end of the seventeenth century, the Parisian theatre not only had shrunk but the remaining troupes held entrenched positions which they were to defend throughout the eighteenth century.

The age of French classicism had brought the theatre of France to maturity. It produced three great playwrights, Corneille, Racine, and Molière, who have remained the primary models for French drama since that time. It had also won complete acceptance for most of the innovations that had originated in Italy during the Renaissance. Consequently, by the late seventeenth century the neoclassical ideal had triumphed. It would continue to dominate theatre and drama until romanticism undermined its appeal in the early nineteenth century.

The Eighteenth Century

7

During the eighteenth century, the theatre extended and consolidated the trends that had begun during the Renaissance. Throughout this century, the neoclassical ideal remained dominant, although its authority was challenged by a number of innovations and minor forms. The theatre also continued to gain in prestige and to expand into new territories. Overall, however, the primary goal apparently was to maintain the standards and conventions that had developed during the preceding century.

GOVERNMENT REGULATION OF THE ENGLISH THEATRE

Charles II was restored to the throne of England in 1660 and with him the theatre regained its place in English life. At that time it was made illegal for anyone to produce plays without a patent from the govern-

137

ment (a monoplistic right that, like property, could be sold or passed on to others). In the early 1660s, the king issued two patents and these remained in effect thereafter.

During the first part of the eighteenth century many attempts were made to circumvent the patents, and eventually the violations, coupled with numerous satirical productions about government officials, provoked the passage of the Licensing Act of 1737. This law reconfirmed the patents and further provided that, prior to production, each play had to be licensed by the Lord Chamberlain (a government official), who thus became the censor of all works intended for the stage. From 1737 until 1843 only two theatres, Drury Lane and Covent Garden, were permitted to produce regular drama throughout the year. (After 1766, the Haymarket Theatre was licensed to perform during the summer months.) The patents were finally rescinded in 1843, but the provisions for licensing plays continued until 1968.

ENGLISH THEATRE ARCHITECTURE

Soon after the English theatre reopened in 1660 new playhouses, incorporating Italianate features, were built. The major difference between English and continental theatres involved the apron (or forestage); continental theatres had aprons but not proscenium doors (that is, doors opening onto the apron). In England during the late seventeenth century, there were two proscenium doors on each side of the stage. This permitted great flexibility in staging, for an actor might exit through one door and reenter immediately at another door on the same side, thus indicating a change in place or lapse of time.

During the eighteenth century, the number of doors on either side was reduced to one and the depth of the apron gradually diminished, but both features were retained well into the nineteenth century. Because in the eighteenth century much of the action took place on the apron, the setting was principally a background rather than an environment for the actor, who performed, for the most part, forward of the proscenium where he could more easily establish rapport with the audience.

The auditorium of the English theatre, with its boxes, pit, and galleries, was similar in all important respects to those then in use on the Continent. Until 1762, spectators were also permitted to sit on the stage.

SCENERY IN THE ENGLISH THEATRE

Scenery in the English theatre between 1660 and 1800 differed in no important respect from that then being used in Italy and France. Scenes

William Hogarth's *The Laughing Pit,* showing spectators in the pit, men of fashion and orange girls in the boxes, musicians in the orchestra pit. Note the spikes to prevent spectators from climbing onto the stage, and the candles on the front of the boxes. (From an eighteenth century engraving. Courtesy of the University of Iowa Library.)

were painted in perspective on wings, borders, and backdrops. Since settings were generalized in accordance with the neoclassical demand for universality, a large number was not needed, and the same setting was used for many different plays. Pantomimes, operas, and a few plays, however, demanded more detailed scenery and elaborate special effects. In these cases, new scenery was specially designed and widely advertised.

The most important eighteenth-century English scene designer was Philippe Jacques de Loutherbourg (1740–1812), who began staging spectacular pieces at Drury Lane in the early 1770s. He complicated the stage picture by adding ground rows (profile pieces shaped and painted to represent rocks, mountains, grassy plots, fences, and similar objects) to the traditional wing-border-drop settings to increase the sense of naturalness and the illusion of space and distance. De Loutherbourg also reproduced likenesses of actual places onstage and thereby helped to create a demand for greater scenic illusion. He improved stage lighting and was able to give the effect of natural light, changes from fair to stormy weather, and similar conditions.

139

THE ENGLISH ACTING COMPANY

When the English theatre was reopened in 1660 its financial structure was considerably altered from that of Shakespeare's day as it came more and more under the control of businessmen. After 1660 actors often served as managers of theatrical troupes, but the majority became employees rather than active participants in management.

Typically, in the English theatre of the eighteenth century an actor was hired for one or two years at a specified salary with the additional guarantee of a "benefit." At a benefit, the receipts (after deduction of operating expenses) went to the beneficiary. After about 1710 every performer had at least one benefit each season, although a lesser actor often had to share his benefit with one or more of his fellows. While a benefit usually brought the actor additional income, it also offered the manager an excuse for paying him a relatively small salary during the rest of the year.

Each actor or actress (actresses were introduced to the English stage in the 1660s and were accepted throughout Europe after that time) was usually employed for a *line of business* (that is, a limited range of parts). An actor learned through experience. As a beginner, he explored lines of business while playing supernumerary roles and after a few years he had usually found his line, which was the one he followed for the rest of his career.

Each actor also *possessed parts.* This meant that once he was assigned a role, it remained his until he left the company. An actor might possess up to a hundred roles, any one of which he could be expected to perform on twenty-four hours' notice.

Many of these practices were determined by the *repertory system* (under which a large number of plays were rotated with some regularity). Between 1660 and 1800 the majority of any company's repertory was made up of plays from the past. A lesser part was composed of works from recent seasons. The smallest part of a company's offerings was new plays.

Plays were rehearsed by the "acting manager," usually a performer in the company who was given additional pay to assume these duties. He took for granted that the actors knew their job, and restricted himself to establishing entrances and exits and to rehearsing difficult bits of stage business. He probably spent little time on blocking (that is, positioning the actors on stage), for performers learned as part of their training to let the major actors have the best stage positions and to move around them inconspicuously. The actor also learned to direct his speeches to the audience as much as to the other characters. The presence of the audience was emphasized by leaving the lights on in the auditorium. Furthermore, since most of the action occurred on the apron, the performer, in

In the intervals between acts a variety of entertainment, such as singing and dancing, filled the stage. Here a ballet performed at a theatre in London in 1791 is seen. Note also the arrangement of the auditorium. (From Thomas Rowlandson's *The Prospect Before Us,* New York Public Library.)

effect, was in the auditorium with the spectators. Rehearsals normally extended over seven to twelve days. By modern standards they were perfunctory, and great reliance was placed on the actor's stage presence and quick wit.

Actors often played more than one role on the same evening because the program was so long and complex. After 1720, a typical evening's bill was arranged as follows: first, there was orchestral music; then came the prologue, followed by a full-length play; the intervals between the acts were filled with variety entertainment (singing and dancing, monologues, acrobatics, trained animals, and so on); following the main piece, an afterpiece (a pantomime, farce, or comic opera) was performed; the evening usually concluded with a song and dance. An actor often appeared in both the main piece and the afterpiece, and he might present one of the variety acts as well.

Acting style was no doubt more exaggerated than modern taste would approve. The actor was said to base his acting on life, but to idealize rather than to copy it. Thus there was careful selection, arrangement, and considerable heightening. Periodically during the eighteenth century, actors supposedly reformed acting in the direction of naturalness, but these actors probably only eliminated some exaggeration. After each effective speech the audience applauded as it does today when a singer

141

Between 1741 and 1776 David Garrick was one of the most renowned English actors. Especially noted for his Shakespearean roles, he is seen here playing Macbeth opposite Mrs. Hannah Pritchard as Lady Macbeth. (From *English Illustrated Magazine*, 1776.)

finishes an operatic aria. This constant interaction between audience and actor made for a more intimate relationship than is typical today.

Among all the English actors, the most famous between 1660 and 1800 were Betterton and Garrick. Thomas Betterton (c. 1635–1710) dominated the English stage from about 1670 to 1710, during which time he played leading roles in almost all the standard plays in the repertory. He excelled in heroic and tragic parts, and his somewhat formal and elocutionary style became a model for many of his successors. David Garrick (1717–1779) was the major actor on the English stage between 1741 and 1776, as well as manager of the Drury Lane Theatre from 1747 to 1776. Through his sound judgment and taste, both in management and acting, he elevated the English theatre to a position of international esteem. Especially noted for his performance of Shakespearean roles, he is generally thought to have been the greatest of all English actors.

ENGLISH PLAYWRITING

The actor's position was more secure than that of the playwright. In the Restoration, writers might be employed by companies on a fixed salary, but this practice was soon replaced by benefits. Under this system, the author received the receipts of the third performance. If a play were especially popular he might also receive benefits on each additional third night of the initial run, although he was fortunate to receive one benefit. After the initial run, the play belonged to the company and the author received no further payment.

The period from 1660 to 1700 is noted particularly for heroic tragedy and the comedy of manners. The heroic play, written in rhymed couplets, usually concerned the necessity of choosing between love and honor and abounded in violent action and startling reversals. Alongside the heroic play another, more vital strain of tragedy developed. Written in blank verse, the outstanding examples are Thomas Otway's (1652–1685) *Venice Preserv'd* and *The Orphan,* both of which held the stage until the nineteenth century. Another example is *All for Love* by John Dryden (1631–1700), a reworking of Shakespeare's *Antony and Cleopatra* to make it conform to neoclassical rules.

The Restoration is principally noted, however, for the comedy of manners, in which characters and events are subordinate to social values and customs. The plays satirize persons who are either self-deceived or are attempting to deceive others. The humor is directed against the fop, the pretender at wit and sophistication, the old woman who is trying to be young, the old man who marries a young wife, and other similar types. The standard is represented by those characters who are truly witty and sophisticated, who see others and themselves clearly, and who act accordingly. Restoration comedy originated with such works as George Etherege's (1634–1691) *The Man of Mode* (1676) and *She Would If She Could* (1668), and reached its perfection in the plays of William Congreve (1670–1729), especially *Love for Love* (1695) and *The Way of the World* (1700).

The Restoration comedy of manners was not calculated to please the Puritan elements in English society. After the return of Charles II in 1660 Puritan influence, which had dominated England during the Commonwealth, was little felt for some time. Furthermore, from 1660 to about 1690 theatre audiences were largely drawn from the upper classes or the more liberal elements of the middle class. A change set in after 1689, however, when William and Mary were crowned rulers of England. Under the patronage of the new rulers, the merchant class came to wield great power, and in the 1690s when it began to attend the theatre in sizable numbers, it exerted pressure for reform. The rise of the middle class coincided with a resurgence of Puritan protests against the theatre, the most powerful of which was Jeremy Collier's *A Short View of the Immorality and Profaneness of the English Stage* (1698), an attack on current plays, particularly the comedies of manners. These factors combined to bring about a change in the subject matter and spirit of English drama after 1700.

The transition to a new outlook can be seen most clearly in such comedies of George Farquhar (1678–1707) as *The Recruiting Officer* and *The Beaux' Stratagem,* which put greater emphasis on a clear-cut set of moral standards and drew its characters less often from fashionable London society.

ENGLISH SENTIMENTAL DRAMA

During the eighteenth century the most important dramatic types were to be sentimental comedy and domestic tragedy. The term *sentimental* indicates an overemphasis on arousing sympathetic response to misfortune. Even comedy became preoccupied with the ordeals of sympathetic characters, and humorous scenes were reserved for minor characters, usually servants. Many plays could be called comedies only because they ended happily. The expressed aim of the dramatist was to draw forth a smile and a tear, or, as one writer put it, to produce "a pleasure too exquisite for laughter."

Today these plays seem highly exaggerated in their depiction of human nature. The characters appear too good and noble and the circumstances too contrived to be convincing. But these plays attracted large audiences, who accepted the works as realistic pictures of human motivations. We need to remember, therefore, that the eighteenth century thought man had an inborn instinct for goodness, that he could be reformed by appealing to his heart, and that those who withstood all trials should be rewarded. Furthermore, the display of concern (especially through tears) at the sight of virtuous characters in distress was thought to be a sign of instinctive goodness in the spectators. Eighteenth-century drama merely reflected these beliefs.

Sentimental comedy received its first full expression in *The Conscious Lovers* (1722) by Sir Richard Steele (1672–1729). In it, the penniless heroine, Indiana, after withstanding many trials, is discovered to be the daughter of a rich merchant, thus making her marriage to the hero acceptable to his father.

Sentimental comedy had its serious counterpart in domestic tragedy, which deliberately avoided the kings and nobility of traditional tragedy and chose its characters principally from the merchant class. It usually painted the horrible outcome of giving in to sin, just as sentimental comedy showed the rewards of resisting sin.

George Lillo (1693–1739) established the vogue for domestic tragedy with *The London Merchant* (1731), a play that shows an apprentice who, led astray by a depraved woman, robs his employer and murders his uncle. It is clearly indicated that had the apprentice resisted temptation he could have married his employer's daughter and become a pros-

144

A scene from *The Conscious Lovers* by Sir Richard Steele. From an edition of the play published in 1816. (Culver Pictures.)

perous merchant. *The London Merchant* exerted great power over audiences throughout the eighteenth century and was a major influence on the drama of France and Germany.

BALLAD OPERA, BURLESQUE, AND PANTOMIME

Sentimental comedy and domestic tragedy are indicative of the weakening of neoclassical standards. Each represents a considerable departure from the "pure" dramatic forms demanded by critics, for they mingled elements formerly associated wholly with comedy or tragedy. Other "illegitimate" forms also appeared, the most important of which were ballad opera, burlesque, and pantomime.

The emergence of ballad opera can be explained in part by the popularity of Italian opera, espcially after George Frideric Handel (1685–1759) came to live in England in 1710. In *ballad opera,* sections of dialogue alternate with lyrics set to already-popular tunes. The first and most important example of the new form was *The Beggar's Opera* (1728) by John Gay (1685–1732), which, though it treated Italian opera humorously, also satirized contemporary politics. At the end, one of the characters observes that it is difficult to tell whether the robbers are imitating the politicians or the politicians the robbers. The ballad opera eventually gave way to the sentimental operetta, or comic opera. The

145

principal writer of this form was Isaac Bickerstaffe (1735–1812), with such works as *Love in a Village* (1762) and *The Maid of the Mill* (1765), the titles of which suggest both the content and tone.

During the 1730s Henry Fielding (1707–1754) turned to writing farces that burlesqued much of the drama of the day and satirized the ruling classes. His *The Tragedy of Tragedies, or, The Life and Death of Tom Thumb the Great* (1730) travesties the tragedies of the time, while his *Pasquin* and *The Historical Register for 1736* ridicule contemporary politics and social conditions. The combination of ballad opera and burlesque did much to motivate passage of the Licensing Act of 1737.

The most popular new form in the eighteenth century, however, was *pantomime*. It came into being around 1715 and was perfected by John Rich (c. 1682–1761), manager of one of the patent companies. The pantomime was composed of dancing and silent mimicry performed to musical accompaniment, set against elaborate scenery, and utilizing special effects. Typically, comic and serious scenes alternated. The comic plot usually involved Harlequin, who by some device has obtained a magic wand by means of which he can transform places, objects, and persons at will. Normally, the serious plot was derived from a mythological or historical subject already known to the audience. Pantomime made its appeal largely to the eye, and great expense was lavished on producing it. It was largely because of the visual requirements of opera and pantomime that stage machinery and scenery became so elaborate in England.

GOLDSMITH AND SHERIDAN

By the 1770s sentimentalism dominated the English stage. At this time two dramatists, Goldsmith and Sheridan, tried to reform public taste. Oliver Goldsmith (1730–1774), especially with *She Stoops to Conquer* (1773), attempted to reestablish what he called "laughing" comedy. His plays are in the tradition of Jonson's more boisterous works or Shakespeare's farces. The plays of Richard Brinsley Sheridan (1751–1816), on the other hand, are in the vein of Restoration comedy. His most famous plays are *The Rivals* (1775) and *The School for Scandal* (1777), the last frequently called the greatest comedy of manners in the English language. It will be examined here as an example of eighteenth-century drama.

THE SCHOOL FOR SCANDAL

Themes and Ideas. *The School for Scandal* is a comedy of manners in which the customs of the day are summed up in the "school for scandal,"

The screen scene from the original production of *The School for Scandal,* 1777. Note the forestage, proscenium doors, stage boxes, clearly defined wings, and the similarity of the actors' costumes to those worn by the spectators. (Courtesy Yale University Library.)

whose members trifle with reputations because they are unable to distinguish between fashion and true virtue. Sheridan places much of the blame for this confusion on the vogue for sentimentalism and makes his principal unsympathetic character, Joseph Surface, a "man of sentiment"—that is, one who mouths moral maxims. Joseph's pious statements are accepted as proof of a virtuous character, while the frank and natural behavior of his brother, Charles, is taken as the sign of a lost soul. Sheridan is ultimately concerned with the distinction between true virtue and pious remarks. His sophisticated and humorous treatment, however, never allows the play's serious aspects to come to the fore.

While Sheridan satirizes sentimental comedy, he has not been able to free his own play from many of its traits. His admirable characters are themselves inclined to moralize or fall into "sentiments," and the play as a whole illustrates the typical lesson of sentimental comedy: true virtue will be rewarded—and with a sizable fortune.

Plot and Structure. *The School for Scandal* is structurally complex since it weaves together the schemes, desires, and cross-purposes of so many characters. Sheridan has solved his problem in part through the relationship he has established among the characters. All move within the same social circle in London and all know each other well. Furthermore, Sir Peter is the guardian of Maria and has been the best friend of the now-deceased father of Charles and Joseph Surface. These close ties allow Sheridan to maneuver his characters more freely and to bring together logically the various strands of the plot as the play progresses. The scandalmongers are among the least important characters, but they are used to great advantage to establish the social background, to give exposition through their gossip, to affect the action through their intrigues, to help in resolving the action when one member defects, and to provoke laughter through their malicious wit.

Sheridan's structural methods often resemble Shakespeare's, especially in the integration of subplot and main plot. In *The School for Scandal* the Sir Peter–Lady Teazle story has little connection with the Joseph–Maria–Charles story in the beginning. As the play progresses, however, the two stories move closer and closer together, and in the "screen" scene the revelation of Joseph's relationship with Lady Teazle leads to the resolution of both the subplot and the main plot.

Sheridan constantly strives for clarity in characterization and situation. In the opening scene he makes it quite plain that Joseph Surface is a hypocrite who is attempting to ruin his brother. Asides to the audience are used throughout the play whenever an action or a motivation might otherwise be ambiguous. In addition, many of the characters have been given names that describe their basic natures: Snake, Sir Benjamin Backbite, Lady Sneerwell, and so on. While Sheridan makes the action completely lucid at any moment, he does not let the audience foresee the way in which it will be resolved.

The high point of the play is the screen sequence, since it brings to a climax almost all of the preceding conflicts and culminates in the discovery of Lady Teazle behind the screen. This brings Lady Teazle to her senses and unmasks Joseph's hypocrisy.

The unities of time and place, as interpreted by English critics, are observed, since all action occurs within twenty-four hours and all places are within easy reach of each other. The close connection between the main plot and the subplot creates unity of action also. *The School for Scandal* is a good example of English neoclassicism, which was considerably more liberal than its French counterpart.

Characters and Acting. In accordance with the neoclassical notion of decorum, the characters in *The School for Scandal* are drawn largely as types. Charles Surface is the natural young man who does those things appropriate to youth. Joseph, on the other hand, pretends to have the characteristics of an older, mature person. Sir Peter observes the proper decorum for a man of his age except in his marriage to a young woman, and it is for this lapse that he is made to suffer. Maria, Sir Oliver, and Rowley represent the ideal standard of behavior, and their conduct is vindicated in the resolution. On the other hand, the scandalmongers clearly deviate from the ideal pattern and are punished. Charles, Lady Teazle, and Sir Peter deviate only in a few respects and, at the end of the play, acknowledge their shortcomings and declare their intentions to reform.

All of the characters—except Old Rowley, Moses, and the servants—are drawn from the leisure class. None is concerned about making a living. They are preoccupied with such matters as marriages, the making of proper impressions, the maintenance and destruction of reputations. To live life pleasurably is the ideal. Sheridan satirizes those who murder reputations and those who are hypocrites, but he does not raise any doubts about the essential rightness of the social system itself. This restricted concern gives the play a tone of lightness and frivolity that is only slightly modified by the moralizing of Maria and Sir Oliver and by the play's ending.

Visual and Aural Appeals. *The School for Scandal* is set in the London of its own time (1777). This is reflected especially in the costumes—those of the upper classes of the day. A contemporary engraving of the "screen" scene (see page 147) shows the production's costumes and setting, the theatre's apron stage, proscenium doors, and members of the audience seated in boxes. The actors' dress corresponds closely to that worn by the audience, and the division of the scenery into two sets of wings and a back-scene is evident.

By the 1770s spectators had been banished from the stage and more emphasis was being placed on the settings. Most of the places required in Sheridan's play are designated merely as a room in Sir Peter's house, at Lady Sneerwell's, and so on, but more specific settings are required for the scene in which Charles sells the family portraits and for the screen scene. All of the settings would have been changed in full view of the audience.

The School for Scandal contains a considerable amount of rather precisely specified business. For example, at Charles Surface's house a supper is in progress during which toasts are drunk and songs are sung. This is followed by an auction of the pictures. Much of the action probably took place on the forestage, and many exits and entrances were undoubtedly made through the proscenium doors. The use of the forestage kept the action close to the audience and made the asides more acceptable.

In the language lies one of the strongest appeals of *The School for Scandal*. Sheridan follows in the tradition of the Restoration by making his characters speak with polish and wit. The dialogue is sophisticated and sparkling; it reflects the same detachment from socioeconomic concerns as does the subject matter.

The School for Scandal has been more consistently popular than any other comedy in the English language. Its story, its wit, and its comic inventiveness have kept it understandable and enjoyable to successive generations.

AMERICA

The theatre first gained a foothold in America during the time it was still a collection of English colonies. Therefore, the American theatre began as an extension of the English, from which practically all of its personnel came. Although there had been sporadic theatrical activity in America during the seventeenth century, it was not until 1752, when Lewis Hallam (1714–1756) brought a company of actors to the colonies, that the professional theatre began to make an impact. Playing first in Virginia, Hallam's company went on to perform up and down the Atlantic seaboard.

During the Revolutionary War theatrical activities were suspended but were revived in the 1780s; by the end of the century they were well established from Charleston, South Carolina, to Boston. Despite its newly won independence, however, the American theatre continued to take its standards from England and it would be many years before a strong native tradition would emerge.

FRANCE

Although today the English theatre of the eighteenth century may seem more interesting than that of other countries, at the time the French theatre dominated Europe. France was considered both the political and cultural center of the Western world.

By 1700 the neoclassical ideal, as embodied in the tragedies of Racine and the comedies of Molière, had become the standard against which European drama was judged, but it also did much to freeze dramatic invention. The only French tragic writer of note in the eighteenth century was Voltaire (1694–1778), who attempted several innovations, such as the use of crowds and ghosts, more spectacle, greater realism in acting and costuming, and a limited amount of violence on stage. But Voltaire's reforms seem slight today, and his influence operated principally to preserve the ideals of Racine. His best plays are *Zaïre* (1732) and *Alzire* (1736).

As the eighteenth century progressed, comedy departed considerably from Molière's pattern. The changes parallel rather closely those already noted in England.

The works of Pierre Carlet de Chamblain de Marivaux (1688–1763) are important forerunners of sentimental comedy, for the dominant theme of his plays is the awakening of love. Typically, the main characters are a couple skeptical about love and marriage. Gradual and subtle changes are traced as the characters are brought to a point at which they must confess the love that has overcome them. Earlier comedy had typically treated characters already firmly in love when the plays opened; the complications arose from their attempts to overcome the opposition of parents or some other external force. In Marivaux' plays, however, the obstacles are psychological and internal. The most famous of Marivaux' works are *The Surprise of Love* (1722), *The Game of Love and Chance* (1730), and *False Confidences* (1737).

True sentimental comedy appeared first in the works of Pierre Claude Nivelle de la Chaussée (1692–1754), whose plays *The False Antipathy* (1733) and *The Fashionable Prejudice* (1735) established the vogue for *comédie larmoyante* (tearful comedy). These plays differed from their English counterparts only by being written in verse, but even this distinction was not maintained by La Chaussée's successors.

Domestic tragedy had no strong advocate in France until Denis Diderot (1713–1784) espoused it in the 1750s. Diderot argued that the traditional classifications of drama into tragedy and comedy should be supplemented by two *middle genres* (which correspond roughly to sentimental comedy and domestic tragedy). It was the middle genres that interested Diderot most, and he advocated many reforms in staging to increase their appeal. He believed that the best drama arouses the greatest emotional response and that the degree of emotion is proportional to the illusion of reality. He therefore argued for the use of prose dialogue and for everyday characters, situations, and settings. He also advocated the "fourth wall" approach, in which the stage is treated as a room with one transparent wall through which the audience looks. The actors then supposedly act as they would in an actual room without taking any note of the audience. Diderot also wrote an important treatise on acting, *The Paradox of the Actor*. In this work he argues that onstage the actor should feel nothing himself but should render the external signs of emotion so compellingly that the audience is convinced of the reality of the fictional situation. Although Diderot's ideas have remained important, they exerted little influence on his contemporaries. His plays, *The Illegitimate Son* (1757) and *The Father of a Family* (1758), were not successful, although they did help to establish the term *drame* as a designation for serious plays which do not fall into the category of traditional tragedy.

The most important French playwright of the late eighteenth century is Pierre Augustin Caron de Beaumarchais (1732–1799), who wrote some *drames* in the fashion of Diderot, but who is remembered primarily for two comedies, *The Barber of Seville* (1775) and *The Marriage of Figaro* (1784). Both center around the character of Figaro. In the first play he is the epitome of all the clever servants of comedy as he aids Count Almaviva in his plan to marry Rosina, the ward of Doctor Bartholo, who wishes to marry Rosina himself. While social satire plays only a small part in *The Barber of Seville,* it is extensive in *The Marriage of Figaro.* In the latter play Figaro is in Count Almaviva's service and on the point of marrying Suzanna, a serving girl in the household. The Count is tiring of Rosina and is attempting to seduce Suzanna. The action of the play is principally taken up with uncovering and thwarting the Count's schemes, which offer many opportunities for comment upon the relative worth of the aristocracy and the lower classes.

France produced a number of outstanding actors in the eighteenth century, the most famous of whom were Clairon, Dumesnil, and Lekain. Claire Hippolyte Clairon (1723–1803) made her debut at the Comédie Française in 1743 in the role of Phaedra. Diderot thought her the ideal actress, and she was also a favorite of Voltaire, who worked with her in making many of his reforms. Her acting was the essence of the carefully

Left: Marie-Françoise Dumesnil in Racine's *Athalie.* In spite of the play's Biblical setting, Dumesnil is wearing an eighteenth-century court dress. (From Pougin's *Dictionnaire Historique et Pittoresque,* 1885.) Right: Costume worn by Mlle. Clairon in *The Orphan of China* (1755). This costume supposedly marked a change toward greater authenticity, though from a modern point of view it is still clearly influenced by eighteenth-century taste. (From a contemporary print.)

planned, "natural" style. Diderot states that Clairon's approach was the opposite of that used by Marie Françoise Dumesnil (1713–1803), who excelled in emotional roles but lacked the control of Clairon. She had no interest in reforming the stage and thought the actor should always be magnificently dressed regardless of the part. Henri Louis Lekain (1729–1778), who was acclaimed the greatest tragic actor of his age, was closely associated with Clairon in making reforms in acting and costume.

In addition to championing a more realistic acting style, Clairon and Lekain abandoned the traditional costumes in favor of others that reflected historical period. These reforms, begun in the 1750s, are symptomatic of innovations which were to undermine neoclassicism. After spectators were removed from the stage at the Comédie Française in 1759, scenic display also increased and began to include historically accurate details.

Perhaps as a result of the growing emphasis on spectacle, the old theatre buildings began to seem inadequate. The Palais-Royal (home of the Opéra) burned in 1763, the Comédie Française abandoned its theatre in 1770, and the Hotel de Bourgogne was not used after 1783. In their places rose buildings that made better provisions for the audience and provided larger stages and more complex machinery.

ITALY

In the eighteenth century Italy continued to be preoccupied with opera, and, as this form spread to other countries, Italian theatrical architecture and scenic design continued to dominate Europe.

In the course of the eighteenth century, design underwent a number of significant changes. Of these, perhaps the most important was the perfection of angle perspective, in which the vanishing point is placed at the sides. Thus, a feeling of space is created by suggesting the continuation of vistas offstage on either side. The development of angle perspective is usually credited to the Bibiena family, of which at least seven members in the seventeenth and eighteenth centuries were scene designers in the principal theatrical centers of Italy, Austria, Germany, Sweden, Russia, Spain, and Portugal.

The Bibienas were also instrumental in popularizing settings conceived on an enormous scale. During the seventeenth century, the stage had been treated as an extension of the auditorium and the scenery had been proportioned accordingly, but in the eighteenth century the wings near the front of the stage were painted as though they were merely the lower portion of structures too large to be contained on the stage. Consequently, settings by the Bibienas often create a mood of fantasy and unreality through their vastness. The Bibienas also continued the

An example of a large-scale set design at the Markgräfliches Opera House, Bayreuth, by Giuseppe and Carlo Galli-Bibiena. This opera house is one of the major surviving examples of the Baroque style of theatre architecture. (Courtesy German Information Center.)

trend toward excessive ornamentation which had begun in the seventeenth century. Columns were twisted and entwined with garlands; S-curved supports were added to beams and pediments; encrustations abounded everywhere.

During the last half of the eighteenth century still other changes were made. As comic opera developed, domestic and rustic scenes became common, while interest in more specific settings led to the inclusion of "local-color" details. After the rediscovery of Pompeii in 1748 had captured the imagination of Europe, interest was aroused in classical ruins. As a result, classical buildings, formerly depicted in pristine condition, were now represented in a state of decay, often over-grown with vines or shrubs. Under the influence of Gian Battista Piranesi (1720–1778), who emphasized extremes of light and shadow in his engravings of prisons and ruins, designers also began to be aware of mood and to depict picturesque places as seen by moonlight or interiors illuminated by only a few shafts of light. Thus, during the eighteenth century scenic design underwent many changes in visual style, although the basic arrangement of wings, drops, and borders continued un-changed.

If the Bibienas are the best known of eighteenth-century Italian designers, they had many rivals. Among these were Filippo Juvarra (1676–1736), the Mauro family (who flourished from the 1650s until the 1820s), the Quaglio family (who worked as designers from about 1650 until 1942), and the Galliari family (who worked from the early eighteenth century until 1823).

In addition to opera, interest in commedia dell'arte continued in the eighteenth century. By the 1730s, however, commedia had become repe-titious and somewhat vulgar, and its emphasis upon farce had begun to be out of tune with the new taste for sentimental drama. Consequently, one of Italy's major playwrights, Carlo Goldoni (1707–1734), attempted

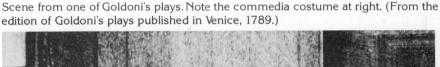

Scene from one of Goldoni's plays. Note the commedia costume at right. (From the edition of Goldoni's plays published in Venice, 1789.)

to reform the commedia. Goldoni began writing commedia scenarios in 1734 and soon set out to substitute written scripts for improvised action. At first he wrote out only a single part, but soon he was able to persuade the actors to accept plays in which all speches were written out. He continued to use traditional characters but sentimentalized them and removed all indecency. *The Servant of Two Masters,* the title of which suggests the basic comic situation, is a good example of Goldoni's commedia plays. But Goldoni was not long able to stop the decline of commedia, and by 1800 this form, one of the most interesting the theatre has produced, had virtually come to an end.

Goldoni also wrote many other kinds of plays, including comedies, comic operas, and tragedies. His comedies usually concern women (who are much more sensible than Goldoni's men) and the middle and lower classes (who are almost invariably depicted as superior to the upper class). Sentimentalism pervades most of his work, but a spirit of fun and lightheartedness keeps it from being cloying. Many of his plays are still highly regarded and frequently performed; the most notable are *The Mistress of the Inn* (1753) and *The Fan* (1764).

In spite of its large role in shaping the European theatre, by the end of the eighteenth century Italy had ceased to develop vital new ideas. In the nineteenth century it was to remain the center of the operatic world but it would play little part in the development of theatre and drama.

GERMANY

The most striking changes in the eighteenth-century theatre occurred in Germanic territories. In 1700 Germany was composed of many small states divided by religious and political differences. The Thirty Years' War (1618–1648) had depleted both its population and its resources, leaving few large cities and little wealth. The theatre was divided between private court productions and public traveling companies, with little connection between the two.

Court theatres arose under the influence of Italian opera. After 1652 the court at Vienna became one of the major theatrical centers of Europe, and its example was imitated throughout Germany, where each court maintained a theatre patterned after those of Italy. Touring companies were the true founders of the professional German stage. The first traveling players in Germany came from England around 1590. Gradually, the English actors were replaced by Germans, and by 1650 there were some all-German companies, although the conditions under which they worked did not change essentially until after 1725. None of the troupes had a permanent home, since no town could as yet support a professional theatre. Touring, therefore, was necessary but costly and

Hanswurst, the clownish character who appeared in most German plays of the early eighteenth century. (From an eighteenth-century engraving; courtesy University of Iowa Library.)

time-consuming. Companies varied their programs as much as possible so as to exert maximum appeal to the limited audience in each town. The low state of the theatre was reflected in the plays, which featured violent action, exaggerated characters, and bombastic dialogue. Hanswurst, a character based on Harlequin of the commedia dell'arte, played a major role in all plays, even serious ones.

All these factors conspired to keep the German theatre in low repute until after 1725, when Johann Christoph Gottsched (1700–1766) and Carolina Neuber (1697–1760) made the first serious effort to reform the German stage. Gottsched, who was interested in improving the level of German literature and in elevating taste and morals, formed a liaison with the acting troupe headed by Carolina Neuber. Gottsched's standards were derived primarily from French neoclassical drama, which was completely unknown to the audiences of popular German theatres.

Nathan the Wise by Gotthold Ephraim Lessing, Germany's first important dramatist (1729–1781). This production was performed on a world tour sponsored by the Goethe Institute. (Courtesy German Information Center.)

Nevertheless, Gottsched and his associates set out to provide a new repertory, much of it either translated or adapted from the French.

Carolina Neuber tried to raise the level of acting and the reputation of the theatrical profession by insisting upon careful rehearsals and a high level of personal morality. She banished Hanswurst from her theatre and revised her repertory to bring it into closer accord with Gottsched's aims. In none of her attempts was she entirely successful, but Gottsched and Neuber's work marks the turning point in the German theatre.

Germany's first important dramatist was Gotthold Ephraim Lessing (1729–1781), who turned attention away from French neoclassicism to English drama as more compatible with German tastes. His *Miss Sara Sampson* (1755), which is set in England, established the vogue for domestic tragedy in Germany. His most popular play is *Minna von Barnhelm* (1767), a comedy that shows how a rich young girl maneuvers an officer into marriage, although he wishes to decline because he has lost his wealth and therefore feels unworthy of her. Lessing's critical writings, especially the *Hamburg Dramaturgy* (1767–1768), also helped to turn attention away from French drama and to establish more defensible standards.

Acting also grew in prestige. Konrad Ekhof (1720–1778) probably did more than any other German performer of the eighteenth century to establish the respectability of his profession. He reformed acting style in the direction of greater naturalness, ran a short-lived training school for actors, and influenced most of the other principal performers of the day. Friedrich Ludwig Schroeder (1744–1816) is generally considered the greatest German actor of the eighteenth century and perhaps of all time. Because of his acting, his managerial skill, and his personal charm, he was for many years considered to be the head of the theatrical profession in Germany.

During the last quarter of the eighteenth century the breach between the court and public theatres was bridged with the formation of subsidized state troupes that served both court and public. The first of the national theatres was formed at Gotha in 1775, and it was soon followed by others at Vienna, Mannheim, Cologne, Weimar, Berlin, and elsewhere. By 1800 almost every Germanic capital had a state theatre organized along lines similar to the Comédie Française.

Although by no means the most prosperous, the best-known state troupe at the end of the eighteenth century was that at Weimar. Here Johann Wolfgang von Goethe, using autocratic methods of directing, welded a company of second-rate actors into the finest ensemble then to be seen in Germany. Goethe's reputation as Germany's greatest poet also served to attract attention to the Weimar theatre, which reached its peak between 1798 and 1805 with productions of Friedrich Schiller's plays. Goethe emphasized grace, harmony, and balance in movement and speech, and sought in every element of production to achieve an idealized beauty. The company's style was to exert strong influence on German theatrical production until well into the nineteenth century.

Thus, by 1800 the German theatre had undergone a revolution. Permanent theatres now housed resident companies, the acting profession was respected, and German drama was beginning to assume international importance. Furthermore, Germany was already in the process of developing a romantic drama that would overthrow those neoclassical ideals that had dominated the stages of Europe for more than a century and a half.

The Nineteenth Century

8

By the beginning of the nineteenth century, a number of forces were combining to break the hold of neoclassicism and to create what is now called romanticism, a movement that flourished between 1800 and 1850. The nineteenth century also saw melodrama emerge as the most popular dramatic form and spectacle become ever more realistic. During this period, the theatre was the major source of popular entertainment for all classes throughout the Western World.

ROMANTICISM

Most of the ideas that shaped romanticism had come to the fore during the eighteenth century as faith in reason, which undergirded neoclassicism, was gradually replaced by trust in natural instinct. In addition, the

161

rise of the middle class prompted a reconsideration of the class structure under which the majority was subservient to the nobility. Gradually, primitive society, as a state in which man had been free to follow the dictates of his own conscience without political and economic strictures, came to be idealized. The American and French revolutions were both based in part on concepts of equality and fraternity.

Equally important, the earlier belief that truth is to be defined in terms of "norms" gradually gave way to the conviction that truth can only be discovered in the infinite variety of creation. According to the romanticists, the universe has been created by God out of himself so that he may contemplate himself. Therefore, everything in existence has a common origin and is a part of everything else. To know ultimate truth, then, one must include as much of creation as possible. Consequently, rather than eliminate details so as to arrive at norms, one should seek to encompass the infinite variety of existence.

Since all creation has a common origin, however, a thorough and perceptive examination of any part may provide insight into the whole. Thus nature (forests, mountains, and so on) reflects something of man, just as man reflects nature. The more unspoiled a thing is — that is, the less it deviates from its natural state — the nearer it comes to truth. This view helps to explain why romantic writers show a marked preference for poetry about nature and for drama about unspoiled man living in primitive times or in rebellion against the restraints imposed by society.

Nevertheless, because truth is infinite, it is ultimately beyond total comprehension. Thus, no matter how hard a writer may strive to record it, he is doomed to fail in part. But the romanticists believed that, despite these limitations, a few rare beings — the geniuses — can perceive far more of the truth than the ordinary man. Genius was said to involve an innate capacity to grasp intuitively the complexity of the universe. But this capacity that sets the genius off from other men frequently makes him appear strange (even dangerous), and thus he is often treated as an outcast. Genius, then, is both a gift and a curse.

According to the romanticists, the genius did not need to be concerned with norms or rules but only with how to express his own perceptions. They soon came to view Shakespeare's plays as ideal models (much as the Renaissance had viewed Greek and Roman plays and the neoclassicists had viewed the works of Racine and Molière) but frequently saw in Shakespeare only freedom from restraint. As a result, they adopted a loose structure in which the unities, sometimes even of action, were abandoned. Since authors frequently ignored the requirements of the stage, because genius should not let itself be restricted by practical demands, many of the plays were never produced and others had to be adapted before they could be staged. About much of the dramatic writing of the period there is an air of impracticality, but the new outlook did serve to free writers from the often-arbitrary demands of neoclassicism.

With the coming of romanticism, the neoclassical doctrine of verisimilitude was firmly rejected. Whereas neoclassicism had sought to eliminate everything that could not logically happen in real life, romanticism tended to emphasize the supernatural and mysterious as essential parts of existence. Thus ghosts and witches, prophecies and curses, coincidence and Providence abound in romantic dramas. Subjects also were chosen from many sources previously ignored, and Greek myths gave way to medieval tales, national or local legends, and stories about folk heroes or rebellions against social or moral codes. These were used to embody themes showing man's attempts to achieve freedom, to find peace of mind or the secret of all being. This fusion of new forms, subjects, themes, and techniques created a drama quite unlike that of the neoclassical age.

MAJOR ROMANTIC DRAMATISTS

Although the romantic ideal was first fully expressed by German theorists around 1800, most of its concepts can be traced to England. Nevertheless, England never experienced a romantic "revolution," probably because the changes in outlook and practice there evolved so slowly as to be almost imperceptible. Furthermore, in England the neoclassical ideal was never so fully entrenched as in France, and therefore the transition to romanticism was more easily made.

In England, romanticism produced few dramas of lasting value. The lack was little felt, however, since in Shakespeare it already had the period's ideal romantic writer. But Shakespeare's influence was not always beneficial, for many promising writers spent their lives turning out imitations of his work. Perhaps the most successful of these playwrights was James Sheridan Knowles (1784–1862) with such works as *Virginius* (1820), *William Tell* (1825), and *The Hunchback* (1832), all of which mingle pseudo-Shakespearean verse and techniques with melodramatic stories. In addition, all of the major English romantic poets — Coleridge, Wordsworth, Byron, Keats, and Shelley — wrote plays, but they made little impact on the theatre.

Germany was more fortunate than England, for its romantic playwrights produced plays of more lasting value. Two of the dramatists who contributed most to German romanticism — Schiller and Goethe — denied any affinity with the movement and preferred instead to be called classicists. Nevertheless, both wrote plays that embody romantic ideals, and other romanticists often acknowledged indebtedness to them.

Friedrich Schiller (1759–1805) began his playwriting career in

A scene from Friedrich Schiller's *Maria Stuart* depicting a confrontation between Elizabeth I and Mary of Scotland. (Courtesy of German Information Center)

1782 with *The Robbers,* a typically romantic work about a good man who is forced by evils around him to become an outlaw. Beginning with *Don Carlos* (1787), Schiller turned principally to moments of crisis in history. *Don Carlos* deals with the awakening aspirations of a Spanish prince to encourage freedom. Opposed by the court and church, he is eventually given up by his father to the Inquisition for punishment. Schiller used English history in *Maria Stuart,* French history in *The Maid of Orleans,* Swiss history in *William Tell,* and German history in his Wallenstein trilogy. Few dramatists have combined such a sweep of historical material with such theatrical power.

Johann Wolfgang von Goethe (1749–1832) is to German literature what Shakespeare is to English, for he is universally considered to be the greatest of German writers. His first play, *Götz von Berlichingen* (1773), deals with the attempts of a German knight of the sixteenth century to remain free in the midst of political and religious intrigues. Goethe underwent a change in the 1780s. Concluding that true greatness lies in an idealized art similar to that of the Greeks, he wrote some plays in the classical manner, the most famous of which is *Iphigenia in Tauris.* But Goethe is best known today for *Faust,* which, like *Götz,* was not conceived with the stage in mind, although it too was soon adapted for theatrical presentation and has been performed frequently since the early nineteenth century.

FAUST

Faust is usually considered the greatest literary work in the German language. Goethe worked on it throughout his life, beginning Part I in the 1780s and completing it only in 1808; Part II was not published until 1831. A "dramatic poem" conceived on a scale too vast for the theatre, it must be adapted and condensed when it is produced.

The "Prologue in Heaven" establishes the basic theme when God states that man cannot avoid making mistakes in his search for fulfillment, but that continuous striving will lead him to the truth. The scenes that follow dramatize the search. Before the search begins, however, Mephistopheles makes a pact to aid Faust in return for Faust's agreement that Mephistopheles can take his soul whenever he finds that moment of fulfillment for which he has been searching and beyond which there will be no point in living.

In this scene from Goethe's *Faust* (Part II), Faust encounters Chiron, a wise Centaur who imparts knowledge to several Greek mythological heros. (From Salzburg Festival, 1963)

Part I shows Faust's search for fulfillment in physical pleasures. Part II shows the completion of Faust's striving. Having found sensual pleasure inadequate, he seeks meaning in ideal loveliness and poetry; eventually he finds the moment for which he has been searching when he renounces his own selfish interests for service to others. But Mephistopheles is thwarted when he comes to take Faust's soul, for Faust has won salvation through that very striving for fulfillment in which Mephistopheles has aided him.

The structure of *Faust* is extremely loose. Although it superficially resembles Elizabethan drama, it lacks the economy of Shakespeare's plays and any compelling unity of action. For example, Shakespeare always makes the dramatic situation clear in the opening scene, but it is not until the fourth scene of *Faust* that the pact with Mephistopheles sets the action in motion. If the two prologues are included, almost one-fourth of Part I is taken up with introductory material.

The principal dramatic questions raised in the play concern Faust's ability to find completion and to save his immortal soul. These questions hold the play together, but the nature of the first is such that Faust may look anywhere for its answer. Goethe chooses to have Faust seek first for fulfillment in material and sensual pleasures, but any other choice could have been made. Furthermore, any phase of Faust's search could be illustrated at length or briefly.

The only sequence that is developed in clear cause-to-effect progression is the Faust–Margarete story. But even this sequence is broken up by the insertion of scenes that illustrate Faust's psychological and philosophical attitudes, Goethe's real concern. Although all of the scenes are thematically related, they are by no means all dramatic. Many could be eliminated without any confusion to an audience, and their removal might actually lead to greater clarity in performance. The major source of unity, then, is thought rather than incident.

The cast of Part I is too vast to count, made up as it is in large part of crowds, choruses, unspecified numbers of witches, wizards, and spirits. Those given any degree of psychological development are few: Faust, Mephistopheles, Wagner, Margarete, Martha, Valentine, and Lieschen. The rest are types or abstractions. Goethe is interested in the range of creation but not concerned with individuals except in a few cases. His principal effort has gone into Faust, and it is only as the other characters illustrate his condition that they are important to the drama.

There is probably no play that allows designers to utilize their gifts so thoroughly as does *Faust*. The costumer must create suitable garments for will-o'-the-wisps, witches, monkeys, and evil spirits as well as for human characters. The lighting designer must suggest the ranges of night and day and the wonders of Walpurgis Night. The scene designer must provide either a single setting capable of suggesting the great variety of places or numerous backgrounds that can be changed rapidly. Sixteen locales are indicated for Part I.

The audience's senses are assaulted through all possible means: speech, song, music, dance, supernatural visions, witches' frolics, folk festivals, and disembodied voices. There is almost endless variety. The proper staging and coordination of all these elements strain the power of any director, even with the full help of many assistants. The task is stupendous, but if properly done *Faust* shows the theatre in its fullest splendor, for it extends the resources of the stage to their breaking point. In its attempt to embody the infinite variety of creation and man's longing for fulfillment, *Faust* is an outstanding example of romanticism.

OTHER DRAMATISTS

Although never a conscious part of the romantic movement, Heinrich von Kleist (1777–1811) is perhaps the best German dramatist of the early nineteenth century. Nevertheless his plays were seldom produced until the late nineteenth century. Today Kleist is remembered principally for one comedy, *The Broken Jug* (1811), and two tragedies, *Penthesilea* (1808) and *The Prince of Homburg* (1811). The last play concerns a young officer who is so bent upon gaining renown that he defies military orders when he sees the chance of winning a victory. Although successful, he had endangered the entire army and is therefore sentenced to die. He is reprieved only after he comes to recognize that his personal goals must be subordinated to service.

By 1815 the strength of the romantic movement in Germany had receded, perhaps because the belief in the possibility of unselfish service to others had been shaken by recent political events. This disillusionment is well illustrated in the plays of Georg Büchner (1813–1837), whose *Danton's Death* (1835) concerns an idealist who, seeing his highest aims wrecked by the pettiness of his fellow men, comes to question the validity of the ideals themselves. Unable to decide whether life has any meaning, he goes to his death with dignity but still in doubt. *Woyzeck* shows a man who, little better than an animal, is led inevitably to his downfall by the social circumstances under which he is forced to live. Both plays are pessimistic and peculiarly modern in their views of human psychology.

Friedrich Hebbel (1813–1863), unlike Büchner (who never passed beyond pessimism), found consolation in view of history as a series of conflicts between old and new ideals through which absolute spirit (or God) works toward perfection. His most famous play, *Maria Magdalena* (1844), is now usually considered a forerunner of realism, since its characters are drawn from ordinary life, its dialogue is in prose, and its story

A production of Georg Büchner's *Danton's Death* (1835) performed by the National Theatre, London, in 1971. (Zoë Dominic, London)

ends in the suicide of the heroine. But it also embodies the conflict of old and new values and suggests that change is on its way. With Hebbel's death in 1863, German drama entered a period of decline from which it was not to recover until after 1890.

The romantic movements in both England and Germany were already declining before romantic drama was accepted in France. Although many strictures on the theatre had been removed during the Revolution, Napoleon reinstituted censorship in 1804 and advocated neoclassicism. In 1807 he issued a decree which established four state theatres (one for major dramatic forms, one for minor dramatic forms, one for comic opera, and one for opera). In many ways, then, Napoleon reinstated the conditions that had existed before 1790. There was one important difference, however—Napoleon allowed private theatres, although the number and repertory were carefully controlled. These nonstate theatres, located largely on the Boulevard du Temple, are the ancestors of today's popular Parisian houses, which are still referred to as "boulevard" theatres.

Despite Napoleon's strictures, the principles of romanticism penetrated France, but it was not until Victor Hugo (1802–1885) published the preface to his play *Cromwell* in 1827 that they were clearly set forth, and romanticism did not triumph in France until Hugo's *Hernani* was produced in 1830.

The French plays of the new movement differ considerably from their German counterparts, and in actuality are more closely related to the melodramas of the day. Many use such melodramatic devices as

168

disguises, hidden staircases, and hairbreadth escapes. They differ from melodrama only in greater depth of characterization, the use of verse and the five-act form, and unhappy endings.

Hernani concerns a man who has become an outlaw because his father has been unjustly accused of treason and his lands confiscated. Hernani loves Doña Sol, who is also loved by her guardian, Don Ruy Gomez, and by Don Carlos, the future Holy Roman Emperor. While Hernani is a guest of Don Ruy, Don Carlos comes seeking him but Don Ruy refuses to reveal Hernani's hiding place. In return for this favor Hernani gives Don Ruy a horn and promises that, if his life is ever needed, Don Ruy need only blow the horn. In the final act, which takes place on the wedding day of Doña Sol and Hernani (now forgiven and no longer an outlaw), Don Ruy, filled with jealousy, blows the horn. Hernani and Doña Sol drink poison and Don Ruy kills himself.

Other important French romantic dramatists were Alexandre Dumas *père* (1803–1870), remembered today chiefly for his novels *The Count of Monte Cristo* and *The Three Musketeers,* and Alfred de Vigny (1797–1863), who translated many of Shakespeare's plays into French and helped to popularize them.

Probably the best dramatist of the time was Alfred de Musset (1810–1857), who was concerned especially with the psychology of lovers. Musset frequently writes of two people in love, each of whom is so afraid of being hurt that he disguises his true feelings; this dissembling serves only to wound the other person, who in striking back widens the breach. Sometimes the breach can be healed to permit a happy resolution, but sometimes it cannot and disaster results. Musset's best-known plays are *No Trifling with Love* and *A Door Should Either Be Shut or Open.*

MELODRAMA

Even as romantic drama was developing, melodrama was also emerging; it was eventually to become the most popular form of the nineteenth century and to hold the stage long after the romantic movement had ended.

Plays have exhibited melodramatic qualities since the earliest times, and examples may be found in every period. But it was not until the eighteenth century that various elements came together to create the conditions out of which a form called melodrama was to emerge. (The principal characteristics of melodrama have already been discussed in Chapter 2; see page 35.) The term *melodrama* means a combination of music and drama, and throughout the nineteenth century a musical score accompanied the action as it does today in movies.

169

In the 1800s melodrama became a highly popular form of theatre. This print, "Le Melodrame," by Daumier, shows both the intensified dramatic action and the enraptured audience's response.

Credit for formalizing melodrama goes to two men: August Friedrich Ferdinand von Kotzebue (1761–1819) and René Charles Guilbert de Pixérécourt (1773–1844). Kotzebue, a German, wrote more than two hundred plays, the most famous of which are *Misanthropy and Repentance* (played throughout the English-speaking world as *The Stranger*) and *The Spaniards in Peru.* He was a master of sensationalism, with which he mixed sentimental philosophizing and startling theatrical effects. But it was Pixérécourt, a Frenchman, who first consciously fashioned his plays as melodramas. He wrote more than one hundred, almost all of which were enormously popular. He did not labor so much over the dialogue as over easily identified character types and startling theatrical effects.

The fortunes of melodrama throughout the world cannot be traced here, but, since the basic pattern was much the same everywhere, the English experience can be cited as reasonably typical. Until the 1820s, the majority of melodramas were rather exotic, either because they were set in some remote time or place or because they featured the supernatural or unusual. In the 1820s, the form took a new turn, however, with the increased use of familiar backgrounds and subject matter: Pierce Egan's *Tom and Jerry, or Life in London* (1821) featured a number of actual places in London; J. B. Buckstone's *Luke the Labourer* (1826) helped to popularize stories about ordinary people; Douglas William Jerrold's *Black-Eyed Susan* (1829) started a vogue for nautical melodramas; and Edward Fitzball's *Jonathan Bradford* (1833) was one of many works based on actual crimes.

In the 1830s, melodrama began to acquire a more elevated tone. Edward George Bulwer-Lytton (1803–1873), already famous as a novelist, helped to establish this "gentlemanly" melodrama with *The Lady of Lyons* (1838) and *Richelieu* (1839). By 1840, melodrama was attracting playgoers of all ranks and had clearly become the most popular of all dramatic forms. Probably the most successful of the later English writers was Dion Boucicault (1822–1890), whose *The Corsican Brothers* (1852), *The Octoroon* (1859), and *The Colleen Bawn* (1860) combine sentiment, wit, and local color with sensational and spectacular endings that tax the full resources of the theatre.

UNCLE TOM'S CABIN

The most popular melodrama of the nineteenth century was the American play *Uncle Tom's Cabin,* based on Harriet Beecher Stowe's novel published in 1852. A number of dramatizations were made of *Uncle Tom's Cabin,* but that by George L. Aiken was to be the most popular. Aiken first constructed a three-act play that ended with the death of Little Eva, then wrote a second play that continued the story until the death of Uncle Tom. They were soon combined to form the six-act play that was presented after that time. When the six-act version was produced in New York in 1853, it played for 325 performances, a phenomenal run for the period. The play was so long that it was presented without the usual afterpiece, an innovation that helped to establish the single-play entertainment.

Themes and Ideas. Mrs. Stowe's novel was in large part a plea for the abolition of slavery. In the play this can best be seen in the story of George Harris and Eliza, which shows how slaveowners (even the best ones) part families by selling members, and how a black is forced to become a fugitive if he rebels against his status as a piece of property. The rights of slaveowners versus the natural rights of man is also debated sporadically in the play.

Uncle Tom's Cabin is also concerned with religion. Uncle Tom is sustained in his trials by his faith. He teaches his religion to Little Eva, aids in St. Clare's conversion, and comforts Cassy with his picture of God's love. This emphasis culminates in the final tableau in which Little Eva, riding on a "milk-white dove," blesses the kneeling figures of St. Clare and Uncle Tom. This final scene also serves as a happy ending to what would otherwise be unhappy and therefore atypical of melodrama.

171

Plot and Structure. *Uncle Tom's Cabin* is composed of a number of loosely connected stories. For example, the subplot dealing with the flight of Eliza and George Harris is related to the main plot only because Eliza and Uncle Tom are owned by the same family. The decision to sell Eliza's child and Uncle Tom to a slave dealer (because of the owner's financial difficulties) initiates both plots, but the two are unrelated thereafter except thematically. Even in the main plot Uncle Tom's life with Little Eva (to whose father he is sold) and his fate under Simon Legree (who later acquires him), are connected only through the character of Uncle Tom. Other scenes, such as those between Miss Ophelia and Deacon Perry, have no discernible purpose except comic relief.

The organization of *Uncle Tom's Cabin,* therefore, is not always that of cause-to-effect relationship among all its parts, although this kind of organization is often found within the individual subplots. Rather they

Uncle Tom's Cabin, by Harriet Beecher Stowe, in its dramatic version was one of the most popular melodramas of the nineteenth century. Here Simon Legree is seen punishing the faithful and patient Uncle Tom. (Theatre and Music Collection, Museum of the City of New York)

are linked because coincidence plays such a large part. But the sprawling form and overuse of coincidence obviously did not detract from the play's appeal. Variety was one of the play's attractions: the story of Topsy serves as an antidote to Little Eva's almost cloying perfection; George and Eliza are suitable contrasts to Uncle Tom in their attitudes toward slavery; and as a slaveowner Simon Legree contrasts strikingly with St. Clare and Shelby. Variety is also achieved through the alternation of comic and serious tone, of quiet and bustling scenes, and in the many reversals of fortune.

Characters and Acting. The play includes approximately twenty-five characters, although a number of additional ones could be used to advantage in such scenes as the slave auction. But, since many characters disappear for scenes at a time, roles can be easily doubled in performance.

All of the characters are types. (The names "Uncle Tom" and "Simon Legree" have passed into popular usage to describe types of behavior.) All are characterized physiologically, sociologically, and in terms of basic attitudes. Much is made of physical appearance, and the division into white and black is important to the play's theme. Sociological roles are also emphasized, since the division into slaves and free men, owners and overseers, workers and the leisure class is important. The chief concern, however, is with the fundamental attitudes of each character. But these attitudes are confined largely to clear-cut moral stances—either good or bad. No character deliberates about what he should do, for his choice is predetermined by his basic moral nature.

Visual and Aural Elements. Melodrama, like romantic drama, placed considerable emphasis upon spectacle. The settings for *Uncle Tom's Cabin* range from the comfortable interiors of wealthy homes to rough cabins; from the idealized landscape of St. Clare's garden to the ice-filled river over which Eliza escapes; from city streets to desolate country scenes. The contrast is made more evident by the rapid changes, for no act of the play has fewer than four scenes (there is a total of thirty scenes).

The basic scenic elements were still wings and drops, with special pieces added as needed. Considerable effort was spent in making such scenes as that in which Eliza crosses the ice as realistic as possible. The popularity of the play led companies to mount rival productions in which they sought to outdo each other with the number of mules, horses, and bloodhounds used in the pursuit of Eliza.

Uncle Tom's Cabin was accompanied by an orchestral score, and at various points songs were inserted. Undoubtedly it was the rich combination of spectacle, music, dance, and story that accounts for the overwhelming success of *Uncle Tom's Cabin,* which was performed continuously until well into the twentieth century.

MAJOR TRENDS IN NINETEENTH-CENTURY THEATRE

Until late in the nineteenth century, the typical producing organization continued to be the resident company performing a large repertory of plays each season. Nevertheless, the system underwent significant changes under the impact of visiting stars, touring companies, and long runs.

Repertory companies had always had their leading players, but the deliberate exploitation of stars was largely an innovation of the nineteenth century. For example, after 1810 major English actors began to tour America in starring engagements, performing a few of their most famous roles with the resident companies they visited. By 1850, the craze for visiting celebrities was universal, and subsequently many of the most renowned performers made round-the-world tours.

Traveling productions were made feasible by the expanding network of railroads. In America, the railroad system extended from coast to coast by 1870 and a comparable growth had occurred in other countries. Perhaps for this reason, the star system gradually expanded after 1860 into the *combination company* (one that toured with stars, complete cast, sets, costumes, and properties and normally a single play rather than a repertory). The impact of the new system is indicated by the rapid decline of resident companies. In America, the fifty resident companies of 1870 had been reduced to four in 1887. A comparable change can be noted in other countries. In England and France, for example, provincial troupes virtually disappeared.

Repertory companies in large cities were little affected by the combination companies. Nevertheless, they too declined, but for another reason—increasingly long runs. Before 1850 successful new plays had usually been performed a few times and then placed in the repertory to alternate with other plays. After 1850, however, the length of runs increased steadily and rapidly, and the size of each theatre's repertory was reduced accordingly, since fewer plays were needed to fill out a season. For example, Wallack's Theatre in New York in the mid-1850s was performing sixty plays each season, but by the mid-1880s only five to ten. This change is explained in part by the enlarged potential audience in urban areas, but also by growing costs of production, for each play had to be performed enough times to recover the investment made in it. The fate of the repertory system was sealed when it became evident that long-term contracts with performers were no longer economically sound, since not all members of a company were cast in each play and therefore some were idle during long runs though still paid. The obvious solution (and the one adopted) was to employ actors only for the run of a play. Thus, by 1900 most producers had given up the repertory system in favor of a single-play, long-run policy. The actor, in turn, had to seek a new engagement each time a play closed. While the new arrangement solved many of the producer's problems, it greatly increased those of the actor.

The decline of the repertory system did not signal a decrease in theatrical activity, however, for the number of new productions continued to increase until well into the twentieth century. The growth in touring, on the other hand, did create many new problems. In America, for example, New York became the center from which all companies originated. Actors therefore had to go there to seek employment, just as local managers did to book attractions. By the 1890s booking was extremely chaotic, since to fill up his season a local manager might have to negotiate with many different producers, each of whom was simultaneously dealing with countless other local managers. Often touring companies defaulted on their contracts, leaving theatres without attractions.

Out of this situation the Theatrical Syndicate grew when six theatre managers and booking agents joined together in 1896 and promised local theatres a full season of plays, complete with stars, on the condition that they book exclusively through it. Although many local managers welcomed the new stability, others resisted this attempt to gain a monopoly. In the latter cases, the Syndicate bought, rented, or built rival houses and gradually drove the recalcitrant managers out of business. After it gained control over a majority of key road theatres, the Syndicate also forced New York producers to sign exclusive contracts with it, since without the Syndicate road companies would not get enough bookings to make tours profitable. Through such devices, the Syndicate dominated theatrical production in America between 1896 and 1915. It also did much to elevate commercial above artistic motives, an attitude from which the American theatre has not yet fully recovered.

AUDIENCES AND ARCHITECTURE

The eighteenth century had seen the middle classes flock to the theatre, and to this group the nineteenth century added the lower classes. A number of factors—among them the industrial revolution (which greatly enlarged the urban population), the expansion of public education, the belief in democracy and equality—served to bring into the theatre many persons who had not previously attended.

The increased demand for theatrical entertainment was met in several ways. First, the number of theatres grew significantly. For example, in London, where there had been only three theatres in the late eighteenth century, there were thirty by 1870. Second, theatre auditoriums were enlarged to hold more spectators. In London Drury Lane and Covent Garden theatres (which each held about two thousand in the

The Bolshoi Theatre in Moscow in 1861. Note the arrangement of boxes, pit, and gallery. (The New York Public Library)

eighteenth century) were enlarged to accommodate more than three thousand. This great size encouraged the use of spectacle, since subtleties in acting were lost in these vast houses. Third, most theatres enlarged the range of entertainment so as to appeal to as wide a range of tastes as possible. Sometimes two full-length plays, plus numerous variety acts, were offered during the same evening on a program that lasted five or six hours.

After midcentury, the situation began to change. First, regular drama and variety acts were separated and theatres came to specialize in one kind of entertainment. Second, as theatres began to specialize, the evening's bill became less complex. Theatres offering drama turned more and more to a single play as the sole attraction and the length of performances changed correspondingly to no more than two to three hours. Third, changes in programming led to alterations in the auditorium. After 1860 there was a trend toward smaller houses. Seating patterns were also altered as the orchestra (rather than the boxes) became the favorite place to sit. This change was brought about by two factors: an increase in democratic sentiment, which made the mingling of classes more acceptable than when the box, pit, and gallery plan had originated; and the trend toward homogeneity within each audience, which was encouraged by programming that limited each audience to those with similar tastes. In the pit (retitled the orchestra) comfortable armchairs gradually replaced the benches previously used there, and in theatres built in the late nineteenth century boxes were omitted entirely and replaced by balcony seating.

STAGING

Developments in staging during the nineteenth century may be attributed primarily to increased interest in historical accuracy and realism. Prior to the late eighteenth century, history was not considered relevant to art, since universal truth, independent of time and place, was said to be the province of drama. During the late eighteenth century, however, the history of architecture, literature, dress, and social customs began to be studied and introduced onto the stage.

This interest extended to the unusual or exotic. Authentic folk dances and costumes of other countries began to creep into productions and picturesque settings became popular. This kind of detail was called *local color*, since it rendered the characteristic features of a specific locale.

At first, historically accurate details and local color were used only sporadically and inconsistently, Charles Kemble's production of Shakespeare's *King John* (produced in London in 1823) was the first in England to claim complete historical accuracy in every detail of costuming. This production was designed by J. R. Planché (1796–1880), who through productions and his histories of costume did more than anyone else in England to promote the trend toward historical accuracy in the theatre. This taste for accuracy flourished in every country, and by 1850 it had become a point of pride to offer productions certified to be completely accurate in every detail of architecture, dress, and accessories.

Once realism of spectacle was accepted as the standard, the wing-and-drop setting could no longer satisfactorily represent interiors. Consequently it was gradually replaced by the *box set*, consisting of three walls and a ceiling. By the early nineteenth century the box set seems to have been in use on the Continent, and it was introduced into England in the 1830s. It was not to be used consistently, however, until the late nineteenth century.

The demand for illusionism also led to the leveling of the stage floor (which, since the Renaissance, had sloped upward toward the rear), as it became increasingly difficult to achieve realistic effects solely through wings and drops (which normally had to be erected parallel to the front of the stage) and increasingly frustrating to maneuver heavy set pieces around the grooves on a sloping floor. Around 1875 the floor began to be leveled and the grooves or chariot-and-pole mechanisms for handling wings removed. Thereafter, scenic units could be placed wherever de-

Steele Mackaye (1842–1894) was an American playwright, actor, director, inventor, and reformer. Shown here is his Madison Square Theatre, which opened in 1880. It featured a double stage, one above the other, on elevators. Settings could be changed in less than one minute. (From *The Scientific American,* April 5, 1884.)

sired, but new methods of shifting scenery had to be devised. The most usual solution was stagehands who moved units manually, but toward the end of the century such devices as the revolving stage, elevator stage, and rolling-platform stage were introduced. (These devices are explained more fully in Chapter 14.

The trend toward realism also brought changes in other theatrical practices. For example, after 1875 the front curtain began to be closed regularly to mask scene changes in order to maintain illusion, which might be destroyed if audiences saw settings being assembled or shifted. The actors also came to perform more and more inside the proscenium, rather than on the apron, and to respect the fourth-wall convention.

Innovations in stage lighting also aided realism. By 1820 gas had begun to replace candles and oil lamps and was in use almost everywhere by the 1840s. For the first time since the theatre had moved indoors the stage could be lighted as brilliantly as desired. Furthermore, by 1850 the *gas table,* a central panel of gas valves, permitted control over all of the stage lights. The perfection of the lime light and the carbon arc, forerunners of the follow spot, also promoted realism, since with them concentrated beams of light could be focused on the stage for the first time. Both were first exploited for such special effects as rays of sunlight, but soon they were used to light acting areas as well. Around 1880 electricity was introduced and rapidly replaced gas as the standard illuminant, since it offered most of the advantages of gas without the major drawback—the constant danger of fire.

The brighter lighting made possible by gas only emphasized the artificiality of painted scenery, and thereafter three-dimensional details began to be added. Real doorknobs were attached to doors and real molding to walls. By the 1870s such realistic business as boiling water, brewing and serving tea had also been introduced.

A lighting controlboard of the late nineteenth century. Note also the prompter at the front of the stage. (From Moynet's *La Machinerie Théâtrale,* 1893)

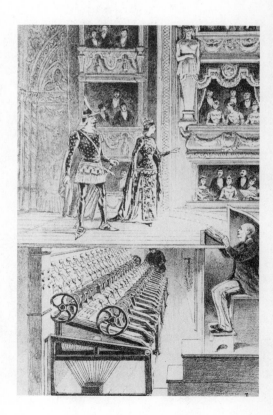

THE ACTOR

The increased concern for realism carried over into acting as well. Many of the developments can best be seen by surveying briefly the careers of a few outstanding English actors of the nineteenth century.

The English stage of the early nineteenth century was dominated by the Kemble family, whose most famous members were John Philip Kemble (1757–1823) and his sister, Mrs. Sarah Siddons (1755–1831). The Kembles aimed at grace, dignity, and beauty in movement, gesture, and voice. Thus, they tended to idealize characters. By 1820, however, the classical style of the Kembles was being challenged by the romantic ideal, epitomized in the acting of Edmund Kean (1787–1833), who often sacrificed dignity and beauty to the depiction of intense emotion. The acting style of William Charles Macready (1793–1873) was a compromise between those of Kemble and Kean, since he worked for beauty and dignity combined with emotional intensity; he planned each detail of

The acting style of William Charles Macready, seen here in the gravedigger scene from *Hamlet*, represented a compromise between that of Kemble and Kean. (From *The Illustrated London News*, 1846)

his characterizations carefully and insisted on painstaking rehearsals. He also did much to popularize historical accuracy in both scenery and costumes.

Mme. Lucia Elizabeth Vestris (1797–1856) did much to turn comic acting away from broad effects to a more natural style. She is also said to have introduced the box set in England and to have shortened evening programs so that audiences could be out of the theatre by eleven.

With his wife, Ellen Tree (1806–1880), Charles Kean (1811–1868), son of Edmund Kean, achieved fame as an actor and manager, principally through his Shakespearean productions at the Princess's Theatre in London between 1850 and 1859. Kean prided himself on the historical accuracy of every detail of his settings, costumes, and properties. It is his productions above all that mark the triumph of historical accuracy in English staging.

Squire Bancroft (1841–1926) and his wife Marie Effie Bancroft (1839–1921), are noted for the many reforms they popularized at the Prince of Wales's Theatre between 1865 and 1880. They concentrated upon plays of contemporary life, especially those by Tom Robertson (1829–1871), to which they applied rigorous standards of realism in every element of production. Their practices helped to popularize the box set and realistic costumes, properties, and acting. Furthermore, they gained acceptance of orchestra seating and helped to popularize matinée performances.

Henry Irving (1838–1905) was the first English actor to be knighted, a sign that the acting profession was at last socially acceptable. With Ellen Terry (1847–1928) he achieved great renown during the final decades of the century. Irving was also a theatrical manager, and it was he who first abandoned the groove method of shifting scenery in England. He placed scenic units onstage wherever needed and employed a vast number of stagehands to make the necessary changes. He was also the first English manager who consistently concealed scene changes from the audience. More than any other producer, Irving synthesized earlier trends toward complexity and realism in staging.

This survey of English actors (most of whom were also managers) by no means exhausts the list of great performers of the nineteenth century. Others include: François Joseph Talma (1763–1826), Rachel (1821–1858), and Sarah Bernhardt (1845–1923) in France; Mikhail Shchepkin (1788–1863) and Prov Sadovsky (1818–1872) in Russia; Tommaso Salvini (1829–1916) and Eleanora Duse (1859–1924) in Italy; Ludwig Devrient (1784–1832) and Fanny Janauschek (1830–1904) in Germany; Helena Modjeska (1844–1909) in Poland; and Edwin Forrest (1806–1872), Charlotte Cushman (1816–1876), and Edwin Booth (1833–1893) in America.

THE PLAYWRIGHT

The nineteenth century brought great improvements in the playwright's financial position, as the *royalty system* of paying authors (a payment either of a fixed sum or a percentage of the receipts for each performance) had been adopted almost universally by the last quarter of the century. The first copyright law designed to give the dramatist control over the production of his plays was passed in France in 1791. In England, a similar law was enacted in 1833. Such laws, however, could not insure the dramatist's rights beyond the boundaries of his own country. Thus, an American might produce a French play without paying its author any fee, or he might translate it and claim it as his own. More effective protection came after 1887, when under the provisions of an international copyright agreement all countries subscribing to it promised to protect the rights of foreign as well as native authors. With rare exceptions, playwrights throughout the world had been accorded legal protection by 1900. The dramatist might still have difficulty getting his plays produced, but when they appeared, either on the stage or in print, his rights were guaranteed by law.

Typically, the culmination of one trend signals the beginning of another. And so it was in the nineteenth century, for romantic drama, melodrama, and illusionistic spectacle laid the groundwork for realism, a movement usually said to mark the beginning of the modern theatre.

The Beginnings of the Modern Theatre

9

By the 1870s the public was becoming aware that significant changes were underway in theatre and drama. Manifested first in realism and naturalism, the new directions were sufficiently lasting that even today the modern theatre is usually dated from that decade. These movements also brought increased demands for unified production, and to meet them the director gradually assumed primary artistic control. By the 1920s, the new conceptions of the theatre's role and means had triumphed almost everywhere.

THE BACKGROUNDS OF REALISM

By the mid-nineteenth century the belief in man's idealistic nature had received many setbacks. After the defeat of Napoleon, around 1815 most European countries reinstated political conditions as oppressive as those of the eighteenth century. In addition, widespread misery accelerated after the industrial revolution caused workers to pour into urban centers where living conditions became increasingly inadequate. Under such political and economic conditions the romanticist's emphasis on the ideal seemed both too vague and too impractical, and many reformers came to demand solutions based on systematic inquiry into facts.

Among the major influences on the changed outlook was Auguste Comte (1798–1857), who believed that sociology is the highest form of science and that all knowledge should be used to improve society. He argued that the key to knowledge is precise observation, since all events must be understood in terms of natural cause and effect.

Comte's philosophy (called positivism) attracted a large following and was soon reinforced by Charles Darwin's *The Origin of Species* (1859), which set forth two main theses: (1) all forms of life have developed gradually from a common ancestry, and (2) the evolution of species is explained by the "survival of the fittest." Darwin's theories have several significant implications. First, they make heredity and environment the causes of everything that man is or does. Second, since behavior is determined by factors largely beyond his control, no individual can be truly held responsible for what he does. If blame is to be assigned, it must go to a society that has allowed undesirable hereditary and environmental factors to exist. Third, Darwin's theories strengthened the idea of progress, since if man has evolved from an atom of being to the complex creature he now is, improvement appears to be inevitable. Nevertheless, it was argued, progress can be hastened by the consistent application of scientific method. Fourth, man is reduced to the status of a natural object. Before the late nineteenth century man had been set apart from the rest of creation as superior to it. Now he lost his privileged status and became merely another object for study and control.

It was out of such beliefs that the movement called realism developed. Like most movements it sought truth, but defined it as that knowledge gained through the five senses (sight, hearing, taste, smell, and touch).

REALISM IN THE THEATRE

As a movement, realism developed first in France, where by 1860 its advocates had stated the following precepts: the playwright should strive to depict truthfully the real world; since he can know the real world only through direct observation, he should write about the society around him and should be as objective as possible.

Given such an outlook, it was only natural that realistic playwrights emphasized the details of contemporary life and introduced subjects not previously seen on the stage. Conservative critics charged that the theatre had become little better than a sewer. To such charges, the realists replied that the plays, as truthful depictions of life, were moral, since truth is the highest form of morality. Furthermore, realists argued, if audiences do not like the life shown onstage, they should change the society that has furnished the models rather than denounce the playwright who has truthfully depicted it.

The visual elements of staging were easily brought into accord with the new demands, since the major steps had already been taken by romantic drama and melodrama, both of which had promoted accuracy in dress and setting. But it was less easy to win acceptance for more realistic subjects. In this, two French playwrights, Alexandre Dumas *fils* (1824–1895) and Emile Augier (1820–1889) were most influential. Dumas *fils* came to the attention of the public in 1847 with a novel, *The Lady of the Camellias,* which he dramatized in 1849. One biographer has said of Dumas that he dared to depict not a legendary courtesan out of history, but a "kept woman" from contemporary life, and made his subject even more realistic by writing in prose. But while its language and subject show a trend toward realism, in over-all tone *Camille* (as the play is usually called) seems merely another romanticized treatment of the "prostitute with a heart of gold." Even so, at the time it was considered so shocking that it was kept off the stage until 1852. Dumas soon became dissatisfied with this work and in 1855 his *The Demi-Monde* denounced the same kind of characters idealized in *Camille.* Thereafter he championed a *theatre of social utility* and wrote plays about contemporary social problems such as divorce, unscrupulous business practices, and the plight of illegitimate children. But he also became increasingly the moralist. As a result, his plays are now usually called *pièces à thèse* (thesis plays).

Augier is noted principally for his political and social dramas about contemporary French conditions. Many of them deal in a less obvious way with problems like those treated by Dumas: the power of money, church interference in politics, and fallen women. Such plays as *Youth* (1858) and *Giboyer's Son* (1862) did much to popularize realism.

IBSEN

But it was with Ibsen that the new methods truly triumphed, so much so that *modern drama* is usually dated from the 1870s, when Ibsen adopted the realistic mode. Henrik Ibsen (1828–1906) began his career about 1850 with dramas based on Norwegian legends. This early work is clearly related to romantic drama, but in 1877 he turned to the problem play with *The Pillars of Society* and continued in that vein with *A Doll's House* (1879), *Ghosts* (1881), and *An Enemy of the People* (1882). With these plays, Ibsen established his reputation as a radical thinker and

Henrik Ibsen, often called "the father" of modern drama.

controversial dramatist. *Ghosts,* especially, raised a storm, for in it Mrs. Alving, against her better instincts, has remained with a depraved husband out of conformity to traditional morality only to have her son go mad, presumably from syphilis inherited from the father. To audiences and critics of the late nineteenth century, *Ghosts* epitomized the "sewer" into which the drama had sunk. Ibsen soon moved away from social problems, and beginning with *The Wild Duck* (1884) concentrated on personal relationships in such plays as *Rosmersholm* (1886), *Hedda Gabler* (1890), and *The Master Builder* (1892). Despite changes in subject matter and style, Ibsen's basic concern remained constant: the struggle for integrity, the conflict between duty to oneself and duty to others.

Much of Ibsen's work is realistic. He discards asides and soliloquies and is careful to motivate exposition. All scenes are causally related and lead logically to the outcome. Dialogue, settings, costumes, and business are selected to reveal character and milieu and are clearly described in stage directions. Each role is conceived as a personality whose behavior can be attributed to heredity or environment.

Ibsen's late plays were to influence nonrealistic drama as extensively as his early prose plays did realistic works. In them, symbols enlarge the implications of the action and many of the plays border on fantasy. The sense of mysterious forces at work in human affairs, so evident in many of Ibsen's late plays, greatly influenced the symbolists at the end of the century.

Almost all later serious playwrights were to be affected by Ibsen's conviction that drama should be a source of insight and a conveyor of ideas rather than mere entertainment. He gave dramatists a new vision of their role.

THE WILD DUCK

The many strands of Ibsen's work are probably brought together most effectively in *The Wild Duck.* In it Gregers Werle returns home after an absence of fifteen years, decides that the lives of all his acquaintances are based on lies, and determines to make them face the truth. His efforts lead to catastrophe.

The principal characters are Old Werle (Gregers' father), Hjalmar Ekdal (Greger's childhood friend), and Old Ekdal, Gina, and Hedwig (Hjalmar's father, wife, and daughter). Old Werle is prosperous, while the Ekdals live in comparative poverty, although years ago Werle and Ekdal were business partners. Ekdal was sent to prison for illegal dealings, and Gregers suspects that his father let Ekdal accept blame that was partially his. Gregers also believes that Old Werle arranged Hjalmar's marriage to Gina, a former maid in the Werle household,

Act III of *The Wild Duck*. Hedwig and Gina serve a meal to Hjalmar , Relling, Molvig, and Gregers. (Courtesy Norwegian Embassy Information Service)

because Gina was pregnant by Werle. Thus, he thinks that Hedwig is not Hjalmar's child.

Gregers takes a room at the Ekdals, in spite of Gina's protest, and through insinuation and leading questions gradually brings his "truth" into the open. After Hjalmar rejects Hedwig, she decides, with a child's simplicity of reasoning, that only some great sacrifice can prove her love for Hjalmar; consequently, she kills herself.

Essentially, *The Wild Duck* is a play about the necessity of illusions. Dr. Relling, another tenant in the Ekdal house, says that most persons need "a saving lie" to help them retain a degree of self-respect. All the characters illustrate this theme, but the opposing positions are most obviously represented by Relling (who believes in the necessity of illusion) and Gregers Werle (who believes in facing the truth).

Ibsen has strengthened his theme through the symbol of the wild duck. First, the duck, happy and carefree, lives in a wild state. Then it is wounded by a hunter, survives, is placed in an artificial environment, and, though crippled, appears to be as happy as in its wild state. Ibsen seems to suggest that the wild duck's experiences parallel those of man, who, wounded by circumstances, constructs a set of delusions by means of which he can regain his sense of purpose.

Characters and Acting. The Ekdal family is reflected in the wild duck, since all in a sense are victims of Old Werle (the hunter). Old

187

Ekdal has lived in an illusory state so long that it has become part of his nature. Since his release from prison he has constructed a make-believe life around the attic, which he treats as a "forest," complete with "wild life" (the duck and the rabbits).

Ibsen has drawn a number of interesting parallels and contrasts between Old Werle and Hedwig. It is possible that Hedwig is the daughter of Old Werle (this is never clarified), both have weak eyesight, both try to make amends to others. But Old Werle has treated life as though it were the sport of hunting, and when he wounds he makes amends through such material compensations as money and arranged marriages. On the other hand, Hedwig responds to life with her whole being and rather than wound others kills herself. Old Werle faces up to his short-comings at the end of the play, but he still believes that material gifts can atone for the wounds he has inflicted on others.

Ibsen's principal effort has gone into the roles of Hjalmar and Gregers. Hjalmar's speeches proclaim his sensitivity, ambition, and idealism, but his actions show that he is insensitive, lazy, and self-centered. Gina runs the photographic studio; she and Hedwig sacrifice every comfort for him. To Hjalmar, Old Ekdal's disgrace is an excuse for easy sentiment, just as Hedwig's death will be in the future. But Hjalmar is perfectly happy in his illusions, for he can indulge himself and, at the same time, find excuses for being ineffectual. That Gregers accepts Hjalmar as a hero demonstrates his own lack of experience. He has hidden away from the world for fifteen years and has avoided becoming involved in life. Although he never attempts to change his own life, he feels free to meddle in the affairs of others.

Relling is used as a foil for Gregers. A doctor, he administers to the psychic wounds of the characters by providing for them "saving lies," while Gregers destroys the illusions that have made life tolerable.

But in spite of the obvious use of characters to illustrate ideas, Ibsen employs realistic techniques in creating roles. Every important characteristic is shown through action. Furthermore, each character's traits are brought out through well-motivated and lifelike speech or action. Ibsen has been careful to fill in the sociological backgrounds of his characters, and each attitude and trait is grounded in particular social circumstances. He has also made his characters complex personalities by showing both good and bad aspects of each.

Plot and Structure. As in most of his plays, Ibsen uses a late point of attack. In *The Wild Duck* Gregers Werle has returned home after a fifteen-year absence, during which he has lived in virtual isolation. Thus he can believably inquire about the past and realistically motivate the complex exposition. Many of Ibsen's plays are written in four acts, but *The Wild Duck* has five, in part because two are required to establish the situation. The need for two acts of preparation is also illustrated by the use of two settings to contrast Old Werle's and the Ekdals' living conditions. By the end of the second act, both situation and characters have been clarified, the symbolism of the wild duck has been introduced, and Gregers has indicated his intention of rectifying the errors of the past. The final three acts grow logically out of the first two.

There are no extraneous scenes and almost nothing could be removed without destroying clarity. At the same time, there is no feeling of haste, for each event seems to develop as it might in real life. Nevertheless, each of the acts is built through a series of complications leading to a high point of suspense near the end of the act, while the play as a whole builds to the climactic scene of Hedwig's death. Ibsen thus achieves great dramatic power while giving the effect of naturalness.

Visual Effects. Ibsen's realistic technique can also be seen in the visual elements of *The Wild Duck.* The influence of environment upon the characters is made clear in part through a detailed representation of the surroundings. The characters seem to live in the settings, for they do everything there they would in a real room. In the studio they eat, retouch photographs, entertain friends, and carry on their daily existence in countless ways. Unlike a neoclassical play in which settings are generalized, *The Wild Duck* demands a stage environment determined by the specific action and characters.

The Wild Duck, with its subject matter drawn from contemporary life, closely observed detail, and avoidance of contrivance, illustrates well the realistic mode as it was practiced in the late nineteenth century.

ENGLAND

The spirit of realism soon spread throughout the world. In England the works of such playwrights as Arthur Wing Pinero (1855–1934), Henry Arthur Jones (1851–1929), and George Bernard Shaw (1856–1950) show in varying degrees the influence of the new trend. Pinero's best-remembered play, *The Second Mrs. Tanqueray* (1893), which concerns a "woman with a past," helped to break down the strictures against frank subject matter, since its ending, in which the woman is punished, upheld traditional morality. Thus, it was simultaneously daring and reassuring. Jones, a didactic and somewhat melodramatic playwright, along with Pinero helped to pave the way for more realistic drama with *Michael and His Lost Angel* (1896) and *Mrs. Dane's Defence* (1900).

George Bernard Shaw was probably the most vociferous and important of Ibsen's admirers. But Shaw's approach differs markedly from Ibsen's, for while his plays are serious in their intent to influence human behavior, they use comic devices to make serious points. In his treatment of problems, Shaw begins with what he thinks is the accepted atti-

At a rehearsal of *Androcles and the Lion* in 1913, George Bernard Shaw demonstrates a point about a fight to Harley Granville Barker and Lillah MacCarthy. (Crown Copyright. Theatre Museum, London.)

tude and then demolishes it before proposing his own solution. Shaw also delighted in using paradoxes to make both characters and audiences reassess their values. Thus *Arms and the Man* (1894) punctures romantic notions about war and love, and *Major Barbara* (1905) depicts a munitions maker as more humanitarian than the Salvation Army, for the former provides his workers with the means whereby to improve their lot whereas the Salvation Army only prolongs the status quo. Ultimately, Shaw wished through his plays to demonstrate the possibility of gradually solving social problems through education, better living conditions, and common sense. But Shaw was no mere propagandist; his plays are theatrically effective and entertaining. Among his many plays, some of the finest are *Candida* (1895), *Caesar and Cleopatra* (1899), *Man and Superman* (1903), *Heartbreak House* (1919), and *Saint Joan* (1923). Perhaps his most popular play is *Pygmalion* (1913), the story of an illiterate flower girl who is transformed by her mentor so thoroughly that she is mistaken for a duchess. (This play is discussed at greater length in Chapter 10 when the musical version, *My Fair Lady,* is considered.)

RUSSIA

Another writer of the late nineteenth century, Anton Chekhov (1860–1904), was to be almost as influential as Ibsen. He began by writing short stories and humorous sketches and moved on to vaudeville skits and one-act farces. His long plays had little success until the Moscow Art Theatre presented *The Sea Gull* in 1898. This company also produced Chekhov's *Uncle Vanya, The Three Sisters,* and *The Cherry Orchard.*

Many qualities relate Chekhov's drama to the realistic-naturalistic school. The subject matter and themes, drawn from contemporary Russian life, show how daily routine gradually shrinks the spirit and drains the will. The characters long for happiness and wish to live useful lives, but they are constantly thwarted by circumstances and their own personalities. Chekhov's realism is further seen in his dramatic form, for the plays have an air of aimlessness which matches that of the characters' lives. All violent deeds and emotional climaxes occur offstage. The action is thus kept in the background while the foreground is occupied by a number of seemingly commonplace details. But, since the characters do not fully understand their own feelings and since they seek to conceal as much as to reveal their responses, it is this seeming trivia that reveals

Act 1 of the first production of *The Cherry Orchard,* 1904. (From Moscow Art Theatre, 1898–1917, 1955)

the dramatic action. Ultimately what happens to each character is a direct result of what he is. Thus, character and fate are one. Chekhov treats all of his characters with tolerance and compassion, but he also makes them both sympathetic and ridiculous. Therefore, the pathetic and comic are mingled, often simultaneously.

Chekhov is not entirely a realistic writer, for like Ibsen he also makes considerable use of symbolism, perhaps most obviously in *The Cherry Orchard,* in which the orchard is a symbol of the Old Russia and the aristocracy. Though it no longer yields fruit, the orchard is clung to by its owners when its sale would save the rest of the estate they so dearly love. In the end, the orchard is bought by a newly rich peasant and is subdivided for a housing development, an action that illustrates the changing social order in which the useless though decorative aristocracy is being displaced by the callous but practical middle class.

NATURALISM

Even as realism was developing, another movement—naturalism—was also emerging. Realism and naturalism are closely related because both demand a truthful depiction of life and are based on the belief that ultimate reality is discoverable only through the five senses. The naturalists, however, insisted that art must become scientific in its methods and depict behavior as determined by heredity and environment.

The major spokesman for the naturalists was Émile Zola (1840–1902), who argued that art should emulate science both in seeking subjects and in treating them. According to Zola, subjects may be of two kinds: those based on scientific findings and those that faithfully record events observed in real life. Zola also argued that the writer should remain detached and never allow his own prejudices to intrude. In practice, naturalism tended to emphasize the more degraded aspects of lower-class life, and consequently much naturalistic drama was preoccupied with human maladies. Zola was fond of comparing naturalistic art with medicine and believed that the dramatist should have the same interest in examining and defining social illnesses as the doctor has in physical ailments.

Zola and his followers were especially opposed to traditional dramatic structure because to them complication, suspense, crisis, and resolution subordinated truth to theatrical effect. One member of the movement suggested that a play should be a *slice of life*—that a dramatist should merely transfer to the stage as faithfully as possible a segment of reality.

Because of its belief in environment as a determinant of character and action, naturalism placed greater emphasis on stage setting than had any previous movement. It wished to see every detail reproduced accurately onstage so as to establish the milieu that determined the characters and their actions. This care extended to costumes, furniture, properties, stage business, and acting.

Though naturalism attracted considerable attention in the late nineteenth century, it produced few dramatists of note. Even Zola was much more successful as theorist and novelist than as playwright. As a dramatist, he is best known for *Thérèse Raquin* (1873), an adaptation of one of his novels, which shows the deterioration and suicide of a couple who have murdered the woman's former husband. A more successful French dramatist in the naturalistic vein was Henri Becque (1837–1899), especially with *The Vultures* (1882), which shows the fleecing of a group of women by their supposed friends after the death of the head of the family.

As a conscious movement, naturalism, like realism, began in France and spread to other countries. Unlike realism, however, naturalism attracted few outstanding dramatists and in most cases even they eventually adopted less extreme approaches. Of the writers in other countries who wrote naturalistic plays, perhaps the best are Gerhart Hauptmann (1862–1946) in Germany and Maxim Gorky (1868–1936) in Russia. Hauptmann, the first important modern German dramatist, is best known for *The Weavers* (1892), which shows an uprising among starving weavers; it is remarkable in part because it has a group protagonist. Gorky is especially remembered for *The Lower Depths* (1902), set in a flophouse peopled with human wrecks.

As a conscious movement naturalism had for the most part run its course by 1900. Nevertheless, it had focused attention on the need for close observation of life, pointed out relationships between environment and behavior, and encouraged greater attention to the details of stage production. In its insistence that reality be reproduced onstage, however, naturalism was unsuccessful and it was gradually absorbed into the realistic movement.

THE EMERGENCE OF THE DIRECTOR

As the demand for greater realism increased, so did the need for more careful rehearsals and better coordination of all elements. As a result, the director gradually assumed full authority over production.

The modern director is usually traced from Georg II, Duke of Saxe-Meiningen (1826–1914), the ruler of a small German state, whose troupe came to public attention through a series of tours between 1874 and 1890. The superior quality of his presentations demonstrated the importance of the director to effective theatrical production. Saxe-Meiningen's troupe performed the same plays (such as those by Shakespeare) seen in the repertory of almost every company of the day. Nevertheless, this troupe, composed almost solely of unknown actors, gave performances that eclipsed those of major theatres. It became clear that the superior qualities of the Meiningen troupe were attributable primarily to its staging methods.

The most important elements of the Duke's approach were his complete control over every aspect of production and his long and careful rehearsals. Rather than using stars, he subordinated all performers to the over-all effect. He drilled his troupe in lengthy rehearsals, paid as much attention to crowds as he did to the principal roles, and worked out the total stage picture as it developed moment by moment.

By the 1880s other groups, insofar as they were able, began applying Saxe-Meiningen's methods. After that time the director steadily gained artistic control over theatrical production. He has retained that power to the present day.

THE INDEPENDENT THEATRE MOVEMENT

By the late 1880s both a realistic-naturalistic drama and realistic staging under the supervision of a demanding director had emerged. The new drama was rarely being performed, however, and the new staging methods were being applied primarily to traditional plays. It remained, therefore, to bring the two together. This was difficult to do because in most countries strict censorship forbade the production of such plays as *Ghosts* on the grounds of moral offensiveness. Eventually the challenge was met by "independent theatres," which began to be established in the late 1880s. Since these organizations were open only to subscribing members, they were not subject to censorship and could perform plays forbidden to other theatres. Therefore, independent theatres were able to accomplish what more established theatres had not, for these new groups embraced the new staging techniques and gave the new drama its chance to be heard.

The first of the independent theatres was the Théâtre Libre, founded in Paris in 1887 by André Antoine (1858–1943). An enthusiastic follower of Zola and Saxe-Meiningen, Antoine sought fidelity to real life. He designed interior settings as though they were real rooms, used real properties (even in one instance carcasses of beef), and tried to reproduce every detail of an environment. He held painstaking rehearsals to achieve the effects he sought.

Antoine's was only the first of numerous independent theatres. In 1889 the Freie Bühne was founded in Berlin by a group headed by Otto Brahm (1856–1912). It made no significant innovations in staging but concentrated on plays denied a public hearing by the censor. By 1894, when Brahm assumed the direction of a commercial theatre, the new drama was being assimilated into the popular theatre throughout Germany. In London the Independent Theatre, founded by J. T. Grein (1862–1935), opened in 1891 with Ibsen's *Ghosts*. It paved the way for the new drama in England and launched Shaw as a dramatist.

Not only did independent theatres meet an important need at the time, they also provided a permanent lesson, for since the late nineteenth century whenever the established theatre has become insufficiently responsive to new demands, a solution has been sought in "art" theatres, "little" theatres, Off Broadway, and so on.

In addition to the independent theatres, another group — the Moscow Art Theatre — was to play a significant role in revitalizing the theatre at the turn of the century. The Moscow Art Theatre was founded by Constantin Stanislavsky (1865–1938) and Vladimir Nemerovich-Danchenko (1859–1943) in 1898, partially under the inspiration of the Meiningen company. Its first major success was won with the plays of Chekhov.

As time went by, Stanislavsky became more and more concerned with the problems of the actor, and eventually evolved one of the most influential approaches ever proposed. This system has been disseminated

Konstantin Stanislavsky as Satin in *The Lower Depths* at the Moscow Art Theatre, 1902.

throughout the world by Stanislavsky's books, *My Life in Art* (1924), *An Actor Prepares* (1936), *Building a Character* (1949), and *Creating a Role* (1961).

Although there has been much disagreement over the essence of Stanislavsky's system, basically it consists of the following principles: (1) The actor's body and voice must be thoroughly trained and flexible so they can respond instantly to all demands. (2) The actor must be a skillful observer of reality so he can build his role truthfully through careful selection of likelike action, business, and speech. (3) The actor needs to be thoroughly trained in stage technique so that he can project his characterization without any sense of artificiality. (4) The actor must be able to imagine himself in the situation of the character he is playing. In doing so he may call on *emotion memory* (the ability to recall emotional responses comparable to those required in the dramatic situation). (5) If the actor is not merely to play himself on the stage, however, he must have a thorough knowledge of the script. The actor needs to define clearly his character's basic motivation in each scene, in the play as a whole, and in relation to other characters. (6) All of his work onstage should be welded together through concentration upon the unfolding events moment by moment so as to convince the audience that he is involved in a situation that is occurring for the first time.

Stanislavsky's entire system urges the need for devoted and constant effort on the part of the actor. He was never fully satisfied with the results and he often cautioned others against trying to take over his system without allowing for differences in artistic needs and cultural backgrounds.

ALTERATIONS IN REALISM

By 1900 realism had become the dominant mode in dramatic writing and in theatrical production almost everywhere. It was to remain dominant until around 1950, even though it underwent alterations.

Many of the alterations can be traced to the influence of Sigmund Freud (1856–1939), whose psychoanalytic theories provided a scientific explanation for much human behavior which previously have been attributed to instinct or supernatural forces and which had thus been placed outside the scope of realism. Freud's conception of the mind (as a faculty that telescopes experience, sublimates and suppresses desires, and often works irrationally) made it possible for dramatists to depart considerably from the early techniques of realism without departing from a scientific outlook. These departures, in turn, moved realism in the direction of the many nonrealistic styles that appeared after 1890 and made it ever easier to assimilate techniques that had originated in revolts against realism.

196

SYMBOLISM

Although realism came to dominate the theatre, it was not universally accepted. The first important revolt against it is usually called symbolism (or—alternatively—neoromanticism, idealism, or aestheticism). As a movement, it appeared in France in the 1880s and had largely expired by 1900. Symbolism is antirealistic in denying that ultimate truth is to be found in evidence supplied by the five senses or by rational thought. Instead, it holds that truth is grasped intuitively.

Since it cannot be logically understood, ultimate truth cannot be expressed directly. It can only be suggested through symbols that evoke feelings and states of mind, corresponding imprecisely to the dramatist's intuitions. As Maeterlinck put it:

> Great drama . . . is made up of three principal elements: first, verbal beauty; then the contemplation and passionate portrayal of what actually exists about us and within us . . . and, finally enveloping the whole work and creating the atmosphere proper to it, the idea which the poet forms of the unknown in which float about the being and things which he evokes, the mystery which dominates them. . . . I have no doubt that this last is the most important element.

Unlike the realists, the symbolists chose their subject matter from the past or the realm of fancy and avoided any attempt to deal with social problems or environment. They aimed to suggest a universal truth independent of time and place that cannot be logically defined or rationally expressed. Symbolist drama, consequently, tends to be vague, mysterious, and puzzling.

By far the most famous symbolist playwright was Maurice Maeterlinck (1862–1949), whose most important works were written in the 1890s. Since his *Pelléas and Mélisande* (1892) is often said to be the best symbolist drama of its time, it will be examined here.

PELLÉAS AND MÉLISANDE

On the surface, *Pelléas and Mélisande* is the story of a young wife who falls in love with her husband's younger brother. The husband kills his brother and the wife dies of grief. This simple story of awakening love and its consequences holds the play together, but mood and feelings are most important. A sense of fate and mystery dominates each scene. The characters are puppetlike, for they do not understand their own actions or motivations. Their backgrounds are never filled in, the precise time and place of the action is left unspecified, and events are not causally related. The play depicts a fairy-tale world in which inexplicable forces control human destinies.

Maeterlinck suggests that life is impenetrably mysterious, but rather than stating his beliefs directly, he implies them through recurring motifs and symbols—water, light and darkness, height and depth. It is impossible to assign a definite meaning to each of these motifs. Rather, the connotations suggested by the context must be examined. Throughout the play, love, happiness, and light struggle with fate, misery, and darkness.

Behind all the happenings, however, there is a sense of mystery and fate. Love comes to Pelléas and Mélisande against their wills, for they are led by forces greater than themselves. At the end of the play both the enigma of the human soul and the meaning of life remain as mysterious as when the play began. Thus, while he rebelled against the outlook of the naturalists, Maeterlinck placed his characters at the mercy of forces just as destructive as heredity and environment in a world that is both unknowable and uncontrollable.

Although *Pelléas and Mélisande* tells a love story, it is unified by themes and ideas. Many scenes are only loosely connected with the main story line. For example, the opening scene—in which the women try to wash the stains from the castle steps—sets a mood of mystery and hopelessness but has nothing to do with the action.

Premonition is used to build and maintain suspense. There is a continual hint of some mystery behind the events which will be revealed, and the characters seem to be led on toward some important discovery that is never forthcoming.

The characters are almost as vague as the ideas. They yearn, love, and die without knowing why. All of the main characters are of the ruling class, but this has little effect upon their actions. Their ages and physical appearance are also of little importance, and even their psychological attributes are vague. None of the characters fully understands his own motivations, and each is driven by forces stronger than himself.

Maeterlinck is less interested in portraying lifelike characters than in suggesting states of feeling that come upon characters mysteriously and lead to mysterious consequences. It is not the texture of daily life but the spiritual realm beyond surface existence that the play seeks to evoke.

In its simplicity and repetitiveness, the language of *Pelléas and Mélisande* suggests a beginning reader. But this repetitiveness helps to emphasize the recurring motifs, and the lack of complexity suggests the need to look beneath the surface.

Antirealism was emphasized in the original production through a number of devices. The stage lighting, very low in intensity, came from directly overhead. A gauze curtain, hung at the front of the stage, made it appear that the entire action was occurring in a mist. The scenery was painted in grayed tones to increase the effect of distance and mistiness. The actors used a singsong delivery and unnatural gestures. The entire production was designed to remove the action from the everyday world; it was as unlike the productions of realists as possible.

Pelléas and Mélisande thus dealt with such universal themes as love, life, and death, and embodied them in symbols and motifs. Perhaps because of its lack of concreteness, symbolism appealed only to a limited audience and produced few plays of lasting interest.

ANTIREALIST THEATRE

The revolt against realism also brought new attitudes toward the theatre. The symbolists drew much inspiration from the German operatic composer Richard Wagner (1813–1883), who sought to fuse all the arts into a masterwork: music drama. Opposed to realism, Wagner argued that music is necessary to the finest drama, which must be "distanced" from actual life. Furthermore, according to Wagner, music offers a means whereby the dramatist-composer may control the performance of the actor-singer, since music can dictate the pitch, duration, and tempo of the words. Wagner also believed that the master artist should retain control

Stage and auditorium of the Bayreuth Festival Theatre. Note the steeply raked auditorium, the double proscenium, and the absence of a center aisle and side boxes. (From Barkhin's *Architectura Teatra*, Moscow, 1947)

over all the other theatrical elements. Thus he was one of the first advocates of unified production.

Wagner argued that the greatest truths cannot be approached through realism, that the theatre should lift the audience out of its humdrum existence through an idealized drama "dipped in the magic fountain of music." To evoke the proper esthetic distance, Wagner used a double proscenium, a curtain of steam, and a darkened auditorium to create a "mystic chasm" between spectators and performers. Because he sought to depict an idealized world, it is not surprising that Wagner should have inspired the symbolists.

The symbolists, encountering many of the same difficulties in getting their plays performed as the realists and naturalists, established independent theatres of their own to gain a heating. The most important of these was the Théâtre de l'Œuvre, founded in Paris in 1892 under the direction of Aurélien-Marie Lugné-Poë (1869–1940). The opening production was *Pelléas and Mélisande.* Until 1897 Lugné-Poë staged all plays in a highly stylized manner that did not attempt to create the illusion of reality, but unity through mood and style.

The symbolists believed that scenery should be confined to draperies or vague forms that evoke a sense of infinite space and time. Historical detail was avoided because it tied plays to specific periods and places rather than bringing out their timeless qualities. Decor was therefore reduced to elements giving a generalized impression appropriate to the atmosphere of a play. Similarly, costumes were usually simple, draped garments of no particular period or place; colors were dictated by the play's mood. For the most part, symbolist productions were too determinedly nonrealistic to attract a wide following, but they laid the foundations for several subsequent developments.

APPIA AND CRAIG

Although not of the symbolist school, two major theorists, Adolphe Appia (1862–1928) and Gordon Craig (1872–1966) were clearly in the tradition of Wagner and the symbolists.

Appia's desire to embody Wagner's ideas led him to articulate for the first time many of the now-accepted ideals of theatrical production. He began with the notion that artistic unity is fundamental, but declared it difficult to achieve because of the diverse visual elements used in the theatre: the moving actor, the horizontal floor, and the perpendicular scenery. Rejecting flat, painted scenery, Appia insisted that three-dimensional structures are the only proper environment for the three-dimensional actor. To reveal the shape and three-dimensionality of the scenery and the actor, light, from various angles and directions, is required. Furthermore, light must change as action and mood change. Constantly changing light fuses the various elements into a unified whole, for it reveals and reflects shifting emotions and ideas. In this way, light becomes the visual equivalent of music, since it welds the elements together visually just as music does aurally.

Appia suggested that, since a unified and artistic performance is the goal, the entire production must be conceived by one person—the director. Appia thus reinforced the trend toward elevating the director to a position of dominance.

Craig was much more militant in his statements and did a great deal more to popularize his theories. He denied that the theatre is a collection of subsidiary arts; rather, he argued, the master theatre artist creates his own art work out of action, words, line, color, and rhythm, just as artists in other fields use the elements appropriate to their art. Because there can only be one master artist in the theatre, Craig once suggested that the actor should be replaced by the marionette, since the marionette cannot inject its own personality into the work and thwart the director's conception.

Opposed to realism, which he called "the theatre of sermons and epigrams," Craig wanted to create works that would transform the theatre into "a place for visions." Like Appia, Craig stood for extreme simplicity in scenery, costume, and lighting, and depended upon line, mass, and color for his effects rather than upon historical accuracy or detailed ornamentation. Also like Appia, he helped to promote the director as the supreme theatre artist. As with Appia, few of Craig's scene designs were ever carried to completion, but his writings inspired many. Together, Appia and Craig exerted untold influence on the modern stage, especially after about 1915.

ECLECTICISM IN THEATRICAL PRODUCTION

By 1900 it had begun to be suggested that each type of play, and even each individual play, has its own style that demands a distinctive stage treatment. This was a revolutionary idea in many ways, for in each period prior to this time a single standard was applied to all productions. For example, in 1850 a Greek drama, a play by Shakespeare, and a melodrama would all have been given the same kind of settings and would have been acted in much the same style. Around 1900 some directors began to argue that the style of a production should be determined by the style of the script and by the theatrical conventions and actor–audience spatial relationships in use at the time the play was written. This eclectic approach, which eventually triumphed, was to be one of the distinguishing marks of twentieth-century directing.

As sometimes practiced, however, eclecticism was merely another version of historical realism, for some directors slavishly copied earlier theatrical conventions (for example, they might stage a play by Shakespeare as nearly as possible as it would have been done in the Elizabethan period). This kind of approach was taken in England by William Poel (1852–1934) between 1894 and 1905 in staging a number of Elizabethan plays. Poel is now remembered almost entirely for his efforts to reconstruct the Elizabethan public stage. Although his productions did not generate widespread enthusiasm, they demonstrated the advantages of unbroken playing and of concentrating attention on the actors.

True eclecticism owes most to the German director Max Reinhardt (1873–1943), who—beginning around 1900—produced plays from all periods and types in a great variety of styles. He believed that some plays require large theatres, whereas others fare best in small houses. (He was one of the first directors to have a small experimental theatre attached to a larger one.) For a medieval pageant drama, he transformed a theatre into a cathedral; to house Greek drama, he remodeled a circus building; and for eighteenth-century plays, he acquired a hall of state in an eighteenth-century palace. He also experimented with all kinds of stage machinery, theatrical devices, and visual motifs in an attempt to create the right atmosphere for each work. With this eclecticism, Reinhardt coupled the belief that the director is the supreme artist of the theatre. He always made a prompt book, in which every detail of movement, lighting, scenery, costume, and sound was recorded with exactness. He coached his actors carefully and controlled each element of his productions.

Reinhardt popularized many ideas that were to be widely accepted and practiced in the twentieth century: the need for a different approach to each play; awareness of the interdependence of theatre architecture and dramatic styles; and the director as the supreme artist of the theatre and as the completer of the playwright's work. Between 1900 and 1933 Reinhardt was one of the world's most prolific and celebrated directors.

But if Reinhardt was the primary popularizer of eclecticism, he was aided by many others. In England, Harley Granville Barker (1887–1946), especially through his work at the Royal Court Theatre between 1904 and 1907, did much to establish the new ideal with plays by authors ranging from Euripides to Shaw. (More than any other producer, Barker won acceptance for Shaw's plays in England.) In France, Jacques Rouché (1862–1957) promoted the eclectic ideal at his Théâtre des Arts between 1910 and 1913. By 1915 eclecticism had been disseminated throughout Europe, although it had not prevailed everywhere on the Continent.

EXPRESSIONISM

After symbolism declined, no strong antirealist movement challenged realism's dominance until expressionism emerged around 1910 in Germany. The expressionists believed that fundamental truth is to be found within man — his spirit, soul, desires, and visions — and that external reality should be reshaped until it is brought into harmony with these inner attributes so that man's spirit may realize its aspirations. Many writers sought merely to express their perceptions of this inner spirit, but others wished to transform society. Consequently some historians have divided the expressionists into two groups, the mystics and the activists. The latter were especially opposed to materialism and industrialism, which they saw as the chief blocks to the expressionist goals and as the major warpers of the soul. Almost all expressionists wrote about the "regeneration of man" and the "creation of the new man." Ultimately, most hoped to build a world free from war, hypocrisy, and hate, where men could express themselves freely and in which humanitarianism would replace materialism.

Expressionist drama tended toward one of two types. Many plays concentrated on the negative aspects of the present in an attempt to show how false ideals have distorted man's spirit until he is little better than a machine. Other plays look forward to the transformation of society and to achieving harmony between man's environment and his spirit. Because the plays are message-centered, they are episodic; many take the form of a search or pilgrimage. Since truth is said to lie in internal vision, the external apearance of things is often distorted. Shape may be altered, color may be abnormal, movement may be mechanical, speech may be reduced to short phrases or single words. Ultimately all the devices of the theatre are employed to project a vision quite unlike that of the realists or the symbolists.

EXPRESSIONIST DRAMATISTS

Among the major influences on expressionist drama are the works of the Swedish playwright August Strindberg (1849–1912). Up to about 1895 his plays, such as *The Father* (1887) and *Miss Julie* (1888), were essentially realistic. But after personal crises drove Strindberg to the edge of insanity his outlook on life and art underwent profound changes. In the late 1890s he began to write a series of plays usually considered to be forerunners of expressionism. These include *The Dream Play* (1902), in his preface to which Strindberg states:

> The author has tried to imitate the disconnected but seemingly logical form of the dream. Anything may happen; everything is possible and probable.

Ingmar Bergman's production of *The Dream Play*, by Swedish playwright August Strindberg, starring Max von Sydow. Royal Dramatic Theatre, Stockholm, 1970. (Courtesy Swedish Information Service)

> Time and space do not exist. On an insignificant background of reality, imagination designs and embroiders novel patterns: a medley of memories, experiences, free fancies, absurdities and improvisations.

In other words, in *The Dream Play* Strindberg tries to destroy the limitations of time, place, and logical sequence by adopting the viewpoint of the dreamer. One event flows into another without logical explanation, characters dissolve or are transformed into other characters, and widely separated places and times blend to tell a story of tortured and alienated mankind. It was to Strindberg that the expressionists turned for many of their dramatic techniques.

Germany produced many expressionist playwrights, but the most widely known are Ernst Toller (1893–1939) and Georg Kaiser (1878–1945). Toller's first play, *Transfiguration* (1918), written while he was in prison for pacifism, is an antiwar drama. Of his later works the most important is *Man and the Masses* (1921), which shows how the machine and factories have come to dominate men's lives. While the play is pessimistic in its outcome, it looks forward hopefully to the day when the workers will be ready for a better life.

Kaiser's best-known work is *From Morn till Midnight*. Written in 1912, it was published in 1916 and first produced (privately) in 1917.

FROM MORN TILL MIDNIGHT

From Morn till Midnight shows the "stations of martyrdom" in the life of modern man. The central character, the Cashier, may be viewed as an Everyman of the modern world, and the time of the action, from morning to midnight, suggests the span of human life. The seven scenes are held together by the central character's search for fulfillment.

The first two scenes are primarily preparatory and expository. Scene 1 establishes the dehumanizing effects of materialism, symbolized by the bank, since the accumulation of wealth is a primary goal of materialism. The effect of materialistic values on the common man is seen in the Cashier, who has been reduced to a soulless machine. Then the Lady from Italy jars the Cashier out of his machinelike state and, in his desire to possess her, he responds as his society has conditioned him to act — he steals money. Scene 2 shows that the Lady is respectable and that the Cashier has irrevocably lost his old place in society.

Scene 3 marks the major transition from the old to the new life. The Cashier now realizes that his past has been empty, and he sets out to find what has been missing. But he still believes that money is the key to success. Scene 3 also prepares for those to follow, for it is out of his decision to search for the meaning of life that the others grow. The scheme of the play is seen further in the appearance of Death, whose invitation to go with him the Cashier declines. In the scenes that follow he makes several visits, and then at midnight reencounters Death.

Although Scene 4 shows the first of his stops, it is still related to the past since it involves the Cashier's home and family. But the home has been as mechanized as the bank, for here even sentiment has been thoroughly standardized.

Scene 5 shows the Cashier's attempt to find meaning in the political and social structure of society, symbolized in the race track. Here the people assemble to watch the contestants — who, no matter how tired

Scene 3 of *From Morn till Midnight* as presented by the Theatre Guild in 1922. Note the tree which has turned into a skeleton. Directed by Frank Reicher; settings by Lee Simonson. (Photo by Francis Bruguiere, The New York Public Library at Lincoln Center)

they may be, race whenever a monetary prize is offered. The race is used to symbolize the drive for monetary gain. The stadium is also segregated in terms of social classes, and the Cashier sets out to break down all the barriers of class and feeling by offering the highest prizes ever heard of. By inducing the fullest expression of emotion, he thinks that he can break down regimentation. But just as the Cashier is about to succeed, the ruler arrives and the spectators resume their conditioned responses.

Scene 6 explores the search for happiness through sensual pleasures. The most exotic foods, plus the suggestion of sexual orgy, are used to represent this goal. But when the Cashier lifts the mask of one of the women she is so ugly that he is repulsed, and another proves to have a wooden leg. The anticipated joys of the flesh turn into disgust and the Cashier rushes out.

Scene 7 brings the Cashier to the end of his journey, as he searches for fulfillment in religion. He has been brought to a Salvation Army hall by the same Salvation Lass who has appeared fleetingly in Scenes 5 and 6. In the meeting that follows, the Cashier realizes that the call of the soul is the true road to happiness. But when he scatters his stolen money about him, the supposedly repentant sinners become beasts striving to tear the money from each other. Since the Salvation Lass does not enter the fight, the Cashier thinks he has found his true mate. But she is merely more cunning than the others, for she turns him over to the police for the reward. In the darkness of the hall a tangle of wires outlines the skeleton of Death, whom the Cashier has eluded in Scene 3. He dies with his arms outstretched on the Cross and his dying sigh echoes words associated with Christ, *Ecce homo* (Behold the man). The lamps explode, and the Policeman says, "We've had a short circuit" — a remark that the audience should interpret as referring to society.

Although the Cashier has seen the way to truth, the people are blind to his values and prefer materialism to his spirituality. He has changed nothing, but he has shown the way. Kaiser expected his audience to see the difference between two sets of values, and to prefer those of the Cashier.

Each of the characters in *From Morn till Midnight* is given only a social designation or type name, for each is intended to embody the characteristics of a group rather than an individual. Most speeches are made up of clichés and the characters perform only stereotyped actions. Only the Cashier (beginning in Scene 3) and the Lady escape stereotyping. The Lady is from another world, and it is her unusualness that jars the Cashier out of the mold into which he has been forced.

The play centers around the Cashier. He is the only truly articulate character and the only one who is able to escape from that machinelike existence that dominates the lives of others. He represents humanity trying to escape the stultifying effects of modern life.

Mechanical qualities are reflected in the scenery, lighting, and costumes, and each represents modern life in its most stereotyped form. The spectacle expresses the Cashier's vision of reality rather than reflecting the everyday appearance of things.

To embody their themes visually, the expressionists frequently used fragmentary rather than full-stage sets. The scenic elements often were given jagged lines, the walls were made to tilt or lean, unnatural color was used; details were enlarged or diminished in size to emphasize the relative importance of each to the play's ideas. Appearances, thus, were distorted to express feelings and ideas.

Costumes, lighting, and stage properties were treated in similar fashion. Many characters often were dressed identically so as to emphasize the uniformity of modern man. (See, for example, the treatment of the Jewish Gentlemen in the race-track scene of *From Morn till Midnight*.) Unnatural color, angle, or intensity in lighting might be used to parallel the distortion of human values depicted in the scripts.

From Morn till Midnight attempts to express the playwright's vision of modern man: the mechanization of feelings and activities and the subjugation of the human spirit. It demonstrates the results and suggests a way out of the dilemma.

EXPRESSIONISM IN THE POSTWAR YEARS

When the German government fell in 1918 only a few expressionist plays had been seen on the stage. Even these had been mounted rather traditionally. Then, beginning in 1919, expressionist drama suddenly came into vogue and a new style of production developed rapidly. Two German directors, Leopold Jessner (1878–1948) and Jurgen Fehling (1890–1968), were expecially instrumental in developing and popularizing expressionist production techniques. Jessner, working in Berlin after 1919, won international fame for his imaginative use of flights of steps (*Jessnertreppen*) as a major scenic and compositional device. He also manipulated color and lighting to reflect the inner feelings of characters and reversals of situation. Jessner worked primarily with older plays, to which he gave new life through his visual approach. Fehling, on the other hand, made his reputation by staging expressionist plays. As the work of Jessner and Fehling became widely known, their practices were adopted elsewhere.

Expressionism in the theatre seems to have reached its peak in 1923. Its desire to transform the world had raised high hopes, but these were dissipated by the wranglings over peace settlements and the aftermath. By 1925 the movement had ceased to be productive.

Expressionism was for the most part a German phenomenon. During

Trial scene from Elmer Rice's *The Adding Machine.* Directed by Gregory Foley.

the 1920s, however, expressionism for a time exerted considerable influence elsewhere. In America, dramas indebted to it include Elmer Rice's *The Adding Machine,* Eugene O'Neill's *The Hairy Ape,* and Marc Connelly's and George Kaufman's *Beggar on Horseback,* all written in the 1920s. After 1925 the influence of expressionism is seen largely in the freer treatment of visual elements, in dream sequences, and in other devices that permit free manipulation of time, place, and appearance.

By the 1920s, Ibsen, Zola, Kaiser, and others had done much to make drama once more a medium for the pursuit of truth and not merely a source of entertainment. Furthermore, producers almost everywhere had been forcefully reminded that theatre is an art, and they had been provoked into debates over its principles, purposes, and techniques. After having been initiated by realism and naturalism, the modern theatre had also begun to undergo that pattern of rapidly changing movements which has characterized it since.

From
the 1920s to
the Mid-1950s

10

Between the 1920s and the
mid-1950s the theatre extended and consolidated the gains of the preceding decades. Probably the most innovative ideas were voiced by Artaud
and Brecht, although neither was widely influential until after 1950, when
the doubts raised by World War II ushered in a new era of experimentation.

THE UNITED STATES

The innovations in playwriting and production that had been introduced
in the late nineteenth century were at first little known in America, partially because until 1915 the Theatrical Syndicate dominated theatrical
production. After 1910, however, the *new stagecraft,* as the European
practices were called in America, began to be imported, in large part

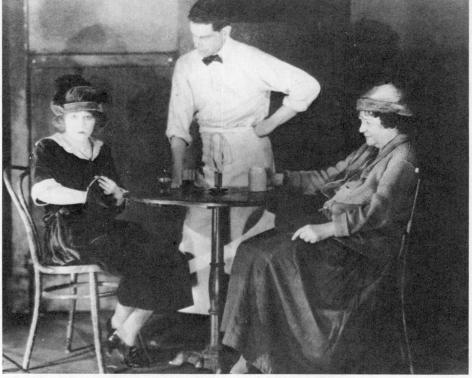

The opening scene of Eugene O'Neill's *Anna Christie* (1921) in its first New York production starring Pauline Lord. (Theatre and Music Collection, Museum of the City of New York)

through the efforts of those who had traveled and studied in Europe, especially designers Robert Edmond Jones (1887–1954) and Lee Simonson (1888–1967).

The new stagecraft was also promoted by "little theatres," which blossomed between 1910 and 1920. The most important of these groups (which resembled European independent theatres) were the Provincetown Players and the Washington Square Players. It was the Provincetown Players, seeking to encourage new American playwrights, that discovered Eugene O'Neill (1888–1953), generally considered to be America's foremost dramatist. Even after O'Neill achieved popular and critical fame with such plays as *Anna Christie* (1921) and *The Hairy Ape* (1922), the Provincetown Players continued to present such commercially unacceptable plays as his *Welded* (1924) and *The Fountain* (1925). It was out of the remnants of the Washington Square Players that the fully professional Theatre Guild came in 1919. Through its choice of plays and production techniques, the Guild did more than any other American company to demonstrate the effectiveness of the new stagecraft.

The influence of these groups was reinforced by Arthur Hopkins (1878–1950), who, in collaboration with Robert Edmond Jones, championed both the new drama and the new visual mode. The success of such producers had by 1925 made the new stagecraft fully acceptable.

The major new American playwrights, including Maxwell Anderson (1888–1959), Elmer Rice (1892–1967), and Thornton Wilder (1897–1975), were related to their European counterparts in their dedication to drama that was more than entertainment. Since none was committed to any particular movement, their work ranged through many styles.

Probably the best American company of the 1930s was the Group Theatre. Modeled on the Moscow Art Theatre, it attempted to apply Stanislavsky's methods in acting and production. It produced some of the finest plays seen in New York, especially Clifford Odets' (1906–1963) *Awake and Sing* (1935) and *Golden Boy* (1937). The Group Theatre also fostered the talents of important directors (among them Harold Clurman and Elia Kazan) and actors (including Lee J. Cobb and Morris Carnovsky). Its members have continued to be the principal promoters of the Stanislavsky system in America.

COPEAU AND THE CARTEL

In France, the acknowledged theatrical leaders after World War I were Copeau and the Cartel. Jacques Copeau (1879–1949) had founded his own theatre, the Vieux-Colombier, in 1913, but had been forced by World War I to close it. He reopened it in 1919 and continued with

Copeau's troupe in their premier performance of *Twelfth Night* at the Garrick Theatre in New York, December 25, 1917. (Courtesy French Cultural Services)

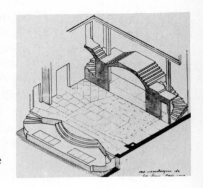

An isometric drawing of Jacques Copeau's stage, the Vieux Columbier in 1919. (From *Theatre Arts*, 1920)

great success until 1924, when he quit to concentrate on his acting school. Copeau declared that the salvation of the theatre lies in a renovated drama and that the director's primary task is to translate faithfully the playwright's script into a "poetry of the theatre." Furthermore, he stated, the actor, as the "living presence of the author," is the only essential element, and the drama can best be served by a return to the bare platform stage. Consequently, at the Vieux-Colombier he removed the proscenium arch to create an open platform, at the rear of which was an alcove surmounted by a balcony reached by steps. This basic structure, which could be altered somewhat by the addition of curtains and set pieces, was used for all productions.

Copeau's single-minded devotion to excellence was carried on by Louis Jouvet (1887–1951), Charles Dullin (1885–1949), Georges Pitoëff (1884–1939), and Gaston Baty (1882–1951), who in 1927 formed an association, usually called the Cartel des Quatre, to assist each other and to promote common ideals. While no member of the Cartel used as simplified a stage as Copeau's, all were opposed to realism and all but Baty accepted Copeau's view of the director's function.

Copeau's influence continues to be felt, as much in England and America as in France, because his actor-training techniques were so widely disseminated by his nephew, Michel Saint-Denis (1897–1971), who founded the Old Vic's theatre school in London, worked with the Royal Shakespeare Company, and helped to plan the national theatre school of Canada and the Juilliard School in New York.

ARTAUD

Another Frenchman, Antonin Artaud (1895–1948), was to exert enormous influence on the theatre throughout the world through the essays he published as *The Theatre and Its Double* (1938). According to Artaud, the Western theatre has been devoted to a narrow range of human experience, primarily the psychological problems of individuals and the social problems of groups, whereas the most important aspects are submerged in the unconscious. Artaud thought this approach mistaken, and he recommended Oriental theatre as a corrective.

Artaud considered the theatre's true mission to be the expulsion of all those things that cause divisions within man and between men and lead to hatred, violence, and disaster. As Artaud put it, "The theatre has been created to drain abscesses collectively."

Artaud was certain that his goal could not be reached through appeals to the rational mind, which has been conditioned to sublimate fundamental human impulses. He was also convinced that it could not be done through language, the primary tool of rational thought. He sometimes called his a "theatre of cruelty," since to achieve its ends it would have to force the audience to confront itself. To do this, he sought to break down the audience's defenses by operating directly on the sensory apparatus in a way that bypasses the conscious mind. He declared that the audience "cannot resist effects of physical surprise, the dynamism of cries and violent movements . . . used to act in a direct manner on the physical sensitivity of the spectators." According to Artaud, we need a new "language of the theatre." He recommended replacing traditional theatre buildings with remodeled factories or airplane hangars, and locating acting areas in corners, on overhead catwalks, and along the walls. In lighting, he called for a "vibrating, shredded" effect, and in sound he favored shrillness, abrupt changes in volume, and the use of the human voice to create dissonances. Thus Artaud wanted to assault the audience, break down its resistance, and purge it morally and spiritually.

These ideas were little heeded until the 1950s but became especially influential during the 1960s with experimental theatre groups.

RUSSIA

The Revolution of 1917 signaled a sharp break with the Russian past, but, since the new Communist leaders were for some time preoccupied with political and economic problems, they permitted the arts considerable freedom until the late 1920s. Furthermore, many of the most enthusiastic supporters of the Revolution were members of avant-garde movements who welcomed the opportunity to break with the past and create new forms. Of this group, Vsevelod Meyerhold (1874–1940) was the leader.

Meyerhold was one of the original members of the Moscow Art Theatre. In 1905 Stanislavsky appointed him director of an experimental group seeking alternatives to the company's realistic methods. But Meyerhold's subordination of the actor to his own directorial concept

213

Meyerhold's production of *The Magnanimous Cuckold* showing his use of a constructivist setting.

led to friction and he soon left. Between 1905 and 1917 he worked with many groups exploring the limits of the theatre as an artistic medium. After 1917 he sought to develop methods that would serve the needs of a revolutionary society, especially through biomechanics and constructivism.

Biomechanics refers to a system of acting through which Meyerhold hoped to make the performer as efficient as a machine in carrying out an assignment. Basically what Meyerhold had in mind is a variation on the James-Lange theory: particular emotions may be elicited by particular patterns of muscular activity. Consequently, the actor, to arouse a desired emotional response, need only enact the appropriate kinetic pattern. Thus Meyerhold sought to replace Stanislavsky's emphasis on internal motivation with one on physical and emotional reflexes. To create a feeling of exuberant joy, Meyerhold thought it more efficient for the actor to swing on a trapeze or turn a somersault than restrict himself to behavior considered realistic.

Constructivism was Meyerhold's attempt to arrive at a setting that would be a "machine for acting" without superfluous details. The term was taken over from the visual arts, where it had been used to describe abstract sculpture composed of intersecting planes and masses. Thus, in both acting and setting Meyerhold was seeking forms appropriate to the new society. He applied his theories most consistently between 1922

214

and 1925 but steadily softened them thereafter. Nevertheless Meyerhold remained the most experimental Russian director, and his fame and influence were international.

Another influential postrevolutionary director was Eugene Vakhtangov (1883–1922), who began as a faithful follower of Stanislavsky and then sought to blend Stanislavsky's and Meyerhold's approaches. From Stanislavsky he preserved the emphasis on concentration, character, and hidden meanings; with this he combined stylized movement and scenic elements not unlike those used by the expressionists. Vakhtangov called his approach "fantastic realism." Perhaps because he insisted that his actors find some justification for whatever they did onstage, his productions appeared unified and coherent. Not only did he win a large following during his lifetime, his influence continues to be strong because so many of his coworkers and students became leading Russian directors.

Next to Meyerhold, the most experimental director of the 1920s was Alexander Tairov (1885–1950), who headed the Kamerny Theatre in Moscow from 1914 until his death. Tairov argued that there is no relationship between art and life, that the theatre is comparable to the sacred dances of an ancient temple. To him, the text was an excuse for creativity. He thought rhythm the most important element and orchestrated his productions almost as if they were musical compositions; speech was a compromise between declamation and song; movement always tended toward dance. The over-all effect was nearer to ritual than to the usual dramatic performance. Although Tairov was to modify his approach somewhat after 1930, he remained the Russian director most concerned with a theatre independent of social or political ideologies.

After Stalin assumed full power in the late 1920s, theatrical workers began to be pressured to uphold Party ideology and to stage productions easily comprehensible to the common man. Soon innovators such as Meyerhold and Tairov were being denounced as "formalists" who failed to understand the people's needs. In 1934, "socialist realism" was proclaimed the appropriate style for all writing. This meant that dramatists not only were expected to reflect the approved ideology but to include in their works a positive hero who points the way toward the triumph of communism. Most subsequent plays are melodramas that denounce opponents of the Party and glorify its supporters.

As the prestige of Meyerhold and Tairov declined, that of the Moscow Art Theatre rose. Following the Revolution, the Moscow Art Theatre at first hesitated, but after 1925 began to stage Soviet plays realistically and with great effectiveness. Consequently, the government regarded the troupe with increasing favor, and by the late 1930s had declared its methods the standard by which all others were to be judged. Thus, by the late 1930s the Russian theatre had been reduced to conformity.

BRECHT AND EPIC THEATRE

During the 1920s one of the most influential of modern movements—epic theatre—took shape in Germany. It is associated above all with Bertolt Brecht (1898–1956), who, to describe his ideal theatre, used three key terms: historification, alienation, and epic.

Unlike the realists, Brecht thought the theatre should not treat contemporary subject matter in a lifelike manner. Rather, the theatre should make actions "strange." One avenue to strangeness is *historification,* or the use of material drawn from other times and places. But contrary to old theatrical practices, which depict historical material in today's pattern, Brecht wanted the dramatist to emphasize the "pastness" of events. The play should make the spectator feel that if he had been living under those conditions he would have taken some positive action to correct them. The audience should then go on to see that, since things have changed, it is possible to reform present conditions.

Historification is part of the larger concept *alienation.* In addition to historification, the playwright may deliberately call attention to the make-believe nature of the work through songs, narrative passages, filmed sequences, and other devices so the audience never confuses what it sees on the stage with reality. Some critics have interpreted alienation to mean that the audience should be in a constant state of detachment, but in actuality Brecht manipulated esthetic distance to involve the spectator emotionally and then jar him out of his empathic response so that he may judge critically what he has experienced.

Each element of production should contribute to alienation. Unlike most modern theorists, Brecht did not envision the theatre as a synthesis of all the arts; he thought each element should comment in its own way on the action. Music, for example, should not merely underscore the meaning of words, and the satirical lyrics of a song which tell of moral degradation may be set to a light-hearted tune; the contrast will force the spectator to consider the song's significance. Similarly, scenery should comment on the action rather than create the illusion of place, although it should indicate locale through fragmentary set pieces, projections, or similar devices. As a further aid in alienation, Brecht wishes the mechanics of the theatre to remain visible. He suggested mounting lighting instruments where they may be seen, changing the scenery in view of the audience, and placing musicians onstage.

Brecht called his plays *epic* because he thought they resembled epic poems more than traditional drama. They are usually composed of alternating sections of dialogue and narration which freely change place and bridge passages of time.

Brecht envisioned the ultimate effect taking place outside the theatre. By stirring up thought and inciting the spectator to implement social reform, he thought the theatre could assume a vital role in daily life. Among Brecht's many plays, some of the best are *The Threepenny Opera, The Caucasian Chalk Circle, Mother Courage,* and *The Good Woman of Setzuan.* The last of these will be discussed as an example of epic theatre.

THE GOOD WOMAN OF SETZUAN

The Good Woman of Setzuan, written between 1938 and 1940 and first performed in 1943, is a parable that has been distanced by setting it in China. The epic nature of the play is established by the prologue, in which narration and dialogue are mingled and in which time and place are telescoped. The prologue also demonstrates the irony that permeates the piece, since Wong assures the Gods that everyone is waiting to receive them—only to have to obtain lodgings from a prostitute. In addition, the prologue establishes the basic situation: the Gods find the good person for whom they have been searching and enjoin her to remain

Scene from Brecht's *The Good Woman of Setzuan,* as presented at the University of Texas. Directed by Francis Hodge; setting by John Rothgeb; costumes by Paul Reinhardt. (University of Texas)

good. At the same time, they refuse to be concerned about how such a difficult assignment is to be carried out—they "never meddle with economics." Herein lies the basic conflict, for economic factors are the very ones that stand in the way of goodness. Thus Brecht implies that the solution to human problems is not to be sought in divine injunctions.

The Good Woman of Setzuan alternates short and long scenes. The short scenes serve two main purposes: to break up and to comment on the action. Both contribute to Brecht's aim of forcing the audience to think by giving it clues about the significance of what it has seen and time in which to reflect upon it.

The long scenes are devoted to the conflict between good and evil as seen in the two aspects of the "good woman." Her better self is shown in the person of Shen Te, while her evil self is embodied in Shui Ta. She assumes the disguise of Shui Ta whenever her goodness has brought her to the edge of destruction. At first the impersonation is for brief periods, but, as the play progresses, she must become Shui Ta for longer periods. Brecht uses this device to show the progressive deterioration of morality. The play ends in a stalemate, for the Gods leave Shen Te with the same message as in the prologue, "Be good." She is still no nearer to knowing how this is to be accomplished, and they are still unconcerned over such practical matters.

Brecht makes no attempt to create the illusion of reality. For example, when Wong says he will find a place for the Gods to spend the night, he suggests the attempt, although the various houses are not represented onstage; the action is outlined, but many details are omitted.

This approach allows Brecht to telescope events and to eliminate transitions, as can be seen clearly in the scene during which Shen Te meets Yang Sun and falls in love. There has been no preparation for this complication, and it is as if a storyteller had said, "One day when Shen Te was out walking in the park she saw a young man trying to hang himself."

Brecht's structural techniques are explained in part by his belief that scenes should be clearly separated as part of the alienation process. They are further explained by his insistence that it should be possible to express the basic social content of each scene in one simple sentence and that all parts of a scene should be clearly related to this simple statement.

Brecht considerably oversimplifies characters, for he is principally concerned with social relationships. He is not interested in total personalities or the inner lives of his characters. Instead of names, the majority of speakers in *The Good Woman of Setzuan* have been given social designations such as Wife, Grandfather, and Policeman. Their desires are also stated in terms of social action: Shen Te wishes to treat all persons honorably, to make it possible for Yang Sun to become a pilot, to provide proper food for children, and so on. Thus, Brecht's characterizations are confined principally to social attitudes. He did not intend to portray well-rounded individuals, but to interpret social forces. The action does not exist to display character, but character to demonstrate social action. The only character who rises to the level of moral decision is Shen Te, and the plot progresses in large part through the series of choices she makes and which show the dilemma of man under existing economic conditions.

Brecht's ideas on acting are in keeping with his over-all approach. He argued that the actor should not impersonate a character but should "present" the role's basic social qualities in a kind of demonstration that comments on the character and action.

Brecht once characterized his use of visual elements as naïve, and added: "The opposite of a naïve approach is naturalism." Fragmentary settings, projections, and captions were his favorite devices. His costumes usually included some historically accurate details, but other parts of the same costumes might be modern or merely expressive of social factors rather than period. He wished all the visual elements to lead the spectator to view reality critically. With every element, then, Brecht sought to transform the old theatre into one in which the spectator could participate actively rather than merely observe passively.

All of Brecht's major works were written before the end of World War II. Living in exile throughout the Nazi regime, Brecht was little known until after 1945. Since that time his plays and theories have been among the most pervasive influences on contemporary theatre.

THE LIVING NEWSPAPER

One of the forms most obviously related to Brecht's Epic Theatre is the *Living Newspaper,* which grew out of the Federal Theatre project in America. During the economic depression of the 1930s, the United States government authorized a Federal Theatre as part of its Works Progress Administration programs, designed to relieve unemployment. Between 1935 and 1939 the Federal Theatre had units in various parts of the country but was most active in New York. It is best remembered for the Living Newspaper, which aimed at achieving in the theatre something similar to the printed newspaper. In actuality it was more closely related to the documentary film, for each play treated a single problem. The most famous examples are *One Third of a Nation* (on slum housing), *Triple-A Plowed Under* (on the farm program), and *Power* (on public utilities and flood control). The plays alternate scenes illustrating social conditions with narrative sequences. Statistical tables, still photographs, and motion pictures were projected on screens; offstage voices, music, and sound effects were used freely. The plays were written by many authors in collaboration and took a definite point of view (in favor of social reform and corrective legislation). This political and social bias

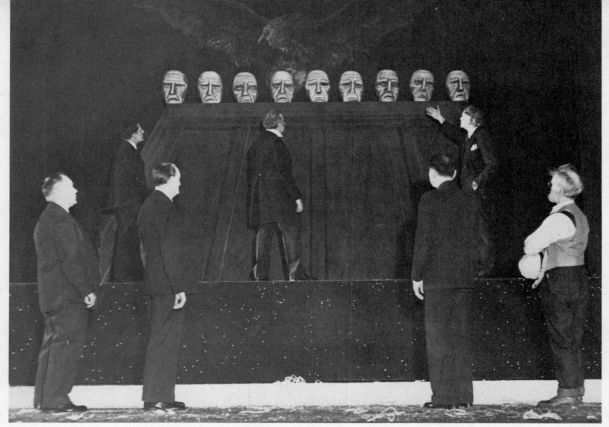

Power, a Living Newspaper production by Arthur Arent. This scene depicts an argument before the Supreme Court about the constitutional validity of the Tennessee Valley Authority. (The New York Public Library at Lincoln Center, Theatre Collection)

eventually led to the discontinuance of the Federal Theatre, for in 1939 Congress refused to appropriate funds to continue it. It was the United States government's first attempt at subsidizing the theatre.

POSTWAR REALISM IN AMERICA

When the Second World War ended in 1945, realism was still the most common theatrical style, but by that time nonrealistic movements had altered tastes sufficiently for simplification and suggestion to become accepted techniques, even in realistic art. Postwar realism therefore fused elements drawn from many sources.

This fusion can be seen most clearly in the work of Tennessee Williams (1914–   ), who came to prominence in 1945 with *The Glass Menagerie* and contributed regularly to the theatre thereafter with such plays as *A Streetcar Named Desire, Summer and Smoke, The Rose Tattoo,* and *Suddenly Last Summer.*

Williams uses many nonrealistic devices. Symbolism is important in almost all of his plays. Normally he also demands fragmentary settings, although each fragment may be realistic. Frequently his sets combine interiors and exteriors to allow fluidity without scene changes. A good example is *Summer and Smoke,* which shows two interiors and a park simultaneously. Time also is fluid in most of Williams' plays. *The Glass Menagerie* is especially noteworthy for its use of memory to motivate calling up scenes from the past.

Williams also draws heavily on realism, especially in character portrayal. He is particularly concerned with suppressed desires, and Freudian concepts undergird many of his works. Williams' characters are often torn between spiritual and material urges, and how a dramatic action is resolved depends upon whether they can reconcile these conflicting sides of human nature.

Williams' realism is also seen in the way he juxtaposes comic and serious elements. Amanda in *The Glass Menagerie,* for example, is admirable and ridiculous, and the scenes in which she appears shift mood rapidly. Williams' portrayal of human limitations in conjunction with high aspirations produce both pathos and humor. Because they mingle such diverse elements, Williams plays sum up many twentieth-century movements prior to the 1950s.

The concern for social issues was best represented in the postwar period by Arthur Miller (1915–   ), who came to prominence with *All My Sons* (1947) and went on to write such plays as *The Crucible, After the Fall, The Price,* and *The Creation of the World and Other Business.* But it is *Death of a Salesman* (1949) that has insured Miller's position, for many consider it the finest American play of its era. It will be examined here as an example of postwar realism.

DEATH OF A SALESMAN

Death of a Salesman dramatizes a primary conflict in the American consciousness: its tendency to measure success in material terms even as this consciousness upholds love as a major value; as a result, it often unconsciously mingles these goals so that approval is withheld from those who have not succeeded materially. Miller has embodied this conflict in Willy Loman's obsessive desire to succeed and his confusion of success with worthiness to be loved.

Willy wants to be liked and admired, and it is his perplexity over the gulf between his accomplishment and his ideal that precipitates the play's action. Because to Willy material success seems so necessary, he believes that his sons cannot love him if he is not successful. He has also conditioned his sons to believe that they do not deserve respect unless they are successful on his terms. It is only when Willy understands that Biff loves him, even though both are failures, that he achieves a degree of insight. Miller has used two characters to represent the poles between which Willy is pulled. Uncle Ben, Willy's brother, epitomizes material success, while Linda, Willy's wife, represents love given without conditions.

The present action occurs during a twenty-four-hour period (with the exception of the funeral), but the scenes from the past range over twenty years. Past and present flow together as Willy tries to find the answers to his questions: Where did I go wrong? What is the secret of success?

The only unusual structural feature of *Death of a Salesman* is the *flashback* technique, for otherwise it is organized conventionally in terms of exposition, preparation, complications, climax, obligatory scene, and resolution. Each flashback is carefully introduced by wandering talk, offstage voices, sound effects, music, or some similar cue. Most productions of the play have also used changes in lighting to lead the audience from the present to the past. The flashbacks are carefully engineered so that each reveals only a small part of the past. The outline gradually emerges but is incomplete until the climactic moment.

Jo Mielziner's sketched idea of the salesman, Willy Loman, and of the set for Arthur Miller's *Death of a Salesman.* (Courtesy of Mr. Mielziner.)

In *Death of a Salesman* psychological realism has replaced external realism and a greater freedom in dramatic structure has resulted. Nevertheless, Miller's aim remains much the same as Ibsen's — to depict with fidelity a contemporary action.

By far the most important character in *Death of a Salesman* is Willy Loman. Now sixty-three years old, he is on the verge of a physical and psychological breakdown. All his life, he has lied to himself and others out of a desire to believe that he is a success. Recent developments, however, have forced him to see that actually he is a failure, although he cannot see where he has taken the wrong path.

Uncle Ben personifies success, and in many ways is merely an extension of Willy's personality. He has gone into the jungle and come out rich; thus he gives a romantic aura to success. Ben also implies that success is bound up with the "law of the jungle," with shady deals and quick-wittedness.

Willy, however, wants to triumph on his own terms — as a salesman liked by everybody. Therefore, he can never completely accept Ben's advice just as he can never give up Ben's ideal. This division is at the root of Willy's character and is seen even in his death, which is a final attempt to achieve material gain and the gratitude of his family simultaneously.

Biff is thirty-four years old but still adolescent in his attitudes. He is irresponsible, a wanderer, and incapable of happiness because of the sense of guilt aroused in him by Willy. From Willy he learned early that the way to success is through lying, stealing, and powerful acquaintances. But the lure of success has been short-circuited in Biff by his disillusionment with Willy, dating from the discovery of his father's unfaithfulness to his mother. Consequently, Biff rebels against success, flouts authority, and tries to punish his father. Biff has his admirable side, nevertheless, for he has a sense of moral responsibility which his brother, Happy, is totally lacking. It is Biff who finally makes his father see the truth as they both come to understand that love is a gift freely bestowed rather than something earned through material success.

Linda understands from the beginning what Willy and Biff learn during the play: love has no conditions. Because she loves so unconditionally, she cannot understand why Willy commits suicide or why the boys have turned out as they have. Success holds no magic for her.

Happy has inherited the worst of Willy's traits without the saving possibility of love. He is entirely selfish and unfeeling; lying and cheating are integral parts of his nature. He is a materialist and sensualist beyond redemption, but devoid of Ben's vision and strength.

Charley and Bernard have succeeded where Willy and Biff have failed; thus, their principal function in the play is to serve as contrasts. Charley's unconscious commitment to *human* above *material* factors is the key to his happiness, just as the reverse is the key to Willy's failure.

In constructing his characters, Miller has concentrated upon sociological and psychological attitudes. His success in creating convincing figures is indicated by the general tendency of audiences to see in the play a reflection of American society.

Miller's ideas about staging *Death of a Salesman* are clearly indicated in the script. Sound is used effectively throughout. Music helps to set the mood and to mark transitions to flashback scenes. Ben has his own special music, played each time he appears; honky-tonk music accompanies Willy's scenes with the Other Woman; music helps to set the locale of the restaurant. The method by which Willy commits suicide is made clear only through the offstage sound of a car driving away.

The continuous presence of the house helps to establish the convention that the flashbacks are fragments of the past and to make clear the simultaneity of the past and the present in Willy's mind. The fragmentary and schematic setting specified by Miller is entirely in keeping with the dramatic techniques, through which the surface is cut away to reveal more clearly the inner reality. *Death of a Salesman* is an excellent example of that modified realism which prevailed in the postwar period.

POSTWAR PRODUCTION STYLE

Largely because of Miller and Williams, American drama seemed especially vital in the years immediately following World War II. Their plays were also instrumental in establishing the major production style of the time, since the approach that dominated the American theatre from the 1940s until about 1960 was popularized by Elia Kazan (1909–   ) and Jo Mielziner (1901–   ) with productions of *A Streetcar Named Desire* (1947) and *Death of a Salesman* (1949). *A Streetcar Named Desire* also popularized a new style of acting with Marlon Brando's (1924–   ) characterization of the inarticulate, uneducated, and assertive Stanley Kowalski. The novelty of serious acting based upon substandard speech, untidy dress, and boorish behavior captured the public imagination and soon became associated with the Actors Studio, at which Brando had worked. The Actors Studio was founded in 1947 by Robert Lewis, Elia Kazan, and Cheryl Crawford, although the dominant figure was its artistic director, Lee Strasberg. Its founders sought to provide selected actors with the opportunity to work and develop according to the Stanislavsky system. In the popular mind, however, it appeared to be a place where actors were encouraged to explore their psyches without regard for the skills needed to project a characterization. This image was mistaken, although major emphasis in training was placed on discovering the "inner truth" of characters rather than on technical skills. The Kazan–Mielziner–Brando style (earthy realism in acting and directing combined with simplified backgrounds) was not seriously challenged in America until the 1960s.

Marlon Brando and Jessica
Tandy in *A Streetcar Named
Desire* in the original
Broadway production.
Directed by Elia Kazan.
(Theatre and Music
Collection, Museum of the
City of New York)

THE MUSICAL PLAY

During and after World War II, the musical play became (and remains)
the most popular of all theatrical entertainments.

The origin of musical comedy is usually traced to the work of George
Edwardes at the Gaiety Theatre in London in the 1890s. His productions, in which sketchy plots provided excuses for songs and chorus-en-
semble numbers, proved so popular that a number of imitations soon appeared. In most of these early musical comedies the stories had little to
do with everyday life and emphasized the romantic appeals of faraway
places and unusual happenings.

Around World War I the vogue for ballroom dancing and ragtime
music turned attention to more familiar characters and surroundings.
Plot remained unimportant, however, and served principally as an excuse
for spectacular settings, songs, dances, and beautiful chorus girls. In the
late 1920s another important change occurred when more concern
began to be paid to plot and psychological motivations. The new stature
of the musical was indicated when *Of Thee I Sing* was awarded the Pulit-
zer Prize in 1931. This evolution was completed in the 1940s in
the works of Oscar Hammerstein II (1895–1960) and Richard Rodgers
(1902–   ), especially with *Oklahoma!*, *Carousel*, and *South Pacific*.
Innumerable fine musicals were written after World War II. They include *Guys and Dolls*, *Pajama Game*, *Damn Yankees*, *West Side Story*, *The
Music Man*, *Hello, Dolly!*, *Mame*, and *Fiddler on the Roof*. One of the

most successful writing teams was Alan Jay Lerner (1918–   ) and Frederick Loewe (1904–   ), with *Paint Your Wagon, My Fair Lady,* and *Camelot. My Fair Lady* will be examined here as an example of the modern musical play. Since it is based on a well-known comedy, it also provides an opportunity to compare the script with its original source and to consider how an existing work is adapted to the musical stage.

MY FAIR LADY

My Fair Lady (1956) is based on George Bernard Shaw's *Pygmalion* (1912), "A Romance in Five Acts." It retells in modern terms the legend of Pygmalion, a sculptor, who falls in love with Galatea, one of his statues. He prays that his statue will come to life, his wish is granted, and he marries Galatea.

Shaw uses this legend only as a point of departure, for he wishes to show that differences in speech undergird the class structure of England. He argues that if everyone were taught to speak English properly the mainstay of the class system would be destroyed. To make his point, he shows how a flower girl is passed off as a duchess by changing her speech. But it is doubtful that the social message contributed significantly to the play's success. Most audiences have seen in it only the romance which the title indicates.

Although *My Fair Lady* follows Shaw's play closely in basic outline, many structural changes have been made. *Pygmalion* is written in five acts, while *My Fair Lady* divides eighteen scenes into two acts. The musical breaks up the acts into short scenes, dramatizes events only talked about in the play, and condenses Shaw's speeches to allow time for songs and dances.

Well over half of the eighteen scenes of the musical have no direct counterpart in Shaw's play, although almost all are based upon things talked about in the play. Many of the additions create variety and spectacle. For example, the slums from which Eliza comes are shown in the musical and offer opportunities for choral numbers. Some additions emphasize the love story: a new final scene has been added, and the role of Freddy, who falls in love with Eliza, is built up to create a threat to Higgins. Some scenes are added to create suspense. For example, at the ball, Karpathy, an expert on speech, repeatedly questions the authenticity of Eliza's title. He vows to find out the truth and as the curtain falls on Act I he is seen dancing with her.

The division of *My Fair Lady* into two acts also marks a change in the plot. Act I is concerned with the decision to pass off a flower girl as a duchess. This purpose has been accomplished when Act II begins. The last half of the musical shows Eliza's refusal to be used and then abandoned.

George Bernard Shaw's *Pygmalion.* Cecil Humphries, Raymond Massey, and Gertrude Lawrence in the 1945 production. (Theatre and Music Collection, Museum of the City of New York)

Many departures from the original play have been dictated by conventions of the musical. In its original form the play requires almost as much playing time as does the musical. Changes had to be made, therefore, to allow for the addition of music, song, and dance. In *Pygmalion* only Act I (outside the Covent Garden Theatre) readily allows for a chorus. In *My Fair Lady,* slum and ballroom scenes are added and a race track is substituted for a drawing room to permit choral numbers.

Thus, while the differences between *Pygmalion* and *My Fair Lady* are numerous, the musical has maintained the essence of Shaw's play while transforming it to meet the demands of the musical stage.

My Fair Lady has only five roles of importance: Higgins, Eliza, Pickering, Doolittle, and Freddy. Of these, Higgins and Eliza are of primary importance, while Pickering, Doolittle, and Freddy are secondary.

Higgins has been made more polished and urbane in the musical than he is in Shaw's play, where he was inclined to be unfashionable in his dress and unconventional in his behavior. The Higgins of the musical is still an individualist, but the rough qualities are gone. Nevertheless, he is still self-confident, selfish, and unfeeling where others are concerned.

The greatest range in acting ability is required of Eliza. She must be able to give a convincing portrayal of a cockney flower girl and must be able to transform herself gradually until the audience is willing to believe

Rex Harrison and Julie Andrews in the opening scene of *My Fair Lady,* the musical version of *Pygmalion.* (Theatre and Music Collection, Museum of the City of New York)

that she might pass as a duchess. Eliza's principal motivation is the desire to be respected. This drives her in the beginning to accept Higgins' offer and later to leave him because he has merely used her for his own purposes instead of considering her feelings as a human being. Ultimately it is her personal integrity that forces Higgins to see himself more clearly and to recognize his need for Eliza.

Although he is onstage during a large part of *My Fair Lady,* Pickering serves principally as a foil for Higgins. It is he who bets with Higgins that he cannot pass Eliza off as a duchess; it is he who treats Eliza as a lady and points up Higgins' indifference to her as a human being.

Doolittle is almost the opposite of Pickering. He is a wastrel and near-drunkard who avoids responsibility. He represents lower-class morality and attitudes, but eventually falls victim to respectability.

Freddy serves as another contrast to Higgins, for he sees Eliza almost completely from a sentimental point of view. He offers Eliza love and respect in large part because she has the strength he lacks. Higgins on the other hand has the strength that Eliza wants in a man, but is lacking in the love and consideration that Freddy offers. It is only when Higgins can make some compromise that the possibility of happiness for Eliza materializes.

Shaw has long been recognized as a master of the English language. The speeches in his plays are sharply outlined, clear and graceful. Much of the dialogue in *My Fair Lady* is taken directly from *Pygmalion;* the rest has been written with Shaw's style in mind and successfully blended with the original.

Nevertheless, much of Shaw's dialogue has been eliminated so that songs and dances may be included. The songs, therefore, must supply much that has been left out. For example, the first three solos (Higgins' "Why Can't the English Learn to Speak?"; Eliza's "Wouldn't It Be Loverly"; and Doolittle's "With a Little Bit of Luck") establish the basic traits of the characters who sing them.

Much time is saved in the musical by capitalizing on the audience's ready acceptance of forthright statements of feelings and intentions in song, Thus, the song is comparable to the soliloquy or aside in its ability to convey a great deal of information in a brief amount of time. Music also makes the condensation of time more acceptable, For example, the lesson scenes in *My Fair Lady* are run together, with the entire sequence building to the song of triumph, "The Rain in Spain," based upon a phrase that has formed the motif of the lessons. Time may also be saved by the effective use of the reprise (the repetition of a song or musical phrase). Such repetitions associate events separated in time and establish connections without the need for lengthy or explicit statement.

Music establishes moods and builds expectations. Even before the curtain opens the overture has given some idea of the general mood and the melodic qualities of the work to follow. Music also helps to establish the mood of individual scenes and to create audience expectation. Music further aids in achieving variety. *My Fair Lady* contains musical numbers of widely contrasting types: songs of delight, love songs, songs of rage and defiance, songs of boisterous enjoyment of life, and songs of longing.

The musical almost always offers great scope to designers. The mingling of song and dialogue usually places a production outside the restrictions of realism and indicates the need for an imaginative use of pictorial elements. A listing of the settings needed for Act I of *My Fair Lady* indicates some of the demands: outside the opera house; the tenement section; Higgins' study; the tenement section; Higgins' study; near the race at Ascot; inside a tent at Ascot; outside Higgins' home; Higgins' study; promenade at the Embassy; the ballroom. Not only is a wide variety of places indicated, but the alternation and frequent repetition of some indicates that they must permit quick changes so that the flow of one scene into another will not be impeded.

The costumes are also numerous and a source of great visual variety and beauty. The time of *My Fair Lady* is 1912, a period noted for elegance. Upper-class characters appear in the Ascot race scenes and at the Embassy Ball, while lower-class characters are seen in the flower market and tenement scenes. Since *My Fair Lady* covers a period of over six months, many costume changes are needed. The transformation of Eliza is indicated in what she wears as well as in how she sounds. Furthermore, the chorus changes its identity often and therefore needs a great variety of costumes: sometimes they represent slum dwellers, at others they are dancers at the Embassy ball or loungers outside the opera house.

Dance adds to the visual effectiveness of the musical play. Like the music, it too comments upon the action and forwards the plot. It is not used extensively in *My Fair Lady,* but in other musicals it has played an extremely important part.

Overall, *My Fair Lady* combines an extremely effective story with interesting and unusual characters, memorable music, and charming and colorful spectacle. It is both a representative and a superior example of the postwar musical.

MOTION PICTURES AND TELEVISION

In the late nineteenth century, the theatre was still the major purveyor of mass entertainment, but since that time its appeal has steadily eroded as competitors have multiplied. One of the most serious challenges has come from spectator sports—baseball, football, boxing, racing, and so on. More direct competition, however, has come from other dramatic media—films and television.

Motion pictures have grown steadily in popularity since penny arcades began to show miniature films soon after Thomas A. Edison demonstrated his kinetoscope in 1894. Motion-picture theatres, seating about a hundred persons and showing short films, were introduced in 1905. In 1914 the Strand Theatre in New York, with its 3300 seats, began the trend toward larger houses, and in 1915 D. W. Griffith's *The Birth of a Nation* inaugurated the full-length film. Two other events—the addition of sound to motion pictures in 1927 and the economic depression of 1929—gave the film such increased appeal that after 1930 the legitimate theatre rapidly declined in popularity.

The weakened theatre was dealt another serious blow after World War II with the introduction of television, for audiences were loath to pay for entertainment when they might have it free in their own living rooms. Thus, television did much to make both film and theatrical producers reconsider the potential of their media. As a result, film-makers became increasingly conscious of the motion pictures as an art form, and theatrical producers sought to revitalize the theatre by offering plays that television, controlled by its advertisers, was reluctant or unable to broadcast. Consequently, much of the experimentation so prevalent since the 1950s has been motivated by the desire to make the theatre a penetrating, relevant, and exciting encounter with significant ideas, issues, and perceptions.

OTHER POSTWAR DEVELOPMENTS

In New York, the theatre's decline in popularity led to the development of Off Broadway in the late 1940s. Believing that financial conditions forced Broadway producers to cater almost exclusively to mass audiences, the new groups sought out-of-the-way buildings where rent was sufficiently low that they might offer short runs of plays to appreciative though limited audiences. Furthermore, since many operated in buildings never intended for theatrical purposes, they almost inevitably had to experiment with such audience-actor spatial arrangements as arena and thrust stages. During the 1950s there were more than fifty Off-Broadway companies, of which the Circle in the Square and the Phoenix Theatre were the most influential. As a whole, they demonstrated that excellence does not depend on material resources.

In France following World War II, the government became concerned about the restriction of theatrical activity to Paris and began to encourage decentralization. Since 1947 it has subsidized "dramatic centers," each based in a large town and serving the adjacent territory; there are now about ten of these scattered throughout France.

The most prestigious French actor-director of the postwar period was Jean-Louis Barrault (1910–   ), who synthesized many earlier developments. From the Cartel he learned respect for a text and for precise workmanship, from Etienne Decroux the power of mime, and from Antonin Artaud the importance of subconscious impulses and nonverbal theatrical devices. Barrault has declared that the text of a play is like an iceberg, since only about one-eighth is visible; it is the director's task to complete the playwright's text by revealing the hidden portions through the imaginative use of all the theatre's resources. Since 1946, Barrault and his wife Madeleine Renaud have headed their own company (bearing their names), with which they have won high critical praise.

Another major director of postwar France, Jean Vilar (1912–1971), remained true to the ideals of Copeau and the Cartel. As head of the Théâtre National Populaire from 1951 to 1963, he won a wide following throughout France with productions simply but imaginatively mounted and powerfully acted.

In England, the war provoked the government to subsidize the arts for the first time in history. After German bombs so damaged the theatres that for a time only one remained open in London, the government sent companies on tour to help build morale. Since that time subsidies have continued, and support, both nationally and locally, has steadily increased.

After the war the English theatre also gained considerably in international repute. Between the wars it had made little impact abroad, since it broke no important new ground. But after the war, the Old Vic (es-

Jean Vilar, head of the Théâtre National Populaire from 1951 to 1963, is seen here with Roger Mollien in the 18th century play, *Le Triomphe de l'Amour* by Marivaux. (Courtesy French Cultural Services)

pecially from 1944 to 1949 under the direction of Laurence Olivier and Ralph Richardson) became the best-known company in the English-speaking world. From 1946 to 1952, the Old Vic also had an excellent acting school run by Michel Saint-Denis. The Shakespeare Festival in Stratford-on-Avon also steadily grew in reputation after the war.

English playwriting demonstrated little strength in the immediate postwar period. Its greatest asset was poetic drama, especially such works as *The Lady's Not for Burning* (1949) and *Venus Observed* (1950) by Christopher Fry (1907–   ) and *The Cocktail Party* (1949) and *The Confidential Clerk* (1954) by T. S. Eliot (1888–1965), who before the war had written *Murder in the Cathedral* (1935). Unfortunately, the appeal of such poetic dramas soon waned, and by the mid-1950s English playwriting seemed at a low ebb.

In Germany, all theatres were closed in 1944. Soon after the hostilities ended, however, they began to reopen and subsidized companies were reestablished throughout the country. Around 1950 new buildings began to replace the more than one hundred theatres that had been destroyed during the war. Consequently, Germany probably now has more up-to-date theatre buildings than any country in the world.

Of the postwar German troupes, the best known was the Berliner Ensemble, founded in 1949 by Bertolt Brecht and his wife Helene Weigel. This troupe was the first to apply Brecht's theories of staging consistently and to make his plays the center of its repertory. Brecht's reputation grew rapidly, and by the time he died in 1956 he was recognized as one of the masters of modern drama and as a major influence on postwar production.

By the 1950s, then, the theatre had almost fully recovered from the effects of World War II. But the war had also raised serious questions about society and morality. Out of this questioning was to come one of the most innovative eras of the modern theatre.

The Contemporary Theatre

11

Since the mid-1950s, virtually all values and practices have been called into question and many innovations attempted. As a result, it has been one of the most exciting, puzzling, and frustrating eras the theatre has known. Only a few of the developments can be considered here, but they should be sufficient to indicate the major directions of change.

ABSURDISM

Absurdism is a term coined by Martin Esslin around 1960 to describe the work of several dramatists who had come to prominence during the preceding decade. These writers were united by a shared view: all ideas about man's significance and behavior are equally illogical. To the absurdists, ultimate truth is the chaos, contradictions, and inanities that make up daily existence — the lack of logic, order, and certainty.

The roots of absurdism go back to the late nineteenth century. It is now usual to label Alfred Jarry's *Ubu Roi* (1896) the first absurdist drama, because of its inversion of conventional values and its determinedly grotesque handling of subject and characters. The most significant forerunners of absurdism, however, are the existentialists, who attracted international attention after World War II. The central problems in existential philosophy are: What does "to exist" mean? and What does "to exist" imply about action?

The best-known existentialist dramatists are Jean-Paul Sartre (1905–   ) and Albert Camus (1913–1960). Sartre has said that in all his work he has attempted to draw logical conclusions from a consistent atheism. He argues that there are no absolute moral values and that man is adrift in a world devoid of purpose. Therefore, each man is free (since he is not bound to a god or a set of verifiable standards) and is responsible only to himself. This viewpoint, set forth in a number of philosophical treatises, forms the basis for such plays as *The Flies* (1943), *No Exit* (1944), and *The Condemned of Altona* (1959). Camus, the first theorist to use the term *absurd,* states that absurdity arises from the gulf between man's aspirations and the meaningless universe into which he has been thrust. Camus' plays illustrating this position include *Cross-Purposes* (1944), *Caligula* (1945), and *The Just Assassins* (1949). Both Sartre and Camus emphasize the necessity for man to find a set of values capable of ordering an otherwise chaotic existence.

The absurdists differ from Sartre and Camus in two important respects: the former emphasize the absurdity of existence rather than the necessity of bringing order to absurdity, and they embody their chaotic subjects in a form which abandons the logical cause-to-effect arrangement used by Sartre and Camus for one based on themes and associations. In France the major absurdist writers were Beckett, Genet, and Ionesco.

Absurdism first attracted wide attention with Samuel Beckett's (1906–   ) *Waiting for Godot* (1953), soon translated into more than twenty languages. In it, two tramps improvise diversions while they wait for Godot, who never comes. Beckett's writings as a whole suggest that it is impossible to be certain about anything. They are rich in implications about human existence, which nevertheless remains mysterious and unexplained. Among Beckett's later plays are *Endgame, Krapp's Last Tape, Happy Days, Not I,* and *That Time.*

Jean Genet (1910–   ), whose major dramas are *The Maids, The Balcony, The Blacks,* and *The Screens,* sees existence as an endless series of reflections in mirrors; each image may for a moment be mistaken for reality, but always proves to be an illusion. Genet suggests that deviation is essential to society, for nothing has meaning without its opposite—law and crime, religion and sin, love and hate. He transforms life into a series of ceremonies and rituals that give a sense of order and importance to what would otherwise be nonsensical.

Eugene Ionesco (1912–   ) wrote his first play, *The Bald Soprano*, in 1950. His subsequent works include *The Chairs, The New Tenant, Rhinoceros, Exit the King, Macbett,* and *The Man with the Suitcases.* Here *The New Tenant* will be discussed as an example of Ionesco's work and of absurdist drama.

THE NEW TENANT

Ionesco, like other absurdists, is convinced that there are no absolutes on which one can base behavior. On the other hand, he believes that all men share certain anxieties—above all, a "true community of fear" about the "void at the center of things," of which the ultimate expression is death. But, though these are universals, they cannot be fully understood

Scene from the first Paris production of Ionesco's *The New Tenant.* Directed by Jean-Marie Serreau; setting by Sine. (Photo by Bernand.)

or explained. Nevertheless, according to Ionesco, even a hint that the world is absurd terrifies the average person, who seeks to reassure himself with material objects, comforting clichés of speech, or rigid ideologies. For Ionesco, the only true solutions are to recognize the need to resist conformity and to go on despite the knowledge that we must all disappear into the void.

The New Tenant develops several themes typical of Ionesco's plays. First, it shows how language has been reduced to empty clichés; rather than being a medium for ideas, it is a way of avoiding thought. A second theme is the displacement of human beings by material objects. In The New Tenant not only is this the dominant motif, it is also the principal action and is closely connected with a third theme—the dehumanization of man through the substitution of objects for people. It is this network of related themes that unifies the play.

The story of The New Tenant is very simple: a Gentleman arrives to claim his apartment, has a brief discussion with the Caretaker, and then supervises two movers who gradually fill the room with furniture and then leave him alone in it. There are no complications, crises, or resolutions in the traditional sense. Rather, themes are introduced and concretized.

The New Tenant includes only four characters: the Caretaker, the Gentleman, and two furniture movers. As their designations suggest, they are not individuals so much as types.

The Caretaker epitomizes the qualities associated with the concierge, whose task it is to oversee the apartment-house domain placed under her charge. She is both obsequious (because she hopes to get something from the Gentleman) and tyrannical (because she is in a position to make life difficult for those who live in her building); she is willing to say whatever she thinks the Gentleman wants to hear, even if it contradicts what she has just said; and, when crossed, she is equally ready to make the most outrageous accusations.

The Gentleman epitomizes middle-class propriety. His manner is reserved and businesslike; at times he can be forceful, especially in rejecting human contacts and in protecting his possessions. In him positive feeling is reserved for things. He speaks only when it is essential and says no more than is necessary.

No information is given about the age or appearance of the two furniture movers, but it is clear that in performance they must contrast sufficiently to be instantly distinguishable. Their primary function is to fill the stage with furniture.

In The New Tenant, spectacle is probably the most important element, for the play is a visualization of how material objects fill space that should be occupied by people. The style of production is summed up in Ionesco's prefatory note: "The action ought to be, in the beginning, very realistic, as should the setting and, later, the furniture that will be brought in. Then the rhythm, almost unnoticed, should imperceptibly impart to the play a certain ritualistic character. Realism should prevail, once more, in the final scene."

As this suggests, in the beginning everything seems completely natural. Only when the furniture begins to arrive does the sense of everyday reality alter. The first change is manifested in the movers' manner of handling objects: straining every muscle in carrying small vases, but moving heavy pieces of furniture with ease. At first the movers work as a team, but then they establish an alternating pattern as one goes out and the other returns; eventually they exit through one door only to return almost immediately, as if on a turntable, through another on the opposite side of the stage. Finally, the furniture begins to enter under its own power. Once the new situation—the dominance of matter—is fully established and accepted, the style becomes realistic again.

The New Tenant has been produced less often than others of Ionesco's plays, probably because of the enormous demands made by spectacle. Nevertheless, it is an excellent example of absurdist vision and method.

RELATED DRAMATISTS

The absurdist mode was to affect the theatre of almost every country. It had a great vogue in West Germany, where French absurdist plays received their greatest number of productions. Nevertheless, few Germans wrote in this style. In England, such early plays as *The Room* (1957) and *The Dumb Waiter* (1957) by Harold Pinter are often called absurdist; and in America Edward Albee's *The American Dream* (1960) and Arthur Kopit's *Oh Dad, Poor Dad, Mama's Hung You in the Closet and I'm Feeling So Sad* (1960) are often placed in this category.

In Eastern Europe, absurdism enjoyed great popularity after Stalinism was denounced in 1956. Many plays from this area have strong political overtones. In Czechoslovakia, for example, Vaclav Havel (1936–   ) launched bitingly satirical attacks on bureaucracy in *The Garden Party* (1963) and *The Memorandum* (1965). In Poland, Slawomir Mrozek (1930–   ) followed a similar path with such plays as *The Police* (1958). He is best known for *Tango* (1965), a parable which suggests that when moral values decline only power remains and that those most willing to exercise it ruthlessly become the rulers of the world.

By the 1960s absurdism had been so widely disseminated that its techniques were being used by those who did not share its philosophical biases. Thus, though its strength waned, it was partially assimilated into other movements.

237

THE ENGLISH REVIVAL

While absurdism was at its peak in France, English drama also began to be revitalized. This resurgence owes most to the English Stage Company (often called the Royal Court after the theatre in which it performs), founded in 1956 by George Devine (1910–1966). Its production in 1956 of John Osborne's (1929–   ) *Look Back in Anger* is usually considered the beginning of the revival. Osborne's play focuses on Jimmy Porter and his dissatisfactions with the class system and the widespread indifference to suffering. It captured the rebellious mood of the time so well that Jimmy came to symbolize the "angry young man."

The English Stage Company has continued to be the principal champion of new playwrights in England. Among its early writers, some of the best known are John Arden (1930–   ), who achieved his greatest success with *Sergeant Musgrave's Dance* (1959), in which a group of men set out to teach a town a lesson about the wastefulness of aggression by killing local residents in turn for those slaughtered abroad, and Arnold Wesker (1932–   ), who in such plays as *Chicken Soup with Barley* (1958) and *The Kitchen* (1958) argues that the working classes have settled for too little and have erred because they have not taken collective action. Although Osborne, Arden, and Wesker continue to write, their recent works have attracted little favorable attention.

Among the English Stage Company's later writers, Bond and Storey have been outstanding. Edward Bond (1935–   ) is one of England's most controversial dramatists because of such plays as *Saved* (1965), in which a baby is stoned to death in its carriage, and *Lear* (1971), a variation on Shakespeare's play. Bond's other works include *The Sea* (1973), *Bingo* (1973), *The Fool* (1975), and *The Woman* (1978). In all of his dramas, Bond is concerned with depicting a world in which the absence of love and compassion have bred a callousness so complete that horror is accepted as normality.

David Storey (1933–   ), in such plays as *The Contractor* (1970), *Home* (1970), *The Changing Room* (1971), and *Life Class* (1974), shows enormous concern for realistic detail. But beneath the surface, he is always concerned with various kinds of alienation: class from class, person from person, man from himself.

In addition to the English Stage Company, the Theatre Workshop played a major role in the dramatic revival. Founded in 1945 by Joan Littlewood (1914–   ) to produce relevant plays for working-class audiences, the Workshop settled in the east London suburb, Stratford, in 1953. In her attempt to make the theatre a place as appealing as fun palaces and penny arcades, Miss Littlewood drew on Brecht and Stanislavsky but above all on popular entertainments. The Theatre Workshop contributed to the dramatic revival primarily through the work of two

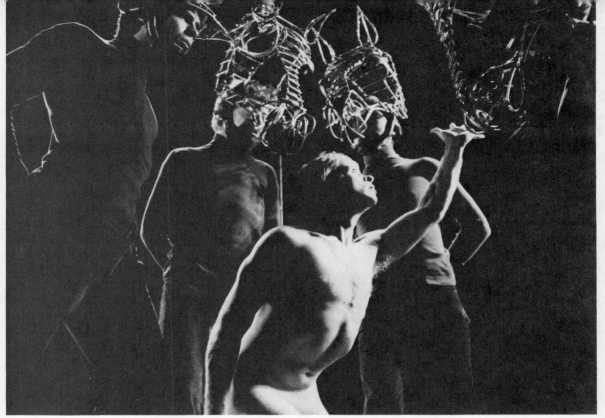

Peter Shaffer's *Equus.* (1974) (Jan A. Wein/FPG)

writers—Brendan Behan (1923–1964) with *The Quare Fellow* and *The Hostage,* and Shelagh Delaney (1939–   ) with *A Taste of Honey.* But the Workshop's greatest success was won with *Oh, What a Lovely War!* (1963), a satirical commentary on World War I done primarily through routines reminiscent of music halls. Though the Workshop still exists, it ceased to be a vital force in English theatrical life in the 1960s.

Because of the support given by the English Stage Company, the Theatre Workshop, and others, competent English playwrights have appeared in considerable number since the late 1950s. Two of the best have been Peter Shaffer (1926–   ) with *The Royal Hunt of the Sun* (1964) and *Equus* (1974) and Tom Stoppard (1937–   ) with *Rosencrantz and Guildenstern Are Dead* (1967), *Jumpers* (1972), *Travesties* (1974), and *Night and Day* (1978).

But of all contemporary English dramatists the most admired has been Harold Pinter (1930–   ), who began his playwriting career in 1957 with *The Room* and continued with such words as *The Dumb Waiter* (1957), *The Birthday Party* (1959), *The Caretaker* (1960), *The Homecoming* (1965), *Old Times* (1971), *No Man's Land* (1975), and *Betrayal* 1978). Although there is much variety among these plays, they share a few characteristics. Almost everything that happens could occur in real life; sometimes the situations and dialogue even suggest naturalism. Neverthe-

239

less, the overall impression is of ambiguity and mystery, primarily because the motivations of the characters are never fully revealed. Most of Pinter's plays occur within the confined space of a single room, where out of quite ordinary events crises arise that force the characters to face their anxieties or inner nature. But often the significance of the dramatic action remains uncertain because so many questions are left unresolved.

Of Pinter's "comedies of menace," *The Birthday Party* is typical. The central character, Stanley, lives in a boardinghouse, where he is mothered by his landlady. Then two men arrive, subject Stanley to intense cross-examination, during which they accuse him of a variety of contradictory acts, and organize a birthday party for him although he insists that it is not his birthday. The next morning they take him away. It is unclear who has sent them or what they intend to do with Stanley. But it is this uncertainty that makes the play so disturbing.

Of the later works, *The Homecoming* is usually considered the best. In it, Teddy (a philosophy professor in an American university) arrives with his wife, Ruth, to visit his family in London. Soon the men in the family suggest that Ruth remain with them as a prostitute; after haggling over the arrangements, she agrees and Teddy calmly returns to America. The dialogue and action seem wholly natural, but the play remains mysterious because so little is revealed about the past or the characters' motivations.

As a dramatist, Pinter seems to fall somewhere between the absurdists and Chekhov. Like the former, he isolates his characters in an unverifiable universe; like Chekhov, he creates a realistic texture of background and dialogue in which both speech and deed are evasions or disguises of deeper conflicts and anxieties.

MAJOR ENGLISH COMPANIES

In addition to its many fine playwrights, the vitality of England's theatre owes much to two groups—the Royal Shakespeare Company and the National Theatre. In 1961, the Memorial Theatre at Stratford was renamed the Royal Shakespeare Company (RSC), recognition that was largely owing to Peter Hall (1930–   ). Upon being named head of the company in 1960, Hall took a lease on the Aldwych Theatre in London and transformed the troupe into a year-round (rather than a summer) operation. Thereafter it divided its program between Stratford and London and produced works from various periods and countries. By 1965 the RSC had become one of the world's finest and most innovative troupes. The Aldwych also became the home of the World Theatre Season, where after 1964 major companies from throughout the world came for brief engagements.

Of the RSC's directors, Peter Brook (1925–   ) was to be the most influential. He began directing while still in his teens and gradually built an outstanding reputation with productions of plays by such authors as Shakespeare, Duerrenmatt, and Genet and with an experimental "Theatre of Cruelty" season done with the RSC in 1963–1964. He is especially well known for his productions of *King Lear* (1962), *Marat/Sade* (1964), *The Tempest* (1968), and *A Midsummer Night's Dream* (1970). Brook is extremely eclectic, borrowing from many sources but always achieving individuality. For example, in *A Midsummer Night's Dream* he drew on Meyerhold, commedia dell'arte, circus, and radical theatre groups of the 1960s, but the results were uniquely his own. Many of his ideas on directing are set forth in his *The Empty Stage* (1968).

In 1971 Brook became director of the International Center for Theatre Research, based in Paris and including participants from all over the world. Here Brook has experimented with acting and directing devices and techniques capable of transcending barriers created by language and culture. His company has also toured much of the world. Without doubt, Brook is now one of the world's most respected directors.

In 1963, England inaugurated its National Theatre. At that time the Old Vic's company was dissolved and its building assigned to the new troupe, under the direction of Laurence Olivier (succeeded in 1973 by

The interior of the Olivier Theatre at the new National Theatre in London. (Photo Donald Mill, courtesy National Theatre)

Peter Hall). Through an extremely varied repertory staged by the most eminent English and foreign directors and designers, the National Theatre rapidly built a reputation for excellence. In 1976 the company moved into its new building, one of the most advanced theatre plants anywhere. It includes three performance spaces: the 890-seat Lyttleton proscenium theatre; the 1160-seat Olivier open-stage theatre; and the 400-seat Cottesloe laboratory theatre.

Outside London there are about fifty resident companies, many of them excellent and practically all subsidized by local governments. Within London there are a large number of "fringe" groups (comparable to American Off-Off-Broadway companies). These groups perform in pubs, meeting halls, playgrounds, schools, or almost anywhere, and at lunch time and late at night as well as more traditional times.

England also has a number of young writers who promise to keep the stage vital. Among the best are Christopher Hampton, David Hare, Trevor Griffiths, and Stephen Poliakoff. Taken as a whole, the English theatre is one of the liveliest anywhere, although like that of many other countries it has been sorely tried by economic inflation.

GERMAN THEATRE AND DRAMA

After World War II Germany was slow to produce significant new dramatists, perhaps because the Nazi era had destroyed so much potential talent. At first, the major German-language dramatists were the Swiss authors Max Frisch (1911–   ) and Friedrich Duerrenmatt (1921–   ). Frisch's reputation rests primarily upon *The Chinese Wall* (1946), *Biedermann and the Firebugs* (1958), and *Andorra* (1961), all posing questions of guilt. In each, as the past is reviewed the characters construct elaborate rationalizations to justify their cowardly actions. Duerrenmatt's fame is based primarily upon *The Visit* (1956) and *The Physicists* (1962). Like Frisch, Duerrenmatt is concerned with moral responsibility. He has stated that plays should frighten audiences and make them face up to the grotesque world in which they live, although the most they can hope for is the courage to endure. Frisch and Duerrenmatt also established the direction that most German drama was to follow thereafter until the 1970s: the exploration of guilt and responsibility.

The best-known German plays of the 1960s—usually called documentary drama or "the theatre of fact"—coupled probing moral questions with subject matter taken from actual occurrences. Among the writers of this form, the best known have been Hochhuth, Kipphardt, and Weiss.

Rolf Hochhuth (1931–   ) came to prominence in 1963 with *The Deputy,* a play that seeks to place much of the blame for the extermi-

Final scene from Friedrich Duerrenmatt's *The Physicists,* as performed at Indiana University. Directed by Gary Gaiser; designed by Richard Scammon. (Indiana University)

nation of German Jews on Pope Piux XII because he did not take a decisive stand against German policies. This was followed by *The Soldiers* (1967), which suggests that Winston Churchill acquiesced in the death of General Sikorski, President of the Polish government in exile, so as not to endanger Anglo-Russian relationships. Heinar Kipphardt (1922–   ) is noted primarily for *In the Matter of J. Robert Oppenheimer* (1964), based on the United States government's hearings into the loyalty of the scientist after he resisted development of the hydrogen bomb.

Somewhat similarly, Peter Weiss (1916–   ) in *The Investigation* (1965) uses as dialogue excerpts from testimony given at the inquiry into Auschwitz, where thousands of German Jews were exterminated by the Nazis during World War II. The best-known of Weiss' plays is *The Persecution and Assassination of Jean-Paul Marat as Performed by the Inmates of the Asylum of Charenton under the Direction of the Marquis de Sade* (usually called *Marat/Sade,* 1964).

MARAT/SADE

Marat/Sade is a play within a play. The main action takes place in 1808 in the asylum of Charenton, where the Marquis de Sade is confined and composes dramas that are performed by the patients for the amusement of a fashionable audience from nearby Paris. On this occasion, de Sade presents his play about the assassination by Charlotte Corday in 1793 of Jean-Paul Marat, a leader of the French Revolution.

Marat/Sade is grounded in historical fact: de Sade was confined at Charenton and he did write and present plays there; the material relating to the French Revolution is also based on fact, though some parts have been altered. Weiss uses this material much as Brecht might, for, though ostensibly writing about France in the years between 1790 and 1808.

The Persecution and Assassination of Jean Paul Marat as Performed by the Inmates of the Asylum of Charenton under the Direction of the Marquis de Sade (usually called *Marat/Sade*), written in 1964 by Peter Weiss. This Royal Shakespeare Company production, directed by Peter Brook, was considered to be an example of Artaud's "Theatre of Cruelty." The principal actors seen here are Patrick Magee, Glenda Jackson, and Ian Richardson. (Jessie Alexander/Nancy Palmer Photo Agency)

Weiss is ultimately concerned about our own times. Just as de Sade in his play looks back on events that have occurred fifteen or more years earlier, so Weiss is looking back on recent bloodbaths, purges, and wars, and he suggests that we are now reassuring ourselves that we have been freed from such barbarities. This idea is pointed up by the Herald's reassurance that these "barbarous displays . . . could not happen nowadays. The men of that time . . . were primitive, we are more civilized."

Weiss' major concerns are summed up in the continuing argument between de Sade and Marat. The former argues that the strong always beat down the weak, that man is essentially selfish, and that it is useless to try to better man's lot. Marat argues that, rather than being paralyzed by conditions, we should invent meanings, help men to overcome selfishness, and learn mutual respect.

The structure of *Marat/Sade* also owes much to Brecht. It is divided into short scenes, each separately titled. Various devices are also used to alienate the spectator from the action: historification; the asylum setting; the play within a play; the Herald who announces scenes; songs that comment on the action; and frequent interruptions and interpolations by various characters. The play is unified in part by the use of historical material and the asylum setting, but most of all by ideas and themes.

Characterization is at once simple and complex: simple because, except for de Sade and Marat, the personages are largely one-dimensional; complex because the play within the play is performed by patients and thus the actors playing these roles must present de Sade's characters without losing sight of the patients' aberrations.

Ultimately the play owes much of its success to spectacle and background action. The setting is an antiseptic room used for baths and massages. The patients not involved in de Sade's play create the appropriate atmosphere through such behavior as hopping about, muttering, screaming, and so on. The patients are kept in order by male nurses with the "appearance of butchers" and by nuns (played by athletic-looking men). The potential of these elements encourages the use of Artaudian techniques, and it was in large part because of them that Peter Brook's production in London and New York was considered by most critics a major example of the "theatre of cruelty."

Perhaps most important, the spectacle becomes a metaphor for the world about which de Sade and Marat argue, one in which the representatives of power keep an eye on any tendency of the people to become restless.

Marat/Sade, with its blend of Brechtian and Artaudian modes, was one of the most successful plays of the decade, and it did much to popularize the approach that was to dominate the 1960s: embedding moral, social, and political themes within highly theatricialized and Artaudian elements.

TRENDS IN DOCUMENTARY DRAMA

Documentary drama made considerable impact in almost every country. As examples one might cite in France Jean Vilar's *The Oppenheimer Dossier* (1965), written out of unhappiness with Kipphardt's play on the same subject; in England, Peter Brook's work on Vietnam, *US* (1967); and in America numerous plays dealing with such incidents as the massacre at My Lai, the *Pueblo* incident, and the trial of the Catonsville Nine. Almost any actual event came to be considered potential material for stage treatment.

The theatre of fact raised a number of ethical issues. Many documentary plays brought public figures onto the stage and attributed immoral or criminal motives to them entirely on the basis of speculation. In such instances, where does poetic license end and libel begin? Much documentary drama was also so partisan as to lose all claim to objectivity. Perhaps for these reasons, the popularity of documentary drama waned for a time, although under the impact of Watergate and similar events it seems to have revived, especially in film and television.

RECENT TRENDS IN GERMAN THEATRE

In Germany during the 1970s, writers seemed to weary of the theme (guilt and responsibility) that had dominated since World War II. Perhaps for this reason, the most admired playwright in Germany now is Peter Handke (1942–   ), who since 1966 has been writing plays that explore the nature of reality and the way language affects behavior. His most popular work has been *Kaspar* (1968), in which a young man who has been brought up in total isolation and without speech is gradually reduced to conformity through language; at the end he is indistinguishable from a host of almost identical figures. In such plays as *The Ride Across Lake Constance* (1971) and *They Are Dying Out* (1974) Handke has explored how human beings are brutalized by language and behavior that reduces everything to uniformity.

In the late 1960s the German theatre was faced by several crises. The source of greatest unhappiness was the almost unlimited power of theatre managers. Actors in several cities demanded a voice in the theatre's affairs. This crisis was met in several ways. Some cities appointed a triumvirate of directors, others a six-member directorate; some adopted a scheme under which every member of a company had to be consulted on all major policy decisions, although the administrative work was left to a small group; in a few instances, communes were formed.

Such controversies raised questions as to whether West Germany needed all of its more than eighty companies that performed on 200

Christopher Lloyd in a scene from the Chelsea Theatre Center's electronic production of Peter Handke's *Kaspar,* directed by Carl Weber. Note the closed-circuit television receivers at top. (Chelsea Theatre Center of Brooklyn)

stages. Inflationary prices created still other problems, especially since in West Germany government subsidies account for approximately eighty percent of all production costs. Threats of closures motivated several schemes for exchanging productions and personnel, sharing information and publicity, and exploring other forms of cooperation.

Overall, the German theatre in the late 1970s was still healthy, but there were signs of changes to come, perhaps most noticeably in the return to a more conservative repertory and a greater concern for entertaining rather than indoctrinating audiences.

247

FRENCH THEATRE AND DRAMA SINCE THE 1960S

After 1960, France declined in influence because few new writers attracted an international following. Perhaps the best was Fernando Arrabal (1932–   ), a native of Spain but a resident of France since 1955.

Arrabal's early plays, such as *The Automobile Graveyard* (1958), tend to emphasize childish and thoughtless cruelty and to employ techniques popularized by the absurdists. Around 1962, Arrabal renounced his earlier approach and declared his concern for a *théâtre panique,* a "ceremony — partly sacrilegious, partly sacred, erotic and mystic . . . part Don Quixote and part Alice in Wonderland." Among Arrabal's later works are *The Architect and the Emperor of Assyria* (1967), *And They Handcuffed the Flowers* (1970), and *Young Barbarians Today* (1975). The first is perhaps the best known. In it two characters enact a series of ritualized situations: master and slave, mother and child, judge and criminal, male and female, and so on. Eventually one is killed and eaten by the other, but then a new figure appears and the process begins all over again. Through such plays Arrabal has called virtually all values and relationships into question and has ferreted out the hidden corners of the human psyche.

During the 1960s decentralization of the theatre continued to be a policy of the French government. In addition to dramatic centers (or regional troupes serving specific areas of the country), it also promoted the concept of municipal cultural centers (*maisons de la culture*) and helped to finance buildings for them, a policy that is still in effect.

During the 1960s, Roger Planchon (1931–   ) came to be considered France's foremost director. In 1957 Planchon founded the Théâtre

A scene from Roger Planchon's production of *Les Folies Bourgeoises.* (Courtesy of French Cultural Services)

de la Cité in Villeurbanne, a suburb of Lyons, where he sought to attract a working-class audience with productions that drew heavily on cinematic and Brechtian techniques. His repertory included plays by Molière, Shakespeare, Racine, and others, but he gave all a proletarian slant. In the early 1970s, Planchon's achievement was acknowledged when the government designated his company the Théâtre National Populaire, a title previously held by a Paris-based troupe.

Like other countries, France has a large number of "alternative" theatres. Perhaps the best known of these is the Grand Magic Circus, headed by Jerome Savary, who first attracted wide favorable attention in 1970 with *Zartan,* "the story of Tarzan's deprived brother," a work described by Savary as the "marvelous story of colonialism from the Middle Ages to the present." He has also produced *The Last Days of Solitude of Robinson Crusoe,* the story of a modern Everyman freed from loneliness and passivity, *From Moses to Mao,* and *Adventures in Love.* But, though Savary's productions comment on social issues, he does not consider this their primary function. Rather, he sees theatre as a "life show"—an excuse for people to come together in joyful celebration. His troupe plays on beaches, in parks, hospitals, and elsewhere, and utilizes techniques associated with children's theatre, circus, and carnivals; there is considerable give and take between audience and performers (but all goodnatured), and the productions are noted for their acrobatic feats, improvisations, and stunning visual effects.

In recent years the French theatre has been plagued by controversies over financial problems, the manner in which subsidies are distributed, and government attempts to shape artistic policies. Although it is still excellent in many respects, France's theatre today does not command the international respect it enjoyed in the 1950s.

BROADWAY

In America, continuously rising costs after 1960 made production on Broadway increasingly risky. By the mid-1970s it cost about $200,000 to mount a one-set dramatic show, while musicals were approaching one million dollars and having to play for more than a year to recover the initial investment. Perhaps for this reason, the 1970s brought attempts (in such musicals as *Company* and *Chorus Line*) to make the principals and the chorus one and the same.

The only new American author of serious plays to win and sustain a high critical reputation on Broadway since 1960 has been Edward Albee (1928–   ). On the basis of his first plays, among them *The Zoo Story* (1958) and *The American Dream* (1960), many critics labeled Albee an absurdist. Then in 1962, with *Who's Afraid of Virginia Woolf?*, his first full-length and most successful play, Albee demonstrated his likeness to Strindberg and Williams with a work about characters who use psycholo-

Edward Albee's first full-length and most successful play, *Who's Afraid of Virginia Woolf?* This photo is of the revival of the play in 1976 which was directed by Albee himself and starred Colleen Dewhurst and Ben Gazzara. (Theatre and Music Collection, Museum of the City of New York)

gical blackmail as their primary tool for dealing with others. In it, two college professors and their wives, during a night spent in drinking and playing cruel games, strip each other of illusions and demonstrate how people create hells for each other out of unwillingness to accept or admit weakness. Since 1962 Albee has written such plays as *Tiny Alice* (1964), *A Delicate Balance* (1966), *All Over* (1971), and *Seascape* (1975), most of them moral parables with a tendency to become overly abstract. For example, *Seascape* suggests that human beings have lost all vitality and that the future belongs to other creatures as they discover love and consideration.

Broadway's shortcomings have prompted many schemes for diversifying the American theatre. Among these has been an attempt to establish permanent companies in New York like those found in major European cities. Consequently, around 1960 plans were launched for the Lincoln Center for the Performing Arts, with facilities for ballet, opera, concerts, and drama. In 1963 a repertory company was formed and in 1965 it moved into the newly completed Vivian Beaumont Theatre in Lincoln Center. Unfortunately, despite a number of changes in management, this theatre has never won high critical praise or strong audience support. Its potential has yet to be realized.

Although Broadway has declined considerably in importance as a producer of new plays, it remains the primary home of America's commercial theatre. In the early 1970s it underwent a considerable slump but since the season of 1974–75 it has recorded the highest box office sales in its history.

OFF-BROADWAY AND OFF-OFF-BROADWAY

In the early 1960s many of the financial pressures that had plagued Broadway began to be felt Off-Broadway. Out of the need to escape these strictures came a new solution—Off-Off-Broadway. The beginning of this trend is usually dated from 1958, when Joe Cino began to welcome various artistic activities into his Café Cino. By the early 1960s groups were performing in all sorts of spaces and under all sorts of circumstances, and by 1965 about four hundred new plays by two hundred new playwrights had been presented by such groups.

Perhaps the most important of the Off-Off-Broadway producers has been the LaMama organization, founded in 1961 by Ellen Stewart. By 1970 LaMama was presenting more plays each season than were seen in all Broadway theatres combined. The LaMama organization also exerted so much influence abroad through tours that it was invited to establish branches in several cities scattered throughout the world. Miss Stewart's primary concern has been to encourage playwrights, and in her theatres have been seen some of the most determinedly innovative contemporary works.

The free-ranging experimentation encouraged in playwriting by Off-Off-Broadway groups also extended to directorial techniques. The results are probably best seen in the work of Tom O'Horgan, who created a stir on Broadway in 1968 with *Hair, Futz,* and *Tom Paine,* and later with *Lenny* and *Jesus Christ, Superstar.* O'Horgan placed primary emphasis on physical activity, lighting effects, amplified music, nonverbal sound, and anti-illusionistic devices of all sorts. His productions were usually colorful and uninhibited, but they also tended to obscure story and idea. Nevertheless, his "physicalization" of dramatic elements has become typical of much directing in recent years, in part because so much contemporary drama is verbally inarticulate.

In the 1970s LaMama has been concerned with developing ensemble companies, some of them ethnic (Black, Puerto Rican, and Native American). The best known of LaMama's recent directors has been Andrei Serban, who has worked with mythic material, invented language, and ritualized action to create productions of great emotional impact in *Medea, The Trojan Women,* and *Electra.* Beginning in 1977, Serban worked with other companies and adapted his techniques in staging such plays as *The Cherry Orchard, Agamemnon,* and *The Ghost Sonata.*

A good example of Andrei Serban's use of ritualized action and of his unique directing techniques may be seen in this scene from the 1977 Lincoln Center production of *The Cherry Orchard.* (Photo by George E. Joseph)

Since the late 1960s the differences between Off-Broadway and Off-Off-Broadway theatres have been so eroded that the two are now often indistinguishable. Among these theatres some of the most important are the Circle in the Square, the American Place Theatre, the Chelsea Theatre Center, the Circle Repertory Company, and the Manhattan Theatre Club.

But the most important of the groups is the New York Shakespeare Festival Theatre, headed by Joseph Papp (1921–   ). After a modest beginning in the 1950s, Papp was able to persuade municipal authorities to let him stage plays in Central Park. This program became so popular that in 1962 the city built an amphitheatre for it. In 1967 Papp acquired the former Astor Library and transformed it into the Public Theatre, with five auditoriums. Many of his productions moved to Broadway, among them Rabe's *Sticks and Bones,* Miller's *That Championship Season,* Shakespeare's *Much Ado about Nothing* and *Two Gentlemen of Verona,* Bennett's *A Chorus Line,* Shange's *For Colored Girls,* and Swados' *Runaways.* From 1973 until 1977 Papp also headed the Lincoln Center Repertory Theatre. With his activities now centered at the Public Theatre, he is probably the most influential force in New York's theatre today.

Off-Broadway and Off-Off-Broadway exerted their greatest influence through their innovative playwrights. Although the accomplishments of these writers as individuals have not been great, as a group they have done much to alter ideas about dramatic structure and to encourage disaffection from accepted life styles. Most of their plays are organized around themes or motifs rather than causally related incidents; characterization is most usually reduced to types; ideas are typically presented through sharply

Joseph Papp persuaded the city of New York to allow him to stage plays in Central Park. In 1962, the Delacorte Theatre, a permanent amphitheatre was built for these successful productions. (George E. Joseph)

Ain't Misbehavin, a musical originally produced Off-Broadway, later moved to Broadway, where it attracted a large audience. (Martha Swope)

253

contrasting (often oversimplified) positions; language is generally down-graded in favor of aural and visual appeals, both of which are exploited extensively. Overall, the trend has been away from realism toward frank theatricality.

The writers who contributed to these changes are too numerous to list. Some of the most successful have been: Sam Shepard, with *The Tooth of Crime, Suicide in B-flat, Seduced,* and *Buried Child;* Rochelle Owens, with *Futz* and *The Queen of Greece;* Paul Foster, with *Tom Paine;* Terrence McNally, with *Sweet Eros* and *Next;* Lanford Wilson, with *The Rimers of Eldritch, Hot L Baltimore,* and *The Mound Builders;* Israel Horowitz, with *The Indian Wants the Bronx* and *Line;* Ronald Ribman, with *Harry, Noon and Night, The Ceremony of Innocence,* and *Cold Storage;* and Robert Patrick with *Kennedy's Children* and *Play by Play.*

BLACK THEATRE

A development related to Off-Broadway was the appearance during the 1960s of a strong black theatre movement. It received its first significant impetus in 1964, when LeRoi Jones and others founded the Black Arts Repertoire Theatre School in New York. This organization soon came to an end, but it inspired others, and by the late 1960s there were more than forty black arts groups in the country. Three of these—the Negro Ensemble Company, the New Lafayette Theatre, and the Spirit House—were of special importance in encouraging playwrights and other organizations.

This upsurge in theatrical activity brought a corresponding increase in the demand for black actors (among the best of whom were James Earl Jones, Ruby Dee, Diana Sands, Claudia McNeill, Ossie Davis, Roscoe Lee Brown, Moses Gunn, Robert Hooks, Ron O'Neal, and Cicely Tyson) and directors (among them Lloyd Richards, Robert Macbeth, Melvin van Peebles, and Michael Schultz).

The number of black dramatists also steadily grew. Among the first to win critical acclaim was Lorraine Hansberry (1930–1965) with *A Raisin in the Sun* (1959) and *The Sign in Sidney Brustein's Window* (1964). The first of these will be examined in detail as an example of black drama.

A RAISIN IN THE SUN

A Raisin in the Sun was the first play by a black woman to be presented on Broadway, where it won the New York Drama Critics Circle Award.

In many respects *A Raisin in the Sun* is traditional, since, like many American dramas, it focuses on the family unit and its dreams. Its straight-forward story is developed through a clear cause-and-effect sequence of

A scene from the original production of *A Raisin in the Sun* at the Ethel Barrymore Theatre in New York, with Claudia McNeil, Sidney Poitier, and Diana Sands. Directed by Lloyd Richards; scenery and lighting by Ralph Alswang. (Jos. Abeles Studio)

exposition, complications, climactic reversal, and denouement. It is divided into three acts, all of which take place in the same setting. Its overall style is realistic with a generous sprinkling of humor in a primarily serious plot.

Plot and Structure. *A Raisin in the Sun* tells the story of the Younger family: the matriarchal Lena, or Mama, a dignified woman in her sixties; Beneatha, her twenty-year-old daughter who hopes to become a doctor; Walter, Lena's thirty-five-year-old son, a chauffeur; Ruth, Walter's wife, who does domestic work for white women; and Travis, the ten-year-old son of Walter and Ruth. All live together on the south side of Chicago in a cramped two-bedroom apartment. There is only one small window for light and air, and the bathroom is shared by all the families on the floor. But, though the space is cramped and the furnishings worn, the apartment is clean and neat; thus, the setting reflects its occupants, who may be poor but are not without pride.

The opening scene of the play introduces the family as they anticipate the arrival of a check of $10,000, the life insurance of the deceased father. To the family the money represents a chance to realize its dreams, the most crucial of which are Beneatha's desire to attend medical school and

Walter's to become a businessman. In the second scene, the money arrives, but by that time friction is beginning to tear the family apart. The opposition of Mama and Ruth to Walter's plan to invest in a liquor store alienates him so fully that Ruth, upon discovering that she is pregnant, makes an appointment to have an illegal abortion.

In Act Two, scene one, Mama, in an attempt to bring her family together, makes a down payment of $3500 on a house that can accommodate everyone comfortably. But it seems certain that trouble lies ahead because the house is located in an all-white neighborhood. Nevertheless, everyone except Walter is overjoyed, for the house will permit them to escape their present environment.

Not until a few weeks later (in Act Two, scene two), when the family is packing to move, does Mama come to understand Walter's deep need to be recognized as a man capable of making his own decisions. As a result, she designates him head of the family and gives him the remaining money with the stipulation that $3000 be put aside for Beneatha's medical education. As the scene closes, Walter, overjoyed, is envisioning his future as an executive.

Act Two, scene three, brings the play's major reversal. Karl Lindner, a white representative of the neighborhood into which the Youngers plan to move, arrives to tell the family of resentment against them and to offer them a sum substantially higher than they have paid for the house. They indignantly refuse. Then Walter learns that one of his prospective business partners has absconded with all the money Mama gave him, including that intended for Beneatha's education. The act ends in despair and recrimination.

At the opening of Act Three, Beneatha is cynical and ready to abandon her dreams. The family is reconciled to remaining in the apartment. But Walter slips out and calls Lindner, intending to sell the new house and play the role of "polite darky" for a white-dominated world. When his plan is revealed, the family is horrified. Lindner arrives just as the moving van does (no one has canceled it), but Walter, forced by Mama to talk to Lindner with Travis present, cannot bring himself to go through with his plan. Recovering his pride, he tells Lindner that the family wants no trouble but insists on moving into its new home. As the play ends, the move is underway. Thus, although the family has realized few of its dreams, it has grown in understanding, dignity, and unity.

Themes and Ideas. Many features place *A Raisin in the Sun* firmly within the American tradition, but others set it apart. Perhaps most significantly, with one exception, all of the characters are black, and their experiences introduce almost every major theme that would be developed extensively by later black playwrights.

The play's title is taken from a work by Langston Hughes, *Montage of a Dream Deferred:* "What happens to a dream deferred? / Does it dry up / Like a raisin in the sun?" Almost everything that happens in the play is related to this concept of the "dream deferred." We learn that Mama and her husband were part of the "great migration" during the early twentieth century when blacks moved north in search of better conditions. But Walter and Beneatha are more concerned about what remains to be done than about what has been accomplished. Of the two, Walter is the more embittered, for as chauffeur to a rich white man he daily sees wealth that lies beyond his reach. Consequently, he all too eagerly leaps at the chance to acquire his own business as the first step toward riches, which he considers the key to happiness. Beneatha, on the other hand, wants to become a doctor so she can ease human suffering, although it is injustice that ultimately bothers her. It one sense, then, Walter represents the selfish and materialistic approach and Beneatha the altruistic and idealistic approach to realizing the dream deferred.

A closely related issue is integration versus separation of the races. This theme is dramatized in part through Beneatha's two suitors—the rich American student George Murchison and the Nigerian student Joseph Asagai. George is interested only with maintaining the security his family has achieved, and he is completely unconcerned about the injustices suffered by other members of his race. Joseph, on the other hand, arouses Beneatha's interest in her African heritage, questions the way she dresses (he calls her straightened hair "mutilated" and he brings her a Nigerian robe), and asks her to return to Africa with him. Above all, in the final act Joseph counters Beneatha's disillusionment by arguing the necessity of living one's dream despite suffering and disappointment.

The theme of integration and separation is also dramatized in the purchase of the house, but the response of whites makes it part of a still larger theme—the exploitation of blacks by whites who still deny blacks full civil rights. Walter's desperation stems in part from his awareness of how many more opportunities are open to white men of his age, and Mama's purchase of the house in a white neighborhood comes about only because "them houses they put up for colored in them areas way out all seem to cost twice as much as other houses." Although there is little direct denunciation of whites (even Lindner is treated objectively), a contrast is continuously implied between exploited blacks and exploiting (or uncomprehending) whites.

Another dominant theme concerns growth and maturity. It is reflected in part by Walter's sense of being denied his manhood both by his mother and by the jobs open to him. The theme is also developed through the repeatedly expressed longing for sunlight and garden space and most forcefully by Mama's spindly plant, which she nurtures in the feeble light of the window just as she has nurtured her family's spirit through all vicissitudes. As the play ends, after everyone has left the apartment, Mama returns for her plant. This final moment implies that neither the plant nor the family will "dry up like a raisin in the sun" but will thrive and grow.

The deferred dream still has not been fully realized, but another step has been taken toward its fulfillment.

Although *A Raisin in the Sun* deals specifically with black life, it is universal in its appeal. Whatever one's race, one can sympathize with the dreams, disappointments, and triumphs of the Younger family. Without bitterness, the play makes clear the injustices done to blacks, and while it offers few solutions, it shows the human consequences of the problems.

OTHER BLACK PLAYWRIGHTS

The black writers who came after Hansberry were increasingly concerned with the injustices of a white-dominated society. Among the most important was LeRoi Jones (Imamu Amiri Baraka, 1934–   ), not only because he was one of the best dramatists of the 1960s but because he represents the trend away from concern with integration to a demand for complete separation. *The Toilet* (1964) is a good example of his early work. It shows a white boy being beaten unmercifully because he allegedly has been attracted to a black boy. Jones uses homosexuality to symbolize the kind of barriers society has erected to make it shameful for races to admit mutual love and respect. After 1965 Jones became increasingly separatist, and since then his plays have been designed either to induce hatred of whites or respect for blacks. One of the most powerful of the later plays is *Slave Ship* (1967), which traces the black experience from Africa to the present.

Scene from LeRoi Jones' *Home on the Range,* as performed at the Spirit House Movers. (© 1968 by Fred W. McDarrah)

258

Vinette Carroll's *When Hell Freezes Over I'll Skate.* (Martha Swope)

The Negro Ensemble Company has fostered the talents of several writers, among them Douglas Turner Ward, whose *Day of Absence* (1967) and *The Reckoning* (1969) use broad caricature to show blacks outwitting whites; Lonne Elder III, whose *Ceremonies in Dark Old Men* (1969) focuses on a family in Harlem and the illegal schemes they are talked into; and Joseph A. Walker, whose *The River Niger* (1972) symbolically traces the African stream flowing all the way to Harlem.

Joseph Papp produced Charles Gordone's *No Place to Be Somebody* (1969), a Pulitzer-Prize-winning drama about a black man's attempt to start his own version of the Mafia, and Ntozake Shange's *For Colored Girls Who Have Considered Suicide When the Rainbow Is Enuf* (1975), a "choreopoem" that explores black women's awareness.

One of the most important and seemingly the most prolific of black writers is Ed Bullins (1935–), for a time resident playwright at the New Lafayette Theatre and editor of *Black Theatre Magazine.* His work is varied in tone and subject but unified by its concern for what it means to be black. He is writing a lengthy cycle about life in the industrial North and West, of which *In the Wine Time* and *In New England Winter* are parts. Others of his plays include *Clara's Old Man* (1965), *The Pig Pen* (1970), and *The Taking of Miss Janie* (1975).

Other black playwrights who deserve mention include Richard Wesley, Melvin van Peebles, Ron Milner, Ossie Davis, Adrienne Kennedy, Ben Caldwell, Vinette Carrroll, and Leslie Lee. In recent years, black playwrights seem to have been moving away from defining black experience through negative pictures of whites and toward depicting blacks in

259

relation to each other. Most encouraging, black theatre and drama seem for the first time in American history to be attracting wide audiences. Many of the plays and musicals seen on Broadway in recent seasons have been by black authors. The number of black companies throughout the country has also greatly increased and are now linked by membership in the Black Theatre Alliance.

Although it is the most extensively developed, black theatre is only one example of the effort to reflect the life of minorities in America. Others who are now developing their own drama include homosexuals, women, and various ethnic groups (such as Puerto Ricans, Native Americans, and Mexican-Americans).

RESIDENT THEATRES

One of the most encouraging trends of the 1960s was a renascence of resident companies outside New York. This form of organization was revitalized in the 1950s by a few groups, most notably the Arena Stage in Washington, the Alley Theatre in Houston, and the Actors' Workshop in San Francisco. It was given a major boost in 1959 when the Ford Foundation made large grants to several existing companies that had won considerable local support. It was further strengthened by the opening of the Tyrone Guthrie Theatre in Minneapolis in 1963, since the example of a major director seeking a home outside established theatre centers led other communities to establish companies of their own. By the late 1970s there were about fifty companies, and for the first time in the twentieth century more actors were employed outside than in New York. These resident troupes, which usually mingle classics with recent works, resemble European subsidized companies more than they do Broadway. But unlike their European counterparts, which can be reasonably certain of continuing government subsidies, most American resident theatres are dependent on box-office receipts, gifts from private donors, or grants from philanthropic foundations, none of which is assured from one year to the next.

A step toward government subsidization of the arts was taken in 1965 when federal legislation established the National Endowment for the Arts to assist projects showing outstanding potential. Money was also appropriated to encourage state governments to form arts councils, most of which have now done so. Thus, larger subsidies are currently devoted to the arts in America than at any time in the past.

In recent years, resident theatres have become increasingly attractive to playwrights, since in them pressures are considerably fewer than on Broadway. Resident companies usually are not concerned with long runs, nor do they expect to succeed or fail on the basis of a single production. Most plays now presented on Broadway have been proved elsewhere,

The Alley Theatre's production of Jack Kirkland's comedy, *Tobacco Road*. (Courtesy Alley Theatre, Houston)

either in the United States or abroad. Several resident theatres have become especially helpful to writers, among them to the Arena Stage in Washington, the Long Wharf Theatre in New Haven, and the Mark Taper Forum in Los Angeles.

THE LIVING THEATRE

One of the greatest influences on the theatre of the 1960s, both in America and elsewhere, was the Living Theatre. Founded in New York in 1946 by Judith Malina (1926–   ) and Julian Beck (1925–   ), it was for many years devoted to poetic drama, although it gradually developed an interest in Brecht, Artaud, and anarchism. In 1963 the Living Theatre was forcibly closed for failure to pay taxes; from 1964 to 1968 it performed in Europe, building a large following, especially among the disaffected. It made its greatest impact with *Paradise Now* (which coincided with and seemed to epitomize the political upheavals then under way in France, America, and elsewhere).

Paradise Now (1968) begins with actors circulating among the spectators and denouncing strictures on freedom. It then continues for four or five hours, and with its final section seeks to move the audience into the streets to continue the work toward revolution begun by the play.

261

To achieve this goal, the actors had to override opposition, and consequently they challenged all real or imagined resistance, often shouting accusations and obscenities at spectators. Thus, performances became a series of confrontations. It was this aggressive behavior toward audiences, combined with its revolutionary stance, that won the Living Theatre its enormous notoriety. Both audience and actors roamed the auditorium and stage indiscriminately, and often several scenes proceeded simultaneously in various parts of the theatre. *Paradise Now* is important in part because it sought to make the audience an integral part of the action.

By 1970 the Living Theatre had begun to disintegrate, and by the time the Becks returned to the United States in 1973 the Living Theatre's popularity had markedly declined. By 1976 it was once more seeking a permanent base in Europe. But, if its influence has subsided, the Living Theatre's importance in the late 1960s cannot be denied, for probably no group was better known or more widely emulated. Of its attitudes and practices, the most influential were: downgrading language in favor of Artaudian techniques; converting all texts into political arguments; insisting on confront-

Members of the San Francisco Mime Theatre in *False Promises,* 1976. (Courtesy San Francisco Mime Troupe)

ing and overriding audiences; establishing an evangelical tone for all activities; and refusing to make any distinction between life style and theatrical style.

Many of the Living Theatre's concerns were reflected in other "radical" groups that sought to use the theatre as a weapon for social change. Among the most important of these were: the Bread and Puppet Theatre (founded by Peter Schumann in 1961 and using both actors and giant puppets to perform plays—based on the Bible or other familiar sources—demonstrating the futility of materialistic concerns); the San Francisco Mime Theatre (which since 1966 has been performing plays on civil rights, women's liberation, and similar subjects); and El Teatro Campesino (founded in 1965 by Luis Valdez to dramatize issues in the California grape pickers' strike but now a bilingual troupe concerned with the heritage and accomplishments of Mexican-Americans).

During the late 1960s, guerrilla theatre also emerged. It took advantage of public gatherings or sites to present unscheduled performances of skits designed to call attention to a specific issue. The decline in the 1970s of demonstrations and confrontations has been paralleled by a decrease in both guerrilla and radical theatre activity.

NUDITY AND OBSCENITY

The numerous assaults made during the 1960s on accepted traditions and standards led to a gradual lessening of strictures on acceptable subject matter, dress, and speech for the stage. The changes are perhaps most graphically demonstrated by the introduction of nudity and obscenity.

The first notable use of nudity came in 1968 in the Broadway production of *Hair*. Obscene language was also sprinkled liberally throughout the play. Both innovations created considerable controversy in America and elsewhere as productions of *Hair* were mounted in various other countries.

Hair's use of nudity and obscenity was soon taken up and considerably extended by such productions as *Che!* and *Oh! Calcutta!*. By the 1970s, though the limits of permissibility were still somewhat vague, almost any subject, behavior, or manner of speaking was potentially acceptable for theatrical use.

GROTOWSKI

During the 1960s a number of persons deplored the tendency of the theatre to borrow from other media and advocated the abandonment of every element not truly required. The outstanding exponent of this view was Jerzy Grotowski (1933–   ), director of the Polish Laboratory Theatre in Wroclaw (Breslau). Grotowski called his a "poor theatre" because he sought to eliminate all technological aids and to concentrate on the two indispensable elements: the actor and the audience. For his productions he used a space that could be rearranged to meet the specific needs of each production; makeup and costumes were purely functional and no actor was permitted to change costume to indicate a change in role or psychological condition; properties were minimal and there was no scenery in the traditional sense; the actors produced all music. Thus the performer was thrown back on his own resources.

For this reason, Grotowski was especially involved in actor training. He coupled intensive physical training with exercises designed to remove psychological barriers, and he sought to develop the voice as an instrument capable of exceeding all normal demands. Ultimately, he wished actors to surpass so completely the spectators' own capabilities as to arouse a sense of magic.

In the beginning, Grotowski tried to involve the audience directly in the action, but he came to believe this only made spectators self-conscious. He then concentrated on creating the proper spatial relationship among spectators and actors so they might interact unself-consciously. For example, in his *Doctor Faustus* the action supposedly occurs at a banquet on the night the devil is to claim Faustus' soul. The audience, seated at long tables on which most of the action occurs, is asked merely to respond as people might at such a function.

Grotowski viewed the theatre as the modern equivalent of a tribal ceremony. He searched in scripts for archetypal patterns independent of time and place and then developed them so as to make both actors and audience confront themselves. Thus, his goals resembled Artaud's, though his means differed markedly.

By 1970 Grotowski had come to believe that his group had reached the end of its search for technical mastery, and he decided to create no new productions. He then set out to eliminate the "idea of theatre," in the sense of an actor playing before an audience, and to find a way of incorporating spectators into the process. His main concern became how to lead participants back into the elemental connections between man and his body, his imagination, the natural world, and other human beings. The first major revelation of the new work came during the summer of 1975 and the experiments still continue. Some of the activities involve groups going into the woods for twenty-four hours during which they are led through ritualized relivings of basic myths, archetypes, and symbols, including fire, air, earth, water, eating, dancing, playing, planting, and bathing. Through this process, participants are expected to rediscover the roots of theatre in pure ritualized experience, as well as to discover their own true being. Thus, it is clear that Grotowski's current approach differs markedly from the one he used in the 1960s. It is the subject of lively debate both in Poland and elsewhere.

Megan Terry's *Viet Rock* as presented at Yale University in 1966. (Courtesy Yale University School of Drama)

THE OPEN THEATRE

Another "poor theatre" is the Open Theatre, based in New York and headed by Joseph Chaikin from its beginning in 1963 until it was disbanded in 1974. Like Grotowski, Chaikin concentrated on those elements peculiar to the theatre. Thus, scenery was usually nonexistent; the actors wore rehearsal or everyday garments in performances; they used no makeup and few properties. But the Open Theatre was not concerned with ritual so much as with contemporary social and moral values. Furthermore, its work was grounded in contemporary theories about role-playing and theatre games. Above all, it was concerned with "transformations"—that is, a constantly shifting reality in which the same performer takes on and discards identities as required by the context. Transformations may involve persons, objects, situations, objectives, time, or place. For example, in Van Itallie's *The Serpent* (1969), the same actor may pass rapidly from being an assassin to part of a tree, to a suitor, to a child, to himself, and from biblical times to the present. Thus, reality is treated not as fixed but as changeable.

The Open Theatre's productions were usually based on scripts evolved in its workshop in close collaboration with its playwrights. Typically, a writer supplied an outline, situation, or idea; then the actors, working through improvisation and other techniques, explored the possibilities, from among which the dramatist selected those that seemed to him most effective. Some of the company's most interesting productions came into being in this way.

Of the writers who worked with the Open Theatre, perhaps the best were Jean-Claude van Itallie (1963–   ) with *Interview, TV,* and *The Serpent,* and Megan Terry (1932–   ) with *Keep Tightly Closed in a Cool Dry Place* and *Viet Rock.*

265

MULTIMEDIA PRODUCTION

Since 1960 approaches to theatrical spectacle have altered significantly. The causes are numerous, but one of the most important involves changes in human perception. Marshall McLuhan argues that, since electronic media have replaced the printed page as the primary means of communication, contemporary audiences are adept at assimilating multiple and concurrent stimuli. Thus, he declares, they no longer demand orderly sequence and a single primary focal point but can take in several things at once.

Many observers agree that the pace of life has accelerated significantly since 1950. This seems to have made audiences impatient with scenic devices that slow the tempo of performance. Furthermore, playwrights have come to assume that time and place should be instantly transformable and infinitely variable. Another factor encouraging change has been the adaptation for theatrical purposes of electronic equipment perfected by wartime and space research. As a result of these and other causes, since 1960 spectacle has come to depend increasingly on light and sound, while three-dimensional elements have been restricted more and more to a few set pieces, furniture, and properties.

Multimedia production designed by Josef Svoboda, scene from Topol's *Their Day* (1959) as presented at the National Theatre, Prague. (Photo © Jaromïr Svoboda.)

Out of these changes have come multimedia productions involving some combination of live actors, projected still or motion pictures, stereophonic sound, light, and music—in other words, elements drawn from several art forms.

The major figure in the development of multimedia production has been the Czech artist Josef Svoboda (1920–   ), probably the best known of contemporary designers. Svoboda's major contributions have been made since 1958, when he began work on two projects, Polyekran (multiple screen) and Laterna Magika. The first of these is restricted to filmed images, but it seeks to overcome the "visual paralysis" of traditional productions by hanging several screens at various distances from the audience and by projecting on each a different image—to give the spectators a choice of things to watch. To this, Laterna Magika adds live performers. In 1959, Svoboda began to incorporate elements from these experiments into his stage work. In addition to projections, he has experimented with movable screens, platforms, and other elements. He has also worked in a great variety of visual styles and for virtually every major company in the world.

Svoboda has not been alone in using multimedia, and since 1960 several techniques have become increasingly common: rapidly changing projections of still pictures on multiple screens; filmed segments; stereophonic sound, the direction, volume, and quality of which may be fully controlled; infinitely varied lighting; close-circuit television; and special effects of all sorts.

HAPPENINGS

During the 1950s impatience with barriers between the arts provoked many attempts to bridge them. Perhaps the best-known result is Happenings, pioneered by Allan Kaprow (1927–   ), a painter who out of his interest in "environments" (that is, in making the entire setting an extension of the artworks on display) came to consider everyone who attended an exhibit a part of the total environment and gave them things to do. In 1959 he published a proposal for an event he called a "happening," and later that year gave the first public showing of *18 Happenings in 6 Parts.* For this work, a gallery was divided into three compartments in which a number of elements were used independently and simultaneously—various actions by participants, multiple projections, recordings, and so on. A number of other persons took up happenings, and soon the label was being applied to any event in which chance or improvisation played a part.

Few happenings were theatrical, but several characteristics associated with them were carried over into the theatre. First, happenings tended to break down the barriers between the arts and to mingle elements borrowed from several; thus, most were multimedia events. Second, happenings were concerned more with participation in a creative process than with arriving at a finished product. Third, rather than attempting to convey an artist's intention, happenings sought to sharpen the sensitivity of participants. Fourth, most happenings had no single, primary focus; rather, many events occurred simultaneously. Fifth, happenings broke down the barriers between art and everyday life by removing art from the context of theatres and museums and taking it into parks, streets, and other ordinary places. Sixth, happenings did much to undermine professionalism and disciplined technique, since anyone could participate and there was no right or wrong way of doing things.

ENVIRONMENTAL THEATRE

The interest in environments that stimulated Kaprow to devise happenings motivated others in the 1960s to promote "environmental theatre"—a term popularized by Richard Schechner. According to Schechner, environmental theatre lies somewhere between happenings and traditional theatre. In it, audiences and actors occupy the same physical space, and the audience is a part of the total event, even if it thinks of itself merely as spectator. The event may take place in "found" space (that is, any kind of unaltered, nontheatrical space) or in a place that has been converted into an environment suited to the event. Consequently, traditional theatre architecture is abandoned for spaces in which audience and actors can intermingle. Focus is flexible and variable, and more than one event may progress simultaneously.

In 1968 Schechner founded the Performance Group to carry out his ideas. It has worked in a converted garage without seats (a few platforms are scattered about on which the audience may sit or which may serve as performance areas). Its productions have included *Dionysus in 69* (a reworking of Euripides' *The Bacchae*), *Commune* (1970), a company-created montage exploring the American past and present, Sam Shepard's *The Tooth of Crime* (1973), which places rivalries in the pop-music world in the context of gangsterism, Brecht's *Mother Courage* (1975), perhaps its greatest critical success, and Seneca's *Oedipus.*

Environmental productions had become common by the late 1960s. In 1969, Luca Ronconi achieved international success with *Orlando Furioso* (adapted from the sixteenth-century narrative poem by Lodovico Ariosto). This production utilized two stages that faced each other across a large open space, occupied by a standing audience and by tall movable platforms that were wheeled in and out at considerable speed. Different scenes were played simultaneously on each of the fixed stages and on one or more wagons in the central area. The audience moved about as it

An example of environmental theatre, Jean-Louis Barrault's *Rabelais* (1968). (Courtesy French Cultural Services)

wished. The total effect was a combination of street pageant, happening, and several playlets all progressing at once.

Another well-known example of environmental theatre is Jean-Louis Barrault's *Rabelais* (1968), given first in a sports arena in Paris and then in Brussels, London, Berlin, New York, and elsewhere. A three-hour-long adaptation of Rabelais' writings, it was performed in a central ring and on ramps extending into the audience.

Still another significant environmental production is *1789* (treating the French Revolution), the creation of the Théâtre du Soleil, a commune under the leadership of Ariane Mnouchkine. For the production, platforms were set up around all four sides of the performance space; the audience, treated as the revolutionary mob, stood in the center. Critics were unanimous in their praise for this production. The company achieved comparable success with *The Age of Gold* (1975), which, as the title suggests, deals with various aspects of materialism.

RECENT TRENDS

By the late 1970s the rather frenetic theatrical experimentation of the preceding decade had subsided considerably. In what remained, a few directions could be discerned. One involved the creation of works composed primarily of hallucinatory visual images. The groups most associated with this approach include the Ontological-Hysteric Theatre (directed by Rich-

Some contemporary companies are primarily concerned with visual images, rather than the spoken text. The Bird Hoffman Foundation's production of *Einstein on the Beach* in 1976 is an example of this school. Directed by Robert Wilson and Philipp Lelan. (Photo © 1976 by Babette Mangolte.)

ard Forman), the Mabou Mines (directed by Lee Breuer), and the Byrd Hoffman Foundation (directed by Robert Wilson). Probably the most distinctive work has been Wilson's in such productions as *Deafman Glance* (1970), *A Letter for Queen Victoria* (1974), and *Einstein on the Beach* (1976). Typically very long (most last around twelve hours but one required 168 hours), Wilson's productions are composed of a slow-moving sequence of images that shift almost imperceptibly (it often takes a character an hour to complete a single movement). Abstract, they are intended to induce contemplation rather than to tell a story. Through such means, Wilson has sought to alter perceptual awareness and place the audience and performers in touch with their own inner consciousness and obsessive fantasies.

Such essentially visual productions are related to happenings and multimedia events. They also continue the downgrading of spoken text as the primary ingredient in drama. Most companies involved in this kind of work have created their own pieces rather than interpreting already existing texts. Thus, their work promotes the concept of playwriting as a visual (rather than linguistic) art.

A related trend could be seen in the increased acceptance of the director as primary artist of the theatre, free to use existing texts however he wished in his own improvisations. In America the best known exponent of this approach is Andrei Serban; elsewhere the number of such directors is

270

large indeed, especially in Germany and France. Thus, the conception of the director as an interpretive artist seeking to translate faithfully the playwright's text into theatrical terms has suffered a major decline.

On the other hand, many new playwrights demonstrated a renewed concern for language and nondidactic storytelling. Among the most prominent of these have been David Mamet with *American Buffalo* and *A Life in the Theatre,* Albert Innaurato with *The Transformation of Benno Blimpie* and *Ulysses in Traction,* Michael Cristofer with *The Shadow Box,* Preston Jones with *The Last Meeting of the White Knights of the Magnolia* and *The Oldest Living Graduate,* and Christopher Durang with *A History of the American Film.* These writers are sensitive to the rhythms and locutions of everyday speech and the mores and values of modern times. Many of the pictures they draw of American life are unflattering, but for the most part these writers avoid the derisory and superior tone often found in the 1960s. Overall, their work suggests that dramatists are returning to a more complex and more objective view of human behavior.

Among the best of the current playwrights is David Rabe, who has been especially concerned with American values. Here his *Streamers* will be examined in detail as an example of contemporary drama.

STREAMERS

Streamers is the third of Rabe's plays to use the Vietnam war as background. *The Basic Training of Pavlo Hummel* (1971) concerns the indoctrination and death of a common soldier, *Sticks and Bones* (1971) shows the aftermath of war as a blinded soldier returns home, and *Streamers* (1976) takes place just before the conflict in Vietnam escalated into a major war. But these plays are not essentially about war. Rather, Rabe uses the warrior mentality to explore significant contemporary attitudes.

Streamers uses an American myth, a variation on that of *Pavlo Hummel:* Army life is the essence of masculinity. This explains Rabe's inclusion of the play's two most prominent (and for many viewers disturbing) features: homosexuality and violence. But, what greater threat to the myth of masculinity than homosexuality, and what more likely than violence from those trained for deadly combat? Although these elements give the play an explosive quality, neither is used sensationally or gratuitously.

The action of the play occurs at a time (1965) when, following a relatively uneventful period, army life is beginning to be dangerous once more. Vietnam is still so remote that it seems a fantasy world (it is referred to repeatedly as Disneyland), but because men on the base are receiving orders to go there, Vietnam brings to the surface anxieties that previously have been hidden.

Streamers is compact and entirely realistic in style. Its language is the vernacular speech of the common soldier, replete with obscenity in almost

271

The two sergeants, Rooney and Cokes, reminisce in this scene from *Streamers*, presented at Lincoln Center, New York. Directed by Mike Nichols. (Martha Swope.)

every line. The story, told chronologically, occurs within the space of a few days. All the scenes are set in the cadre room of a barracks shared by three Specialists (Billy, Roger, and Richie), around whom the action centers. Billy and Roger accept the myth of the army, although with a measure of humor. Nevertheless, they voluntarily do pushups, compulsively clean the room, and spend their spare time in sports or on the town. Richie, on the other hand, declares: "There's no point to any of it." He makes playful sexual overtures to Billy, who at first ignores and then is outraged by them. Thus, Richie is the principal threat to the myth and becomes one of the prime elements in the explosive action.

All of these characters are complex. Billy acts the role of an ordinary, uneducated young man, but eventually he admits that he is a college graduate who has had problems because he "overcomplicates" everything; furthermore, his reponses to Richie seem to reveal an uncertainty about his own sexual preferences. Roger, a black, has grown up in a ghetto and has been under psychiatric care for severe headaches. His primary goal has become to avoid all personal conflicts. When Richie was a child, his father abandoned the family, leaving his son to be brought up by a rich and indulgent mother. He has always followed his impulses. Thus, all three are evading self-knowledge. Billy and Roger see the army as a male preserve and a proving ground for masculinity. And about Vietnam, Billy declares: "Be a great place to come back from, man, you know? I keep thinkin' about that. To have gone there, to have been there, to have seen it and lived." Despite their anxieties, then, for Billy and Roger the trademark of the authentic hero is survival in combat.

Those who best represent the army (and who have been in combat and returned) are the two sergeants, Rooney and Cokes, parachutists in World War II and Korea. When the play opens, Rooney has just been ordered to Vietnam, and Cokes has just returned—sent back because he has leukemia. Both are rather pathetic men in their fifties, passing their time in childish games of hide-and-seek or in drinking and reminiscing about the past. Still, they consider themselves to be authentic heroes and real men, in contrast to Billy, Roger, and Richie who are not "regular army." While reminiscing, Cokes tells the story of how during the Korean War he threw a hand grenade into a bunker and sat on the lid while the North Korean soldier inside tried desperately to get out.

The sergeants also provide the title of the play, taken from the song they sing (set to the tune of "Beautiful Dreamer" and attributed to soliders whose parachutes fail to open): "Beautiful streamer, / Open for me, / The sky is above me, / But no canopy." This title is appropriate since the play ultimately is concerned with questions about the nature of the canopy that suspends us and keeps us from crashing fatally. Most of the men in the play have chosen the army as a kind of parachute, for all are seeking that which sustains an illusion of happiness.

If the sergeants represent one extreme, Carlyle, a recent black draftee, represents another, opposite one. He is the most crucial character in the play—the catalyst who disrupts the relatively stable situation and turns it to violence. Carlyle has no interest whatever in the myth of masculinity. He is like a free animal who has been captured and placed in a zoo. This sense of being trapped and wanting out makes him alternately affable and enraged. Like Richie he is an outsider, and Rabe uses this affinity to draw them together in a sexual liaison that leads to the violent and bloody climax. Billy, outraged and unheeding of Roger's frantic appeals for him to leave the room, tries to prevent Richie and Carlyle from going through with their sexual encounter; Caryle draws a switchblade, cuts Billy across the palm of the hand, and then stabs him in the stomach. When the drunken Sergeant Rooney wanders in, Carlyle also kills him and insists that he has resigned from the army. After the bodies have been removed, Roger, typically and mechanically, mops up the blood and tidies up the room.

The play might have ended here, since the major action is over, but there follows a lengthy scene which gives shape and meaning to the play. Cokes, oblivious to all that has happened, comes looking for Rooney, with whom he has been playing hide-and-seek. His drunken monologue, in which he describes his day with Rooney, shows that his army life has been an eternal adolescence. But his awareness that he now has incurable leukemia makes him ponder his own existence and begin to see things in a new light. To comfort Richie, he says: "There's a lotta worse things in this world than bein' a queer. I seen a lot of 'em too." Haunting his consciousness is something as deadly as the leukemia in his blood—the memory of the North Korean soldier he killed with a hand grenade. "I'd let him out now, he was in there. Oh, how'm I ever gonna forget it?" And the play ends as he sings "Beautiful Streamer" in a makeshift language imitating Korean. Streamers, then, do not concern only parachutists but all humanity. The awareness of human waste created by this final scene gives the play true tragic dimension.

Rabe is nondidactic in his handling of his subject. For this reason, many viewers have been conscious only of the sensational and violent elements and have been repelled by them. But *Streamers* is neither an antiwar play nor a defense of homosexuality. Rather, it is a perceptive observation of one human institution and the myths that have grown up around it. The meaning of the play is conveyed primarily through implications that raise fundamental questions: What does it mean to be "a man"? Is not the love of one man for another preferable to the killing described by Cokes? These questions are asked without bitterness. All the characters are treated compassionately; all have weaknesses, sometimes giving rise to humor, but none is ever ridiculed. They share in common their need for love and understanding—symbolized by the open parachute ("Just like a mother / Watching o'er me"), which prevents "streamers," the metaphor for desperation and destruction.

POSTSCRIPT

Today the theatre seems to be in a period of reassessment and consolidation. Most of the extremes of the 1960s have disappeared, and much of what then was innovative has become standard practice. As are the other arts, the theatre today is attracting a larger audience than at almost any time in history. Its most pressing problems are not artistic but financial and organizational: How can theatre be supported, and how can it be made accessible in many more geographical locations?

What the future will bring can only be a subject for speculation, for accurate prediction would require the ability to foresee the course of events. Western drama has always reflected changing views about human beings and their world. Thus, as conceptions within the fields of psychology, morality, sociology, and politics have altered, so too have conceptions within the field of drama changed. Many recent innovations that now seem important will in the future no doubt fade into oblivion, whereas others, perhaps unnoted in this book, will in retrospect be recognized as forerunners of major changes. Only conceptions of human beings in the future— what sort of creature they will be; what kinds of appeals must be made to their senses; what kind of personal, moral, social, and political ideals they will be capable of understanding and sustaining—will determine the direction to be taken by theatre and drama. And these conceptions are yet to evolve.

THE THEATRE ARTS IN AMERICA TODAY

PART **3**

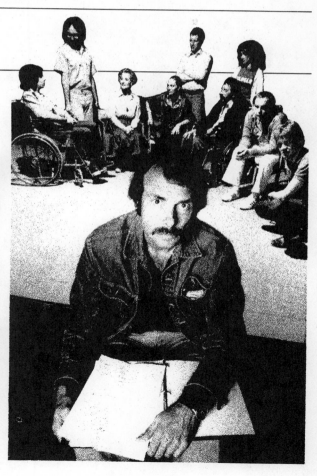

The
Playwright,
Producer,
and Director

12

As the preceding survey has shown, theatrical practice has varied widely from one era to another. How plays are mounted at any point in time depends on many factors: the audience, the prevailing views about psychology and reality, theatrical conventions, the managerial and financial procedures, the available technology and materials, and so on. Several of these determinants have been discussed briefly as they relate to the contemporary theatre, but to understand how the various theatre arts function today it will be necessary to treat them in greater detail. What follows, therefore, is an explanation of the purposes, principles, materials, and working procedures of each major aspect of theatrical production in America today.

THE PLAYWRIGHT'S WORKING METHODS

Since the script (or a working outline of some sort) is the usual starting point for a theatrical production, its creation is of primary importance.

277

Playwright Arthur Kopit
with cast of his play
Wings (1979). (© Jack
Mitchell)

(The playwright's means have already been discussed in Chapter 2.) The inspiration for a play may come from almost any source. Sometimes a writer starts with an idea and then works out an action—comic or serious, episodic or tightly structured. Another writer may start with an amusing, complex, or abnormal character, or he may be stimulated by a situation based on a newspaper article, a personal experience, or an anecdote. Since the possibilities for drama are ever-present, almost anything can stimulate a dramatist's creativity.

Just as plays stem from various impulses, so, too, methods of writing vary. Some dramatists prefer to work from a scenario and make an outline of the entire plot before writing any dialogue. Other writers find a scenario too inhibiting, since their interests shift and grow as they write. A procedure that has worked well for some is to write the scene of crisis first and then to work out those scenes that precede and follow it, since the crisis is the point to which the entire action builds and out of which the resolution grows.

Other writers prefer to make a large number of notes about characters, situations, and ideas, and the actual writing may not start until the whole play has taken shape in the mind. Another favorite method is to "think on paper." That is, the writer begins composing with only a vague idea of how he wishes the play to conclude, and lets the characters and situations develop as he goes along.

In recent years, numerous plays have been written with the aid of

278

group improvisations. Using this method, a writer supplies an outline, situation, or idea; the actors then explore, through improvisation or other techniques, multiple possibilities. Gradually situation, movement, and dialogue evolve, and the dramatist selects and arranges what seems to him most effective.

No doubt there are other ways in which playwrights work. The common goal, however, is to organize and reduce to effective form the many elements that go into a play.

Seldom does a playwright arrive at the final version on the first try. Most finished works represent many revisions, sometimes made over a period of years. Furthermore, since plays are intended for the stage, most writers need to see their works performed before they can be sure they have accomplished what they intended.

GETTING THE PLAY PRODUCED

If the dramatist wishes to see his play performed, he must find a producer. The problems are so complex that most writers work through agents, who understand the market and can devote the necessary time to selling a play. Most professional playwrights also belong to the Dramatists Guild, whose purpose is to protect the author and secure for him the best possible contract.

If a producer is interested in a work, he may take an option on it by paying a sum to the playwright for the possibility of performing the play and to prevent others from doing so. A time limit is set; if the play is not produced during that period or if the option is not renewed, all rights revert to the playwright.

If a producer decides to present a play, the dramatist is given a contract (most of the provisions are specified in a standard form prepared by the Dramatists Guild). The playwright seldom relinquishes television, motion-picture, amateur, or foreign rights to the producer. The playwright's contract usually specifies that he must be available for consultation and to make revisions throughout the rehearsal period.

The playwright is constantly under pressure to make changes in his script. Even before a producer sees a play, a dramatist's agent may suggest a number of alterations. A producer may express an interest if certain revisions are made. Frequently a well-known actor will agree to appear in a play if it is rewritten to show off his abilities to greater advantage.

For New York it has been customary to have a series of out-of-town tryouts during which critical notices and audience response are carefully studied. On the basis of these, the play is reworked, often after each performance. Sometimes a play is almost completely rewritten during this process. In recent years, some producers have replaced the out-of-town tryout with preview performances in New York, but the purpose remains the same — to allow for revision of the play on the basis of response before the formal opening.

The pressures on the dramatist are more pronounced on Broadway than in any other situation, and for this reason Broadway has recently declined as a producer of new plays. The majority of the works now seen there were first presented elsewhere, many of them abroad or by resident companies outside New York or in Off-Off-Broadway houses, where the playwright usually can retain greater control over his work than on Broadway.

Many playwrights are loath to let any nonprofessional group present their works so long as there is any hope for professional production. This situation is unfortunate, for a dramatist needs to see his plays performed if he is to progress, and many nonprofessional organizations in America can and do produce original plays effectively.

THE PRODUCER

The ultimate fate of a play depends much on the producer, who is concerned primarily with financing and selling it. The producer options the play and secures a director, theatre, and the necessary financial backing; he publicizes the production, sells tickets, and handles all other business arrangements. While he is not directly responsible for the artistic aspects of performance, he exerts considerable influence on them.

The producer's work varies according to the type of organization, but his responsibilities are most clearly defined in the Broadway theatre. The Broadway producer may be a group or an individual. In most cases, a special corporation or partnership is formed for each play so as to limit the financial liability of investors. The cost of producing a play on Broadway has become exceedingly high, sometimes running to more than a million dollars. One of the producer's first jobs, then, is to convince others that a play will be a worthwhile investment. He provides prospective investors with a proposed budget up to the opening and a statement about how profits will be divided.

After the money has been raised, the producer proceeds with the actual business of preparing the play for performance. He negotiates contracts with all the persons involved. This phase is difficult because he must deal with eleven different unions — representing playwrights, directors and choreographers, actors, musicians, stagehands, wardrobe attendants, press agents and managers, treasurers, ushers and doormen, porters and cleaners, and engineers. He rents space for tryouts and rehearsals and leases a theatre for performances. He also arranges for out-of-town tryouts or previews. He keeps financial records, which are submitted to all investors at regular intervals. He handles the payroll and closes down the show at the end of its run. Given the handicaps under which he works, it is remarkable that anyone attempts to stage a play on Broadway.

In other kinds of theatres, the producer's job is not so clearly defined. Since such groups normally present a number of programs each year, many of the problems are simplified. For example, a group may use the same theatre for several years and therefore need not rent one for each new production.

Like the Broadway producer, Off-Broadway, Off-Off-Broadway, resident, and summer stock companies must raise money, but as a rule the investment is made in the organization rather than in a single play. Because these groups usually are not wholly commercial in their goals, many have been able to obtain sizable grants from foundations, the National Endowment for the Arts, state arts councils, or private donors.

Most permanent organizations are headed by an artistic director (who is primarily responsible for the staging of the plays) and a managing director (who is primarily responsible for the theatre's business affairs). Both are usually involved in determining policies, in raising money, and in choosing the repertory. Once plays are in production, however, the managing director is normally responsible for those functions performed on Broadway by the producer.

In community theatres, the organization is usually considered the producer, but the actual duties are often divided among several persons. Most hire only a director and a designer-technician. Other duties typically are assumed by volunteers under the supervision of the director or unpaid members (such as a board of directors, a president, or a committee).

In educational theatre, responsibilities may be divided in still other ways. Some university theatres have a paid business manager who is responsible for arranging publicity, selling tickets, placing purchase orders, and keeping accounts. In small schools, a director may have to perform virtually all the functions of a producer. Since his salary is usually paid by the school and since most of the other work is done by students or faculty, the expenses are confined to such items as royalties, publicity, programs, and the materials for building costumes and scenery. Furthermore, the use of the theatre building does not normally cost the group anything.

If a nonprofessional group produces an original script, the arrangements are usually made directly with the author or his agent. The amateur-production rights to previously produced plays are handled by agencies (such as Samuel French or Dramatists Play Service). Older plays may not require a royalty payment if the copyright has expired.

Most permanent organizations present several plays each year. In planning a season, a group may consider: (1) variety in the type of plays; (2) the available actors; (3) the requirements of each play in terms of scenery, costumes, and lighting; (4) the total cost; and (5) the taste of local audiences. The amount of weight given to each of these factors varies from group to group.

THE DIRECTOR

Just as the producer is concerned with the financial aspects, the director is responsible for the artistic elements of a production. He decides how the script is to be interpreted and coordinates the efforts of all the other theatre artists into a unified performance.

There are two basic conceptions of the director's function. One sees him as an interpretive artist who serves the playwright by translating the script as faithfully as possible into theatrical form. The other views him as a creative artist who uses all the elements of the theatre, of which the script is merely one, to fashion his own work of art. Those who hold the latter view argue that the director may alter a play in any way he wishes, just as he is free to shape the visual elements to suit his goals. In other

Director Frank Corsaro working with actors and boxers for *Knockout*. (© Jack Mitchell)

words, he becomes his own playwright or adapter. Although this view is less common, it has been increasingly accepted in recent years.

Ordinarily the director performs these functions: (1) he decides upon the interpretation to be given the script, (2) he casts the actors, (3) he works with the other theatre artists in planning the production, (4) he rehearses the actors, and (5) he coordinates all of the elements into the finished stage performance.

UNDERSTANDING AND INTERPRETING THE SCRIPT

The director must familiarize himself thoroughly with the script. He must understand how the play is organized, including the over-all pattern of preparation, complication, crisis, and resolution. (The principal elements of dramatic structure have been outlined in Chapter 2). He may wish to divide the play into short segments (often called French scenes) marked off by the entrance or exit of characters, and examine each in terms of its major functions. In this way he becomes aware of the strengths and weaknesses of the script and the problems he must solve. The director must also understand each character, both its function in the play and the physical, vocal, and emotional demands it makes on the actor who will play the part. The director must understand the scenic, costume, and lighting requirements, so he can talk intelligently and persuasively with the designers and technicians about anything in his conception that depends on design.

In addition to studying the script, the director may need to acquire information about the author, the period in which the play was written, or the period or environment depicted. If the play has been produced previously, he may wish to read what critics have said about it or about how audiences responded to it.

When he undertakes a play from the past, the director must make sure it will be comprehensible, moving, and entertaining to a present-day audience. He may seek to clarify it by substituting current words and phrases for those now obsolete, by omitting subplots, or by rearranging scenes. He may decide that a play can be made more meaningful by changing the time and place to one more familiar to the audience. He may wish to give a fresh interpretation of the play as a whole. For example, Peter Brook, in directing *A Midsummer Night's Dream,* wished to avoid the romantic aura traditionally associated with it, so he used devices reminiscent of Meyerhold's productions (such as an abstract setting, trapezes, and circuslike costumes) in order to make his audiences see the play in a fresh light.

The style of a play can sometimes be made more understandable by adapting the staging methods — the acting techniques, the costume and scenic conventions, and the physical arrangement of the stage — in use at

Shakespeare's *Much Ado About Nothing,* with the action transposed to c. 1900. Production by the New York Shakespeare Festival Theatre. (George E. Joseph)

the time the work was written. For example, the architectural and scenic conventions of the Elizabethan public theatre are often used in current productions of Shakespeare's plays.

The director may also encounter difficulties with contemporary plays if they are novel in content, structure, or technique. Although audiences are now accustomed to departures from tradition, the director still often must serve as a mediator between playwright and viewer. Thus, he needs to understand the views that have shaped the script and find appropriate theatrical techniques for projecting them.

In producing new plays, the director often works directly with the playwright, who may be making revisions up to the opening night. The presence of the playwright may simplify problems of interpretation, but the director must see that the author is making himself clear to audiences and must suggest revisions when he senses confusion.

Regardless of the type of play and the problems it poses, a director usually arrives at a central concept around which he organizes his production. The suitability of the concept will depend much on the director's sensitivity, perceptiveness, and intelligence.

THE DIRECTOR AND THE DESIGNERS

Before rehearsals begin the director usually meets with the designers to discuss and agree on the production concept. Although he should listen carefully to all suggestions, the director ultimately must decide on the interpretation to be used, and the designers must work within that framework.

If the director has any specific requests, he should make them at this meeting. For example, the floor plan does much to determine the movement of the actors. The director may therefore wish to have a setting of a particular shape, or a door or sofa located at a specific place.

After the production concept and requirements are clarified, the designers must be allowed time in which to visualize the production and make sketches. At subsequent meetings designs are considered and revisions requested until the result is satisfactory.

Before giving final approval to the designs, the director must be sure that he has anticipated all needs. Do the proposed settings and lighting suit the play's action, mood, theme, and style? Is the setting functional? How long will scene changes require? Will the proposed costumes enhance the actors' movements? The director should consider these and other questions if he is to avoid costly last-minute changes.

After the plans are approved there may be occasional conferences, but each artist works more or less independently thereafter until the final rehearsals. The director meantime turns his attention primarily to the actors.

CASTING

Normally it is the director who casts the play. Some groups may cast several plays simultaneously, but most often plays are cast one at a time.

In casting, various methods are employed. Perhaps the most usual is the open tryout, which permits all those interested to apply. If the applicants are numerous, some may be eliminated on the basis of résumés or interviews. Even those remaining usually have only a few minutes in which to demonstrate their talents. In such circumstances, choice is often made on the basis of personal and physical attributes rather than proven ability.

Another common approach is the closed or invitational tryout. Following open tryouts (or on the basis of information from another source) only those thought qualified are invited to continue. Some educational theatres restrict casting to those majoring in theatre, and some community theatres only use members.

Tryouts are conducted in various ways. Sometimes actors are able to study a script in advance; at others they are asked to read material they have not previously seen. Some directors ask actors to memorize scenes and perform them. Others use pantomimes to test imagination, inventiveness, and movement. The director may give explanations and ask the actors to read with these in mind; he may stop the reading to give further instructions. In this way, he tests the actors' ability to assimilate direction.

Many factors determine the final casting. Some roles demand specific physical characteristics (size, race, or appearance), quality of voice, or accent. The director must also keep in mind the range of qualities demanded by each role and the potential of an actor to project these qualities. The total effect must also be considered. In romantic roles, lovers often have to be paired or contrasted with others. The director also tries to avoid using too many persons of the same physical type or with similar vocal qualities.

After weighing all the demands, the director eventually chooses those actors he believes most capable of embodying the qualities he sees in the script.

WORKING WITH THE ACTOR

The director next sets out to mesh actors with roles so as to bring the script to life. He supervises rehearsals, explains his concept of the play, criticizes performances, and makes suggestions for improvements. He attempts to create an atmosphere free from unnecessary tensions in which the actors may explore and develop their roles. The director needs to be flexible, tactful, and understanding, since each actor has his own problems and favorite working methods. Some take public criticism gracefully, while others may become embarrassed or argumentative.

Because the actor can never see his own performance from the point of view of the audience, the director must try to do this for him. He attempts to assess the probable effect of the performances and to alter, correct, or intensify characterizations in order to achieve the proper emphasis. Although as an efficient executive he must make all important decisions, the director should avoid seeming arbitrary and unfeeling. He must be a critic, teacher, friend, and disciplinarian.

THE DIRECTOR'S MEANS

The director's means include the entire resources of the theatre: the script; the voice, speech, physical appearance, movement, and psychological and mental attributes of the actors; the stage space, scenery, and properties; costumes and makeup; electronic equipment and lighting; and sound. Since each of these elements is discussed elsewhere in this book, the emphasis here is on the director's work with actors: (1) creating the stage picture, (2) movement, gesture, and stage business, and (3) voice and speech.

In all of these, the director is concerned with one overriding problem—how to control emphasis and subordination—for it is in this way that he projects his directorial concept and controls the audience's attention.

Balance in stage composition may be achieved in many ways. In this scene from *The Wiz,*
director Geoffrey Holder uses varying bodily heights and positions to attain a balanced yet
dynamic composition and to focus on the monkey in the foreground. Choreography by
George Faison. (Martha Swope.)

The Stage Picture. Each moment of a performance may be thought
of as a picture capable of communicating with the audience apart from
speech or movement. The director must therefore carefully arrange the
visual elements moment by moment so as to embody the situation, dominant emotion, and character relationships. In doing this the director uses
various devices for achieving emphasis. (These will be described first in
terms of the picture-frame stage and then as they relate to other types of
stages.)

One of the most important sources of emphasis is the *bodily positions*
of the actors in relation to the audience, for—all other factors being
equal—the actor most nearly facing the audience will be the most
emphatic. (Various bodily positions are explained in greater detail in
Chapter 13).

A second source of emphasis is *height*. All other factors being equal,
the tallest character will be the most emphatic. To vary height, the
director may have actors sit, stand, kneel, lie down, or mount steps or
platforms.

A third device for achieving emphasis is the use of *stage areas*. Since
an actor tends to become more emphatic as he moves toward the center

287

of the stage or toward the audience, the director may shift emphasis by manipulating the actors in relation to the audience or the stage space. (One division of the proscenium stage into areas may be seen in the chart below.)

Emphasis may also be gained through *focus*. If all the actors look at the same thing or person, so will the audience. In this way attention may be shifted rapidly.

Emphasis may result from *spatial relationships*. If a number of actors are grouped on one side of the stage and a single actor is placed on the other, attention will be directed to the isolated character. *Contrast* may also be used. If all actors but one face in the same direction, the contrast will direct attention to the one who is different.

Other ways of gaining emphasis include the use of *costume* (a brilliantly colored garment in the midst of drab clothing), lighting (contrasting colors or a spotlighted area), and *scenery* (placing a character in a doorway or against a piece of furniture to strengthen the visual line).

Seldom does a director depend upon a single source of emphasis. He may use several simultaneously and he avoids repeating the same ones too often. Furthermore, since emphasis may need to be divided between two or more characters, several devices may have to be employed.

When one moves from the proscenium to the thrust stage (which is normally viewed from two or three sides) or the arena (seen from four sides), some devices for gaining emphasis are no longer very useful. For example, bodily position becomes relatively meaningless, since an actor facing one part of the audience may have his back to another. Similarly, stage area loses its effectiveness. But most of the other devices of emphasis still apply, although it may be difficult to compose pictures that are expressive from every angle, and compositions may need to be altered often so that no part of the audience is neglected.

Since emphasis and subordination clarify situations, character relationships, and emotional tone, the stage picture should be composed with these elements in mind. (For example, in a love scene nearness in

To facilitate positioning of actors, the director usually speaks of the stage as though it were divided into many small areas. The diagram shows typical subdivisions on a proscenium stage.

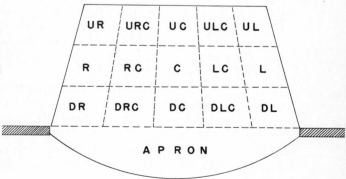

288

space may be used to indicate the emotional relationship of the characters.) In arranging the stage picture, the director should make sure the composition is balanced in terms of line, mass, and proportion and that it creates a harmonious effect.

The stage picture depends to a large degree upon the setting. The placement of doors and furniture permits some compositional patterns and impedes others. The absence of furniture in many period plays (such as Greek and Shakespearean tragedies) rules out certain kinds of pictures that would be normal in serious modern plays set in living rooms. Picturization is also affected by the type of play, since devices appropriate to farce might be completely out of keeping in tragedy.

Some directors question the importance of picturization and composition, arguing that they are legacies of the picture-frame stage now better forgotten. Others believe that concern for picturization leads to self-conscious posing which distracts attention from the dramatic situation. Still others argue that if the actors understand the dramatic situation they will instinctively group themselves properly.

The most extreme challenge to the concept of picturization has come from environmental theatre, since it presents scenes simultaneously in various parts of a space shared by audience and performers. Thus it rejects the traditional idea that each moment in a play should have a single primary focus to which the audience's attention is directed and which should be visible and audible to every member of the audience. Although the environmental approach marks a radical break with many past practices, it does so primarily in offering the spectator multiple focal points among which to choose. In each of the simultaneous scenes of an environmental production, however, emphasis and subordination are used, whether planned or unplanned. The devices discussed above thus still apply.

Movement, Gesture, and Business.   So far, the stage picture has been treated as though each moment were frozen in time, but in performance an impression of movement, rather than of stillness, dominates. Movement blends one stage picture into another and creates a sense of flow, change, and development. It is one of the director's most powerful means of expression.

Movement may be divided into three main types: *from place to place, gesture,* and *business.* Each type may be dictated by the script or may be invented by the director or actors. Many movements (such as entering and exiting, dancing, or lighting lamps) may be specified by stage directions or dialogue. Many plays, on the other hand, indicate no action beyond the arrival and departure of characters.

Since a completely static stage picture soon becomes boring, the director usually makes considerable use of physical action. In doing so, he takes his cues from the script so that movement will appear motivated

Gesture is especially important as a means of gaining emphasis, as may be seen here in the well-known grave-digger's scene from *Hamlet,* with Stacey Keach. (George E. Joseph)

rather than aimless. Character relationships and emotional connotations are among the most frequent motivations for movement. Surprise, anger, and eagerness normally make persons move closer to each other, while disgust, fear, and reluctance separate them. Thus, movement can illustrate inner feelings.

Several factors help the director to determine which characters should move and how they should move. First, movement can be used for *emphasis.* Since it catches the eye of the spectator, it directs attention to the actor whose movement is strongest.

Second, movement should be *appropriate to the characters.* An elderly person normally uses fewer and slower movements than a young person; the nervous or angry person responds differently than the casual or relaxed person. Movement, then, is an important part of characterization.

Third, movement should be *appropriate to the situation.* Highly emotional scenes normally demand more movement than do quiet moments—and in the first it is apt to be more rapid and sharply defined.

Fourth, movement must be *appropriate to the type of play.* The movement for *Oedipus the King* should be more stately and formal than that for *The New Tenant.* Furthermore, certain kinds of movement may be associated with a given period or style. For example, *The School for Scandal* deals with a society noted for its elegance of dress, walk, and gesture. Other plays, such as *From Morn till Midnight,* deliberately distort or stylize movement in their conscious departure from realism.

Fifth, movement may be used for *building scenes to a climax,* for *contrast,* and for *rhythmical effects.* In any type of production the amount and size of movement may help to achieve a sense of growing confusion or conflict, or of development and change. Even in a play with a small cast, the feeling of building toward a high point of interest may be achieved by a steady increase of movement. A contrast in movement from one scene to the next can point up differences in mood and situation and can provide variety as well.

Much stage action does not require movement from place to place. Nevertheless, *gesture, facial expression,* and *bodily attitude* are of special importance in achieving subtlety and clarity.

Although gestures normally involve the hands and arms, they may also be movements of the torso, head, feet, or legs. Gesture is especially important as a subtle means of gaining emphasis, since a gesture preceding speech is usually sufficient to shift attention to an actor at just the right moment. Gesture can indicate basic psychological traits. A large number of spontaneous gestures can create the impression of an uninhibited, outgoing personality, while few and awkward gestures may create the opposite effect.

Bodily attitude — stiffly upright, slumping, relaxed, and so on — is an especially useful means for displaying emotional states and for indicating immediate reactions. So is facial expression, which, though it is not always visible in a large auditorium, should not be overlooked as a supplementary aid in projecting emotion.

Another kind of movement is *stage business* (detailed actions such as filling and lighting a pipe, arranging flowers, wrapping packages, eating and drinking, dueling and fighting). It should be carefully rehearsed, timed to make appropriate points, and coordinated with dialogue to avoid distracting attention from more important action or lines. Much of the business in a play is prescribed by the script, but much of it may be invented by the director or actors, for carefully chosen business can clarify and enrich characterization.

In recent years, several nontraditional uses of movement, gesture, and business have become increasingly common. Actors now writhe on the floor in tangled masses, crawl about the set, and climb onto various structures. Popular music (especially rock) has also encouraged uninhibited movement. As a result, mood, emotion, and psychological states are now likely to be expressed through techniques more reminiscent of Meyerhold (such as swinging on trapezes, shooting down slides, and doubling up into balls) than those realistically motivated ones recommended by Stanislavsky. Pantomime has also increased in importance. Thus the range of movement has been considerably extended in the contemporary theatre.

Voice and Speech. The director's means also include the voice and speech of the actors. Just as innovative movement has become increasingly important, so too has nonverbal vocal sound. Consequently, directors now often use voice to create dissonances, modulations ranging from the loudest to the softest, cries, yelps, and so on. Nevertheless, the director is still most commonly concerned with voice as a medium for language. Since voice is usually considered primarily the actor's concern, the variable factors in voice and speech will be discussed more fully in Chapter 13. Nevertheless, the director needs to understand voice and speech thoroughly so he can manipulate them for his purposes and aid the actors in creating their roles.

The director must make sure the dialogue is both audible and intelligible, that there is variety in the use of voice, and that vocal patterns are appropriate to character, situation, and type of play. As with movement, he may also use voice and speech in building scenes or entire plays to a climax.

Thus, the director's means are varied. With them he seeks clarity and a sense of progression from beginning through middle to end.

REHEARSING THE PLAY

Rehearsals can seldom be held in surroundings that approximate those used in performance. As a rule, the scenery, costumes, lighting, and properties are not available until dress rehearsals, and the rehearsal space is seldom the stage upon which the play will be presented. Therefore, the director and actors must rely heavily upon imagination during rehearsals.

For adequate rehearsal space, a room at least as large as the stage is required. The ground plan of the set is usually marked out on the floor with paint or adhesive tape. If there is more than one set, each is indicated with different colors. Chairs, tables, and improvised doors and levels help the actors become familiar with the setting.

If actors have complex stage business (serving drinks, wrapping packages), temporary properties that approximate those to be used in the actual production must be supplied. Comparable problems are raised by period costumes. The convincing use of trains, unusual headdresses, swords, and similar articles requires considerable practice, and actors need to be supplied rehearsal garments and props if they are to become accustomed to unfamiliar dress.

The director must know approximately how much rehearsal time he will have. In the nonprofessional theatre, actors are usually available for rehearsals only in the evenings for three or four hours and for a period of four to eight weeks. In the professional theatre a rehearsal period of about four weeks is usual, but actors are available approximately eight hours each day. A group that evolves its scripts primarily through improvisation may require several months in which to ready a performance.

Knowing approximately how many hours of rehearsal time he will have, the director works out a schedule that will utilize the time to maximum advantage. Since he cannot work on all problems simultaneously, the director usually breaks down the schedule in terms of phases and objectives.

Before they begin work on the actual script, many directors devote some time to theatre games, improvisations, or similar activities designed to break down the actors' inhibitions, to build trust and a sense of ensemble among the cast, to encourage concentration, and to prepare the actors for the work to come.

The first phase of actual rehearsals is usually devoted to reading and analyzing the script. The amount of time spent on textual study varies from director to director, with the complexity of the script, and with the experience of the cast. During this period the director makes sure that each actor understands his role and its function in the play; he tries to make clear his own interpretation of the script and to clarify the objectives toward which everyone must work.

The next period is usually devoted to blocking (indicating movement from place to place on the stage and the position of each actor moment by moment). For example, an actor may be directed to enter up center, to cross slowly to the sofa down left, and to stand facing front. Normally the director is concerned at this point only with the gross patterns of movement; subtleties and refinements are left until later. When the blocking for an act or scene is clear, the director moves on to the next portion and repeats the process until the entire play is blocked.

If this is the most typical approach, it is far from universal. Some directors argue that movement should evolve out of character relationships and the actors' feelings about them. When the latter approach is used, patterns of movement may become fixed only after numerous rehearsals.

The next period is usually devoted to dialogue. The director normally sets a date by which the actors must know their lines for each act. Actors should learn lines early, for it is extremely difficult for them to achieve subtlety and polish if they must continually consult their scripts.

Once the actors are sure of movement and lines, the director may proceed to the next phase — detailed work on characterization, line readings, business, transitions, progression, and ensemble playing. The director may need to explore their motivations with the actors; he may wish to question the interpretation of certain lines; he may have to go over the same scene repeatedly to achieve the proper timing or build in intensity. He must make sure that there is variety and he must work for ensemble playing as opposed to isolated performances.

If the production is musical, the director's task can become especially complex during this and the succeeding phase of rehearsals. For a musical, a choreographer normally creates and rehearses the dances, just as the musical conductor rehearses the singers and chorus. It remains, however, for the director to integrate music and dance into the whole and to devise the transitions from spoken lines into song and from stage movement into dance.

The final phase of the rehearsal schedule is devoted to integrating all of the elements of production. For the first time the actors are able to rehearse in their costumes and makeup and with the scenery, lighting, sound, and music that will be used in performance. Frequently, these rehearsals also mark the first time that the actor has rehearsed onstage. Consequently, changes may have to be made.

It is usual to have at least one technical rehearsal, to work out problems with scene changes, lighting cues, costume changes, sound, music, and properties. Typically there are two or three dress rehearsals, intended to approximate as nearly as possible the conditions of performance. Difficulties are noted and corrected. Some directors invite a number of people to the dress rehearsals as a way of getting indications of probable audience response and as a way of preparing the actors for a larger audience.

In the professional theatre, out-of-town tryouts may function as a series of dress rehearsals, after each of which changes may be made. The alterations are then tried out on other audiences until the play is opened in New York.

When the play opens, the director's job is usually considered to have ended, although he may hold additional rehearsals from time to time to keep the performance up to the mark.

THE DIRECTOR'S ASSISTANTS

In carrying out his duties, the director usually calls on several assistants, the most important being the rehearsal secretary, assistant director, and stage manager.

The *rehearsal secretary* takes notes for the director during rehearsals so he can remember points he wishes to discuss with the actors, designers, or technicians. The *assistant director* performs tasks assigned him by the director: he may attend conferences, serve as liaison with designers, coach actors, or rehearse scenes. His function is to ease the director's task.

The *stage manager* is responsible for running the show during each performance after it has opened. He compiles a prompt book in which he records all blocking, stage business, lighting, sound, and other cues—whatever is needed to run the show. In the professional theatre, he may organize and run tryouts, and after the show opens he rehearses the actors as necessary. He is the person most responsible for seeing that performances continue to follow the director's plans.

While this discussion has not covered all that might be said of the director, the nature of his work should be clear. Only he can create a truly integrated production. His job requires insight, taste, tact, organizational ability, leadership, and perseverance.

The Actor

13

Of all theatre workers, the actor most nearly personifies the stage for the general public—he is the only one the audience normally sees. The actor lends his body and voice to the character and makes it live and breathe.

The actor is one of the few artists whose basic means of expression cannot be separated from himself: he must create with his own body and voice out of his own psychological and intellectual endowments. The director, designers, and playwright can sit in an auditorium and watch their work, but the actor can never completely separate himself from what he creates. Thus, for the actor the task of assessing his own accomplishments is extremely complex.

In many ways acting is an extension of everyday human behavior. Almost everyone speaks, moves, and interacts with others, and each plays many "roles" each day as he adjusts to the demands of changing contexts: home, business, school, celebrations, and so on. Perhaps not surprisingly, then, it is not always easy to distinguish acting talent from personality traits or to convince would-be actors that rigorous training is necessary.

Acting is nevertheless an art, and the ability to use behavior expressively in the theatre differs from the ability to function adequately in daily life. There are three basic ingredients in the actor's development — native ability, training, and practice. Native ability is perhaps most essential, but it is not enough in itself; it must be developed through extensive training and constant practice.

THE ACTOR'S TRAINING AND MEANS

Probably no aspect of the theatre has undergone so much change in recent years as acting. Until the mid-1960s it was assumed that good acting meant a convincing imitation of real-life behavior. In actor training, Stanislavsky was usually considered the best guide. But in the 1960s these earlier assumptions were challenged and approaches became extremely diverse.

Acting has changed since the mid-1960s in part because playwrights have been less concerned with highly detailed characterization than with boldly drawn attitudes and character types. Instead of taking time to motivate speech and movement realistically, they are apt merely to provide essential information and then go directly to the heart of some attitude or behavioral pattern. Thus they have encouraged acting in which a few broad strokes replace an accumulation of specific details — a style in which a type of behavior is presented rather than a fully rounded character represented. Furthermore, the tendency during the 1960s to reject the past led many performers to concentrate entirely on new works and to ignore earlier plays and conventions.

In the 1960s the tendency to analyze the training process into parts and then to pursue each part independently (movement, voice, psychological preparation, and so on) came under heavy fire. Consequently attempts were made to devise more unified approaches. Most took their cues from Gestalt psychology, since they insisted that all the basic processes — physical, vocal, and psychological — must be involved simultaneously because the actor is a unified being who cannot be compartmentalized. These new approaches have altered old ones to some extent, although new and old are now often intertwined.

Body, Voice, and Inner Impulse. Since they are his primary means of communicating with an audience, an actor's body and voice should be flexible, disciplined, and expressive. Flexibility is needed so the actor can express physically or vocally a wide range of attitudes, traits, emotions, and situations. But body and voice must also be under conscious control, which comes through understanding, practice, and discipline.

The expressiveness required of an actor can be seen here in Glenda Jackson in the role of Charlotte Corday in *Marat/Sade*. (Jessie Alexander/Nancy Palmer Photo Agency)

The first step involves understanding. The actor's primary problem is to understand how his own body and voice function. This in turn may be divided into two stages: learning how the human body and voice operate in a general, physiological sense; and learning how his own body and voice actually are functioning. If he can discover what his normal body alignment is, how his centers of balance are functioning, how he is breathing, what patterns of tension he is subject to, and so on, he will then be able to work toward gaining effective control over his physical and vocal equipment. The aim is to eliminate inhibiting tensions so he can move freely and effortlessly and achieve a resonant, musical voice; the ultimate goal is control over both body and voice for expressive use in performance.

Since body and voice are integral parts of a total system and are consequently deeply affected by psychological factors, it is usually impossible to achieve freedom and expressiveness without some concern for those psychological processes that create tensions and blocks. Therefore, actor training in recent years has become much concerned with self-knowledge, and the devices used to increase it have been numerous. Perhaps the most popular has been improvisational theatre games designed to break down inhibitions and build confidence and trust. Others have drawn on "sensitivity training" and "role-playing" and have used various exercises borrowed from Oriental and Western sources. All tend to treat inner impulse, body, and voice as extensions of one another.

Most of these new approaches do not deny the traditional goals of training: to produce actors who are sensitive, skilled, and expressive. Many aspects of earlier approaches may consequently be used effectively with or as supplements to the newer exercises. For example, once he understands the integrated approach outlined above, the actor may benefit from instruction in dancing, fencing, oral reading, and singing.

The actor must also be concerned about his powers of imagination and observation. He may strive to develop emotion memory so he can recall how he felt in a given situation and utilize that memory in building a characterization. Since he learns about others principally through observation, he needs to develop the habit of watching those around him (how each type and age group walk, sit, and react when happy, surprised, and so on). While the results cannot be transfered directly to the stage, they can be a helpful resource in creating believable characterizations.

The actor must also develop his imagination so he can project himself into the lives of others and into fictional situations; unless he can enter fully into a dramatic action, he is unlikely to give an effective performance.

Control and Discipline. No matter how well an actor has mastered these basic skills, he is unlikely to be effective onstage unless he has learned to control, shape, and integrate them as demanded by the script and the director. Control is usually achieved only through daily practice and disciplined effort over a long period of time.

One essential mark of control and discipline is concentration—the actor's ability to immerse himself in the situation and to shut out all distractions. In performance some actors, because of overfamiliarity with the play, seem mere automatons. The good actor, on the other hand, creates the illusion that this is the first time he has experienced each situation no matter how often he has performed the role. To give such a performance, he must concentrate on what is happening around him, not in a general sense but on specific phrases, intonations, gestures, and movements, and he must respond in the appropriate key and at the appropriate moment. This involves the ability to immerse oneself in the "here and now" of whatever is taking place on the stage.

Technique, or Stage Shorthand. Experience has shown that some ways of doing things onstage are more effective than others, and over the years many of the actor's routine tasks have been reduced to a set of conventions. Most of these serve as a kind of shorthand that saves time and effort, and most directors assume that the actor has mastered this elementary information.

The actor should be familiar with stage areas, since in productions on proscenium and thrust stages directions are usually given in relation to

In the early twentieth century William Gilette (seated center) internalized the role of Sherlock Holmes to such an extent that in his personal life as well he enjoyed and created intrigue and mystery. (The New York Public Library at Lincoln Center, Theatre Collection, Astor, Lenox, and Tilden Foundations)

them. *Upstage* means toward the rear of the acting area; *downstage* means toward the front; *right* and *left* refer to the actor's right or left as he faces the audience. The stage floor may also be spoken of as though it were divided into squares, each with its own designation: *up right, up center, up left, down right, down center,* and *down left.* The actor's knowledge of this terminology is usually taken for granted.

For work on the proscenium stage, the actor should be familiar with body positions. *Full front* means facing the audience; the *one-quarter* position means turned approximately 45 degrees away from the audience; *one-half* or *profile* means turned 90 degrees away from the audience; *three-quarter* means turned 135 degrees away from the audience; and *full back* means turned completely away from the audience.

Other terminology may supplement designations of area and bodily position. *Open up* means to turn slightly more toward the audience; *turn in* means to turn toward the center of the stage; *turn out* means to turn toward the side of the stage. Two actors are sometimes told to *share a scene,* meaning that both should play in the one-quarter or profile position so that they are equally visible to the audience. To *give stage* means that one actor gives the dominant stage position to another by facing away from the audience more than the other actor. In most scenes, emphasis shifts frequently from one character to another, and the actors may constantly be giving and taking the stage according to which needs to be more emphatic at a specific moment.

An actor may be told to *dress the stage,* which means that he should move to balance the stage picture. Experienced actors make such movements almost automatically, and without being obtrusive. To *focus* means to look at or turn toward a person or object to direct attention to it.

Some devices are commonly used to emphasize or subordinate business. A letter that is to be important later may be *planted* in an earlier scene. To draw attention to it, the actor may hesitate or start to put it somewhere else before selecting the final spot. On the other hand, many actions need to be masked from the audience. Eating, for example, must be faked to a large degree, since actors can seldom eat the actual food designated in the script. Scenes of violence such as stabblings, shootings, and fist fights must also be faked. They require careful rehearsal to appear convincing.

In whatever he does the actor normally strives to be graceful since gracefulness is usually unobtrusive, while awkwardness is distracting. His movements should also be precise and clear; vagueness creates the impression of indefiniteness. In addition, he should study all aspects of theatrical production, since the more he knows about scenery, costumes, and lighting, the better he will be able to use them in his work.

CREATING A ROLE

Each time he undertakes a new role, the actor must solve a number of specific problems. First, he must analyze his role. (For a discussion of dramatic structure and characterization, see Chapter 2.) In doing so, it is helpful to look at levels of characterization: What does the playwright reveal about the character's physical makeup; his profession, social class, economic status, and family background; his basic attitudes, likes, dislikes, and general emotional makeup; his ways of meeting crises and conflicts? Which characteristics are most important? The actor must decide which traits to emphasize and which are relatively unimportant.

Sometimes a script fails to provide a well-rounded characterization and the actor must supply many details (for example, certain physical traits and psychological attitudes). In filling in missing information, however, the actor must be careful to take his cues from the script and to invent nothing that contradicts what the author has said.

Second, the actor must define the goals of the character he is to play. To begin, he should isolate the major over-all goal. He then should de-

The first day of rehearsal of Thomas Babe's *Taken in Marriage,* at the Public Theatre, 1979. (© Jack Mitchell)

termine how this goal is manifested in each scene and how it evolves and changes. In defining major and minor goals, it is usually helpful to break the play into short units and isolate the character's motivations in each. This will help the actor find the right focus for each scene, just as examining individual scenes in relation to the whole play will show how the characterization must build and grow.

Third, the actor should study character relationships. He must determine how his character is viewed by all the others; what a character thinks of himself may not accord with the image he tries to project to others. The actor also must analyze his character's attitudes about each of the other characters.

Fourth, the actor should examine how his role relates to the play's dramatic action and themes. If the play is from a past period, involves an unfamiliar environment, or deviates from the realistic mode, it may require special effort on the actor's part to understand the script, the period, and the appropriate acting style.

Finally, the actor must examine his role in terms of the director's over-all concept. If necessary, he must adjust his interpretation until it is appropriate to the production as a whole.

Psychological and Emotional Preparation. In addition to understanding a play, the actor must also be able to project himself imagina-

301

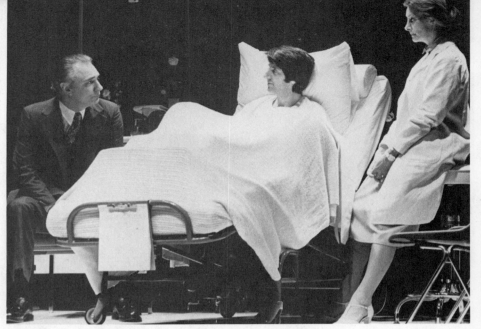

An actor must be able to project himself imaginatively into any situation. Here Tom Conti (center) appears as a paralytic in *Whose Life Is It, Anyway?* (Courtesy Bill Evans)

tively into the situation, the environment, and any conditions laid down by the director.

At times it is difficult for the actor to imagine himself as the character or as involved in the circumstances, and he may need to experiment with ways of inducing belief in himself. Common aids are emotion memory and observation of similar persons and situations. Perhaps even more popular now are improvisations and theatre games, through which the actor explores multiple possibilities in cooperation with his fellow performers, each of whom may also be seeking his own solutions.

Movement, Gesture, and Business. As a rule, blocking is done early in the rehearsal period. The director usually indicates where the character is to be at each moment, but the actor should speak out whenever he finds a direction contrary to his understanding of the role. Conflicts over stage positions and movement can usually be resolved by discussing the character and his motivations.

Even when the director specifies stage and body positions, the actor must fill in many details—the character's walk, posture, bodily attitudes, and gestures. (For a fuller discussion of movement and its purposes, see Chapter 12.)

Movement is either specified by the script or invented. In either case it may be used for several purposes: to tell a story; to establish character; to clarify motivations, attitudes, and emotional responses; to establish mood and style; to create variety; to secure and hold attention; and to compose a stage picture. While some of these purposes are not directly

Even when the director specifies stage and body positions the actor must fill in many details. This is a scene from *Fortune and Men's Eyes* by John Herbert, produced by the Mini Theatre in Ontario. (Carolyn A. McKeone/FPG)

related to characterization, all movement is executed by actors and should therefore be appropriate to the characters and the play's style.

In analyzing the appropriateness of his physical characteristics, the actor may find it helpful to examine it in relation to three levels. First, he should make sure that he has taken into consideration the physical attributes demanded by the part and the changes that occur during the action. Second, out of the over-all traits, the actor may need to assess which are appropriate at any given moment. It is sometimes helpful to think of the play as though it had no words, in which case the actor would have to express visually the situation, motivations, and emotional responses. This approach can stimulate the actor's imagination in working on his physical characterization. Third, within the limits imposed by the script and the role, the actor should work for distinctiveness, since the best acting is usually free of clichés. Overall, then, the criteria for judging a physical characterization are appropriateness, clarity, expressiveness, and distinctiveness.

Vocal Characterization. The actor's analysis of his role should also extend to its vocal demands. Although as a rule actors cannot radically change their dominant vocal traits during a rehearsal period, they may, if they have well-trained voices, modify their vocal patterns considerably.

The variable factors in voice are *pitch, volume,* and *quality,* and each may be used to achieve many different effects. In some contemporary productions, the voice is treated as a type of nonverbal gesture to create

Concern for articulation, pronunciation, duration, inflection and projection, factors of speech, are especially evident in *My Fair Lady*, in which changes in speech patterns are the crucial element in transforming a flower girl into a duchess. (Theatre and Music Collection, Museum of the City of New York)

dissonances, harmonies, and rhythmic effects. More typically, however, the voice is used as a medium for language that evokes or defines emotions, ideas, or situations.

The variable factors of speech are *articulation, pronunciation, duration, inflection,* and *projection* (or audibility). *Articulation* involves the production of sounds, while *pronunciation* involves the selection of sounds. A person may articulate sounds clearly but mispronounce words. The well-trained actor should be able to speak clearly or to alter articulation and pronunciation as needed to suit character and situation.

Duration refers to the length of time assigned to any sound, *inflection* to rising and falling pitch. Both duration and inflection are used to stress some syllables and subordinate others. Without correct stress, words may be unrecognizable. (For example, in *probably* the first syllable is normally emphasized through duration, but if the stress is shifted to the second syllable, the word becomes unintelligible.) Duration also refers to the number of words spoken per minute. Slowness can create the impression of laziness, old age, or weakness, while a rapid rate may suggest tension or vivacity.

Inflection, change in pitch, is one of the principal indicators of meaning. Surprise, disgust, indifference, and other reactions are usually indicated by tone of voice, and the sense of a sentence can often be completely altered by changing an inflection.

In performance actors must strive above all for *audibility* (projection) and *intelligibility,* for unless the audience can both hear and understand the actors the play will have little chance of success.

Actors must also be concerned with *variety.* Nothing is more deadening than all lines delivered at the same speed and with the same emotional intensity. Clear understanding of the function and emotional content of speeches and scenes is usually the best guide to good vocal characterization, since any change in thought or feeling motivates changes in volume, pitch, or quality.

Memorization and Line Readings. One of the technical problems facing every actor is memorization. In this process it is usually helpful to memorize speeches and action simultaneously, since they reinforce each other. Furthermore, because blocking is done in relation to specific speeches, this conjunction ultimately becomes fused in the actor's memory.

In solving the problem of memorization there are a few simple rules. First, since it is impossible to memorize everything at once, it is necessary to divide the play into sections and to master them one at a time. Second, the actor should begin by familiarizing himself with the sequence of ideas and motivations—the sense of a scene—for this greatly facilitates memorizing individual lines. Third, the actor should be familiar with the lines of all the other actors in his scenes, and he must memorize *cues* (the words or actions of others which immediately precede each of his own lines) as thoroughly as he does his own speeches.

In addition to actions and words, the actor must be concerned with the meaning of what he memorizes. Therefore, he must analyze his speeches carefully and call upon his knowledge of the variable factors of voice and speech to set off one idea from another and to make transitions clear. This is especially important in long speeches, where both monotony and confusion in thought or feeling are most apt to occur. He should also be concerned with creating a sense of spontaneity and conviction.

Conservation and Build. The actor must learn to conserve his powers and build his role in a climactic order. Virtually every play moves from the less to the more interesting as it progresses. Similarly, an actor's performance should grow in intensity and complexity.

The need to sustain and build a part is greatest in highly emotional roles or in those demanding a high level of energy. If the actor begins at too high a pitch, he may soon be unable to build the intensity further, and the rest of his performance will remain on a level and become monotonous. The actor must learn to judge his power and plan a performance so that it builds throughout the play.

Ensemble Playing. No single role (except in those rare plays written for one character) is complete by itself, and its effectiveness must be judged in part by how well it is integrated with other performances. The sense of wholeness that results from the cooperative efforts of an entire cast is called *ensemble playing.*

Ensemble playing comes only when each actor is willing to subordinate himself to the demands of the play. Each must be willing to fade into the background when unimportant, refrain from trying to steal scenes, and put the good of the production above winning plaudits for himself. Ensemble playing depends in part on each actor's awareness of what he can expect of others, where he needs to compensate for their shortcomings, and how they may help him. Probably the most important factor in ensemble playing is concentration. The most believable actors are those who appear really to listen, see, and respond moment by moment, and the best performances come when all the actors concentrate so completely on the stage events that the action seems to be unfolding spontaneously and for the first time.

Dress Rehearsals and Performances. As a rule, not until dress rehearsals is an actor able to work with all properties, settings, costumes, makeup, and stage lighting. He can do much to ease the transition from rehearsal to performance if he takes time to familiarize himself thoroughly with the designs and total stage environment.

Of special importance to the actor is his costume. He should find out everything he can about it—which movements it enhances or restricts, its possibilities for stage business, and the like. If stage garments are significantly different from ordinary dress, the actor should be provided suitable rehearsal costumes from the beginning. He should also have given considerable thought to his makeup. He should know what effects he wishes to create and should have experimented with achieving them if they are in any way unusual. In addition, he should have rehearsed extensively with reasonable facsimiles of all properties.

Performance, of course, is the goal. The better rehearsed the actor is, the more certain he will feel when opening night comes. It is a rare actor, however, who does not experience some stage fright—which can be beneficial if it keeps him alert and ready to meet any emergency. Many actors, especially those in long runs, tend to let down after they begin to feel comfortable in their roles. The actor should remember that each performance is the first for that audience. Concentration is the best insurance of continued quality. Ultimately performance offers the actor one of his greatest opportunities for learning, since the ability to affect or control an audience's responses is the ultimate test of his skill.

Acting is one of the most glamorous of professions, but it is also one of the most difficult in which to secure a foothold. Yet the actor is the artist most necessary for the existence of theatre. Given the conditions under which he must work in America today, he needs not only great talent but also unflagging perseverance and dedication.

Scene Design and Architecture

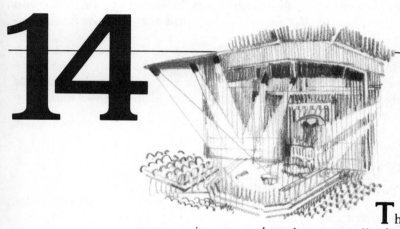

14

The director and actor use the stage environment, but they normally depend on others to design it. All theatrical design has common aims and uses similar means; in some situations the same person creates all the visual elements. Since, however, scenery, costumes, and lighting have their own distinctive features, they will be treated separately.

THE FUNCTIONS OF SCENE DESIGN

The basic functions of scene design are to define and characterize the stage space and to facilitate the dramatic action.

The floor plan of a setting should help clarify both the onstage and the offstage space. In a realistic living-room setting, for example, the arrangement of the rest of the house (the location of the main entrance, the kitchen, bedrooms) should also be implied. In other plays the nature of the stage space may not be specific, but the arrangement should allow the director to work out a pattern of exits, entrances, and action that is consistently logical. The stage space should also permit variety in grouping actors. Platforms and steps offer opportunities for creating emphases and compositions that clarify relationships and situations. Furthermore, since the floor plan of any setting allows certain patterns of movement and restricts others, it should be arranged to encourage the smooth flow of action.

The stage setting may define time and place. The amount of emphasis placed on period and locale varies considerably from one script to another. Some plays (such as *The Wild Duck*) specify rooms similar to those typically used in real life at the time of the action. Others, such as those by Molière and Sheridan, indicate period and country but do not emphasize them. Still others, such as *Waiting for Godot,* leave time and place indefinite. The designer may or may not follow the playwright's directions, but whatever he does comments in some way on place and time—even if it tells us that in this production they are mere abstractions.

The stage setting should be expressive of a play's basic artistic qualities. It should help to answer the question: With what kind of world are we in contact (a reasonable facsimile of everyday existence; a world of fantasy; an absurd world)? Thus the setting should give some indication of the mood, style, and theme of the play.

THE ELEMENTS OF DESIGN

All visual design uses the same basic elements—*line, shape, space, color, texture,* and *ornament.*

Line defines boundaries. There are two basic kinds—straight and curved—and these may be combined to form zigzags, scallops, and other variations. The dominant lines in stage settings are horizontal (the stage floor and overhead masking) and vertical (the upright scenery). This dominant pattern is varied by furniture and other elements.

Line is normally thought to elicit emotional responses. Straight lines connote stability, curved lines grace. Two lines that move farther apart as they rise vertically can generate a feeling of openness, while those that come closer together may create a sense of oppression. Thus, line is important in creating mood and atmosphere as well as in defining shape.

Shape and *space* are closely related and are frequently treated together as a single element—*mass.* While line has only direction or length, mass involves three dimensions. It identifies shape (square, round, oblong) and size (height, width, and thickness).

Designer Ruddi Barch designed this curvilinear set for a German production of *Iphigenia in Tauris.* (German Information Center)

A setting may be thought of as a hollow cube, the inside of which can be organized in a variety of ways. By altering the shape and size of the individual elements and their relationship to each other, almost any effect may be achieved. Thick, horizontal forms (for example, a low ceiling with thick beams) may create an effect of compression, while narrow, vertical, and pointed forms (thin, tall columns and high Gothic arches) may create a sense of openness and grace.

Color may be described in terms of three basic properties: *hue, saturation* or *intensity,* and *value. Hue* is the name of the color. *Saturation* or *intensity* refers to the relative purity of a color (its freedom from gray or its complementary hue). *Value* is the lightness or darkness of a color—its relation to white or black. A color that is light in value is usually called a tint, while one dark in value is called a shade.

Colors may be classified as *primary, secondary,* or *intermediate.* The *primary* colors are those that cannot be created by mixing other colors, but from which all other colors are derived. The primary colors in pigment are yellow, red, and blue. The *secondary* colors—orange, violet, and green—are created from equal mixtures of two primary colors. The *intermediate* colors are mixtures of a primary with a secondary color. These colors may be arranged around a wheel to indicate their relationships. Those opposite each other on the wheel are called complementary, those next to each other analogous. Colors may also be described as warm or cool. Red, orange, and yellow are warm; green, blue, and violet are cool. Almost any combination of colors may be used together if saturation, proportion, and value are properly controlled.

Mood and atmosphere depend much on color. Many people believe that light, warm colors are more likely to evoke a comic response than are dark, cool colors. Some color combinations are garish, others sophisticated. The designer, therefore, may use color to create the right mood and atmosphere and to establish the taste of the characters who inhabit the settings.

Texture may help establish the appropriate feelings through smoothness, roughness, shininess, softness, or graininess. Some plays seem to demand rough textures, others smooth. Such qualities as sleaziness, fragility, or richness depend much on the textures used in the setting.

Ornament includes the pictures hung on walls, decorative motifs, wallpaper patterns, moldings, and similar items. It is one of the chief means for achieving distinctiveness, for it adds touches that complete the picture. For example, even if all the other elements of design have been used skillfully, the walls of a living room will appear barren without ornament. Furthermore, devices such as banners, statuary, or thrones are often used to give temporary particularity to otherwise nonrepresentational settings.

THE PRINCIPLES OF DESIGN

In applying the elements of design, certain artistic principles must be used if the results are to be pleasing and effective. The principles of design are *harmony, balance, proportion, emphasis,* and *rhythm.*

Harmony creates the impression of unity. All of the elements of each setting should be harmonious and the various settings for the same play should be related so all are clearly parts of a whole. If monotony is to be avoided, however, some variety is needed. Thus a designer seeks a double effect of unity and variety.

Balance is that sense of stability which results from the apparent equal distribution of weight on either side of a central axis. The stage may be thought of as a fulcrum with the point of balance at the center. The scenic elements placed on each side of that line should appear equal in weight; if they do not, an uneasy response may be aroused. Apparent weight is not the same as actual weight. A large, light-colored object may appear to weigh no more than a small, dark-colored object, and a small object near the outer edge of a set may be used to balance a large object near the center.

There are two basic kinds of balance: symmetrical and asymmetrical. Symmetrical balance means that each side of the stage is a mirror image of the other. It is easily achieved, but not always desirable, since it seems formal and sometimes contrived. Asymmetrical balance, through irregular placement of elements, creates the effect of informality. It requires subtlety, for it must give the appearance of being unplanned while being perfectly balanced.

Proportion involves the relationship between the parts of a design: the shapes; the scale of each element in relation to the others; and the division of the space (for example, if a wall is to be painted two colors, the amount of space devoted to each). Proportion can help create the impression of stability or instability, of grace or awkwardness. Furniture that is too large in proportion to the size of a room may give a cramped feeling, whereas furniture that is too small may appear meager. The beauty or ugliness of a setting depends in large part on the proportion of its parts.

A design should also have a focal point, or *center of emphasis.* A well-composed design will direct the eye to the most important point immediately and then to each of the subordinate parts. Emphasis may be achieved in several ways. Line may be used. For example, a triangular platform with its apex at center stage will lead the eye to that point. The line of walls, furniture, steps, and decorative motifs may similarly be utilized to create focal points. Emphasis may also be achieved by the placement or grouping of objects. A sofa may be made emphatic through its position, or a series of similar objects may lead the eye to the last in the series. Color may be used to achieve emphasis: a brighter saturation, a hue that contrasts with others around it, or a difference in value may direct the eye to a point of interest. Unusual texture or ornamentation may also give emphasis.

Rhythm is that factor which leads the eye easily and smoothly from one part of a picture to another. All the elements of design may be used for rhythmic purposes. Lines and shapes may be repeated; the size of objects may be changed gradually so as to give a sense of progression; gradations in hue, saturation, and value may lead the eye from one point to another; changes or repetitions in texture and ornament may give a sense of flow and movement.

The ways in which the elements and principles of design can be utilized are inexhaustible, and knowledge of their potential is an indispensable part of the scene designer's training.

WORKING PROCEDURES AND PLANS

Like other theatre workers, the designer should first study the script. He should begin by analyzing the play in terms of action, characters, themes, language, and spectacle: he needs to understand the play's over-all qualities. Only then should he be concerned with the specific scenic demands.

The designer looks for information of various kinds: the number of settings required; the kinds of setting (exterior, living room, prison, abstract, and so on); the space needed for the action; the physical arrangement of the settings (placement of doors and furniture, the need for platforms and steps); indications of period, place, social and economic background; indications of type and style (tragedy, comedy; expressionism, realism, and so on).

The designer may need to do research about manners and customs, decorative motifs, architecture, furnishings, and the use of color in the period of the play's action. He may wish to explore the staging conventions for which the play was written. Although he may not use all of this information, it can stimulate his imagination, and it will make for accuracy if authenticity is desired.

Before the scene designer makes sketches and plans, he usually meets with the director and other designers in order to clarify the interpretation and the production concept to be followed. At this initial conference the designer should note any specific requirements of the director (such as placement of entrances and exits, the amount of floor space needed for each scene, business that will demand a specific arrangement of furniture, and so on). If he does not already know, he must also find out how much money is available for the scenery, what stage or kind of space is to be used, and what equipment will be available.

The script, the interpretation, and the financial and physical arrangements provide the limitations within which the designer must work. With these in mind, he can proceed.

After he has settled on designs he thinks right for the play, his ideas are discussed at other conferences with the director and designers. Some ideas may have to be abandoned and new ones proposed. Before final approval is given, the designs must be rendered in color and drawn in perspective to show how the finished settings will look onstage when lighted. Since sketches can be deceptive, the designer also supplies floor plans that show the arrangement of each setting, and he may be asked to construct three-dimensional scale models which show in miniature each set as it will appear when completed.

After his designs have been accepted, the designer must make working drawings. The number and type of drawings required vary from one organization to another, but the designer may have to provide any or all of the following: (1) perspective sketches in color showing the finished settings; (2) a floor plan of each setting; (3) a scale model of each setting; (4) rear elevations, which indicate the construction, materials, and methods to be used in assembling each unit; (5) front elevations, which show each unit in two dimensions from the front with indications of such features as molding, baseboards, and platforms; (6) side elevations, which show units in profile and indicate the thickness and shape of each unit; (7) detailed drawings, which show the methods by which such units as platforms, steps, trees, columns, and similar objects are to be built; and (8) painter's elevations of each unit, showing the color of the base coat and any overpainting to be used. With the exception of the perspective sketches, all of the plans are drawn to scale so that the exact size of any object may be determined. In addition to the drawings listed above, the designer may also need to provide special plans showing how the scenery is to be shifted and stored when not in use.

After the plans are completed, the process of execution begins. While he may not be directly involved in carrying out the plans, the designer must approve all work, for it is his responsibility to see that the finished settings conform to his specifications.

BASIC SCENIC ELEMENTS

Since World War II, a combination of rising costs, changing tastes, and new materials and equipment has steadily diminished concern for full-stage realistic settings. Although the traditional box set is still used, it is now far less common than formerly. The majority of settings today are composed of a few set pieces and stage properties, or steps and levels. In other words, they tend to be fragmentary and suggestive rather than fully representational. Furthermore, during the 1960s the use of projected images on various types of surfaces and such new materials as Styrofoam and other plastics encouraged the exploitation of effects previously little attempted. Nevertheless, traditional stagecraft still dominates practice and consequently it will be treated most fully in the following discussion.

In carrying out his plans, the scenic designer utilizes two basic types of units: standing (those that rest on the floor or on other parts of the set) and hanging (those suspended from above).

Standing Units. The basic standing unit is the flat (a wooden frame over which canvas or muslin is stretched). Flats of almost any width or height may be made, but if they are too large they become unstable. Therefore, the height of flats usually ranges from eight to sixteen feet, and the width from one to six feet.

Probably the most common piece of scenery is the plain flat—a rectangle without an opening. Other types of flats include: the door flat (with an opening into which a door frame may be set); window flat; fireplace flat; and arch flats (with openings shaped to simulate Roman, Gothic, or other arches). There are many variations on these basic types. They may be constructed with slanting sides, with edges shaped to simu-

313

late trees, rocks, distant mountains, ruined arches, and so on. Flats are used in many kinds of setting, but they are of special importance for interiors. A living-room set, for example, is normally assembled by hinging together a number of flats of the right type and size.

Other standing units are: door frames, with doors; window frames, with windows; fireplace units; platforms; steps and staircases; rocks; mounds; tree trunks; and columns.

It is not within the scope of this book to indicate how these units are built; the processes are described in detail in a number of books on stage scenery.

Hanging Units. Hanging units include ceilings, drops, curtains, borders, screens for projections, and cycloramas. A ceiling is usually constructed in two parts approximately equal in size, covered with canvas, and hinged together. It is suspended above the setting and let down onto the flats that compose a room. The hinges allow it to be folded and drawn up out of sight when not in use.

The most common overhead masking both for interior and exterior scenes is the border—a short curtain or piece of painted canvas. Borders are hung parallel to the front of the stage and in series from front to back of the stage. They may be made of black cloth or painted and shaped to represent foliage, the beams of a ceiling, or other objects.

A drop is made by sewing together enough lengths of canvas to create an area of the desired size. Most typically, it is then attached at the top and bottom to wooden battens that support it and keep it free of wrinkles; occasionally it is framed on all four sides. The drop's surface can be painted as desired.

Draperies may be hung parallel to the proscenium on either side of the stage in a series from front to back to mask the sides of the stage in the manner of flat wings. Black draperies are often used to surround the acting area or to create an enclosing void for a fragmentary setting. A scene (such as a forest or distant view of a city) may be painted on canvas draperies and hung in folds as a stylized background.

Scrim, a curtain made of gauze, appears opaque when lighted from the front only but becomes transparent when light is placed behind it. It is used for apparitions, for showing first the outside and then the inside of a building or object, for creating effects of fog or mist, and for a number of other purposes. Plastic may be sprayed on scrim and painted, then parts of the scrim may be cut away to create settings of great delicacy and apparent depth and complexity from materials of very light weight.

A cyclorama is any arrangement of curtains or other materials that surrounds the stage area on three sides. It may be composed of draperies or a plaster dome, but typically it is a continuous, tightly stretched curtain suspended on a U-shaped batten that curves around the back and sides of the stage. It is usually neutral or gray so its apparent color may be changed through lighting. It is used to represent the sky, to give the effect of infinite space, and to allow the maximum use of stage space without the need for numerous masking pieces. It may also be used as a surface for projections.

In recent years, the increased use of projections has made the screen a common scenic element. A screen may be used alone or in conjunction with others. They may rest on the floor, but usually they are flown. Some may be relatively near the audience, others far upstage; they may be rigged so they can be raised, lowered, or moved laterally during a performance; they may be of any size or shape and made from almost any material—wide-mesh netting, translucent plastic, textured cloth, and so on. Some surfaces blur images, some let projections bleed through onto other surfaces; some permit the use of images from the front, others from the rear; the variations and range of effects are wide.

New Directions. In recent years, experiments with nontraditional materials have been numerous. Metal pipes and welding have been used to create intricate towers and structures of various shapes. Fiberglass treated with chemicals has been molded into rocks, mounds, and similar structures to create very lightweight pieces able to support heavy loads. Such materials as Styrofoam have been incised to create the three-dimensional form of molding, bricks, and carvings or sculptured to create figurines and other properties formerly very difficult to construct. Vacuform molds, which permit the easy duplication in plastic of almost any shape, have become relatively common.

ASSEMBLING SCENERY

The designer must decide both what scenic units to use and how these units are to be assembled. The method chosen will depend in part on how the scenery is to be transported from the scene shop to the theatre, and whether or not it needs to be shifted. Sometimes, scenery must be transported from one town to another and must therefore be assembled in small units. If the scenery is to be shifted manually when in use on the stage, it may need to be put together in smaller units than if it is to be moved by other methods.

The typical methods of assembling scenery are hinging, permanent joining, and lashing. Hinges are used most often to join flats into walls. The hinges and cracks between flats are then covered with strips of muslin (or *dutchmen*) and painted. Braces may be attached to the back of the assembled units to make them rigid and to prevent them from folding. Temporary hinging (using hinges with removable pins to hold the two halves together) is sometimes used where two units meet at 90-

degree angles, to join platforms and steps, or to attach one unit to another.

Permanent joining is done with screws, bolts, and nails, or occasionally by welding. This kind of assembly is used for heavy units that do not need to be shifted, or for those that are shifted by means that do not require the units to be taken apart. Because it is most stable, permanent joining is used whenever possible.

Lashing is a method of joining scenic units temporarily with lines or ropes drawn around cleats attached to the backs of units. It allows settings to be assembled and dismantled rapidly during performances.

When assembled, the scenery is then ready for painting.

PAINTING SCENERY

Scene shops normally stock dry pigment in a wide range of colors from which any hue, saturation, and value may be mixed. When the desired color has been achieved, the dry pigment is combined with a binder—a liquid solution that binds the pigment to a surface after it is dry. The most common binder is a glue-and-water solution, but others may also be used.

Ordinarily, new flats are first painted with a solution of glue and pigment to stretch and seal the cloth. This process is called *sizing.* After sizing, a prime coat, near in color to the final coat, is applied. It is usually mixed from cheap pigments to reduce the cost.

Next, the *base coat* is applied. The result should be a uniform color of smooth texture. The final step is usually some modification of the base coat through *overpainting* designed to simulate textures (such as plaster, brick, or wood) or to soften a surface that appears flat. Overpainting may also be used to shade the upper portions of settings to decrease their prominence; to emphasize the shape and form of objects by giving emphasis to corners or curves; to counterfeit three-dimensional details, such as molding, paneling, bark, or mortar.

Painting may be done with a variety of techniques. The prime and base coats normally employ a technique called *flat painting* (intended to give an even surface) done with a large brush or a spray gun. Since *overpainting* adds texture, shading, or details, it requires colors different from the base coat. The degree of contrast depends on the purpose. For example, the texture of relatively smooth plaster may be achieved by *spattering* (that is, by flicking small drops of paint from a brush onto the base coat) with one color that is slightly lighter and a second that is slightly darker than the base coat itself to create the effect of raised and receding surfaces. Rough plaster may be simulated through *rolling.* This involves the use of a rolled-up piece of burlap or other rough-textured cloth which is dipped in paint and rolled over the base coat in irregular patterns. Other common painting techniques include *sponging* (in which a natural sponge is dipped into paint and patted on the surface of the base coat) and *scumbling* (the simultaneous application and blending of more than one shade of paint on the same surface to give a mottled effect to simulate foliage or walls on which the paint is fading, mildewing, or crumbling).

The appropriate painting techniques must be specified by the designer on his painter's elevations. He must also approve the finished job.

ASSEMBLING AND SHIFTING SCENERY ONSTAGE

After the scenery has been painted, it is transported to the stage on which it will be used. In the nonprofessional and most resident theatres this may merely mean moving the scenery from one part of the building to another. In the Broadway theatre, however, transportation by truck is usually involved.

How scenery is to be assembled onstage depends on the method of shifting to be employed. A single setting may be set up permanently, whereas multiple settings may need to be planned so the individual units can be assembled quickly and quietly, moved easily, and stored economically.

There are many methods of shifting scenery, of which the most common are: by hand, flying, wagons, elevators, and revolving stages.

The simplest procedure (in the sense that no mechanical devices are needed) is to change all elements *manually*. In this case, each part of a set is moved by one or more stagehands to some prearranged storage space offstage, and the elements of a new setting are brought onstage and assembled. Parts of almost every setting must be moved manually, even when the major shifting is done by other means. Since manual shifting can be used on any stage, however simple or complex, a designer can always rely on it, though a large crew may be required to carry it through efficiently. Its drawbacks are its relative slowness and the need to break the setting into small units.

Another common method of shifting scenery is by *flying*. In this case, elements are suspended above the stage and raised or lowered as needed. Flying is normally reserved for such elements as drops, curtains, ceilings, borders, cycloramas, screens for projections, and small units of flats.

The lines for flying scenery are normally attached to steel pipes or battens which extend across the width of the stage and at regular intervals from front to back so that scenery may be flown at any spot. The lines that support the battens run upward to the top of the stagehouse, where they pass over pulleys resting on the gridiron (a network of steel girders); they then continue to one side of the stagehouse, where they pass over another set of pulleys and turn downward, where they are attached to the top of a cradle or frame; into this cradle weights (in the amount needed to balance whatever is being flown) are placed. To the bottom of the cradle are attached ropes that continue downward to the flyrail, where the ropes are tied off securely when not in use and from which stagehands operate the entire system. With a good counterweight system of this type, a single stagehand can easily raise and lower scenic elements of any size. Some newer flying systems utilize electrically controlled winches without counterweights and a more flexible arrangement of lines which allows scenery to be flown at angles rather than parallel to the front of the stage.

The *wagon* is a platform on casters. The larger the platform the more scenery it can carry, but many stages do not have enough wing space to allow large wagons to be maneuvered or stored. Some stages have permanently installed tracks which guide wagons on- and offstage with precision, but this does not permit flexibility in positioning onstage. The top surface of a wagon is normally raised above the stage floor about one step so that actors may get on and off easily.

A *revolving stage* may be either permanently or temporarily installed. If permanent, a circle of the stage floor (normally larger in diameter than the width of the proscenium opening) is mounted on a central supporting pivot so that the entire circle may be rotated. Because of the weight, it is rotated electrically. A temporary revolving stage may be constructed by mounting a low circular platform on casters and attaching it at its center to the stage floor. One or more small revolving units may also be used at almost any place on the stage.

The revolving stage allows a number of settings to be erected simultaneously; individual sets are placed so that each faces the circumference. To shift scenery, the stage is revolved until the desired setting faces the audience. Settings may be changed on the backstage part while another setting is being used onstage.

With an *elevator stage,* sections of the stage floor may be raised and lowered vertically. In some theatres, portions of the stage may be lowered to the basement, where scenery can be mounted and then raised to the stage level. Each segment of the stage floor may be mounted on a lift that allows that section to be raised, lowered, or tilted so that ramps, platforms, and levels can be created without the necessity of building and shifting them in the usual ways. In a number of recently constructed theatres, the orchestra pit is on lifts and may be raised to form a forestage or used at auditorium level for audience seating when not needed for musicians.

Seldom is one method of shifting used exclusively. The designer must know what methods are available to him and must decide how each unit is to be moved.

SET DECORATION, PROPERTIES, AND FURNITURE

When the scenery is assembled onstage, set decoration, properties, and furniture are added. Although these are part of the basic design, they are not structural parts of the setting.

Set decoration and properties include such items as banners, pictures, draperies, books, and lamps—anything that completes a setting. Properties are frequently subdivided into *set props* and *hand props*. A *set prop* is one that is attached to the setting or that functions as a part of the design. A *hand prop* is principally used in the actor's stage business.

The designer is always responsible for the selection of set properties and may choose the hand props, but more frequently hand props are considered the director's responsibility, since they are so intimately connected with acting. In the nonprofessional theatre, the responsibility for obtaining properties of both types may be assigned to a property crew.

The appropriate pieces may be bought, made, rented, or borrowed. Regardless of how furniture and properties are obtained, the designs are not complete without them.

TECHNICAL REHEARSALS, DRESS REHEARSALS, AND PERFORMANCES

Most organizations schedule technical rehearsals to make sure the settings and scene changes function as planned. Adjustments are made as needed, although it is extremely difficult to make major changes in settings at this point.

Since dress rehearsals approximate performances, they offer an opportunity to see the settings as the audience will. The designer must be available for consultation and changes until the play has opened. On opening night, responsibility for the scenery passes to the stage crew and the stage manager.

THE DESIGNER'S ASSISTANTS AND COWORKERS

In carrying out his duties, the designer may be aided by a number of persons.

In the professional theatre, well-established designers often employ one or more assistants who make working drawings, search for furniture and properties, act as liaison between the designer and the scenic studios—anything the designer may request.

In the nonprofessional theatre, the technical director is likely to perform many of these functions. In many theatres, however, the technical director's job is quite independent of the designer's and of equal status.

When a permanent organization produces a number of shows each year, the designer's job may be divided into its artistic and practical aspects. A designer may then conceive the designs and the technical director execute them. The technical director may also purchase all materials and supervise the backstage operation of the theatre.

The scenery is built, assembled, and painted in a scene shop (or another work space which fills that function). In the professional theatre, all persons involved usually must be union members. In other types of organizations, this work is done by assigned or volunteer helpers under the supervision of the designer or technical director.

When the scenery is delivered to the stage for rigging and shifting, scenery and property crews take over. In the professional theatre, all such persons must be union members; a master carpenter travels with a show on tour and makes sure the scenery is kept in good condition. In the nonprofessional theatre, scenery and props are usually handled by volunteers or assigned crews, but in all types of theatre the heads of stage crews operate under the supervision of the stage manager. Their duties include the efficient movement and accurate placement of scenery and properties during performances and the upkeep of materials during the run of the show.

The designer's helpers frequently go unnoticed by the public since little is done to draw attention to them. They are, nevertheless, also indispensable members of the production team.

THEATRE ARCHITECTURE

Every theatre has three basic parts: that intended for the audience; the stage; and the work areas. Facilities designed for the audience include the box office, lobby, rest rooms, corridors, exits, and refreshment stands.

From the standpoint of theatrical production, the auditorium is the most important of audience facilities. It should be designed to insure optimum seeing and hearing. Unfortunately these demands are frequently subordinated to others, among them that some or all seats be removable because the space must be used for other purposes, that the seating capacity be as great as possible for maximum box-office receipts, and that the auditorium be fitted into an already existing structure.

Auditoriums vary widely in their basic characteristics. They may be large or small; all seats may be on the same level (although normally the floor is then raked), or there may be one or more balconies; the audience may view the acting area from one side, or it may be seated on two, three, or four sides, or even intermingled with the performers; the distance of spectators from the acting area may vary from a few to hundreds

An open or thrust stage. (From Parker and Smith, *Scene Design and Stage Lighting,* 3rd ed. Courtesy Mr. Parker.)

of feet; sightlines may be such that all members of the audience may see all of the acting area, or they may prevent some members of the audience from seeing large portions of the performance area.

There are three basic stage forms: proscenium, open (or thrust or platform), and arena (or in-the-round). Each creates a different audience-actor relationship, each has different facilities, and each promotes a different approach to production.

The proscenium stage is designed to be viewed from the front only. Since the stage action is oriented in one direction, the designer may utilize three sides of the stage for the scenery, entrances, and exits. The scenery may be as tall as the designer wishes and he may use few or many units. There is only one basic restriction: the view of the audience must not be blocked from the front.

The proscenium stage is usually equipped with a curtain that may be used to conceal or reveal the stage. It ordinarily has a counterweight system, wing space, and other features that allow for a wide variety of scene-shifting methods.

In the proscenium theatre, the action and scenery are usually removed a greater distance from the audience than in other types of theatres. There may be an orchestra pit or forestage between the first row of seats and the setting. Since scenery is not viewed at close range, it may be treated differently than were it viewed close-up.

With an open or thrust stage, the seats are usually arranged around three sides of a raised platform that juts into the auditorium. (A good example may be seen on page 321.) Less frequently, an open stage is viewed from only one side, but in this case it is essentially the traditional stage without its proscenium arch.

Most open stages permit only a restricted use of scenery. Tall units must be kept to the rear of the platform so as not to interfere with sightlines. Some thrust stages are backed by an area equipped with a cyclorama and other features typical of the proscenium stage. Others, however, have a permanent architectural facade at the back which can be altered only slightly.

The open stage may or may not have a curtain; if there is one, it is usually mounted in the ceiling on a recessed track, shaped to follow the contours of the stage. Often there is no provision above the stage for flying scenery, drops, or curtains; lighting instruments are mounted in recesses in the ceiling. Modified thrust stages may have a stage house at the rear of the main platform, and this may include flying equipment and lighting positions. As a rule, scenic units on the main platform are shifted manually. Wagons may be thrust out onto the platform from the rear, and occasionally a revolving or elevator stage may be installed, or there may be a number of traps. Nevertheless, scenery is usually relatively simple.

The basic purposes of the open stage are to bring the audience and the actors into more intimate relationship and to do away with the trappings of realism. Since three sides of the stage are usually surrounded by seats, even if the auditorium is large audience members are closer to the actors than in a proscenium theatre with the same seating capacity. Because the open stage is usually seen from three sides, it is in most respects more three-dimensional than the proscenium stage; acting and other elements of theatrical production must project in three directions simultaneously.

In the typical theatre-in-the-round, there is no stage as such (that is, there is no raised platform). Rather, an open space is left at floor level in the middle of the auditorium. The seats for the audience are set up in a bleacherlike arrangement around all four sides of the acting area. In most theatres of this type, the acting area and the seats are not permanently installed and the arrangement may be varied at will.

An arena theatre restricts the scene designer considerably in the amount and kind of scenery he can use, since it must allow the entire acting area to be seen from every angle. The designer, therefore, may use a few open structures such as trellises or pavilions through which the audience can see, but he must rely principally on furniture and properties or on scenic units not more than two or three feet high, most typically placed around the outer edge of the acting area. Since there is no curtain, all changes are made either in darkness or in full view of the audience. All shifting, as a rule, must be done manually. Units often must be moved through the aisles of the theatre, although recently built arena theatres have passageways running beneath the auditorium and giving directly onto the acting area. While lighting instruments are suspended overhead, provision is seldom made for flying scenery. Screens for projections are occasionally suspended at various spots over the acting area, the audience, or around the walls but, as a rule, the designer for the arena stage must suggest locale, period, mood, and style with a few touches. Even so, both scenery and actors must be expressive when viewed from any angle.

The amount of work space provided in theatres varies widely. A well-designed, self-contained theatre (one that has facilities for preparing productions as well as performing them) will include the following: a scene construction shop (with space to store equipment and materials), painting facilities, an area for assembling scenery, sufficient offstage space for storing and shifting scenery during performances, and permanent storage space for scenery when it is not in use; a property room near the stage, and another area for the permanent storage of furniture and bulky props; a costume shop; laundry, dyeing, cleaning, and pressing facilities, and an area for permanent storage of costumes; a work space for lighting personnel, a storage area for lighting equipment, a large room to house the remote-control lighting board, and a lighting booth for the control-board operator during performances (ideally with full view of the stage); a number of large rehearsal rooms; a number of dressing rooms, each with makeup facilities (unless a separate makeup room is provided); adequate showers and rest rooms for the actors and crews, and an area (the *green room*) where all the actors and crew members can assemble to receive instructions or relax; space to house sound equipment and from which to operate it; and adequate office space.

During the 1960s there was a movement to reject altogether theatre buildings of the traditional type. Some argued that, like museums and concert halls, theatres tend to discourage all except a cultural elite. They sought instead to take the theatre into parks, streets, and other places where theatrically unsophisticated spectators might discover the theatre. Instead of a building, they advocated the use of "found" space—either adapting a production to fit into already existing areas or altering existing areas to fit the needs of productions. The results tended to fall into one of the three categories discussed above, for though the equipment often was minimal, the arrangements resembled proscenium, thrust, or arena stages since productions were usually seen from the front, two or three sides, or in the round.

Advocates of "environmental" theatre, on the other hand, proposed an essentially new arrangement: a large open space without stage or fixed seating and in which actors and spectators intermingle. In this type of theatre, different scenes are often performed at various places within the space simultaneously, and the audience moves about as it wishes. Sometimes the spectators participate in the action—an approach that breaks down the traditional barriers between performers and viewers. Rather than using scenery in the usual sense, the entire space becomes the setting, with perhaps a few posters or slogans on the walls.

What all these variations demonstrate is that theatre architecture— the physical relationship of stage and audience—inevitably is an integral part and major determinant in every theatrical production.

Costume
and Makeup

15

The scene designer creates the stage environment in which the actors perform; the costumer is concerned with the visual appearance of the actors themselves.

THE FUNCTIONS OF COSTUME DESIGN

The functions of costume design are to characterize the personages and to clarify the interpretation being given the script. Costumes usually indicate sex and may establish the age of characters, since some garments are conventionally thought appropriate to the young and others to the old. In some cases, clothing may indicate that characters are trying to appear older or younger than they are.

Costumes may establish the social and economic status of characters by distinguishing between lower and upper classes, between rich and poor, or between more and less affluent members of the same class. Costume often identifies occupation (nurse, milkman, soldier) or life style (conservative middle-class, modish leisure-class, disaffected youth, "street people").

Costumes can also help clarify character relationships. For example, in Shakespeare's plays, warring factions may be identified by using the same color scheme for all members of the same faction. Similar devices may be used to show a sympathetic or antipathetic relationship among characters in any play. Likewise, changes in costume may be used to indicate an alteration in relationship among characters or in the outlook of an individual.

Each costume should indicate the psychological nature of its wearer (extroverted or introverted, fastidious or careless, open and frank or deceptive). The costumer usually seeks to project the truth about a character while allowing him to wear clothing that he might credibly have chosen for himself.

Through emphasis and subordination, costume may indicate the relative importance of characters in the play's action. A woman in black entering a scene in which all others are in pastels, for example, immediately becomes emphatic.

Costumes may identify the period in which the action occurs, and they may establish the general locale (throne room, battlefield, farm, city) or a particular country or region. Costumes may identify the time of day and clarify the occasion (an informal morning at home or a formal evening dance).

The costume designer also seeks to reflect the appropriate mood (both overall and in individual scenes), style (realistic, expressionistic, absurdist, or other), and themes.

During the 1960s, a number of groups questioned the need for stage costumes or makeup at all. Arguing that the theatre has come to depend too much on nonessentials, they sought to eliminate everything not absolutely needed: all but the actor and the audience. In such groups, actors wore the same casual clothing in performance as at rehearsals or on the street. They used neither makeup nor costumes as aids in characterization or in changing roles. Since 1968 a few productions have also introduced total nudity, but this too merely becomes a variation on dress. Such new approaches have served primarily to enlarge concepts of costuming rather than to displace old ones.

THE ELEMENTS OF COSTUME DESIGN

Like the scene designer, the costumer utilizes the basic elements of design — line, mass, color, texture, and ornament — in various combina-

Painted lines are used to create emphasis on this costume for Eve in the *Creation of the World and Other Business* by Arthur Miller. (Inge Morath/ Magnum)

tions. Since each of these elements has already been defined in the chapter on scenery, only their application in costuming will be discussed here.

Line is manifested in costume primarily in the silhouette of garments and in darts, ornamentation, seams, and other features that create visible lines.

Shape and size (*mass*) are reflected by the over-all configuration of costumes and the space they occupy. The dress of each period has its own distinctive mass. For example, the Greek woman wore a garment that fell in loose folds about the body, whereas the mid-nineteenth-century woman wore a tight-fitting bodice and a bell-shaped skirt. In studying the dress of a period, the characteristic treatment of each part of the body should be considered: head, arms, upper torso, lower torso, feet, and legs.

Hair styles and head coverings vary markedly from one period to another. For example, the man of the 1950s with his close-cut hair had little in common with his late-seventeenth-century ancestors, who wore full-bottomed wigs hanging in curls about the shoulders. In considering the head, beards and mustaches should not be forgotten.

Arms may be uncovered, partially covered, or fully covered with close-fitting sleeves, with puffed sleeves, or with sleeves as full as those of an academic gown. The covering of the upper torso may be tight or loose. Shoulders may be bare or covered; the bust and waist may be

327

emphasized or masked. In many periods, corsets have considerably altered the natural shape of the body.

The appearance of the lower torso may be changed more easily than the rest. Tights or bathing suits may reveal the form, while garments of various shapes and lengths may mask it. For example, skirts may be hung over variously shaped foundation garments to make them resemble bells, barrels, or a variety of other objects.

Foot and leg coverings have also varied widely through history. Men have worn high-heeled shoes, sandals, and wide-topped, knee-length boots. At times the legs have been revealed, at others concealed. Thus the natural lines of the human body may be altered in many ways and the costumer can manipulate line and mass to convey the qualities he thinks appropriate.

Color is one of the most powerful means available to the costumer for expressing mood and character. Although it is difficult to specify connotations, different colors clearly can arouse different responses. Hues that are grayed in saturation and dark in value may establish a somber mood, while those light in value suggest gaiety or delicacy.

The colors of each costume should reflect the traits of its wearer. A character's lack of taste may be indicated through inharmonious colors, a defiant nature by clothing at odds with the occasion; the relative conservatism of an individual can be implied by subdued tones.

Color can point up relationships among characters. Those closely related through sentiment or politics may be costumed in the same basic color scheme, while antipathy may be indicated through contrasting colors.

Line, mass, and color are abstractions, however, until embodied in materials, each with its own *texture* and weight. Heavy threads and loose weaves have a homespun quality associated with the working classes, whereas the smooth texture of silk suggests the upper classes. Each material has a texture that the designer can use to achieve desired effects.

Ornament includes such items as ruffles, buttons, fringe, and lace. It may not be essential to good design, but it usually adds a special touch that brings the whole to life. For example, the white collar and cuffs give variety and distinction to the dress of the Puritan. A red rose on a black mourning dress not only sets off the black but may also indicate that the wearer is not totally engrossed in grief.

Ornament can also be used to indicate a lack of taste. Too many ruffles, or too much ornamentation of any kind, may indicate a person without restraint. Likewise, too many kinds of ornament may create a cluttered and disorganized effect. Ornament thus gives variety, sharpens effects, and helps to characterize.

Costumes are complemented or completed by such accessories as canes, swords, purses, and jewelry. In many cases, accessories perform the same function as ornamentation. They should be appropriate to the character and the costumes they accompany.

PRINCIPLES OF DESIGN

The costumer also utilizes the principles of design — harmony, balance, proportion, emphasis, and rhythm. *Harmony* makes a garment seem a complete whole rather than a collection of disparate parts. But to avoid monotony, variety as well as unity is needed both in individual costumes and in the total collection of costumes used for a production.

Balance is relatively easy to attain in costuming since in most cases garments are symmetrical — that is, both sides are alike. The costumer may nevertheless use asymmetrical balance effectively (a drapery may hang down the back on one side only; ornamentation may be placed so as to alter an otherwise symmetrical arrangement).

Proportion is of great importance in clothing. The amount and distribution of color, the length of the bodice in relation to the skirt, the width of the shoulders in relation to the hips, bust, and waist are some of

Masks may become an integral part of costuming as can be seen here in the mime production, *Mummenschanz.* (Jeffrey Richards Assoc.)

the factors involved in proportion. Through the manipulation of proportion much can be done to change an actor's appearance. By emphasizing vertical lines, a plump actor may be made to appear more slender, just as emphasis on width may make an actor seem stocky. Grace and beauty in large part result from right proportions, whereas awkwardness and ugliness come from wrong proportions.

A costume also needs a point of *emphasis* to which the eye is directed first. It may be created by a patch of color, converging lines, a change in texture, or by ornament. The skillful costumer can direct attention to an actor's good points and away from his poor features. He can also help the audience perceive each character's basic psychological qualities. Furthermore, when the costumes are viewed together, some should be more important than others, since attention should be directed to the principal rather than the subordinate actors.

Finally, to achieve *rhythm* the parts of a costume should be related in such a way that the eye travels easily from one part to another and from the major point of interest to subordinate ones.

Like the scene designer, the costumer should have a thorough knowledge of the elements and principles of design. In his work, he organizes elements (line, mass, color, texture, and ornament) in accordance with principles (harmony, balance, proportion, emphasis, and rhythm) to fulfill the purposes of design in costuming.

WORKING PROCEDURES AND PLANS

Like other theatre workers, the costumer should analyze the script thoroughly, for costumes should be appropriate both to individual characters and to the over-all qualities of the script. After he understands the play as a whole, he should then look at the specific costuming demands.

The costumer may also need to do considerable research. If he decides to use garments like those worn at the time of the play's action, he should become thoroughly familiar with that period's characteristic silhouettes, typical textures and materials, dominant colors, ornamental motifs, and usual accessories. He should learn as much as possible about the manners and customs of the day so he will understand how each garment and accessory was used.

Before he begins his designs, the costumer meets with the director and the scenic and lighting designers to discuss the script and the interpretation being given it. If he does not know already, he should find out how much money is available for costumes, how many costume changes are envisioned for each character, and any special demands that must be met—the director may have business in mind that requires a particular garment or cut. The costumer should know the kind of performance space in which his work will be seen, since small details that would be totally ineffective in a large auditorium may be used to advantage in an intimate theatre. The costumer must find out as much as he can about the plans of the other designers since the scenery, costumes, and lighting should be unified.

With these limitations in mind, the costumer may begin his designs. When he is ready to show his work, additional conferences are held with the director and other designers; revisions may be requested, and still other conferences may be needed before final approval is given. Before the designs can be accepted, they must be rendered in color and in a manner that conveys a clear impression of the final product.

The designer then must provide working sketches and plans. The costumer's basic working drawing is a color sketch showing the lines and details of each costume. If there are unusual features, details are shown in special drawings (usually in the margins of the color sketch). At times it may be necessary to show more than one view of a costume if the front, back, or sides have distinctive features. Samples of the materials to be used in making the garment are attached to each drawing.

A costume chart is also needed. This is made by dividing a large

Costume chart for *Othello*. (Courtesy of Paul Reinhardt.)

ROLE	I-7 (184 Lines)	I-2 (99)	I-3 (410)	II-1 (321)	II-2 (12)	II-3 (394)	III-1 (60)	III-2 (6)	III-3 (479)		III-4 (201)	IV-1 (293)	IV-2 (252)	IV-3 (106)	V-1 (129)	V-2 (371)
DUKE OF VENICE			Duke 1 Red													
BRABANTIO	1 Change to 2 add Jerkin, Hat, Gloves	Bra.	Bra.													
GRATIANO															Grat. 1 Black Gown	Grat.
LODOVICO												Lodovico 1 Gown Boots		Lod.	Lod.	Lod.
OTHELLO		Othe. 1	Othe. White & Gold	Othe. 2 Armor		3 Brown Dressing Robe		Othe. 4 Armor	Othe. 5 White Doublet		6 Dark Brown Doublet-Jerkin	Othe.	Othe.	Othe. Jerkin Off	Othe.	Othe.
CASSIO		Cas. 1	Cas. Olive & Gold	Cas. 2 Armor		Cas. Stripped of Rank	Cas.		Cas.	INTERMISSION	Cas.	Cas.			Cas.	Cas.
IAGO	Iago 1 Black Cape	Iago	Iago Black & Green	Iago 2 Armor		Iago	Iago	Iago	Iago		Iago	Iago	Iago		Iago in Shirt	Iago
MONTANO				Mont. 2 Armor		Mont.										Mont.
RODERIGO	Rod. 1 Black Cape	Rod.	Rod. Brown & Coral	Rod. 2 Armor		Rod.							Rod.		Rod.	
CLOWN				Clow.		Clow.	Clow.				Clow.					
DESDEMONA			1 Brown with Red Trim	1a Blue Gown over Brown		2 Tan Negligée			3 Rose with Tan Jacket		Des.	Des.	Des. Remove Jacket	Des.		Des. 4 Nightgown
EMILIA			Emi. 1 Green Dress	Emi.		2 Negligée	Emi.		Emi.		Emi.		Emi. Remove Oversleeves	Emi.	Emi.	Emi.
BIANCA											1 Bian. Dk. Red & Brown	Bian.			Bian.	

sheet of paper into squares. Down the side the name of one character (and usually that of the actor playing the role) is listed in each square. In like manner each scene (or act) is listed across the top. Thus there will be one square for each actor in each scene of the play. In each square the designer indicates the costume items (including accessories) to be worn in that scene and may attach color samples of each garment. The range of colors and the over-all color scheme can thus be seen at a glance, and the list of costume items can be used as a guide for dressing the actors and for keeping the costumes organized for running the production efficiently. A sample costume chart is shown on page 331.

CARRYING OUT THE DESIGNS

Costumes may be borrowed, rented, assembled from an existing wardrobe, or made new. When costumes are borrowed, the designer looks for garments that fit his conceptions, but often he must accept clothing that is less than ideal.

Borrowed clothing can be altered only slightly, since as a rule its owner expects it to be returned in much the same condition as when taken. Much can be done, however, to alter its appearance through the imaginative use of accessories or ornamentation. The practice of borrowing clothing is restricted principally to nonprofessional theatres and short-run productions.

Costumes from rental houses vary considerably. Some of the larger agencies buy the costumes of a Broadway or road show when it closes and rent these costumes as a unit. Other houses employ staff designers who create costumes for frequently produced plays. In still other cases, costume houses merely assemble a large variety of costumes for each period. From this stock, the most appropriate garments are selected for any given show.

When costumes are rented, the costume house assumes many functions of the designer. The director or costumer may write at length about his interpretation of the play and request specific colors and kinds of garments, but usually he must accept what is sent. Sometimes a costume agency is located nearby and the costumes can be selected or approved on the spot, but rented costumes normally arrive at the theatre only in time for one or two dress rehearsals and there is seldom time to obtain replacements or do more than make minor changes. The better costume houses provide good service, but the work of even these cannot match well-designed garments made with the needs of a specific production in mind. Even groups that normally make their own costumes sometimes nevertheless rent articles such as military uniforms that are extremely difficult to construct.

Costumes created for the 1978 Broadway production of *Zoot Suit,* reminiscent of the 1940s. (Martha Swope)

Permanent theatre organizations that make their own costumes usually maintain a wardrobe composed of items from past productions. In this way a large stock of garments is built up over a period of time. When garments are taken from stock, the costumer designs the play with this in mind. He knows what is available and can choose in advance. Furthermore, existing costumes can be remade or altered to fit new conceptions. As a rule, the costumes worn by the principal characters are new, even in productions otherwise costumed from existing stock.

The procedures and working conditions for creating new costumes vary from one kind of organization to another. In the Broadway theatre, the producer contracts with a costume house to execute the costumes. The designer must approve the finished products but has little to do with the actual work itself beyond supervising fittings. He does not supply patterns or cutting, sewing, and fitting directions, since the costume house does all this.

In resident and nonprofessional theatres, the designer may supervise the construction of his own costumes; if so he must be skilled in pattern drafting, draping, and fitting. Whether or not he supervises the construction, he should understand the techniques used to carry out his designs so he will know what effects can be accomplished and by what means.

Regardless of who actually makes the costumes, a number of standard procedures are involved. First, accurate measurements must be made of all the actors. (The stage manager or assistant director usually makes appointments for measurements and fittings.) Second, materials must be bought. While the designer specifies materials, it may be difficult to find precisely the same cloth or color. Either the designer or some other authorized person may need to search at length for the specified materials or acceptable substitutes.

Next, patterns must be drafted as guides for cutting and shaping the material. It is at this point that the technical knowledge of the tailor and seamstress is of greatest value. Some costumes can be made more easily through draping than from patterns. For example, the typical Greek garment, which hangs from the shoulders in folds and is not fitted to the body, is most easily made by draping the material on the actor or on a mannequin.

After the patterns are completed, the material is cut and the parts basted together. The first fitting usually takes place before sewing is completed. Each garment is put on the actor who is to wear it and fit and appearance are checked by the designer. It is easy at this point to make many alterations or changes which would be impossible or extremely troublesome after the garment is entirely finished.

Next, the garment is finished and ornamentation and accessories are added. Another fitting is then arranged to assure that the costume looks and functions as planned.

THE COSTUME PARADE, DRESS REHEARSALS, AND PERFORMANCES

When all costumes are finished, it is usual to have a dress parade during which each scene of the play is covered in sequence so that the actors may appear in the appropriate costumes under lights that simulate those to be used in performance. The actors may be asked to perform characteristic portions of each scene to make sure the costumes are functional. The dress parade allows those concerned to see and evaluate the costumes without the distractions of a performance. Difficulties can be noted and corrected before dress rehearsals begin. In the professional theatre, the dress parade is held at the costume house; in other organizations it usually occurs onstage. It is normally supervised by the costumer.

After problems have been corrected, the costumes are moved to the dressing rooms in the theatre to be used for performances. If no dress parade is held, its functions must be accomplished during the dress rehearsals.

Dress rehearsals allow the costumes to be seen under conditions as nearly like those of performance as possible. Changes at this time should be few, but those necessary must be made speedily so the actor is not confronted with new details on opening night.

Once dress rehearsals begin, a wardrobe mistress or costume crew usually assumes responsibility for seeing that costumes are in good condition and that each actor is dressed as planned. In the nonprofessional theatre, the costumer frequently assumes these duties. In most situations, however, the costumer's work is considered to be over after opening night.

THE COSTUMER'S ASSISTANTS

In carrying out his work, the costumer needs a number of helpers. The costumer's assistant may make sketches, search out appropriate materials, supervise fittings, or act as liaison with the other theatre workers.

Cutters, fitters, and seamstresses make the costumes. In the professional theatre, such workers must be union members. In the nonprofessional theatre, much of this work is done by volunteer or student labor, although occasionally a paid seamstress may be hired to sew and to supervise the work of others.

When the costumes are finished, a wardrobe mistress takes charge. It is her responsibility to see that costumes are ready for each performance. She may need to mend, launder, clean, or press them. She must see that garments are replaced when they begin to be shabby so that the show will continue to look as the designer intended. She is directly responsible to the stage manager during performances.

The number of dressers depends on the size of the cast and the number and rapidity of costume changes. Sometimes actors need very little help, but quick changes and complicated garments may require more than one dresser to aid a single actor. There must be a sufficient number to keep the show running smoothly during performances and to keep the costumes in shape at all times.

THE COSTUMER AND THE ACTOR

The costumer must work very closely with the actor, for many of their problems are shared. First, the costumer should consider the strengths and weaknesses of each actor's figure when designing costumes. For example, if an actor's thin legs are out of keeping with the role he is playing, they can be covered or attention drawn away from them by boots, a cape, or some other device.

The costumer should also keep in mind the physical actions demanded of the actor. For example, it is difficult to climb steps in a tight skirt, and fencing may be dangerous when an actor wears billowing sleeves, but these same garments can enhance movement in other situations.

335

Almost any unfamiliar garment will seem awkward to the actor until he becomes aware of its possibilities. The characteristic features of clothes in each period emphasize qualities that were admired at the time and allow movements that were socially useful, beautiful, or desirable. For example, the sleeves on a fashionable man's coat in the eighteenth century will not allow the arms to hang comfortably at the sides (they must be bent at the elbows and held away from the body) whereas the modern suit coat is cut so that the arms are most comfortable when hanging at the sides (but outward and upward movement is restricted). The costumer must understand the relationship between cut and movement, and he can help the actors get the feel of the time by making garments from authentic period patterns.

The costumer should also aid the actor with movement appropriate to a style or period by proper attention to shoes and undergarments. The height of the heel on shoes is of special importance in stage movement (a high heel throws the weight forward onto the balls of the feel while flat shoes bring the weight back). Similarly, underclothing such as a hooped crinoline will not allow the same kind of movement as modern underwear. Corsets can also force the body into certain configurations and thereby inhibit some actions.

If the costumer's designs encourage suitable movement, they can be of enormous help to the actor. For maximum effectiveness, however, the actor and director must be willing to explore the possibilities of garments and allow time for rehearsal in them.

MAKEUP

Traditionally, makeup has been considered the actor's responsibility, and often each actor is assumed to be capable of achieving any desired effect. This is not always true, however, and it is especially questionable in the nonprofessional theatre. For this reason, in many organizations makeup is under the supervision of the costumer, director, or some other specially skilled person. In the professional theatre, each actor is expected to create his own makeup. Makeup is discussed here in connection with costuming because of its intimate connection with the actor's appearance.

Purposes. Makeup should characterize personages and be appropriate to the play's artistic qualities. It can establish the age of a character, his state of health, and his race; within limits it may suggest profession (outdoors versus indoors), basic attitude (such as grumpiness shown through facial lines), and self-regard (pride in personal appearance).

Makeup may be used to establish psychological qualities and to make the face more expressive. It also restores to the face color and form that are diminished by stage lighting.

336

Mime applying make-up. (Andrew Rakoczy/EPA)

Makeup may indicate style. In a realistic drama, age is modeled as much as possible after life, whereas in an expressionistic play primary attention may be given to an idea such as suggesting that all the characters are merely living corpses.

The Makeup Plot. When makeup is designed and supervised by one person, a plot and sketches are normally used. A chart is made on which to record basic information about the makeup of each actor: the base, liners, eye shadow, and powder; any special features such as a beard; any changes to be made during the play. It serves both as a guide for applying makeup and as a check on how the makeup of each actor relates to that of all the others. Sometimes a sketch is also made of each actor's face to show how the makeup is to be applied.

337

Types of Makeup.   In makeup, effects may be achieved in two basic ways: by painting, and by adding plastic or three-dimensional pieces. Painting involves the application of color, highlights, and shadows to the face or other parts of the body. Plastic makeup includes such items as beards, wigs, false noses, and warts.

Painted makeups may be divided into a number of subcategories: age groups; straight and character makeups; racial types; and special effects.

If an actor is to portray a character whose age is significantly different from his own, he must alter his appearance. Like the actor, then, the makeup artist may need to observe the characteristic distinctions among various ages. He should study each part of the face to see the typical coloration, highlights, shadows, and lines. He should not neglect the hands, arms, and other parts of the body that may destroy the illusion created by facial makeup if not also treated properly.

Makeups may also be classified as *straight* or *character*. With a *straight* makeup, the actor's own basic characteristics are utilized without significant change. A *character* makeup is one in which the actor's appearance is altered. The change may be one in age, but it may also involve making the actor seem fatter and coarser or more lean and wizened, or emphasizing some distinctive facial characteristic.

Frequently scripts require a clear differentiation of races. Again, the makeup artist should observe or discover the characteristic differences among such races as Chinese, Indian, Polynesian, Caucasian, and Black.

Special painted effects include clown makeups, distortions for stylistic effects, or decorative designs painted on the face (such as might be used in a tribal ritual).

The number of effects that can be achieved by painting are almost limitless. Significant transformations in an actor's appearance, however, may be more easily accomplished with three-dimensional elements. For example, a change in the shape of the nose and the addition of a beard and bushy eyebrows can mask an actor's features more completely than painting can. Prominent cheeks, hanging jowls, a protuberant forehead, fleshy jaws, warts, or large scars may be used to change the shape of the face or to give an unsightly appearance.

The actor may grow his own beard and mustache, but these can also be made with relative ease. Many styles of hair can be achieved readily only with the aid of wigs. Baldness can also be simulated with a "bald wig." Much can also be done to alter the actor's own hair.

Makeup materials.   To accomplish these and other effects, a variety of makeup materials is available from manufacturers and makeup supply houses.

Most makeups begin with a base (pigment suspended in an oily solution, usually a pastelike substance in tubes). A very wide range of base colors is available: various shades of pink, suntan, yellow, beige, brown, black, and white. Each color may be used as it comes or it may be mixed with one or more additional colors to achieve the desired shade. The base color is applied over the exposed portions of the face, neck, and ears. A range of colors is available in liquid form for application to large surfaces of the body such as the arms, legs, and torso.

A base color alone is apt to make the actor's face appear flat and uninteresting. Over this base, therefore, lines, highlights, and shadows are applied. For this purpose a thick paste, normally called *liner,* is available in small tins and in a wide variety of colors such as white, light brown, dark brown, blue, green, red, gray, and black. Like the base colors, liners may be mixed to create any shade. They are used for shadows under the eyes, hollows in the cheeks or temples, for furrows in the forehead or for creases which spread outward and downward from the nose — for any high- or low-light. Red liner may be used for lipstick or rouge.

Crepe hair is used to make beards and mustaches. It comes in a wide range of colors, which may be combined to achieve more accurate representations of mottled human hair.

For beards and other items such as mustaches and bushy eyebrows, liquid adhesive is needed. This is a plastic substance which becomes solid, though flexible, when exposed to the air. It may be applied to the face (usually several layers are built up) to form a base to which crepe hair can be attached with the same liquid adhesive. When a beard of the desired shape and size has been made, the whole structure, including the base and hair, can be removed. This permanent beard can be reused at each performance by reattaching it to the face with liquid adhesive.

Nose putty is used for changing the shape of the nose, chin, cheek bones, or forehead. It may be shaped as desired and then attached to the face. It is not very satisfactory when applied to flexible parts, however, since it is likely to loosen with movement and fall off. For plastic effects on flexible parts of the face, gauze may be stretched over pieces of cotton and glued to the face with liquid adhesive. These are then covered with the same base as that on the rest of the face. Liners may be used to make them appear more realistic.

In addition to dye, various materials may be employed to alter hair color. A white liquid, usually called hair whitener, may be combed through the hair to gray it. More realistic effects can be achieved by combing aluminum or copper metallic powders through oiled hair.

Wigs have become so common in recent years as to be readily available in many styles at local stores. They may also be rented from costume supply houses or made from the type of plastic hair used on store-window models. Wigs made from anything other than plastic or human hair are seldom satisfactory if a natural appearance is desired. If naturalness is not a consideration, wigs may be made from hemp, crepe hair, or a variety of other materials.

After the makeup is complete, the painted portions must be powdered, for otherwise the actor under stage lights will appear greasy. Powder comes in the same variety of shades as base paints. It should be applied freely and the excess brushed off. For removing makeup, cold cream and facial tissues are used.

It should be the aim of the costumer and makeup artist to aid the actor in transforming himself into the character he is playing. Above all, they must integrate their work into the total design, in which it plays a key role.

The *Book of Job* is a stage play based on the eighteenth book of the Old Testament, using narration and poetic dialogue. The combination of makeup and costume creates the striking mosaic effect. The costumes by Irene Corey imitate fifth century designs with multicolored bits of satin on black robes with black hoods and gloves. The makeup is based on portraits of saints from Gothic stained glass windows. Application takes over an hour. The play was originally commissioned by the Free Church Federal Council in England. It was developed by Orlin Corey who was also responsible for directing the play and arranging the text. This production was performed by the Everyman Players. (© Dennis Stock/Magnum, 1961)

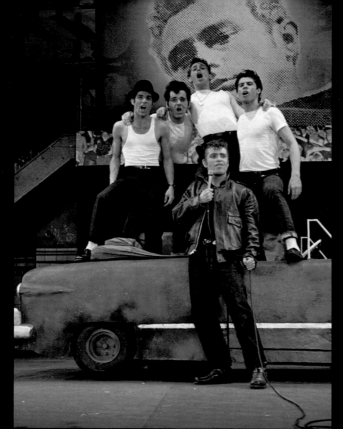

Set designs are created out of the script, the time, theatrical influences, and personal vision. Each of these sets reflects one way of presenting a play.

Grease (top left, opposite page), a musical set in the 1950s, recreates that era with an old car, a projection of James Dean, t-shirts, and a leather jacket. (From the touring company production, photo © Sy Friedman)

Crucifer of Blood (top right, opposite page), a Sherlock Holmes mystery, builds suspense with the mist and fog of a London night in a dark theatre. (photo, Martha Swope, 1978)

The Wiz (bottom, opposite page), a musical version of *The Wizard of Oz*, uses bright, vivid color and swirling designs to transport the audience to the land of Oz. (photo, Martha Swope, 1978)

The Royal Shakespeare Company's production of *Marat/Sade* directed by Peter Brook (below), considered an example of Artaud's "Theatre of Cruelty," presents stark, angular sets and clothes the actors in hospital gowns. (photo, © Dennis Stock/Magnum)

This presentation of Shakespeare's *A Midsummer Night's Dream* (bottom), performed by The Royal Shakespeare Company and directed by Peter Brook, places bright solid colors against a white background to alter the audience's perception of a familiar play. (photo, © Max Waldman/Magnum)

Costuming affects the tone of a production.

Shakespeare's *Merry Wives of Windsor* (top), produced at the American Shakespeare Festival Theatre, dresses the principal characters in startling black and white, while the supporting actors in this scene are in gray. (American Shakespeare Festival Theatre, photo, Martha Swope, 1971)

The New York Shakespeare Festival's production of *Taken in Marriage* (middle) by Thomas Babe uses contemporary clothing in a modern setting. (photo, Martha Swope, 1979)

For Colored Girls Who Have Considered Suicide When the Rainbow is Enuf (bottom) by Ntozake Shange relies on the color from costumes and lighting to set the tone. Each actress wears a distinctively colored dress; in this scene note the women in red, maroon, orange, green, blue, and yellow. (photo, Martha Swope, 1976)

Lighting,
Sound,
and Multimedia

16

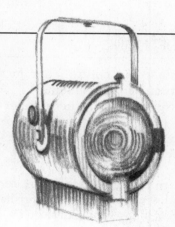

One of the least publicized but most important theatre artists is the lighting designer, for without his work that of the others would not be seen. His designs can either enhance or seriously distort the action, scenery, costumes, and makeup.

Perhaps his work is little known because light is intangible, takes up no stage space, and is visible only when it strikes a reflecting surface. Thus, lighting is usually ignored unless it is obviously inadequate or obtrusively spectacular. Since lighting also requires a knowledge of complex instruments and controlboards, electricity and electronics, optics and physics, to many it sometimes appears more the province of the electrical engineer than the theatre artist. In practice, the lighting designer needs to be both an able technician and an artist of high caliber.

341

FUNCTIONS OF STAGE LIGHTING

The functions of stage lighting are to aid understanding and to express a play's artistic values. First, and most basically, lighting aids understanding by making the other elements visible. In addition, it can establish the time of day, the source of the light (sun, lamps, firelight), and weather conditions. The play's period may be indicated by the lighting fixtures seen onstage. Light may further aid understanding through special effects (lightning, offstage fires, rainbows).

Lighting is a compositional element, since it can lead the eye to see what is important and subordinate what is less significant. It also helps establish mood and atmosphere, style, and themes. Normally, bright, warm colors are associated with gaiety, cool colors with somberness. Intensity, color, and direction of lighting may be combined in numerous ways to create such widely varying moods as foreboding, mystery, romance, and joy. Lighting can help to express style through its effect on form, for though stage space, actors, and furniture are three-dimensional, their shapes may be revealed or distorted through lighting.

THE CONTROLLABLE FACTORS OF LIGHT

In lighting, the designer can control four factors: intensity (or brightness), color, distribution, and movement.

Intensity depends primarily on the number and wattage of lamps. It may be modified in several ways: a color filter reduces the amount of light that passes through it; distance diminishes brightness; few or many instruments may be directed at the same area; or dimmers may be used to vary brightness.

The visible spectrum of light includes red, orange, yellow, green, blue-green, blue, and violet, each distinguishable from the others because it is composed of light waves of a given length. *Color* is attributed to objects because of their capacity to absorb some wave lengths and to reflect others.

To control color in stage lighting, filters are used. A filter is based on the principle of selective transmission — it allows only certain wave lengths to pass through. A blue filter, for example, screens out the majority of other rays. This process considerably reduces the amount of light that reaches the stage. Furthermore, if a red object is lighted only with a blue light, its apparent color will be magenta. To avoid such distortions, filters of different colors are placed on other lighting instruments so that light from a number of sources may be mixed on the stage. The primary colors of light — red, blue, and green — may be mixed to obtain white light. More frequently, however, a variety of subtle tints and shades is employed.

Color in light has three basic qualities: *hue, saturation,* and *brightness.* *Hue* is the name of the color. *Saturation* is the relative purity of the color—its concentration around a specific wave length. *Brightness* is the darkness or lightness of the color, or its component of white light. The addition of white light produces tints, while taking it away makes shades. Since the color filters available from manufacturers combine these three qualities in many ways, it is relatively easy to obtain filters appropriate to any effect.

Distribution depends upon the direction from which light comes and the way it is spread over the stage: all may be directed at one area or evenly distributed over the entire stage. Direction is determined by the position of the light source. Almost any placement is possible, for instruments may be mounted in the auditorium, above the stage, on the floor, or on vertical pipes or stands.

Movement refers to alterations in any or all of the other controllable factors. The principal device for achieving movement is the control board. With it, lamps may be brightened or dimmed to control intensity, color, or distribution. Movement allows light to change moment by moment in accordance with shifting moods and the dramatic action. Movement also makes lighting one of the most flexible of all production elements.

THE PRINCIPLES OF DESIGN

Stage lighting is governed by the same principles of design as other visual arts: harmony, balance, proportion, emphasis, and rhythm.

The lighting for an entire production should be unified and harmonious but must also have variety. Balance, proportion, and emphasis are closely related in lighting, since each is achieved largely through the proper handling of the others. Lighting should give primary emphasis to the acting areas; the brightest light is usually focused there, with proportionately less on the background. Proportion must be handled, however, so all parts of the stage blend together smoothly as a unit. As a rule, light on the acting areas should be evenly distributed so that the actors do not pass through distracting dark and bright spots as they move about the stage. This usual handling of balance, proportion, and emphasis can be altered, of course, as the script demands.

Rhythm is that factor that makes attention flow effortlessly from the main center of emphasis to the subordinate parts. In lighting. it results from gradations in intensity and the proper handling of color and distribution.

The lighting designer shapes the controllable factors of light in accordance with the principles of design to achieve the purposes of stage lighting and to meet the demands of the production.

WORKING PROCEDURES

The lighting designer should begin by analyzing the script thoroughly; after he understands the play as a whole, he is ready to investigate how to embody its qualities through light.

The designer should note the nature of the light: the sources of illumination (lamps, sunlight); changes in intensity (growing darkness, lamps being lighted); variations required for different parts of the stage; the direction of light (moonlight through a window, sunlight from one side of the stage); any special effects (such as lightning or fire); and coloration (firelight, lamplight, sunlight). Such practical considerations often are helpful and cannot be ignored if essential parts of the action.

Above all, the designer should be concerned with mood and style. In a realistic drama, the source of light may need to be clear and all changes motivated. If the script is nonrealistic, light can be used more arbitrarily. The designer can also underline the play's structural development by underscoring changes, such as that from happiness to despair.

The lighting designer may do research to determine the typical lighting fixtures of a period, the kinds of light derived from each, and the way each fixture was used. If the production utilizes earlier staging techniques, he may need to study the stage-lighting practices of the time.

At the initial conference with the director and other designers, he participates in discussions of the production concept and outlines his ideas about the lighting. He must be particularly concerned with the plans of the scene designer and costumer since their work affects his own. There may be a series of conferences before final accord is reached.

To create the documentary style for Brecht's play *The Measures Taken,* the designer used stark, colorless lights from exposed sources. (Designer, Frederick Youens; Photo, Nelson)

In the professional theatre, the lighting designer must make sketches showing the stage as it will look when lighted. In the nonprofessional theatre, a general agreement is reached about the qualities of the lighting to be used — its intensity, coloration, and distribution — but the specific design is often tentative.

LIGHT PLOTS AND INSTRUMENT SCHEDULE

The lighting designer should be able to outline his plans by means of sketches, light plots, and an instrument schedule.

Light plots usually include a floor plan and a vertical section plan. The floor plan shows, as seen from above, the layout of the entire stage, the setting, and pertinent parts of the auditorium. A section shows the vertical arrangement of the stage, the scenery, and the auditorium. On each of these the following are also shown: the type, size, and position of each instrument and the area to be lighted by each.

It is usually necessary to make a separate light plot for each setting and, in addition, a composite plot that shows all of the settings simultaneously and the relationship of the lighting for each scene to all the others. This is necessary because as a rule some of the same instruments must be used to light more than one set.

Lighting for the stage may be divided into specific illumination, general illumination, and special effects. Specific illumination is confined to a very limited area; general illumination spreads over a large part of the stage; and special effects are out-of-the-ordinary demands such as projections, fires, rainbows, and lightning.

Specific illumination is used principally for lighting the acting areas, which need greatest emphasis and often require much variety in intensity, color, and distribution. Spotlights, the principal sources of specific illumination, are designed to emit a concentrated beam that can be confined.

Since a single spotlight can illuminate only a small segment of the stage, the total acting space is normally divided into smaller areas. For an average-size setting, three or more areas are needed across the forward part of the stage and an equal number at the rear. Each area may then be lighted separately. At least one spotlight should be focused on an area from each side so as to strike it at an angle of 45 degrees both horizontally and vertically. Nowadays, several instruments (mounted at varying levels and angles) are often focused on a single area. The lighting for each area should overlap the other sufficiently to insure even distribution of light.

Where instruments are mounted depends in part on the type of stage. In the proscenium theatre, since forward acting areas cannot be

Capturing the feeling of light coming from chandeliers is a specific design problem as can be seen in this design by Robert Edmond Jones for Congreve's *Love for Love.*

lighted effectively from behind the arch, some instruments are hung in the auditorium — in ceiling apertures, in vertical apertures at the sides, or on the front of the balcony. The upstage acting areas are normally lighted by instruments hung back of the proscenium — on a light bridge just behind the opening, on vertical pipes at either side of the proscenium, on pipe battens suspended over the stage at intervals from front to back, or on stands or the floor.

In the arena theatre, all instruments are mounted above the acting area or the audience. Since performances are viewed from four sides, the acting areas must be lit from all directions. On the thrust stage, most of the instruments are mounted over the platform or above the audience, but there may be a stagehouse back of the main platform where others are hung. This, plus the fact that performances are normally viewed from three sides, makes lighting for thrust stages a compromise between that used for proscenium and for arena stages.

General illumination is exploited most fully on the proscenium stage, where it serves three basic functions: to light all of the background elements (cyclorama, ground rows, drops) not illuminated by spotlights; to blend acting areas together and to provide a smooth transition from the high intensity of the acting areas to the lower intensity of the background; and to enhance or modify the color of settings and costumes.

General illumination is provided primarily by striplights and floodlights. Although this light cannot be confined to small areas, its direction can be partially controlled. Footlights are pointed upward and backward from the front edge of the stage. Border lights may be hung over the acting area and pointed downward or tilted. Other striplights may be placed on the floor to light ground rows or the cyclorama. Floodlights may be suspended on battens, placed on stands, or situated on the floor to illuminate drops or the cyclorama.

On the arena stage, general illumination plays a minor role, since usually there is no background to light and since the specific illumination covers the entire acting space. On the thrust stage, general lighting may play a somewhat larger role, especially if there is a stagehouse.

Special effects cover a variety of miscellaneous lighting requirements, including lightning, fog and smoke, bright rays of light (to simulate moonlight or sunlight), fires and firelogs, explosions, rainbows, "strobe" lights (rapid on-off lighting varying markedly in intensity), and "black" light (ultraviolet light used to pick out specially treated substances on an otherwise dark stage).

In making a light plot, specific illumination, general illumination, and special effects should be considered separately and then as a unit. The instruments, the placement of each, the area to be lighted by each, and the color of filters to be used must be indicated on the lighting plan.

After the lighting plots are completed, an instrument schedule is made. This is a table that lists separately each lighting instrument and indicates specifications (wattage, lens, reflector, lamp, and any other pertinent information), mounting position, color filter, area to be lighted, the circuit into which it is plugged, and the dimmer to which it is connected. It summarizes in tabular form all the technical information needed for acquiring and setting up lighting instruments.

LIGHTING INSTRUMENTS, ACCESSORIES, AND CONTROLBOARDS

To carry out his plans, the lighting designer needs instruments, accessories, and a controlboard.

Most resident and nonprofessional theatres own a supply of lighting equipment sufficient to meet the demands of their productions. Also as a rule, they use buildings that have permanently installed electrical circuits and controlboards.

Most commercial theatre buildings in New York, as well as most used by touring companies elsewhere, do not have controlboards or even permanently installed electrical circuits into which lighting instruments may be plugged. In these instances, the designer must list (with exact specifications) every item necessary for lighting a show. This material may be rented or bought. Because most productions tour (if only for out-of-town tryouts), the lighting equipment must be easily transportable and capable of quick installation. These requirements have kept Broadway productions from using much complex equipment, especially some of the more recent kinds of controlboard.

Lighting Instruments. Lighting instruments may be divided into a number of categories: *spotlights, striplights, floodlights,* and *special lighting equipment.*

Spotlights are designed to illuminate restricted areas with a concentrated beam of light. Any good spotlight has a metal housing, lamp socket, reflector, lens, color-frame guide, mounting attachments, and some device for adjusting focus. Spotlights are normally classified according to wattage, lenses, and reflectors. They range from 100 to 10,000 watts in size, the average being 1000.

A lens gathers the light from a lamp and bends it into parallel rays to create a concentrated beam. Two types of lenses, plano-convex and Fresnel, are most commonly used in spotlights. A plano-convex lens is flat on one side and convex on the other; it gives a sharp, distinct beam of light. In a Fresnel lens, one surface is flat, the other composed of concentric rings of differing diameters; it is ridged on its convex side and is much thinner than a plano-convex lens; it diffuses the light so as to avoid the sharp edges typical of the plano-convex lens. Each spotlight is designed to utilize one type of lens and will not operate efficiently with any other.

Lenses are also described in terms of diameter and focal length. The most common diameters are six, eight, ten, and twelve inches. The focal length of a lens (also stated in inches) indicates the distance that the filament of the lamp should be from the axis of the lens. Each spotlight is designed to use a lens of a specified diameter and focal length.

A reflector is placed behind or around the lamp to throw forward light which would otherwise be wasted and thereby increases efficiency (the ratio between the amount of light emitted by a source and the amount that reaches the stage). Reflectors are made of metal and in various shapes, although those used in spotlights are either spherical or ellipsoidal.

Spotlights are usually divided into three types: *Fresnel, plano-convex,* and *ellipsoidal.* The differences between the Fresnel and plano-convex spotlights result principally from their lenses, since otherwise their basic parts, including a spherical reflector, are similar. The Fresnel is the more popular of the two. The ellipsoidal spotlight may be equipped with a lens of either type; its distinctive qualities are determined by its reflector.

The ellipsoidal spotlight is by far the most efficient type. It is also the most expensive and largest. It is used primarily where the distance between the instrument and the stage is great and where mounting space is not at a premium. Its major use has been to light acting areas from the auditorium.

All spotlights have a number of other features: guides forward of the lens to hold color frames; a mounting that allows the instrument to be rotated from side to side and up and down; and adjustable focus that changes the relationship of lamp, lens, and reflector to each other.

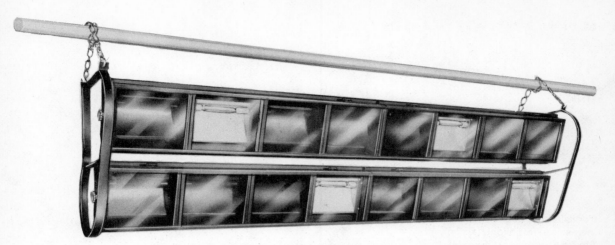

These two striplights may be focussed independently of each other. Each has four-color circuits and uses 300-500 watt lamps. (Courtesy Kliegl Brothers)

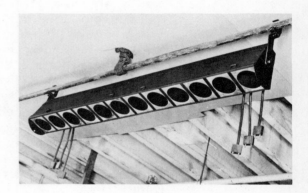

Six-foot portable borderlight.
(Courtesy Kliegl Brothers)

A *striplight* is a series of lamps set into a narrow rectangular trough. It is used for general illumination.

As a rule, each strip is wired with three or four separate circuits. Each third or fourth lamp is on the same circuit and may be controlled together. All of the lamps on the same circuit are covered with filters of the same color. Thus, each strip can produce three or four different colors when each circuit is used alone or it can combine circuits to produce a wide range of additional colors. Striplights therefore can be used to "tone" the settings, costumes, and makeup.

Striplights vary considerably in length from those having only three or four lamps to those that cover the entire width of the stage. They also vary considerably in wattage, using individual lamps ranging from 75 to 500 watts.

Striplights are often subdivided into three categories: footlights, borderlights, and miscellaneous striplights. Footlights normally are recessed in a slot at the front of the stage. They may be used to eliminate shadows

349

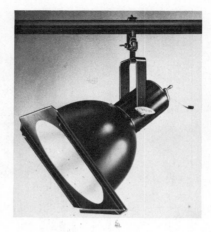 

Focusing floodlight and sixteen-inch scoop floodlight. (Courtesy Strand Century and Kliegl Brothers.)

cast by large hats, to blend the specific and general illumination, and to enhance color. Borderlights are hung from battens above the stage; there may be several rows from front to back. They are used more often than any other instrument for blending together the acting areas and for toning the settings and costumes. Miscellaneous striplights may be placed on the floor to light ground rows and drops and around the base of the cyclorama (as "cyc foots") to create various sky effects. Small strips may be used to light backings for doors and windows.

The floodlight, designed to give general illumination, uses a single lamp as its source. It has a housing with a large opening; there is no lens. Most floodlights have either ellipsoidal (the most typical) or parabolic reflectors. Wattage varies from 250 to 5000. A frame is provided to hold color filters.

Floodlights may be used singly or in combination. They may be suspended above the stage to substitute for borderlights. Like striplights, they may be placed on the floor to light drops and ground rows, and they may be used to light backings and other scenic units. Floodlights are used most frequently to light the cyclorama (several may be used to achieve smooth, even light over the entire visible surface).

It is impossible to specify all special effects that are sometimes called for. Perhaps the most common special equipment is the projector. For still pictures, commercially available, 35-mm. slide projectors are often satisfactory. Since these are not designed for stage use, however, it is sometimes desirable to employ lens projectors bought or rented from lighting supply houses or made by knowledgeable stage technicians. Some projectors are designed for use with moving, circular discs on which such images as clouds, waves, rain, smoke, or fire have been painted; a motor revolves the disc at a constant speed to create the effect of movement. Motion-picture projectors of various types may be used with filmed sequences.

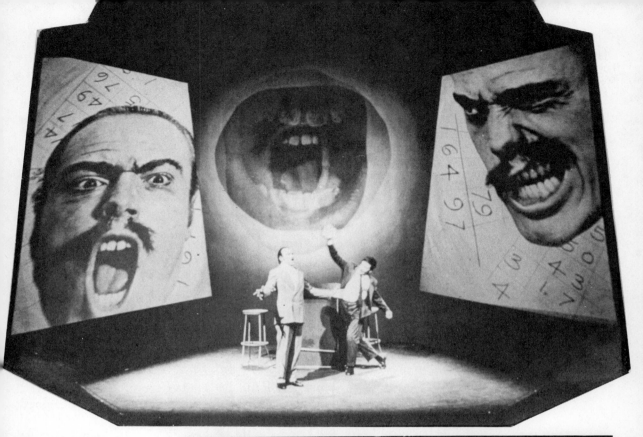

Projectors are used to create the scenic background in this production of Elmer Rice's *The Adding Machine.* The bottom figure shows the screen arrangement: two small downstage front-projection screens backed by a large rear-projection screen.

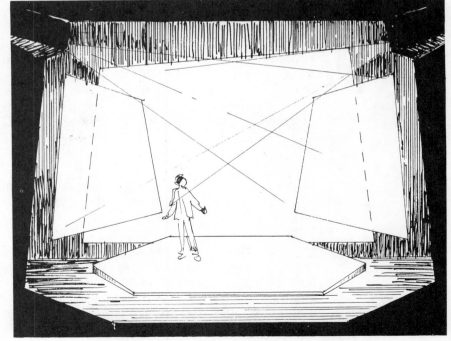

Lightning can be produced by bringing into close proximity two carbon sticks to each of which an electrical terminal is attached; as the current leaps between the two, a bright light, as in welding, produces a realistic lightning effect.

For fireplaces or campfires, prop logs or coals may be constructed and painted appropriately. A lamp is placed inside and the light allowed to shine through holes covered with transparent orange and amber material. Flames may be simulated by a revolving multicolored disc moving in front of a light or by irregular strips of colored silk, chiffon, or plastic kept in motion by a fan.

These common special effects may be supplemented by anyone with a knowledge of electricity and stage-lighting instruments. Additional equipment is also available from lighting-supply houses.

Accessories. A number of accessories—lamps, electrical cable and connectors, color frames and color media—are needed. Each instrument is designed to use a particular lamp. Similarly, each lamp is designed for specific purposes. Lamps vary according to type of base, filament, wattage, whether gas-filled (and if so the kind of gas), shape, treatment of the glass, and position in which it should be used (base up or base down). Manufacturers' catalogues give complete details about lamps designed for stage use.

Electrical cable for the stage should be heavily insulated since it must withstand much wear. It is available in a number of sizes, each designed to carry a maximum electrical load.

Almost every lighting instrument is equipped for color filters and consequently color frames and color media are needed. A frame is usually made of metal, with an opening of the same size and shape as that of the instrument with which it is to be used.

A number of color media are used in stage lighting. The most common is gelatin, a transparent material available in a wide range of hues, saturations, and intensities. It may be cut to any desired shape, but it is fragile and fades with use. Plastic media such as roscolene, cinemoid, and cinabex are also common. They are similar to gelatin in all important respects but are thicker, more durable, and more expensive. Glass is often used with striplights; it is the most durable medium, but is available in only a limited range of colors.

Connecting Panels and Controlboards. No lighting system is complete without some means of control. Instruments and color filters provide the possibilities for control, but before they can be exploited, a board is needed. A board permits some instruments to be on while others are off or partially dimmed, and allows mixing colors from a number of instruments.

This controlboard operator has an unimpeded view of the stage and can easily see the results of her work. (Courtesy Kliegel Brothers)

For a controlboard to be efficient, it must be possible to connect each instrument to it. For this is required a connecting panel to which all stage circuits and controlboard dimmers run so that any circuit may be connected to any dimmer.

Technically, a controlboard can be merely a panel of switches for turning lights on and off. If control is to be subtle, however, dimmers are required. Dimmers are of many types, the most important of which are *resistance, autotransformer,* and *electronic.* Each works on a different principle, but each allows a gradual increase or decrease in the electrical power reaching the lamps so they may be dimmed or brightened.

It is not within the scope of this book to explain how each type of dimmer works. The resistance dimmer is now generally considered outmoded, although it continues to be used in many Broadway theatres and elsewhere. In theatres with restricted space and budgets, the autotransformer has largely supplanted the resistance dimmer. In those with sufficient space and funds, the favorite type by far is the electronic dimmer (especially the silicon controlled rectifier or SCR).

As the number of dimmers increases so does the problem of control

353

by an operator. If each dimmer had to be adjusted manually and individually, several persons would be required to operate a large bank of dimmers. To avoid this, all types of dimmer boards are equipped with master controls that allow some or all of the dimmers to be connected so that a single handle can operate all. An efficient controlboard allows dimmers to be connected in almost any combination.

Another problem is the size of a bank of dimmers. Most electronic units, for example, are so bulky that they must be installed in another part of the building, with a remote-control console located near the stage. Since neither type can be operated by remote control efficiently, resistance and autotransformer dimmers must be installed in the stage area. On the other hand, resistance and autotransformer dimmers can easily be put together in "packages" that can be moved readily and are thus useful where portability is desired. Recently, packaged SCR dimmers have also become available and, though more bulky than other types, are growing in popularity.

The placement of the controlboard console is of considerable importance. The most common locations are: at one side of the stage; in the orchestra pit; at the back of the auditorium; and in a booth built into the face of the balcony. The ideal arrangement is one that permits the operator to see the stage from much the same vantage as the audience.

With some controlboards, dimmers may be preset, with lighting for one or more scenes set up in advance. Then, with a master dimming device, lights for one scene may be faded out and another brought up simultaneously, or changes within a scene may be set on the board beforehand. The ability to preset controls eliminates many mistakes. In recent years, computers have been used to extend the potential for presetting scenes. Consequently, all major manufacturers now offer with their SCR systems a "memory bank" capable of storing several hundred cues or preset scenes. The settings for all of the lighting in an entire show or even in several shows can be recorded, stored, and called up as desired.

Few aspects of theatrical production have undergone so many changes in recent years as lighting control. It is advisable to make frequent inquiries about new developments. The lighting designer should have detailed knowledge of both the range of equipment and its possible applications so that he may select wisely and work efficiently.

REHEARSALS AND PERFORMANCES

Typically, the theatre is not available for work on lights until a few days before the production opens. Regardless of how much time is available, however, the procedures are reasonably standard. Using the light plot

(a) A sketch of the setting.

(b) The layout of the
lighting instruments for the
setting.

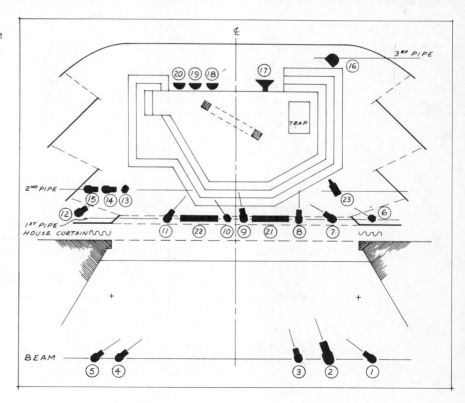

No.	INSTRUMENT	LOCATION	PURPOSE	LAMP	COLOR	REMARKS
1	6" ELLIPS'L-REF'R SPOTLIGHT	BEAM-L	DR SPECIAL	500 T 12	29	
2	8" " " "	" "	FOLLOW SPOT	750 T 12	54	
3	6" " " "	" "	R-CENTER SP.	500 T 12	NONE	
4	" " " "	BEAM-R	DL SP. #1	"	57	
5	" " " "	" "	" " #2	"	26	
6	6" FRESNEL-LENS SPOTLIGHT	1ST PIPE-L	L-STEPS	500 T 20	3/62	KEEP OFF CYC.
7	6" ELLIPS'L-REF'R SPOTLIGHT	" " "	UC SPECIAL	500 T 12	NONE	
8	" " " "	" " "	"HORROR SP."	"	41	FRAME TO TRAP
9	" " " "	1ST PIPE-C	ARCH SP. #1	"	58	
10	6" FRESNEL-LENS SPOTLIGHT	" "	R-STEPS	500 T 20	17	
11	6" ELLIPS'L-REF'R SPOTLIGHT	1ST PIPE-R	ARCH SP. #2	500 T 12	30	FRAME TO ARCH
12	" " " "	PLATFORM-DR	FOLLOW SPOT	"	26/29	
13	6" FRESNEL-LENS SPOTLIGHT	2ND PIPE-R	UR STEPS	500 T 20	18	
14	6" ELLIPS'L-REF'R SPOTLIGHT	" " "	DS STEPS #1	500 T 12	26	
15	" " " "	" " "	" " #2	"	57	
16	16" BEAM PROJECTOR	3RD PIPE UL	ARCH BACKLIGHT	1000 G 40	54	FOCUS THRU ARCH
17	LINNEBACH PROJECTOR	BEHIND PLATFORM-L	PROJECTION ON CYC	1500 G 40	SLIDE	HIDDEN OPERATOR-- ADDITIONAL SLIDES
18	14" ELLIPS'L-REF'R FLOOD	BEHIND PLATFORM-R	FIRE GLOW ON CYC	500 PS	60	}
19	" " " "	"	"	"	67	} GANG TOGETHER
20	" " " "	"	"	"	63	}
21	6" x 4'-6" STRIPLIGHTS	1ST PIPE-L	X-RAYS	150 PS	29 / 58	3-COLOR CIRCUIT FEED THROUGH
22	" "	" " -R	"	OR R40-FL.	41	
23	SLIDE PROJECTOR	2ND PIPE-L	PROJECTION ON CYC	1000 G 40	SLIDE	8" PLANO-CONVEX SPOT WITH EFFECT HEAD

(c) The instrument schedule with numbers corresponding to the layout (b).

and the instrument schedule as guides, technicians mount each instrument and direct it toward the stage area specified by the light plot. The correct color filter is added, then the instrument is plugged into the proper circuit and connected to the designated dimmer. The instruments may be focused tentatively at this time, but the final touches must wait until the scenery is in place.

Setting and focusing instruments is time-consuming and sometimes disheartening, for it is difficult to confine light exactly as desired. Unwanted lines, shadows, and bright areas may appear and, when the same instruments must be used to light more than one setting, an ideal adjustment for one scene may not be right for another.

In the professional theatre, the lighting designer often sits in the auditorium, where he may see the stage from the spectator's point of view, and calls out directions to the lighting crew. Sometimes as many as twenty-four continuous hours are spent adjusting the lighting. In the nonprofessional theatre, this process is seldom compressed into a continuous session of such length, but it is rarely simple.

Cue sheets—indicating the setting of lights at the beginning of each scene (the dimmer to be used and the intensity setting of each), any changes to be made during the scene, and the cues for the changes—must also be made. If there is a memory bank or other preset device, information must be fed into it.

During the technical rehearsal, lighting is integrated with the other elements for the first time. Alterations may be required, and further adjustments may be needed after dress rehearsals. Changes should be made as quickly as possible.

After the play opens, responsibility usually passes to the lighting crew.

THE LIGHTING DESIGNER'S ASSISTANTS

The lighting designer is aided by a number of persons. He sometimes has an assistant who may make drawings for light plots, compile instrument schedules, find the necessary equipment, act as liaison between the lighting designer and the rest of the production staff, and aid in setting up the lights and in compiling the cue sheets.

The master electrician or lighting-crew head works closely with the designer when equipment is being installed and instruments adjusted. After the show opens, he must see that all materials are properly maintained, and that the lighting operates as planned. He is directly responsible to the stage manager.

The lighting crew installs, operates, and maintains all lighting equipment and shifts electrical equipment that must be moved during scene changes. The controlboard console operator is of special importance, since he actually controls the lighting during performances. In the professional theatre, the crew must belong to a union. In the nonprofessional theatre, crews are most frequently assigned.

SOUND

Like other theatrical elements, sound makes its greatest contributions when it is designed as a unit and carefully integrated with the production as a whole. It may be divided into three categories: the actors' voices, music and abstract sounds, and realistic noises. The first category has already been dealt with in the chapters on acting and directing. Music, if recorded, is handled by the sound crew; if played live, by musicians. Ab-

357

stract sound is nonmusical and nonverbal noise without recognizable origin. Realistic sound effects are those readily associated with a natural or man-made phenomenon, such as thunder or an airplane.

Sound fulfills two basic functions: it helps establish mood and style, and it serves as exposition. Music and abstract sound serve the first function by creating the appropriate atmosphere and by underlining important qualities in scenes. For example, strange, hollow noises might be used in a nonrealistic play to support the theme. Realistic sounds may also be used for mood. Thunder and rain can set the background for a murder mystery, while birdsong may establish a quiet, pastoral scene.

Expository sound is most frequently realistic. Gunshots, crashing dishes, doorbells, and similar sounds may prepare for onstage action or suggest offstage happenings. Sound may identify time and place (certain noises may be associated with different times of the year and day); they may place the action in the city or the country near a river or a railroad.

Sound may be live or recorded. Since live sound is created anew at each performance, it may vary considerably from one night to the next. Its major advantage is its adaptability to variations in performances. In recorded sound, effects are created and then placed on records or tape. Barring human or mechanical errors, recorded sound is the same at each performance.

A wide variety of effects can be obtained on commercially made tapes, but these are not always appropriate to specific plays. Since most organizations now own some kind of taping equipment, they usually can record their own effects. Such noises as doorbells and telephones can be produced so easily with electrical buzzers that to record them would be inefficient.

Sound systems vary widely in complexity and quality. Some groups must make do with the simplest of record players or tape-recorder/playback units; others have very elaborate systems. A completely effective system allows all of the controllable properties of sound — pitch, quality, volume, direction, and duration — to be varied in relation to each other and in accordance with the demands of a script. For example, complete flexibility in direction requires a series of amplifiers located at various spots on the stage and in the auditorium so that a sound such as of an airplane can begin on one side, seem to approach, pass over the set, and go out of hearing on the other side. A truly efficient system, therefore, should include the following: a number of tape-recorder/playback units — so that sound may be recorded and then mixed from more than one tape played simultaneously; microphones and turntables — for taping live sound and musical selections, and for use during performances as needed; a speaker system of high quality and with considerable versatility — so that sound at any volume can be reproduced effectively and so the direction of sound can be controlled fully; a patch bay—so that sound sources such as tapes or microphones can be connected to any outlet; and a control console—so that the entire system can be operated efficiently.

Normally the only plan for sound is the cue sheet. It indicates each sound, when it is to begin, how it is to build, and when it is to end. It may also specify the method by which the sound is to be produced and, where electronic equipment is involved, sound levels. If elaborate and extensive sound equipment is available, it may be necessary to make a chart similar to an instrument schedule for stage lighting. It should list each piece of equipment (with specifications), and indicate for each its placement, use, and control.

As with other elements, sound must be rehearsed and integrated carefully with the production as a whole. It must be adjusted in relation to the stage and auditorium, the actors' voices, and the requirements of the script.

MULTIMEDIA PRODUCTIONS

In recent years, multimedia productions have become increasingly common. Combining live action with projected still or moving pictures, stereophonic sound and music, they mingle elements from several media.

Several factors explain the increased popularity of multimedia devices. First, wartime and space research brought significant advances in electronics that have been adapted to theatrical production. Second, escalating costs in the theatre have created a demand for means less expensive than full-stage, three-dimensional settings. Third, artistic taste and audience perception have changed so that rapid shifts in time, place, and focus are expected. Playwrights also have come to take it for granted that time and place can be altered instantaneously. For these and other reasons, settings of the traditional sort have been partially supplanted by those created primarily through light and sound.

The most characteristic feature of multimedia productions is the liberal use of projections—usually of still pictures, although several slides may be shown simultaneously on a number of screens and changed rapidly. All the slides may represent fragments of the same picture, or each may be wholly unlike the others. All are usually chosen because of their appropriateness to the mood or dramatic action; some may suggest comparisons between the stage events and those of other times and places. Filmed sequences may be used narratively to show offstage action or for the same purposes as still pictures. Closed-circuit television can show views of the action as seen from various angles, or the audience itself. Projections are usually accompanied by stereophonic and directional sound—varying in volume from the loudest to the softest, from the most realistic to the purely abstract, from the atmospheric to the psychologically jolting.

In these and other ways, multimedia productions have enlarged the range of theatrical techniques, and probably will continue to do so.

POSTSCRIPT

This book has surveyed the theatre in its varied aspects—theoretical, historical, practical, artistic—as a basis for better understanding, continuing study, and practice. The theatre of today is the inheritor of a tradition that stretches back to the beginning of recorded history. Between its origins and the present, many changes have taken place. On the basis of these, a number of conclusions may be hazarded.

First, both the theatre and the value placed on it vary as historical and social conditions change. Second, the theatre reflects the outlook of its time. Each theatrical style is an attempt to express adequately a view of the world and man's place in it. Third, there is always a close relationship between the drama and the theatrical conventions of an age. The dramatist's conception of the theatre's potential dictates in part the demands he makes on it. Fourth, while social conditions, ideas, and theatrical conventions influence dramatic expression, the playwright's vision is ultimately the source of greatness.

Fifth, although every play is clearly a product of its age, the great plays are timeless. Great drama provides a means through which we in the present can feel our way into the past, comprehend it, and perceive the continuity of human experience. Sixth, theatre and drama are important ways of knowing about man's ideas and feelings. Seventh, the dramatic inpulse seems too deeply ingrained in man ever to be eradicated. The theatre may fluctuate in popularity, and the pleasures it offers may be fulfilled at times by other activities, but the theatre in one form or another remains a vital part of human society.

Appendix:
Opportunities to Work in the Theatre

There are more producing groups in America today than ever before. The outlets for theatrical talent are numerous, although a large proportion do not carry prospects of a living wage. The professional theatre can absorb relatively few of those who seek employment. Fortunately, there are other rewarding outlets—in community theatre, education, and various other activities.

THEATRE AS AN AVOCATION

The majority of students who receive theatrical training in colleges do not enter the theatre after graduation. To most, theatre is a means for acquiring a liberal education just as English, philosophy, or history might be. The opportunities for working in the theatre as an avocation are many, since the majority of theatrical organizations in America rely upon

361

unpaid personnel. The demand for actors is great, and almost anyone with an interest in scenery, costumes, lighting, properties, makeup, sound, dance, or music can find ample opportunities to express it.

THEATRE IN EDUCATION

Probably the largest number of paying jobs in the theatre are in education. As a rule, theatre workers are employed in schools for two purposes: to teach and to produce plays. Sometimes it is possible to specialize in directing, costuming, lighting, or some other area, but to be assured of employment one should be prepared to undertake almost any assignment.

The educational theatre may be divided in terms of levels: *children's theatre, secondary school theatre,* and *college and university theatre.*

Children's Theatre. Children's theatre may operate within any of three frameworks: professional, community, or educational. Its distinguishing characteristic is its intended audience.

A related area is creative dramatics, although technically it is not a theatrical activity. Children are stimulated to improvise dramatic situations based on stories, historical events, or common social situations. It is used to help children feel their way into fictional and real-life situations, to make learning more concrete, to allow children an outlet for their responses and feelings, and to stimulate imagination. Thus it is an educational and developmental tool rather than a product intended for an audience. Normally creative dramatics is handled by the classroom teacher, who should have specialized training in its techniques.

Theatre as such is seldom taught in elementary schools. Children are instead offered plays through a variety of channels: the recreation program in most large cities includes children's theatre; many community theatres, high schools, colleges, and universities produce plays for children; and several professional organizations specialize in plays for children.

There is a fairly large demand for persons with some training in children's theatre and creative dramatics. Some colleges and universities employ specialists in these areas; school districts may hire a person who can demonstrate and supervise creative dramatics; some community theatres employ a director whose sole responsibility is the production of children's plays; public recreation programs often employ a specialist in this area. In addition, there are a number of professional troupes who perform only for child audiences.

The worker in children's theatre needs all the same basic training required by any other theatre worker. In addition, he should receive some specialized instruction in child and developmental psychology and in the specific techniques of children's theatre.

The Paper Bag Players, a very successful children's theatre group, take their name from their use of simple props, often made from paper bags. This scene is from their production *Grandpa*. (The Paper Bag Players)

Secondary School Theatre. Almost every high school in the United States produces one or more plays each year. Relatively few offer courses in theatre and drama, and plays frequently are directed by persons with no theatre training at all. On the other hand, some secondary schools have excellent theatre programs.

The teacher in the secondary school should understand the adolescent and usually must be certified to teach subjects other than theatre, such as speech and English.

Undergraduate Colleges and Universities. The majority of colleges and universities in the United States offer some coursework in theatre. In most cases theatre courses are included in the liberal arts curriculum, but the production program is extracurricular.

The teacher in a liberal arts college may have a chance to specialize in such areas as directing or design but often he must teach and supervise several areas of production. Those undergraduate programs that offer the BFA degree in theatre usually admit students only after auditions and interviews have established their talent and commitment. Since these programs are usually oriented to the professional theatre, instructors must be able to set high standards through their own work.

A scene from the Indiana University Theatre's production of Harold Pinter's *The Birthday Party*. (Courtesy Indiana University Theatre)

Graduate Schools.   The graduate school is designed to give specialized training. It therefore requires a staff of experienced specialists and employment is usually available only to those who have demonstrated considerable ability in specific aspects of the theatre. The graduate school is crucial to the theatre, for most practitioners now receive their basic training in colleges and universities, and graduate schools supply most of the teachers.

University Resident Theatres.   About thirty colleges and universities currently support resident theatre companies. Many of these companies are made up of students; some mingle students and professionals and a few are wholly professional. Most typically each group produces plays of many types and from many periods.

The majority of each company's members are actors, but a director, a few technicians, and sometimes a designer are usually included. Each spring those companies belonging to the University/Resident Theatre Association (U/RTA) hold joint auditions. The number of students from each school who can try out is limited. When professional actors are included, they are usually selected through auditions conducted in New York or a few other locations.

THE COMMUNITY THEATRE

Almost every town with a population of more than thirty thousand has a community theatre. Many of these theatres are operated entirely by volunteers; others pay the director of each play and may provide a small sum for the designer and other key workers. Most typically, a community theatre employs a full-time director who supervises all productions. The more prosperous groups also have a full-time designer-technician, and some hire a children's theatre director as well.

Because of their purpose, however, community theatres usually do not hire persons other than in supervisory capacities. The primary function of community theatre, in addition to providing theatrical entertainment for local audiences, is to furnish an outlet for the talents of adult volunteers.

Anyone who seeks employment in the community theatre therefore needs to be a leader. He should be diplomatic, able to cooperate with diverse personalities, and know a great deal about public relations.

SUMMER THEATRES

Summer theatres are now numerous and scattered throughout the country. They usually perform between late June and early September. Most present a different play each week or every two weeks; during the run of a show, one or more additional scripts are usually being rehearsed.

There are many kinds of summer companies. Some are entirely professional and hire only professional actors, designers, and directors. Others mingle professionals and nonprofessionals. (Actors Equity classifies companies according to the number of professional actors employed, minimum salaries, and working conditions.) Companies employing professional actors may hire designers and directors who are not union members. Some summer theatres are operated by educational institutions and give college credit for participation.

Many summer theatres have apprenticeship programs. Apprentices may receive room and board and even a small weekly salary; seldom is the pay more than enough for living expenses. Some organizations ask apprentices to pay a fee, but this practice is generally frowned upon.

There are many varieties of summer theatre. Some companies perform a single work for the entire summer. Some specialize in plays by a single author, such as Shakespeare. Some perform only musicals. Still others employ only a nucleus company and import well-known motion picture, television, or stage actors to play leading roles. Occasionally summer theatres try out new plays for Broadway producers.

Most hiring for professional and semiprofessional summer theatres is done in New York and a few large cities. Those summer theatres run by colleges may hold auditions on campus. In any case, summer theatre can only provide seasonal employment.

PROFESSIONAL COMPANIES OUTSIDE NEW YORK

Most of the permanent companies outside New York (there are now about fifty-five) belong to the League of Resident Theatres (LORT), which assists them in various ways with common problems.

Normally the same staff—designers, directors, business and promotional personnel—continues throughout the season. Several companies import guest directors for some productions, and most companies engage a new group of actors for each new production.

The LORT companies secure their personnel in various ways. They usually hold joint auditions each year in a number of cities. Personnel other than actors are usually employed on the basis of interviews, recommendations, and demonstrated aptitude or achievement. Some companies are willing to audition applicants from colleges and universities, although usually only if they have been screened in advance.

Other than resident troupes, the professional theatre outside New York is represented primarily by touring companies. Since these are usually cast in New York, they are essentially an extension of Broadway.

PROFESSIONAL THEATRE IN NEW YORK

The jobs most difficult to get are those on Broadway, not only because opportunities are few but because of union control. Some of these conditions apply elsewhere than Broadway but seldom so fully.

Directors. The director is employed by the producer. He must be a member of the Society of Stage Directors and Choreographers, which has worked out standard contracts to specify the director's rights and working conditions.

Actors. Actors (including dancers and singers) must belong to Actors Equity Association. A performer may be cast without being a member of Equity but must join before he can be given a contract.

Actors Equity requires producers to devote a minimum of eight hours to open interviews or auditions for each show. This screening may be done by an assistant, and few of the applicants may actually be permitted to try out. Many actors obtain auditions through agents, and others are invited by the producer to try out.

Actors Equity also controls contracts beyond Broadway. It classifies companies according to production conditions, prescribes the percentage of actors who must be members of Equity, and sets the minimum wage scale.

Stage Managers.   Stage managers must also belong to Actors Equity. Most begin as performers and for extra pay take on the job of assistant stage manager; large shows usually have several. If they are reliable, they may subsequently be employed as principal stage manager. In addition to his other tasks, the stage manager sometimes plays a minor role, and after the show opens he may rehearse the cast as needed.

Designers.   The designers are employed by the producer. All must belong to the United Scenic Artists Union, the most difficult of all stage unions to gain admission to. Applicants must pay an examination fee and, if he passes the rigorous exam, a sizable initiation fee. This union also controls design in television, films, opera, and ballet. A designer may be admitted to the union as a scenic, costume, or lighting designer, or he may qualify in two or all of these areas. All contracts must meet the union's minimum requirements. Many younger members of the union work as assistants to well-established designers.

Scenery, Costume, Lighting, and Property Crews.   Members of the various crews that run shows must belong to the International Alliance of Theatrical Stage Employees. Crews are very carefully separated, however, so that no one will perform more than one function. This union restricts admission to make sure most of its members will be employed. Acceptance depends as much on knowing the right persons as on training. Those who have been through theatre programs do not normally enter this union.

Others.   Each production must have a company manager and a press agent, who work directly with the producer. The manager aids in letting contracts, arranges for rehearsal space and out-of-town tryouts, and handles the payroll. The press agent is concerned principally with selling the show. Both must be members of the Association of Theatrical Press Agents and Managers.

Any theatrical worker may have an agent, whose job it is to market his client's services. He can be crucial in getting a hearing for clients, who might otherwise never be able to display their talents. For his services an agent is paid a percentage of his client's earnings on each contract he negotiates. Agents customarily must be approved by the client's union.

The number of job opportunities in New York is very small in relation to those seeking employment. Usually fewer than one-fourth of the members of Actors Equity are employed at one time; fewer than twenty-five designers in each of the fields of scenery, costume, and lighting design all the shows seen on Broadway each year; and fewer than fifty directors direct all the shows. Most work on no more than one show each season.

The bleakness of this picture is relieved somewhat by Off-Broadway and Off-Off-Broadway, which provide as many jobs as Broadway. In Off-Off-Broadway companies, especially, the unions' demands are less than on Broadway, but they are increasing. Still, it is almost as difficult to get a job off as on Broadway, and the pay is usually as low as circumstances will permit.

Many people do their best to discourage would-be professionals from going to New York, but nothing can keep many from doing so. It is nevertheless becoming increasingly common for aspirants to look to resident theatres and other organizations outside New York as their best hope.

SPECIAL EMPLOYMENT OPPORTUNITIES

In addition to the more obvious opportunities already discussed, a number of related activities should be mentioned. First, television and motion pictures offer additional possibilities. Without them, many professionals would lead a difficult life indeed. But these supplementary fields have their own unemployment problems, and they merely relieve some of the pressures.

Second, a number of industrial and commercial firms stage special shows to publicize their products. Frequently these productions are lavish and some tour to major cities. These shows normally play for invited audiences only; they pay extremely well but provide little further recognition. Most are cast in New York.

Third, the United States Army employs a large number of civilian specialists to stage plays and other entertainment. Many of the positions also offer the opportunity of living and working abroad.

Fourth, many municipal recreation departments employ persons trained in theatre. To be eligible, one must usually have had some training in the field of health, physical education, and recreation.

Fifth, theatre for the aging seems to be emerging as a field. As the average age of retirement is lowered and as life expectancy increases, the potential of this field should expand.

Sixth, theatrical techniques have been adapted for a number of nontheatrical uses. For example, they are now used therapeutically with emotionally disturbed persons. To work in such a field, sound training in psychology as well as in drama and theatre is needed.

When the variety of theatrical activities — in both the nonprofessional and professional theatre — is considered, the employment opportunities are considerable. There are by no means as many jobs as there are applicants, especially in the professional theatre, but the theatre has never been an easy profession. Still, there is always a demand for talented and dedicated persons, and the future of the theatre depends on this select few.

Bibliography

This bibliography lists some important works on the theatre. It is divided to correspond with the divisions in the text. All works are in English.

PART ONE

1: Theatre, Audience, and Critic

Crane, R. S. *The Language of Criticism and the Structure of Poetry.* Toronto: University of Toronto Press, 1953.

Esslin, Martin. *An Anatomy of Drama.* New York: Hill and Wang, 1976.

Fergusson, Francis. *The Idea of a Theater.* Princeton, N.J.: Princeton University Press, 1949.

Granville-Barker, Harley. *The Uses of Drama.* Princeton, N.J.: Princeton University Press, 1945.

Lahr, John, and Price, Jonathan. *Life-show: How to See Theatre in Life and Life in Theatre.* New York: Viking Press, 1973.

Langer, Susanne K. *Problems of Art.* New York: Charles Scribner's Sons, 1957.
Littlewood, Samuel R. *The Art of Dramatic Criticism.* London: Pitman, 1952.
Styan, J. L. *Drama, Stage and Audience.* New York: Cambridge University Press, 1975.
Wickham, Glynne. *Drama in a World of Science.* Toronto: University of Toronto Press, 1962.
Winnicott, D. W. *Playing and Reality.* New York: Basic Books, 1971.

2. The Script: Dramatic Structure, Form, and Style

Barry, Jackson G. *Dramatic Structure: The Shaping of Experience.* Berkeley: University of California Press, 1970.
Beckerman, Bernard. *Dynamics of Drama: Theory and Method of Analysis.* New York: Alfred A. Knopf, Inc., 1970.
Gross, Roger. *Understanding Playscripts: Theory and Method.* Bowling Green, Ohio: Bowling Green University Press, 1974.
Hayman, Ronald. *How to Read a Play.* New York: Grove Press, 1977.
Heffner, Hubert. *The Nature of Drama.* Boston: Houghton Mifflin Co., 1959.
Kerr, Walter. *Tragedy and Comedy.* New York: Simon & Schuster, Inc., 1967.
Nicoll, Allardyce. *The Theory of Drama,* rev. ed. London: Harrap and Co., Ltd., 1931.
Olson, Elder. *The Theory of Comedy.* Bloomington: Indiana University Press, 1968.
_____. *Tragedy and the Theory of Drama.* Detroit: Wayne State University Press, 1961.
Pollard, Richard N. and Hazel M. *From Human Sentience to Drama: Principles of Critical Analysis, Tragic and Comedic.* Athens: Ohio University Press, 1974.
Smiley, Sam. *Playwriting: The Structure of Action.* Englewood Cliffs, N.J.: Prentice-Hall, Inc., 1971.
Styan, J. L. *The Elements of Drama.* New York: Cambridge University Press, 1960.
Tennyson, G. B. *An Introduction to Drama.* New York: Holt, Rinehart and Winston, Inc., 1967.
Weales, Gerald. *A Play and Its Parts.* New York: Basic Books, 1964.

PART TWO

General Works Applicable to Part Two

Brockett, Oscar G. *History of the Theatre,* 2d ed. Boston: Allyn & Bacon, Inc., 1974.
Duerr, Edwin. *The Length and Depth of Acting.* New York: Holt, Rinehart and Winston, Inc., 1962.
Gassner, John. *Masters of the Drama,* 3rd ed. New York: Dover Publications, Inc., 1954.
Izenour, George C. *Theatre Design.* New York: McGraw-Hill, 1977.
Laver, James. *Drama: Its Costume and Decor.* London: Studio Publications, 1951.

McGraw-Hill Encyclopedia of World Drama. 4 vols. New York: McGraw-Hill, 1972.

Nicoll, Allardyce. *World Drama from Aeschylus to Anouilh.* Rev. ed. London: Harrap and Co., 1976.

Oenslager, Donald. *Stage Design: Four Centuries of Scenic Invention.* New York: Viking Press, 1975.

Oxford Companion to the Theatre, 3d ed. London: Oxford University Press, 1967.

Southern, Richard. *The Seven Ages of the Theatre.* New York: Hill & Wang, 1961.

Stuart, Donald C. *The Development of Dramatic Art.* New York: Appleton-Century-Crofts, 1933.

3: The Theatre of Ancient Greece and Rome

Allen, James T. *Stage Antiquities of the Greeks and Romans and Their Influence.* New York: Longmans, Green, 1927.

Arnott, Peter D. *Greek Scenic Conventions in the Fifth Century, B.C.* Oxford: Clarendon Press, 1962.

————. *The Ancient Greek and Roman Theatre.* New York: Random House, Inc., 1971.

Beare, William. *The Roman Stage: A Short History of Latin Drama in the Time of the Republic,* 3d ed. London: Methuen & Co., Ltd., 1963.

Bieber, Margarete. *The History of the Greek and Roman Theater,* 2d ed. Princeton, N.J.: Princeton University Press, 1961.

Butler, James H. *The Theatre and Drama of Greece and Rome.* San Francisco: Chandler Publishing Co., 1972.

Deardon, C. W. *The Stage of Aristophanes.* London: Athlone Press, 1976.

Duckworth, George E. *The Nature of Roman Comedy.* Princeton, N.J.: Princeton University Press, 1952.

Hanson, J. A. *Roman Theater-Temples.* Princeton, N. J.: Princeton University Press, 1959.

Harsh, Philip W. *A Handbook of Classical Drama.* Stanford, Calif.: Stanford University Press, 1944.

Kitto, H. D. F. *Greek Tragedy,* 2d ed. London: Methuen & Co., Ltd., 1950.

Lawler, Lillian B. *The Dance of the Ancient Greek Theatre.* Iowa City: University of Iowa Press, 1964.

Lucas, Frank L. *Seneca and Elizabethan Tragedy.* Cambridge: The University Press, 1922.

Pickard-Cambridge, A. W. *Dithyramb, Tragedy, and Comedy,* 2d ed., rev. by T. B. L. Webster. Oxford: Clarendon Press, 1962.

————. *The Dramatic Festivals of Athens,* 2d ed., rev. by John Gould and D. M. Lewis. Oxford: Clarendon Press, 1968.

————. *The Theatre of Dionysus in Athens.* Oxford: Clarendon Press, 1946.

Segal, Erich W. *Roman Laughter: The Comedy of Plautus.* Cambridge, Mass.: Harvard University Press, 1968.

Sifakis, Gregory M. *Studies in the History of Hellenistic Drama.* London: Athlone, 1967.

Taplin, Oliver. *The Stagecraft of Aeschylus.* Oxford: The Clarendon Press, 1977.

Vitruvius. *The Ten Books of Architecture.* Trans. by M. H. Morgan. Cambridge, Mass.: Harvard University Press, 1914.

Webster, T. B. L. *Greek Theatre Production,* 2d ed. London: Methuen & Co., Ltd., 1970.

4: Medieval Theatre and Drama

Bevington, David. *From Mankind to Marlowe: Growth in Structure in the Popular Drama of Tudor England.* Cambridge: Harvard University Press, 1962.

Chambers, E. K. *The Mediaeval Stage.* 2 vols. Oxford: Clarendon Press, 1903.

Collins, Fletcher. *The Production of Medieval Church Music-Drama.* Charlotte: University of Virginia Press, 1971.

Craig, Hardin. *English Religious Drama of the Middle Ages.* Oxford: Clarendon Press, 1955.

Craik, Thomas W. *The Tudor Interlude: Stage, Costume, and Acting.* Leicester: The University Press, 1958.

Kolve, V. A. *The Play Called Corpus Christi.* Stanford, Calif.: Stanford University Press, 1966.

Nagler, A. M. *The Medieval Religious Stage: Shapes and Phantoms.* New Haven: Yale University Press, 1976.

Nelson, Alan H. *The Medieval English Stage: Corpus Christi, Pageants and Plays.* Chicago: University of Chicago Press, 1974.

Nicoll, Allardyce. *Masks, Mimes and Miracles.* New York: Harcourt Brace Jovanovich, Inc., 1931.

Potter, Robert. *The English Morality Play: Origins, History and Influence of a Dramatic Tradition.* London: Routledge and Kegan Paul, 1975.

Salter, F. M. *Medieval Drama in Chester.* Toronto: University of Toronto Press, 1955.

Wickham, Glynne. *Early English Stages, 1300–1660.* 2 vols. New York: Columbia University Press, 1959–72.

———. *The Medieval Theatre.* London: Weidenfeld and Nicolson, 1974.

Williams, Arnold. *The Drama of Medieval England.* East Lansing: Michigan State University Press, 1961.

Woolf, Rosemary. *The English Mystery Play.* Berkeley: University of California Press, 1972.

Young, Karl. *The Drama of the Medieval Church.* 2 vols. Oxford: Clarendon Press, 1933.

5: Elizabethan England

Adams, John C. *The Globe Playhouse: Its Design and Equipment,* 2d ed. New York: Barnes & Noble, 1961.

Adams, Joseph Q. *Shakespearean Playhouses: A History of English Theatres from the Beginnings to the Restoration.* Boston: Houghton Mifflin Co., 1917.

Baldwin, T. W. *The Organization and Personnel of the Shakespearean Company.* Princeton, N.J.: Princeton University Press, 1927.

Barroll, J. L., et al. *Revels History of Drama in English.* Vol. 3: 1576–1613. New York: Barnes and Noble, 1975.

Beckerman, Bernard. *Shakespeare at the Globe, 1599–1609*. New York: The Macmillan Company, 1962.

Boas, Frederick S. *An Introduction to Stuart Drama*. London: Oxford University Press, 1946.

Gildersleeve, Virginia. *Government Regulation of the Elizabethan Drama*. New York: Columbia University Press, 1908.

Harbage, Alfred. *Shakespeare's Audience*. New York: Columbia University Press, 1941.

Hodges, C. Walter. *The Globe Restored*, 2d ed. London: Oxford University Press, 1968.

Joseph, Bertram. *Elizabethan Acting*, 2d ed. London: Oxford University Press, 1964.

Nagler, A. M. *Shakespeare's Stage*. New Haven, Conn.: Yale University Press, 1958.

Nicoll, Allardyce. *Stuart Masques and the Renaissance Stage*. London: Harrap & Co., Ltd., 1937.

Orgel, Stephen. *The Illusion of Power: Political Theatre in the English Renaissance*. Berkeley: University of California Press, 1975.

Reynolds, George F. *The Staging of Elizabethan Plays at the Red Bull Theatre, 1605–1625*. New York: Modern Language Association, 1940.

Rossiter, A. P. *English Drama from Early Times to the Elizabethans: Its Background, Origins and Developments*. New York: Hutchinson's University Library, 1950 (Reprinted, New York: Barnes & Noble, 1959).

Smith, Irwin. *Shakespeare's Blackfriars Playhouse: Its History and Its Design*. New York: New York University Press, 1964.

Southern, Richard. *The Staging of Plays before Shakespeare*. New York: Theatre Arts Books, 1973.

Speaight, Robert. *Shakespeare on the Stage: An Illustrated History of Shakespearean Performance*. London: Collins, 1972.

Strong, Roy. *Splendor at Court*. Boston: Houghton Mifflin Co., 1973.

Welsford, Enid. *The Court Masque*. New York: Russell and Russell, 1962.

Wickham, Glynne. See under Chapter 4.

6: From the Renaissance to Neoclassicism in Italy and France

Bjurstrom, Per. *Giacomo Torelli and Baroque Stage Design*. Stockholm: Almqvist and Wiksell, 1961.

Duchartre, Pierre L. *The Italian Comedy: The Improvisation, Scenarios, Lives, Attributes, Portrait and Masks of the Illustrious Characters of the Commedia dell'Arte*. Trans. by R. T. Weaver. London: Harrap & Co., Ltd., 1929.

Herrick, Marvin. *Italian Comedy in the Renaissance*. Urbana: University of Illinois Press, 1960.

———. *Italian Tragedy in the Renaissance*. Urbana: University of Illinois Press, 1965.

———. *Tragicomedy: Its Origin and Development in Italy, France, and England*. Urbana: University of Illinois Press, 1955.

Hewitt, Barnard (ed.). *The Renaissance Stage: Documents of Serlio, Sabbattini, and Furttenbach.* Coral Gables, Fla.: University of Miami Press, 1958.

Jeffery, Brian. *French Renaissance Comedy, 1552–1630.* Oxford: Clarendon Press, 1969.

Kernodle, George. *From Art to Theatre: Form and Convention in the Renaissance.* Chicago: University of Chicago Press, 1943.

Lawrenson, T. E. *The French Stage in the XVIIth Century: A Study in the Advent of the Italian Order.* Manchester: Manchester University Press, 1957.

Lea, Kathleen M. *Italian Popular Comedy: A Study of the Commedia dell'Arte, 1560–1620.* 2 vols. Oxford: Clarendon Press, 1934.

Lough, John. *Paris Theatre Audiences in the Seventeenth and Eighteenth Centuries.* London: Oxford University Press, 1957.

Nagler, Alois M. *Theatre Festivals of the Medici, 1539–1637.* New Haven, Conn.: Yale University Press, 1964.

Nicoll, Allardyce. See under Chapter 5.

Turnell, Martin. *The Classical Moment: Studies in Corneille, Molière and Racine.* New York: New Directions, 1948.

White, John. *The Birth and Rebirth of Pictorial Space,* 2d ed. London: Faber & Faber, Ltd., 1967.

Wiley, W. L. *The Early Public Theatre in France.* Cambridge, Mass.: Harvard University Press, 1960.

Worsthorne, S. T. *Venetian Opera in the 17th Century.* Oxford: Clarendon Press, 1954.

Wright, C. H. C. *French Classicism.* Cambridge, Mass.: Harvard University Press, 1920.

7: The Eighteenth Century

Baur-Heinhold, Margarete. *The Baroque Theatre.* New York: McGraw-Hill Book Co., Inc., 1967.

Boas, Frederick S. *An Introduction to Eighteenth Century Drama, 1700–1780.* New York: Oxford University Press, 1953.

Booth, Michael, et al. *Revels History of Drama in English.* Vol. 6: 1750–1880. New York: Barnes and Noble, 1975.

Bruford, Walter H. *Theatre, Drama, and Audience in Goethe's Germany.* London: Routledge & Kegan Paul, Ltd., 1957.

Goldoni, Carlo. *Memoirs of Carlo Goldoni.* Trans. by John Black. New York: Alfred A. Knopf, Inc., 1926.

Highfill, Philip H., et al. *A Biographical Dictionary of Actors, Actresses, Musicians, Dancers, Managers, and Other Stage Personnel in London, 1660–1800.* Carbondale: Southern Illinois University Press, 1973–. (In progress.)

Hotson, Leslie. *The Commonwealth and Restoration Stage.* Cambridge, Mass.: Harvard University Press, 1928.

Joseph, Bertram. *The Tragic Actor.* New York: Theatre Arts Books, 1959.

Krutch, Joseph W. *Comedy and Conscience after the Restoration.* New York: Columbia University Press, 1949.

Loftus, John, et al. *Revels History of Drama in English.* Vol. 4: 1660–1750. New York: Barnes and Noble, 1976.

The London Stage, 1660–1800. 11 vols. Carbondale: Southern Illinois University Press, 1960–1968.

Lough, John. See under Chapter 6.

Mayor, A. Hyatt. *The Bibiena Family.* New York: H. Bittner, 1945.

Melcher, Edith. *Stage Realism in France from Diderot to Antoine.* Bryn Mawr, Pa.: Bryn Mawr College, 1928.

Nicoll, Allardyce. *History of English Drama, 1660–1900.* 6 vols. London: Cambridge University Press, 1955–59.

Odell, G. C. D. *Shakespeare from Betterton to Irving.* 2 vols. New York: Charles Scribner's Sons, 1920.

Price, Cecil. *Theatre in the Age of Garrick.* Oxford: Blackwell, 1973.

Prudhoe, John. *The Theatre of Goethe and Schiller.* Oxford: Blackwell, 1973.

Rankin, Hugh F. *The Theatre in Colonial America.* Chapel Hill: University of North Carolina Press, 1965.

Scholz, Janos. *Baroque and Romantic Stage Design.* New York: E. P. Dutton & Co., Inc., 1962.

Sherbo, Arthur. *English Sentimental Drama.* East Lansing: Michigan State University Press, 1957.

Southern, Richard. *Changeable Scenery: Its Origin and Development in the British Theatre.* London: Faber and Faber, Ltd., 1952.

Speaight, Robert. See under Chapter 5.

8: The Nineteenth Century

Birdoff, Harry. *The World's Greatest Hit: "Uncle Tom's Cabin."* New York: S. F. Vanni, 1947.

Bogard, Travis, et al. *Revels History of Drama in English.* Vol. 8: American Drama. New York: Barnes and Noble, 1977.

Booth, Michael, et al. See under Chapter 7.

Booth, Michael R. *English Melodrama.* London: Herbert Jenkins, 1965.

Carlson, Marvin A. *The French Stage in the Nineteenth Century.* Metuchen, N.J.: Scarecrow Press, Inc., 1972.

————. *The German Stage in the Nineteenth Century.* Metuchen. N.J.: Scarecrow Press, Inc., 1972.

Cross, Gilbert. *Next Week "East Lynne": Domestic Drama in Performance, 1820–1874.* Lewisburg, Pa.: Bucknell University Press, 1976.

Donohue, Joseph W. *Theatre in the Age of Kean.* Oxford: Blackwell, 1975.

Hewitt, Barnard. *Theatre USA, 1668–1957.* New York: McGraw-Hill Book Co., Inc., 1959.

Joseph, Bertram. See under Chapter 7.

Kaufmann, F. W. *German Dramatists of the Nineteenth Century.* Los Angeles: Lymanhouse, 1940.

Lacey, Alexander. *Pixérécourt and the French Romantic Drama.* Toronto: University of Toronto Press, 1928.

Mammen, Edward W. *The Old Stock Company School of Acting.* Boston: The Public Library, 1945.

Melcher, Edith. See under Chapter 7.

Moynet, Jean-Pierre. *French Theatrical Production in the Nineteenth Century.* Binghamton, N.Y.: Max Reinhardt Foundation, 1976.

Nicoll, Allardyce. See under Chapter 7.

Odell, G. C. D. See under Chapter 7.

Prudhoe, John. See under Chapter 7.

Quinn, Arthur H. *A History of the American Drama from the Beginning to the Civil War,* 2d ed. New York: Appleton-Century-Crofts, 1943.

————. *A History of the American Drama from the Civil War to the Present Day,* 2d ed. New York: Appelton-Century-Crofts, 1949.

Rowell, George. *The Victorian Theatre.* London: Oxford University Press, 1956.

Southern, Richard. See under Chapter 7.

Speaight, Robert. See under Chapter 5.

Vardac, A. N. *Stage to Screen: Theatrical Method from Garrick to Griffith.* Cambridge, Mass.: Harvard University Press, 1949.

Walzel, Oskar F. *German Romanticism.* New York: G. P. Putnam's Sons, 1932.

Watson, Ernest B. *Sheridan to Robertson: A Study of the Nineteenth Century London Stage.* Cambridge, Mass.: Harvard University Press, 1926.

Witkowski, Georg. *The German Drama of the Nineteenth Century,* 2d ed. New York: Benjamin Blom, 1968.

9: The Beginnings of the Modern Theatre

Antoine, André. *Memories of the Théâtre Libre.* Trans. by Marvin Carlson. Coral Gables, Fla.,: University of Miami Press, 1964.

Appia, Adolphe. *The Work of Living Art and Man Is the Measure of All Things.* Coral Gables, Fla.: University of Miami Press, 1960.

Bablet, Denis. *Edward Gordon Craig.* New York: Theatre Arts Books, 1967.

Bentley, Eric. *The Playwright as Thinker: A Study of Drama in Modern Times.* New York: Reynal & Company, Inc., 1946.

Brockett, Oscar G., and Findlay, Robert R. *Century of Innovation: A History of European and American Theatre and Drama Since 1870.* Englewood Cliffs, N.J.: Prentice-Hall, Inc., 1973.

Brustein, Robert. *The Theatre of Revolt: An Approach to Modern Drama.* Boston: Little, Brown and Co., 1964.

Carter, Huntly. *The Theatre of Max Reinhardt.* New York: Benjamin Blom, 1964.

Carter, Lawson A. *Zola and the Theatre.* New Haven, Conn.: Yale University Press, 1963.

Cornell, Kenneth. *The Symbolist Movement.* New Haven, Conn.: Yale University Press, 1951.

Craig, Edward Gordon. *On the Art of the Theatre,* 2d ed. Boston: Small, Maynard, 1924.

Garten, H. F. *Modern German Drama.* New York: Essential Books, 1959.

Gorchakov, Nikolai A. *The Theater in Soviet Russia.* Trans. by Edgar Lehman. New York: Columbia University Press, 1957.

Gorelik, Mordecai. *New Theatres for Old.* New York: Samuel French, 1940.

Matlaw, Myron. *Modern World Drama: An Encyclopedia.* New York: E. P. Dutton & Co., Inc., 1972.

Miller, Anna Irene. *The Independent Theatre in Europe, 1887 to the Present.* New York: Ray Long and Richard R. Smith, 1931.

Rischbeiter, Henning. *Art and the Stage in the 20th Century.* Greenwich, Conn.: New York Graphic Society, 1968.

Roose-Evans, James. *Experimental Theatre: From Stanislavsky to Today,* new rev. ed. London: Studio Vista, 1973.

Slonim, Marc. *Russian Theatre from the Empire to the Soviets.* Cleveland: World Publishing Co., 1961.

Stein, Jack M. *Richard Wagner and the Synthesis of the Arts.* Detroit: Wayne State University Press, 1960.

Valency, Maurice. *The Flower and the Castle: An Introduction to Modern Drama.* New York: Grosset & Dunlap, Inc., 1963.

Volbach, Walther. *Adolphe Appia, Prophet of the Modern Theatre.* Middletown, Conn.: Wesleyan University Press, 1968.

Waxman, S. M. *Antoine and the Théâtre Libre.* Cambridge, Mass.: Harvard University Press, 1926.

Willett, John. *Expressionism.* New York: McGraw-Hill Book Co., Inc., 1970.

10: From the 1920s to the mid-1950s

Artaud, Antonin. *The Theatre and Its Double.* Trans. by Mary C. Richards. New York: Grove Press, 1958.

Bradshaw, Martha. *Soviet Theatres, 1917–1941.* New York: Research Program on the USSR, 1954.

Braun, Edward. *Meyerhold on Theatre.* New York: Hill and Wang, 1969.

Brecht, Bertolt. *Brecht on Theatre.* Trans. by John Willett. New York: Hill & Wang, 1965.

Brockett, Oscar G., and Findlay, Robert R. See under Chapter 9.

Brustein, Robert. See under Chapter 9.

Clurman, Harold. *The Fervent Years: The Story of the Group Theatre in the Thirties.* New York: Hill & Wang, 1957.

Davis, Hallie Flanagan. *Arena.* New York: Duell, Sloane and Pearce, 1940.

Downer, Alan S. *Fifty Years of American Drama, 1900–1950.* Chicago: Henry Regnery Co., 1951.

Fuerst, Walter R., and Hume, Samuel J. *Twentieth Century Stage Decoration.* 2 vols. New York: Alfred A. Knopf, Inc., 1928.

Garten, H. F. See under Chapter 9.

Gorchakov, Nikolai A. See under Chapter 9.

Gorelik, Mordecai. See under Chapter 9.

Greene, Naomi. *Antonin Artaud: Poet without Words.* New York: Simon & Schuster, 1970.

Guicharnaud, Jacques. *Modern French Theatre from Giraudoux to Beckett.* New Haven, Conn.: Yale University Press, 1961.

Hainaux, René (ed.). *Stage Design throughout the World since 1935.* New York: Theatre Arts Books, 1956.

Hoover, Marjorie L. *Meyerhold: The Art of Conscious Theatre.* Amherst: University of Massachusetts Press, 1974.

Houghton, Norris. *Moscow Rehearsals: An Account of Methods of Production in the Soviet Theatre.* New York: Harcourt Brace Jovanovich, Inc., 1936.

Innes, C. D. *Erwin Piscator's Political Theatre.* New York: Cambridge University Press, 1972.

Knowles, Dorothy. *French Drama of the Inter-war Years, 1918–39.* New York: Barnes & Noble, 1967.

Krutch, Joseph W. *The American Drama since 1918,* rev. ed. New York: G. Braziller, 1957.

Ley-Piscator, Maria. *The Piscator Experiment: The Political Theatre.* New York: James H. Heineman, Inc., 1967.

Matlaw, Myron. See under Chapter 9.

Rischbeiter, Henning. See under Chapter 9.

Roose-Evans, James. See under Chapter 9.

Saint-Denis, Michel. *Theatre, the Rediscovery of Style.* New York: Theatre Arts Books, 1960.

Slonim, Marc. See under Chapter 9.

Smith, Cecil. *Musical Comedy in America.* New York: Theatre Arts Books, 1950.

Strasberg, Lee. *Strasberg at the Actors Studio.* New York: Viking Press, 1965.

Symons, James M. *Meyerhold's Theatre of the Grotesque: The Post-Revolutionary Productions, 1920–32.* Coral Gables, Fla.: University of Miami Press, 1971.

Tairov, Alexander. *Notes of a Director.* Trans. by William Kuhlke. Coral Gables, Fla.: University of Miami Press, 1969.

Willett, John. *The Theatre of Bertolt Brecht.* New York: New Directions, 1959.

11: The Contemporary Theatre

Abramson, Doris E. *Negro Playwrights in the American Theatre.* New York: Columbia University Press, 1969.

Addenbrooke, David. *The Royal Shakespeare Company: The Peter Hall Years.* London: William Kimber, 1974.

Ansorge, Peter. *Disrupting the Spectacle: Five Years of Experimental and Fringe Theatre in Britain.* London: Pitman, 1975.

Biner, Pierre. *The Living Theatre,* 2d ed. New York: Horizon Press, Inc., 1972.

Brockett, Oscar G., and Findlay, Robert R. See under Chapter 9.

Brook, Peter. *The Empty Space.* New York: Atheneum, 1968.

Browne, Terry. *Playwrights' Theatre: The English Stage Company at the Royal Court.* London: Pitman, 1975.

Brustein, Robert. *Revolution as Theatre: Notes on the New Radical Style.* New York: Liveright, 1971.

Burian, Jarka. *The Scenography of Josef Svoboda.* Middletown, Conn.: Wesleyan University Press, 1971.

Chaikin, Joseph. *The Presence of the Actor.* New York: Atheneum, 1974.

Chiari, Joseph. *The Contemporary French Theatre: The Flight from Naturalism.* London: Barrie and Rockliff, 1958.

Cook, Judith. *The National Theatre.* London: Harrop, 1976.

Croyden, Margaret. *Lunatics, Lovers and Poets: The Contemporary Experimental Theatre.* New York: McGraw-Hill Book Co., Inc., 1974.

Engel, Lehman. *American Musical Theatre.* Rev. ed. New York: Macmillan, 1975.

Esslin, Martin. *The Theatre of the Absurd,* rev. ed. Garden City, N.Y.: Doubleday & Company, Inc., 1969.

Freeman, E. *The Theatre of Alfred Camus.* London: Methuen, 1973.

Garten, H. F. See under Chapter 9.

Grotowski, Jerzy. *Towards a Poor Theatre.* New York: Simon & Schuster, 1968.

Hainaux, René (ed.). *Scene Design throughout the World, 1960–1970.* New York: Theatre Arts Books, 1972.

———. *Stage Design throughout the World since 1950.* New York: Theatre Arts Books, 1964.

———. *Stage Design Throughout the World Since 1970.* New York: Theatre Arts Books, 1976.

Hinchliffe, Arnold. *British Theatre, 1950–1970.* Totowa, N.J.: Rowman and Littlefield, 1975.

Kienzle, Siegfried. *Modern World Theatre: A Guide to Productions in Europe and the United States Since 1945.* New York: Frederick Ungar Publishing Co., 1970.

Kirby, Michael. *Happenings.* New York: E. P. Dutton & Co., Inc., 1965.

Kostelanetz, Richard. *The Theatre of Mixed Means.* New York: The Dial Press, 1968.

Lesnick, Henry. *Guerilla Street Theatre.* New York: Avon Books, 1973.

Little, Stuart. *Enter Joseph Papp: In Search of a New American Theatre.* New York: Coward, McCann and Geoghegan, Inc., 1974.

Marowitz, Charles, and Trussler, Simon. *Theatre at Work: Playwrights and Productions in the Modern British Theatre.* New York: Hill & Wang, 1967.

Matlaw, Myron. See under Chapter 9.

Neff, Renfreu. *The Living Theatre USA.* Indianapolis: Bobbs-Merrill, 1970.

Novick, Julius. *Beyond Broadway.* New York: Hill & Wang, 1968.

O'Connor, Garry. *French Theatre Today.* London: Pitman, 1975.

Pasolli, Robert. *A Book on the Open Theatre.* Indianapolis: Bobbs-Merrill, 1970.

Patterson, Michael. *German Theatre Today.* London: Pitman, 1976.

Rischbeiter, Henning. See under Chapter 9.

Roose-Evans, James. See under Chapter 9.

Sainer, Arthur. *The Radical Theatre Notebook.* New York: Avon Books, 1975.

Schechner, Richard. *Environmental Theatre.* New York: Hawthorn Books, Inc., 1973.

———. *Public Domain: Essays on the Theater.* Indianapolis: Bobbs-Merrill, 1969.

Schevill, James. *Breakout! In Search of New Theatrical Environments.* Chicago: University of Chicago Press, 1972.

Taylor, John R. *The Angry Theatre,* rev. ed. New York: Hill & Wang, 1969.

———. *Second Wave: British Dramatists for the Seventies.* New York: Hill & Wang, 1971.

Temkine, Raymond. *Grotowski.* New York: Avon Books, 1972.

Vinson, James, ed. *Contemporary Dramatists.* 2d ed. New York: St. Martin's Press, 1977.

Weales, Gerald. *American Drama since World War II.* New York: Harcourt Brace Jovanovich, Inc., 1962.

_____. *The Jumping Off Place: American Drama in the 1960s.* New York: The Macmillan Company, 1969.

Ziegler, Joseph. *Regional Theatre: The Revolutionary Stage.* Minneapolis: University of Minnesota Press, 1973.

PART THREE

12: The Playwright, Producer, and Director

Brook, Peter. See under Chapter 11.

Capbern, A. Martial. *The Drama Publicist.* New York: Pageant-Poseidon, 1968.

Clurman, Harold. *On Directing.* New York: The Macmillan Company, 1972.

Cohen, Robert, and Harrop, John. *Creative Play Direction.* Englewood Cliffs, N.J.: Prentice-Hall, Inc., 1974.

Cole, Toby (ed.). *Playwrights on Playwriting.* New York: Hill & Wang, 1961.

_____, and Chinoy, Helen K. (eds.). *Directors on Directing,* rev. ed. Indianapolis: Bobbs-Merrill, 1963.

Dean, Alexander. *Fundamentals of Play Directing,* revised by Lawrence Carra, 3d ed. New York: Holt, Rinehart and Winston, Inc., 1974.

Engel, Lehman. *Planning and Producing the Musical Show.* Rev. ed. New York: Crown Publishers, 1966.

Farber, Donald C. *From Option to Opening: A Guide for the Off-Broadway Producer,* rev. 3d ed. New York: DBS Publications, 1977.

_____. *Producing on Broadway.* New York: DBS Publications, 1969.

Hodge, Francis. *Play Directing: Analysis, Communication, and Style.* Englewood Cliffs, N.J.: Prentice-Hall, Inc., 1971.

Langley, Stephen. *Producers on Producing.* New York: DBS Publications, 1976.

_____. *Theatre Management in America, Principles and Practice: Producing for Commercial, Stock, Resident, College and Community Theatre.* New York: DBS Publications, 1974.

Reiss, Alvin. *The Arts Management Handbook,* rev. ed. New York: Law-Arts Publishers, Inc., 1973.

Staub, August. *Creating Theatre: The Art of Theatrical Directing.* New York: Harper & Row, 1973.

Wills, J. Robert, ed. *The Director in a Changing Theatre.* Palo Alto: Mayfield Publishing Co., 1976.

See also the works listed under Chapter 2.

13: The Actor

Albright, Hardie. *Acting: The Creative Process,* 2d ed. Encino, Calif.: Dickenson, 1974.

Benedetti, Robert L. *The Actor at Work.* Rev. ed. Englewood Cliffs, N.J.: Prentice-Hall, Inc., 1976.

Blunt, Jerry. *The Composite Art of Acting.* New York: The Macmillan Company, 1966.

Cole, Toby, and Chinoy, Helen K. (eds.). *Actors on Acting: The Theories, Techniques, and Practices of the Great Actors of All Times as Told in Their Own Words.* New York: Crown Publishers, Inc., 1949.

Hagen, Uta. *Respect for Acting.* New York: The Macmillan Company, 1973.

King, Nancy. *Theatre Movement: The Actor and His Space.* New York: DBS Publications, 1972.

Lessac, Arthur. *The Use and Training of the Human Voice.* New York: DBS Publications, 1967.

McGaw, Charles J. *Acting Is Believing,* 2d ed. New York: Holt, Rinehart and Winston, Inc., 1966.

Machlin, Evangeline. *Speech for the Stage.* New York: Theatre Arts Books, 1966.

Rockwood, Jerome. *The Craftsmen of Dionysus: An Approach to Acting.* Chicago: Scott, Foresman and Company, 1966.

Spolin, Viola. *Improvisation for the Theatre.* Evanston, Ill.: Northwestern University Press, 1963.

Stanislavsky, Constantin. *An Actor Prepares.* Trans. by Elizabeth Reynolds Hapgood. New York: Theatre Arts Books, 1936.

_____. *Building a Character.* Trans. by Elizabeth Reynolds Hapgood. New York: Theatre Arts Books, 1949.

_____. *Creating a Role.* Trans. by Elizabeth Reynolds Hapgood. New York: Theatre Arts Books, 1961.

Strasberg, Lee. See under Chapter 10.

Turner, J. Clifford. *Voice and Speech in the Theatre.* 3d ed. rev. by Malcolm Morrison. New York: DBS Publications, 1977.

14: Scene Design and Architecture

American Theatre Planning Board. *Theatre Check List: A Guide to the Planning and Construction of Proscenium and Open Stage Theatres.* Middletown, Conn.: Wesleyan University Press, 1969.

Bablet, Denis. *Stage Design in the Twentieth Century.* New York: Leon Amiel, 1976.

Bay, Howard. *Stage Design.* New York: Drama Book Specialists, 1974.

Bellman, Willard F. *Scenography and Stage Technology: An Introduction.* New York: Harper and Row, 1977.

Burdick, Elizabeth B., *et al.* (eds.). *Contemporary Stage Design.* Middletown, Conn.: Wesleyan University Press, 1975.

Burris-Meyer, Harold, and Cole, Edward C. *Scenery for the Theatre,* 2d rev. ed. Boston: Little, Brown and Co., 1972.

_____. *Theatres and Auditoriums,* 2d ed. with supplement. Huntington, New York: Robert E. Krieger Publishing Co., 1975.

Cogswell, Margaret (ed.). *The Ideal Theater: Eight Concepts.* New York: The American Federation of Arts, 1962.

Corey, Irene. *The Mask of Reality: An Approach to Design for the Theatre.* Anchorage, Ky.: Anchorage Press, 1968.

Izenour, George C. *Theatre Design.* New York: McGraw-Hill, 1977.

Jones, Robert E. *The Dramatic Imagination.* New York: Meredith Publishing Co., 1941.

Joseph, Stephen. *New Theatre Forms.* New York: Theatre Arts Books, 1968.

Larson, Orville K. (ed.). *Scene Design for Stage and Screen: Readings on the Aesthetics and Methodology of Scene Design for Drama, Opera, Musical Comedy, Ballet, Motion Pictures, Television and Arena Theatre.* East Lansing: Michigan State University Press, 1961.

Mielziner, Jo. *Designing for the Theatre.* New York: Atheneum, 1965.

———. *Shapes of Our Theatres.* New York: Potter, 1970.

Oenslager, Donald. *Scenery Then and Now.* New York: W. W. Norton & Company, 1936.

———. *Stage Design: Four Centuries of Scenic Invention.* New York: Viking Press, 1975.

Parker, W. Oren, and Smith, Harvey K. *Scene Design and Stage Lighting,* 3d ed. New York: Holt, Rinehart and Winston, Inc., 1974.

Pecktal, Lynn, *Designing and Painting for the Theatre.* New York: Holt, Rinehart and Winston, Inc., 1975.

Schubert, Hannelore. *Modern Theatre Buildings: Architecture, Stage Design, Lighting.* New York: Praeger, 1971.

Selden, Samuel, and Rezzuto, Tom. *Essentials of Stage Scenery.* New York: Appleton-Century-Crofts, 1972.

15: Costume and Makeup

Barton, Lucy. *Historic Costume for the Stage.* Boston: Baker's Plays, 1935.

Corey, Irene. See under Chapter 14.

Corson, Richard. *Stage Make-up,* 5th ed. Englewood Cliffs, N.J.: Prentice-Hall, Inc., 1975.

Jones, Robert E. See under Chapter 14.

Komisarjevsky, Theodore. *The Costume of the Theatre.* New York: Holt, Rinehart and Winston, Inc., 1932.

Motley. *Designing and Making Stage Costumes.* London: Studio Vista, Ltd., 1964.

Payne, Blanche. *History of Costume from the Ancient Egyptians to the Twentieth Century.* New York: Harper & Row, 1965.

Prisk, Berneice. *Stage Costume Handbook.* New York: Harper & Row, 1966.

Russell, Douglas, *Stage Costume Design: Theory, Technique and Style.* New York: Appleton-Century-Crofts, 1973.

Smith, C. Ray (ed.). *The Theatre Crafts Book of Make-up, Masks and Wigs.* Emmaus, Pa.: Rodale Press, 1974.

16: Lighting, Sound, and Multimedia

Bellman, Willard F. *Lighting the Stage: Art and Practice,* 2d ed. San Francisco: Chandler Publishing Co., 1974.

———. *Scenography and Stage Technology.* See under Chapter 14.

Bergman, Gosta M. *Lighting in the Theatre.* Totowa, N.J.: Rowman and Littlefield, 1977.

Burian, Jarka. See under Chapter 11.

Collision, David. *Stage Sound.* New York: DBS Publications, 1976.

Jones, Robert E. See under Chapter 14.

Jones, Tom Douglas. *The Art of Light and Color.* New York: Van Nostrand, Reinhold, 1973.

McCandless, Stanley R. *A Method of Lighting the Stage,* 4th ed. New York: Theatre Arts Books, 1958.

Parker, W. Oren, and Smith, Harvey K. See under Chapter 14.

Rosenthal, Jean, and Wertenbaker, Lael. *The Magic of Light.* New York: Theatre Arts Books, 1972.

Rubin, Joel E., and Watson, Leland. *Theatrical Lighting Practice.* New York: Theatre Arts Books, 1954.

Schechner, Richard. *Environmental Theatre.* See under Chapter 11.

Sellman, Hunton D. *Essentials of Stage Lighting.* New York: Appleton-Century-Crofts, 1972.

Appendix: Opportunities to Work in the Theatre

Allosso, Michael. *Exploring Theater and Media Careers.* Washington: U.S. Government Printing Office, 1976.

Babcock, Dennis and Boyd, Preston. *Careers in the Theatre.* Minneapolis: Lerner, 1975.

Matson, Katinka. *The Working Actor.* New York: Viking Press, 1976.

Index